THREE TREATISES

THREE TREATISES

THE ANNOTATED LUTHER STUDY EDITION

EDITORS
Timothy J. Wengert
Erik H. Herrmann
James M. Estes
Paul W. Robinson

Fortress Press
Minneapolis

THREE TREATISES

The Annotated Luther Study Edition

Cover design: Kristin Miller
Cover image: Illustration of a Martin Luther, 1483–1546. "Disputation between Luther and Eck on the Pleißenburg in Leipzig" | Nastasic via Getty Images

Print ISBN: 978-1-5064-8830-1
eBook ISBN: 978-1-5064-8831-8

Contents

Publisher's Note

About the Annotated Luther Study Edition

The volumes in the Annotated Luther Study Edition series have first been published in one of the comprehensive volumes of The Annotated Luther series. A description of that series and the volumes can be found in the Series Introduction (p. ix). While each comprehensive Annotated Luther volume can easily be used in classroom settings, we also recognize that treatises are often assigned individually for reading and study. To facilitate classroom and group use, we have pulled key treatises along with their introductions, annotations, and images directly from the Annotated Luther Series volumes.

To the Christian Nobility of the German Nation, 1520,
was first published in The Annotated Luther series,
Volume 1, *The Roots of Reform* (2015).

The Babylonian Captivity of the Church, 1520,
was first published in The Annotated Luther series,
Volume 3, *Church and Sacraments* (2016).

The Freedom of a Christian, 1520,
was first published in The Annotated Luther series,
Volume 1, *The Roots of Reform* (2015).

Series Introduction

Engaging the Essential Luther

Even after five hundred years Martin Luther continues to engage and challenge each new generation of scholars and believers alike. With 2017 marking the five-hundredth anniversary of Luther's *95 Theses*, Luther's theology and legacy are being explored around the world with new questions and methods and by diverse voices. His thought invites ongoing examination, his writings are a staple in classrooms and pulpits, and he speaks to an expanding assortment of conversation partners who use different languages and hale from different geographical and social contexts.

The six volumes of The Annotated Luther edition offer a flexible tool for the global reader of Luther, making many of his most important writings available in the *lingua franca* of our times as one way of facilitating interest in the Wittenberg reformer. They feature new introductions, annotations, revised translations, and textual notes, as well as visual enhancements (illustrations, art, photos, maps, and timelines). The Annotated Luther edition embodies Luther's own cherished principles of communication. Theological writing, like preaching, needs to reflect human beings' lived experience, benefits from up-to-date scholarship, and should be easily accessible to all. These volumes are designed to help teachers and students, pastors and laypersons, and other professionals in ministry understand the context in which the documents were written, recognize how the documents have shaped Protestant and Lutheran thinking, and interpret the meaning of these documents for faith and life today.

The Rationale for This Edition

For any reader of Luther, the sheer number of his works presents a challenge. Well over one hundred volumes comprise the scholarly edition of Luther's works, the so-called Weimar Ausgabe (WA), a publishing enterprise begun in 1883 and only completed in the twenty-first century. From 1955 to 1986, fifty-five volumes came to make up *Luther's Works* (American Edition) (LW), to which Concordia Publishing House, St. Louis, is adding still more. This English-language contribution to Luther studies, matched by similar translation projects for Erasmus of Rotterdam and John Calvin, provides a theological and historical gold mine for those interested in studying Luther's thought. But even these volumes are not always easy to use and are hardly portable. Electronic forms have increased availability, but preserving Luther in book form and providing readers with manageable selections are also important goals.

Moreover, since the publication of the WA and the first fifty-five volumes of the LW, research on the Reformation in general and on Martin Luther in particular has broken new ground and evolved, as has knowledge regarding the languages in which Luther wrote. Up-to-date information from a variety of sources is brought together in The Annotated Luther, building on the work done by previous generations of scholars. The language and phrasing of the translations have also been updated to reflect modern English usage. While the WA and, in a derivative way, LW remain the central source for Luther scholarship, the present critical and annotated English translation facilitates research internationally and invites a new generation of readers for whom Latin and German might prove an unsurpassable obstacle to accessing Luther. The WA provides the basic Luther texts (with some exceptions); the LW provides the basis for almost all translations.

Defining the "Essential Luther"

Deciding which works to include in this collection was not easy. Criteria included giving attention to Luther's initial key works; considering which publications had the most impact in his day and later; and taking account of Luther's own favorites, texts addressing specific issues of continued importance for today, and Luther's exegetical works. Taken as a whole, these works present the many sides of Luther, as reformer, pastor, biblical interpreter, and theologian. To serve today's readers and by using categories similar to those found in volumes 31–47 of Luther's works (published by Fortress Press), the volumes offer in the main a thematic rather than strictly chronological approach to Luther's writings. The volumes in the series include:

Volume 1: *The Roots of Reform* (Timothy J. Wengert, editor)
Volume 2: *Word and Faith* (Kirsi I. Stjerna, editor)
Volume 3: *Church and Sacraments* (Paul W. Robinson, editor)
Volume 4: *Pastoral Writings* (Mary Jane Haemig, editor)
Volume 5: *Christian Life in the World* (Hans J. Hillerbrand, editor)
Volume 6: *The Interpretation of Scripture* (Euan K. Cameron, editor)

The History of the Project

In 2011 Fortress Press convened an advisory board to explore the promise and parameters of a new English edition of Luther's essential works. Board members Denis Janz, Robert Kolb, Peter Matheson, Christine Helmer, and Kirsi Stjerna deliberated with Fortress Press publisher Will Bergkamp to develop a concept and identify contributors. After a review with scholars in the field, college and seminary professors, and pastors, it was concluded that a single-language edition was more desirable than dual-language volumes.

In August 2012, Hans Hillerbrand, Kirsi Stjerna, and Timothy Wengert were appointed as general editors of the series with Scott Tunseth from Fortress Press as the project editor. The general editors were tasked with determining the contents of the volumes and developing the working principles of the series. They also helped with the identification and recruitment of additional volume editors, who in turn worked with the general editors to identify volume contributors. Mastery of the languages and unique knowledge of the subject matter were key factors in identifying contributors. Most contributors are North American scholars and native English speakers, but The Annotated Luther includes among its contributors a circle of international scholars. Likewise, the series is offered for a global network of teachers and students in seminary, university, and college classes, as well as pastors, lay teachers, and adult students in congregations seeking background and depth in Lutheran theology, biblical interpretation, and Reformation history.

Editorial Principles

The volume editors and contributors have, with few exceptions, used the translations of LW as the basis of their work, retranslating from the WA for the sake of clarity and contemporary usage. Where the LW translations have been substantively altered, explanatory notes have often been provided. More importantly, contributors have provided marginal notes to help readers understand theological and historical references. Introductions have been expanded and sharpened to reflect the very latest historical and theological research. In citing the Bible, care has been taken to reflect the German and Latin texts commonly used in the sixteenth century rather than modern editions, which often employ textual sources that were unavailable to Luther and his contemporaries.

Finally, all pieces in The Annotated Luther have been revised in the light of modern principles of inclusive language. This is not always an easy task with a historical author, but an intentional effort has been made to revise language throughout, with creativity and editorial liberties, to allow Luther's theology to speak free from unnecessary and unintended gender-exclusive language. This important principle provides an opportunity to translate accurately certain gender-neutral German and Latin expressions that Luther employed—for example, the Latin word *homo* and the German *Mensch* mean "human being," not simply "males." Using the words *man* and *men* to translate such terms would create an ambiguity not present in the original texts. The focus is on linguistic accuracy and Luther's intent. Regarding creedal formulations and trinitarian language, Luther's own expressions have been preserved, without entering the complex and important contemporary debates over language for God and the Trinity.

The 2017 anniversary of the publication of the *95 Theses* is providing an opportunity to assess the substance of Luther's role and influence in the Protestant Reformation. Revisiting Luther's essential writings not only allows reassessment of Luther's rationale and goals but also provides a new look at what Martin Luther was about and why new generations would still wish to engage him. We hope these six volumes offer a compelling invitation.

Hans J. Hillerbrand
Kirsi I. Stjerna
Timothy J. Wengert
General Editors

Abbreviations

BC	*The Book of Concord*, ed. Robert Kolb and Timothy J. Wengert (Minneapolis: Fortress Press, 2000).
Brecht 1	Martin Brecht, *Martin Luther: His Road to Reformation, 1483–1521*, trans. James L. Schaaf (Minneapolis: Fortress Press, 1985).
CIC	*Corpus Iuris Canonici*, ed. Emil Louis Richter and Emil Friedberg, 2 vols. (Graz: Akademische Druck- u. Verlagsanstalt, 1959)
CSEL	*Corpus Scriptorum Ecclesiasticorum Latinorum*
Friedberg	*Corpus iuris canonici*, ed. Emil Friedberg, 2 vols. (Leipzig: Tauchnitz, 1879-1881).
LW	*Luther's Works* (American edition), ed. Helmut Lehmann and Jaroslav Pelikan, 55 vols. (Philadelphia: Fortress Press/St. Louis: Concordia Publishing House, 1955-1986).
MLStA	*Martin Luther: Studienausgabe*, ed. Hans-Ulrich Delius, 6 vols. (Berlin/Leipzig: Evangelische Verlagsanstalt, 1979-1999).
MPL	*Patrologiae cursus completus, series Latina*, ed. Jacques-Paul Migne, 217 vols. (Paris, 1815-1875).
NPNF	*Nicene and Post-Nicene Fathers*, ed. Philip Schaaf and Henry Wace, series 1, 14 vols.; series 2, 14 vols. (London/New York: T&T Clark, 1886-1900).
RTA	Adolf Wrede et al., eds., *Deutsche Reichtagsakten, jüngere Reihe*, 20 vols. (Gotha: Perthes, 1893-2009).
STh	Thomas Aquinas, *Summa Theologica*
TAL	The Annotated Luther
WA	*Luthers Werke: Kritische Gesamtausgabe* [*Schriften*], 73 vols. (Weimar: H. Böhlau, 1883-2009).
WA Br	*Luthers Werke: Kritische Gesamtausgabe: Briefwechsel*, 18 vols. (Weimar: H. Böhlau, 1930-1985).
WA DB	*Luthers Werke: Kritische Gesamtausgabe: Deutsche Bibel*, 12 vols. (Weimar: H. Böhlau, 1906-1961).
Wander	Karl F. W. Wander, ed., *Deutsches Sprichwörterlexikon: Ein Hausschatz für das deutsche Volk*, 5 vols. (Leipzig: Brockhaus, 1867-1880; reprint Aalen: Scientia, 1963).

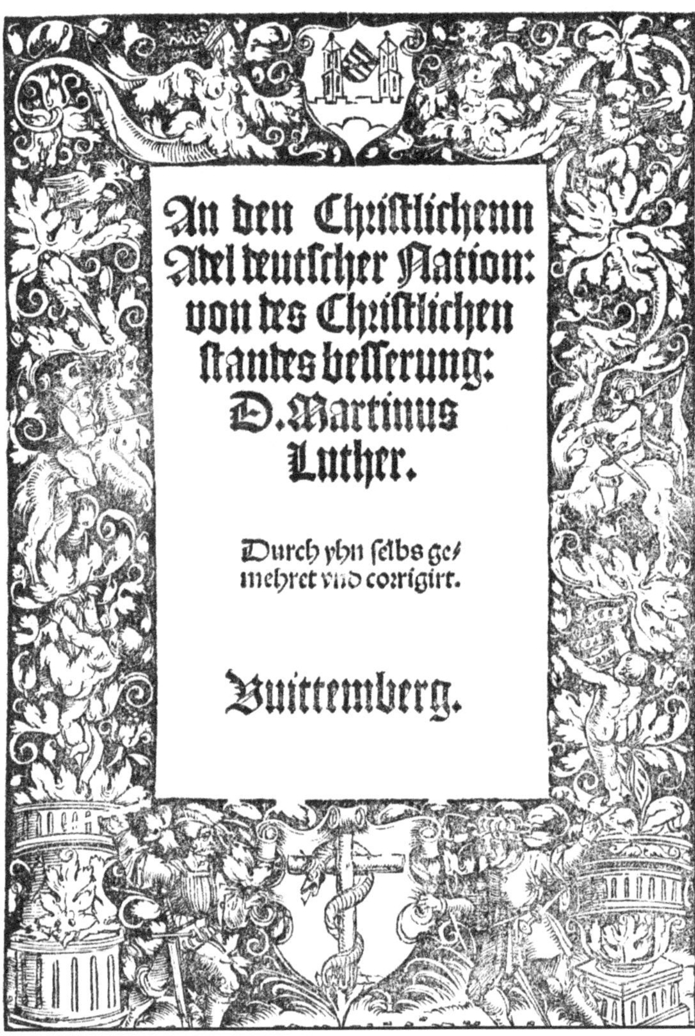

An den Christlichenn
Adel teutscher Nation:
von des Christlichen
standes besserung:
D. Martinus
Luther.

Durch yhn selbs ge/
mehret vnd corrigirt.

Wittemberg.

Title page of *Address to the Christian Nobility*. This historiated title page border features the arms of the city of Wittenberg at the head and the crest of the printer, Melchior Lotter the Younger, at the foot. The woodcut has been attributed to Lucas Cranach the Elder.

To the Christian Nobility of the German Nation Concerning the Improvement of the Christian Estate

1520

JAMES M. ESTES

INTRODUCTION

This treatise is Luther's first appeal to secular authorities for help with the reform of the church. For more than two years, starting with the *95 Theses* in 1517, Luther's appeals for reform had been addressed to the ecclesiastical hierarchy, whose divinely imposed responsibility for such things he took for granted. By the early months of 1520, however, Luther had come to the conclusion that nothing could be expected from Rome but intransigent opposition to reform of any sort.[a] It was only at this point that he began to write of the need for secular rulers to intervene with measures that would clear the way for ecclesiastical reform. In the *Treatise on Good Works* (in print by 8 June 1520), Luther argued that the abuses of "the spiritual authorities" were causing "Christendom to go to ruin," and that, in this emergency, anyone who was able to do so should help in whatever way possible. Specifically, "The best and indeed the only remaining remedy would be for kings, princes, the nobility, cities, and communities

a See James M. Estes, *Peace, Order, and the Glory of God: Secular Authority and the Church in the Thought of Luther and Melanchthon, 1518–1559* (Leiden: Brill, 2005), 7–17. See also Brecht 1:369–79.

to take the first step in the matter so that the bishops and clergy, who are now fearful, would have cause to follow."[b] He made the same point in the treatise *On the Papacy in Rome* (in print by 26 June 1520), asserting that "the horrible disgrace of Christendom" has gone so far "that there is no more hope on earth except with secular authority."[c]

Meanwhile, just as the *Treatise on Good Works* was coming off the presses, Luther received a copy of the *Epitome of a Response to Martin Luther* (*Epitoma responsionis ad Martinum Lutherum*) by the papal theologian Silvester Prierias (c. 1426–1523).[1] The *Epitome* was a bold assertion of papal absolutism, insisting that papal authority was superior to that of a council and even to Scripture itself. To Luther, this "hellish book" was conclusive evidence that the Antichrist was reigning in Rome and that there was no possibility of a reform initiated or approved by it. It was therefore necessary to abandon "unhappy, hopeless, blasphemous Rome" and seek reform elsewhere.[d]

It was in this frame of mind that on 7 June 1520 Luther announced to Georg Spalatin (1484–1545) his intention "to issue a broadside to [Emperor] Charles and the nobility of Germany against the tyranny and baseness of the Roman Curia."[e] By 23 June, the "broadside" had grown into a major treatise, the manuscript of which Luther sent to his friend Nicholas von Amsdorf (1483–1565), together with the letter that became the preface to the treatise when it was published in mid-August.[f] In the letter, Luther describes the treatise as "a few points on the matter of the improvement of the state of Christendom, to be laid before the Christian nobility of the German nation, in the hope that God may help his church through the laity, since the clergy, to whom this task more properly belongs, have grown quite irresponsible."[2] What could the laity do to remedy the failure of the clergy?

b See the *Treatise on Good Works* in *The Annotated Luther*, Volume 1, p. 342.

c LW 39:102–3.

d WA 6:328–29 (Luther's preface to the annotated edition of the *Epitome* that he published in mid-June 1520).

e WA Br 2:120.

f See below, pp. 8–10.

1. The Dominican, Silvestro Mazzolini, known as Sylvester Prierias (after his birthplace Priero in Piedmont), was "master of the sacred palace" at the Roman Curia, which meant that he was the pope's theological adviser and censor of books. Given charge of the Luther case in 1518, he became Luther's first Italian literary opponent, publishing four polemical treatises against him in the years 1518–1520. The third of these, the *Epitome*, was published at Perugia in 1519.

2. See below, p. 8. Offers of support, including armed protection, received in the early months of 1520 from the imperial knights Ulrich von Hutten (1488–1523), Franz von Sickingen (1481–1523), and Silvester von Schaumberg (c. 1466–1534) appear to have given Luther a sense of political support outside Saxony that encouraged him to hope that an appeal to the nobility might well produce a positive response; see Brecht 1:369–70.

Luther's answer was that the leaders of the lay community could summon a church council.[g] But how could that be done against the will of the pope? Luther's answer to that question was a fundamental contribution to the thought of the Reformation.

The treatise itself is divided into three sections. In the first, Luther attacks the "three walls" behind which the "Romanists" have shielded themselves from reform: (1) the claim that spiritual authority is higher than secular authority and therefore not subject to secular jurisdiction; (2) the claim that the pope alone has the authority to interpret the Scriptures; and (3) the claim that only the pope can summon a council. The second section is a brief discussion of measures to be discussed at councils to curb the "thievery, trickery, and tyranny" of Rome. The third and by far the longest of the three sections, which appears to have been tacked on at the last moment, is a set of twenty-seven proposals for action by either secular authority or a council (as appropriate) for improving "the dreadful state of affairs" in Christendom. In these last two sections, Luther denounces a long list of ecclesiastical abuses, particularly those of the Roman Curia, which would have been familiar to his readers. Many of them are taken directly from the lists of "*Gravamina* [grievances] of the German Nation Against Rome" that had been brought forward at virtually every meeting of the imperial diet since the middle of the fifteenth century, most recently at the Diet of Augsburg in 1518.[h] In so doing, Luther identified himself with the conciliarist, patriotically German, anti-Roman sentiment that pervaded German ecclesiastical and political life at the time. This was well calculated to secure widespread popular approval for the treatise, but

g For Luther's suspicions about church councils, see the *Treatise on Good Works* in *The Annotated Luther*, Volume 1, p. 341.

h See Martin Luther, *Sämmtliche Werke*, ed. Johann Georg Walch et al., 2d ed., vol. 15: *Reformations-Schriften, erste Abtheilung, zur Reformationshistorie gehörige Documente: A. Wider die Papisten aus den Jahren 1517 bis 1524.* (St. Louis: Concordia, 1899), 453–71. For the more extensive list presented at the Diet of Worms in 1521, see RTA 2:661–718.

it is Luther's attack on the three walls that accounts for the enduring importance of the treatise. In that attack he redefines the relationship between clergy and laity and elaborates the view of the role of secular government in church reform to which he would adhere virtually without change for the remainder of the 1520s, before adapting it to new circumstances in the 1530s.

To the Christian Nobility has often been described as the work in which Luther called upon the German princes to assume responsibility for the reform of the church.[i] In fact, however, the most striking feature of the treatise is Luther's refusal to attribute to secular rulers any authority at all in matters of faith or church governance. Although the classical formulation of what is sometimes labeled the "Doctrine of the Two Kingdoms" was still three years in the future,[j] Luther was already clearly committed to the view that secular authority extends only to the secular realm of human affairs and that it has no jurisdiction in the spiritual realm. As he put it in the *Treatise on Good Works*, secular jurisdiction is limited to matters covered by the Second Table of the Decalogue (the commandments regulating the conduct of human beings toward one another), and that it has nothing to do with the First Table (the commandments regulating the duties of human beings toward God).[k] How, then, could Luther justify any role at all for secular government in the reform of the church? The answer, already prefigured in the *Treatise on Good Works* and *The Papacy at Rome* and now fully elaborated in *To the Christian Nobility*, was necessarily somewhat complicated.

i See, e.g., John Dillenberger's introduction to the treatise in *Martin Luther: Selections from His Writings* (New York: Random House, 1961), 403: "In this work of 1520 . . . Luther calls upon the ruling class to reform the Church, since the Church will not reform itself." See also Roland Bainton, *Here I Stand: A Life of Martin Luther* (New York/Nashville: Abingdon, 1950), 152: "[B]y what right, the modern reader might well inquire, might Luther call upon [the German nobility] to reform the Church?"

j In the treatise *On Secular Authority, To What Extent It Should Be Obeyed* (LW 45:75–129).

k See the *Treatise on Good Works* in *The Annotated Luther*, Volume 1, pp. 342–44.

First of all, many of the most glaring ecclesiastical abuses in need of correction fell into the category of secular crimes (robbery and theft) committed by "spiritual" persons (the clergy and monks). Thus defined, such abuses (e.g., raising money by peddling indulgences) could be viewed as the direct responsibility of secular rulers, to whom God had assigned the duty of protecting the goods and property of their subjects. One had only to dispose of the claimed exemption of "spiritual" persons from secular jurisdiction. "Spiritual" crimes, on the other hand, were a more difficult matter. Given his definition of the limits of secular authority, Luther could not appeal to secular rulers *as such* to deal with such matters. He could, however, argue that, *as baptized Christians*, secular rulers shared in the right and duty of all Christians to interpret Scripture and to adhere to the correct interpretation if the pope errs. This meant that in an emergency with which the pope could not or would not deal, they shared in the right and duty of all baptized Christians to do what they could to restore ecclesiastical authority to its proper function. It meant further that, *because of their commanding position in society*, they had a special obligation to do so. On this basis, Luther could appeal to the emperor and the German princes to serve their fellow Christians in an emergency by summoning a church council, in which "bishops and clergy," hitherto intimidated and frustrated by papal opposition to reform, would be free to do their duty to provide reform. The aim, in other words, was to restore the proper functioning of established ecclesiastical authority, not to transfer it to secular rulers.[l]

The response to Luther's appeal to "the Christian nobility of the German nation" came at the Diet of Worms in 1521. Instead of summoning a reform council, the assembled princes outlawed Luther and his followers. But the reform movement continued to spread rapidly, particularly in cities and towns, and Luther defended the right of such communities to reform themselves despite the objections of

l See Estes, *Peace, Order, and the Glory of God*, 17–30.

Luther is shown as an Augustinian monk debating the pope, a cardinal, a bishop, and another monk.

ecclesiastical authority.[m] When, moreover, hostile Catholic governments tried to suppress these reform efforts, Luther angrily denounced them for arrogating to themselves a power in spiritual matters that was not theirs by right.[n] By the late 1520s, however, the spontaneous spread of the Reformation in Saxony had reached the point at which church life urgently needed to be regulated in the interest of unity and good order. But Saxony had no bishop to provide the

m See LW 39:305–14 (*That a Christian Assembly or Congregation Has the Right and Power to Judge All Teaching and to Call, Appoint, and Dismiss Teachers, Established and Proven by Scripture*, 1523).

n *On Secular Authority* (1523).

necessary leadership. In this emergency, Luther once again appealed to secular authority for help with ecclesiastical reform, using essentially the same arguments that he had advanced in 1520. He called on the elector, in his capacity as Christian brother, to serve his fellow Christians by appointing an ecclesiastical visitation commission that would establish uniformity of doctrine and practice on the churches in his domains.[o] Since, however, Luther expected the elector *as prince* to enforce the established uniformity, it was clear that his distinction between the prince *as prince* (secular authority *as such*), without authority in spiritual matters, and the prince as Christian brother, entitled to intervene only in emergencies, no longer fit the situation as well as it had at the beginning of the decade. Luther himself was aware of this and, starting in 1530, he rethought his position in conversation with Philipp Melanchthon (1497–1560). By 1534 he and Melanchthon were in agreement that, the necessary distinction between secular and spiritual authority notwithstanding, it was the duty of a Christian prince to establish and maintain true religion among his subjects.[p]

o LW 40:263–320.

p See Estes, *Peace, Order, and the Glory of God*, ch. 5. In Luther's case, the key texts are his commentaries on Psalms 82 (1530) and 101 (1534–35), particularly the latter; see LW 13:51–60, 166–201.

Portrait of Nicholaus von Amsdorf, whom Luther consecrated as bishop of Naumburg in the 1540s, by the German painter and printmaker Peter Gottlandt.

TO THE CHRISTIAN NOBILITY OF THE GERMAN NATION CONCERNING THE IMPROVEMENT OF THE CHRISTIAN ESTATE, 1520[3,4]

JESUS.[q]

TO THE ESTEEMED and Reverend Master, Nicholas von Amsdorf, Licentiate of Holy Scripture, and Canon of Wittenberg, my special and kind friend, from Doctor Martin Luther.

The grace and peace of God be with you, esteemed, reverend, and dear sir and friend.[r]

The time for silence is past, and the time to speak has come, as Eccles. [3:7] says. I am carrying out our intention to put together a few points on the matter of the improvement of the state of Christendom, to be laid before the Christian nobility of the German nation, in the hope that God may help his church through the laity, since the clergy, to whom this task more properly belongs, have grown quite irresponsible. I am sending the whole thing to you, reverend sir, [that you may give] an opinion on it and, where necessary, improve it.

I know full well that I shall not escape the charge of presumption, because I, a despised, cloistered person, venture to address such high and great estates on such weighty mat-

3. The present translation is a twice-revised version of that by Charles M. Jacobs in *Works of Martin Luther with Introductions and Notes*, ed. Luther Reed et al., 6 vols. (Philadelphia: Holman, 1915), 2:61–164. The first revision was by James Atkinson for LW 44:123–217. The German text used is that of MLStA 2:96–167, edited by Karlheinz Blaschke. Much information from Blaschke's notes has found its way into this translation. See also WA 6:381–469, and Karl Benrath, ed., *An den christlichen Adel deutscher Nation von des christlichen Standes Besserung* (Halle: Verein für Reformationsgeschichte, 1884), referred to below as Benrath.

q Following a monastic tradition, Luther began many of his early writings and letters with this word.

r An early example of Luther's use of a "Pauline greeting" (cf. 1 Cor. 1:3) here combined with an older form where he simply employed the word "Jesus." By 1522 this new form, an indication of identification of his office with that of the Apostle Paul, would completely replace the other.

ters, as if there were nobody else in the world except Doctor Luther to take up the cause of Christendom and give advice to such highly competent people. I make no apologies no matter who demands them. Perhaps I owe my God and the world another work of folly. I intend to pay my debt honestly. And if I succeed, I shall for the time being become a

A fool is pictured with a feather hat, about to trip himself with a cane; one shoe on and one off; and three children running about him.

court jester. And if I fail, I still have the one advantage that no one need buy me a cowl or provide me with a cockscomb.[5] It is a question of who will put the bells on whom.[s] I must fulfill the proverb, "Whatever the world does, a monk must be in the picture, even if he has to be painted in."[t] More than once a fool has spoken wisely, and wise men have often been arrant fools. Paul says, "He who wishes to be wise must

s I.e., who will declare whom to be a clown.

t The proverb *monachus semper praesens* is attested in Wander, 3:703, n. 130.

4. In the German phrase *der christliche Stand* ("the Christian Estate"), the word *stand* can mean "estate" as used in such phrases as "estates of the realm" or "imperial estates," but it can also mean "status" in the sense of standing or rank, as well as "state" in the sense of condition or walk of life. Nowhere in the treatise does Luther address himself to a Christian or "spiritual" estate that stands apart from another, presumably secular or worldly estate in society. Indeed, one of his principal arguments is that all baptized Christians are of the same "spiritual status" and that there is no distinction in this regard between clergy and laity (see below, pp. 13–15). Moreover, the list of reforms that he proposes requires action by both spiritual authority and secular authority, which he views as Christian. "The Christian estate," in other words, is the entire body of Christians viewed as one entity, often referred to as Christendom, in which all are of the same spiritual rank or standing. Luther finds that entity to be in terrible condition and thus sorely in need of reform. Bertram Lee Woolf captured this meaning when he took the liberty of turning *von des christlichen Standes Besserung* into "as to the Amelioration of the State of Christendom"; see Woolf, *Reformation Writings of Martin Luther* (New York: Philosophical Library, 1953), 101.

5. A cowl and a red rooster's comb were traditional signs of a clown or jester. Luther did not need them because he was already equipped with a monk's cowl and tonsure.

become a fool" [1 Cor. 3:18]. Moreover, since I am not only a fool, but also a sworn doctor of Holy Scripture, I am glad for the opportunity to fulfill my doctor's oath,[6] even in the guise of a fool.

I beg you, give my apologies to those who are moderately intelligent, for I do not know how to earn the grace and favor of the super-intelligent. I have often sought to do so with the greatest pains, but from now on I neither desire nor value their favor. God help us to seek not our own glory but his alone. Amen.

At Wittenberg, in the monastery of the Augustinians, on the eve of St. John Baptist [June 23] in the year fifteen hundred and twenty.

To His Most Illustrious, Most Mighty, and Imperial Majesty, and to the Christian Nobility of the German Nation, from Doctor Martin Luther.

Grace and power from God, Most Illustrious Majesty, and most gracious and dear lords.

It is not from sheer impertinence or rashness that I, one poor man, have taken it upon myself to address your worships. All the estates of Christendom, particularly in Germany, are now oppressed by distress and affliction, and this has stirred not only me but everybody else to cry out time and time again and to pray for help. It has even compelled me now at this time to cry aloud that God may inspire someone with his Spirit to lend a helping hand to this distressed and wretched nation. Often the councils have made some pretense at reformation, but their attempts have been cleverly frustrated by the guile of certain men, and things have gone from bad to worse.[7] With God's help I intend to expose the wiles and wickedness of these men, so that they are shown up for what they are and may never again be so obstructive and destructive. God has given us a young man of noble birth as our ruler,[8] thus awakening great hope of good in many hearts. Presented with such an opportunity we ought to apply ourselves and use this time of grace profitably.

The first and most important thing to do in this matter is to prepare ourselves in all seriousness. We must not start

6. Luther's authority to speak on controversial matters of doctrine and practice derived from his status as a doctor of theology. In the process of being awarded his doctorate (19 October 1512), he took a solemn oath to teach the Holy Scriptures faithfully and to combat heresy and error. With the doctorate, moreover, he acquired full academic freedom to discuss without hindrance all questions of scriptural interpretation. See Brecht 1:126–27.

7. During the Great Schism in the Western church (1378–1417), when there were two (and, for a time, three) rival popes, and ecclesiastical abuses (most of them rooted in the ruthless exploitation of papal authority to raise money) got worse, a sustained attempt was made to deal with the situation by means of a general council. Canonists argued that supreme authority in the church rested not with the pope, but with the universal community of believers, and that in an emergency that authority could be exercised by a council, which could be convoked by some authority (e.g., the emperor) other than the pope. The resulting "conciliar movement" assigned to a general council the task of restoring the unity of Christendom under one pope and of reforming the church, beginning with a thorough reform of the papacy itself. The Council of Constance (1414–1417) managed to restore unity under one undisputed pope, but it did not successfully address the problem of church reform. There followed a struggle

something by trusting in great power or human reason, even if all the power in the world were ours. For God cannot and will not suffer that a good work begin by relying upon one's own power and reason. He dashes such works to the ground; they do no good at all. As it says in Ps. 33[:16], "No king is saved by his great might and no lord is saved by the greatness of his strength." I fear that this is why the good emperors Frederick (I) Barbarossa and Frederick II and many other German emperors, even though all the world feared them, were in former times shamefully oppressed and trodden underfoot by the popes.[9] It may be that they relied on their own might more than on God, and therefore had to fall.

Frederick I Barbarossa.

between the restored papacy, which rejected the very idea of conciliar supremacy and feared reforms that would reduce papal income, and the conciliarists, who were numerous among theologians, bishops, and secular rulers, and who continued to call for limitations on papal authority and a thorough reform of the church "in head and members." With the help of Europe's secular rulers, to whom they made far-reaching concessions of authority to appoint bishops and other clergymen as well as of a share of ecclesiastical revenues, the popes defeated the conciliar movement, which had its last stand at the Council of Basel (1431–1449). But because of abuse and lack of reform in the "Renaissance papacy," conciliarism retained widespread appeal, particularly north of the Alps.

8. Charles V (1500–1558) was now twenty years old.

9. The Hohenstaufen emperors Frederick (I) Barbarossa (1152–1190) and his grandson, Frederick II (1212–1250), the last of the Hohenstaufens, both pursued dynastic and imperial interests in Italy that brought them into conflict with the cities of Lombardy and the popes (in their capacity as Italian territorial rulers). Both were excommunicated, and Frederick II was even deposed; both experienced catastrophic losses on the battlefield at the hands of their Italian enemies. Meanwhile, particularly in the reign of Frederick II, the German princes secured concessions that put an end to all hope of the establishment of a powerful national monarchy hereditary in the Hohenstaufen family.

Imperial authority survived in northern Italy and Germany but real power was in the hands of the great commercial cities of Italy and the German territorial princes.

10. Known as "the warrior pope," Julius II (1443–1513) spent much of his reign (1503–13) personally leading military campaigns aimed at recovering papal territory that had been alienated by his predecessors or annexed by Venice. In these struggles, France and Venice numbered among his enemies, but the German emperor Maximilian I (1459–1519) was his occasional ally.

11. I.e., the advocates of papal supremacy in the church.

What was it in our own time that raised the bloodthirsty Julius II to such heights? Nothing else, I fear, except that France, the Germans, and Venice relied upon themselves.[10] The children of Benjamin slew forty-two thousand Israelites because the latter relied on their own strength, Judg. 20[:21].[u]

That it may not so fare with us and our noble Charles, we must realize that in this matter we are not dealing with human beings, but with the princes of hell. These princes might well fill the world with war and bloodshed, but war and bloodshed do not overcome them. We must tackle this job by renouncing trust in physical force and trusting humbly in God. We must seek God's help through earnest prayer and fix our minds on nothing else than the misery and distress of suffering Christendom without regard to what evil men deserve. Otherwise, we may start the game with great prospects of success, but when we get into it the evil spirits will stir up such confusion that the whole world will swim in blood, and then nothing will come of it all. Let us act wisely, therefore, and in the fear of God. The more force we use, the greater our disaster if we do not act humbly and in the fear of God. If the popes and Romanists[11] have hitherto been able to set kings against each other by the devil's help, they might well be able to do it again if we were to go ahead without the help of God on our own strength and by our own cunning.

The Romanists have very cleverly built three walls around themselves. Hitherto they have protected themselves by these walls in such a way that no one has been able to reform them. As a result, the whole of Christendom has fallen horribly.

In the first place, when secular authority has been used against them, they have made decrees and declared that secular authority has no jurisdiction over them, but that, on the contrary, spiritual authority is above secular authority.[v] In the second place, when the attempt is made to reprove

u The biblical text mentions only twenty-two thousand slain.

v See p. 16, n. 18.

them with the Scriptures, they raise the objection that only the pope may interpret the Scriptures.[w] In the third place, if threatened with a council, their story is that no one may summon a council but the pope.[x]

In this way they have cunningly stolen our three rods from us, so that they may go unpunished. They have ensconced themselves within the safe stronghold of these three walls so that they can practice all the knavery and wickedness that we see today. Even when they have been compelled to hold a council,[12] they have weakened its power in advance by putting the princes under oath to let them remain as they were.[y] In addition, they have given the pope full authority over all decisions of a council, so that it is all the same whether there are many councils or no councils. They only deceive us with puppet shows and sham fights. They fear terribly for their skin in a really free council! They have so intimidated kings and princes with this technique that they believe it would be an offense against God not to be obedient to the Romanists in all their knavish and ghoulish deceits.

May God help us and give us just one of those trumpets with which the walls of Jericho were knocked down [Josh. 6:20] to blow down these walls of straw and paper as well and set free the Christian rods for the punishment of sin,[13] [as well as] bring to light the craft and deceit of the devil, to the end that through punishment we may reform ourselves and once more attain God's favor.

Let us begin by attacking the first wall. It is pure invention that pope, bishop, priests, and monks are called the spiritual estate while princes, lords, artisans, and farmers are called the secular estate. This is indeed a piece of deceit and hypocrisy. Yet no one need be intimidated by it, and for this reason: all Christians are truly of spiritual status, and there is no difference among them except that of office. Paul says in 1 Cor. 12[:12-13] that we are all one body, yet every

12. The most recent was the Fifth Lateran Council, 1512–1517. See n. 40, p. 30.

13. "Rod" is used in the Bible to mean an instrument of God's wrath; see, e.g., Ps. 2:9 and Rev. 2:27.

w For the claim of sole authority to interpret Scripture, see Friedberg 1:58–60 (*Decret. prima pars*, dist. 19, can. 1f).

x See n. 37.

y See the *Treatise on Good Works* in *The Annotated Luther*, Volume 1, p. 341f.

member has its own work by which it serves the others. This is because we all have one baptism, one gospel, one faith, and are all Christians alike; for baptism, gospel, and faith alone make us spiritual and a Christian people.

But if a pope or bishop anoints, tonsures, ordains, consecrates, and prescribes garb different from that of the laity, he can perhaps thereby create a hypocrite or an anointed priestling, but he can never make anyone into a Christian or into a spiritual person by so doing. Accordingly, we are all consecrated priests through baptism, as St. Peter says in 1 Pet. 2[:9], "You are a royal priesthood and a priestly realm." And the Apocalypse says, "Thou hast made us to be priests and kings by thy blood" [Rev. 5:9-10]. For if we had no higher consecration than that which pope or bishop gives, such consecration by pope or bishop would never make a priest, and no one could say Mass or preach a sermon or give absolution.

Therefore, when a bishop consecrates it is nothing else than that in the place and in the name of the whole community, all members of which have the same power, he selects one person and charges him with exercising this power on behalf of the others. It is just as if ten brothers, all the sons and equal heirs of a king, were to choose one of their number to rule the inheritance for them: even though they are all kings and of equal power, one of them is charged with the responsibility of ruling. To put it still more clearly: suppose a group of earnest Christian laypeople were taken prisoner and set down in a desert without an episcopally ordained priest among them. And suppose they were to come to a common mind there and then in the desert and elect one of their number, whether he were married or not,[z] and charge him to baptize, say Mass, pronounce absolution, and preach the gospel. Such a man would be as truly a priest as if he had been ordained by all the bishops and popes in the world. This is why in cases of necessity anyone can baptize and give absolution.[14] This would be impossible if we were not all

14. On emergency baptism see, e.g., the bull *Exultate Deo* (1439), which decreed that in case of necessity anyone, "not only a priest or deacon but also a woman or, indeed, even a pagan or a heretic, has the power to baptize" (Carl Mirbt and Kurt Aland, eds. *Quellen zur Geschichte des Papsttums und des römischen Katholozismus*, 6th ed. (Tübingen: Mohr Siebeck, 1967), 485, no. 774, §10). The idea that in an emergency when no priest is available an ordinary layperson can hear confession and pronounce absolution can be traced to a statement of St. Augustine (354–430) that was incorporated into the *Decretum Gratiani* (cf. following note); Friedberg 1:1374.

z The word here translated as "married," *ehelich*, can also mean "of legitimate birth." Canon law made both marriage and illegitimate birth a disqualification for ordination.

priests. Through canon law[15] the Romanists have almost destroyed and made unknown the wondrous grace and authority of baptism and Christian status. In times gone by, Christians used to choose their bishops and priests in this way from among their own number, and they were confirmed in their office by the other bishops without all the fuss that goes on nowadays. St. Augustine, Ambrose, and Cyprian each became [a bishop in this way].[16]

Since those who exercise secular authority have been baptized with the same baptism, and have the same faith and the same gospel as the rest of us, we must admit that they are priests and bishops, and we must regard their office as one that has a proper place in the Christian community and is useful to it. For whoever has crawled out of the water of baptism can boast that he is already a consecrated priest, bishop, and pope, even though it is not seemly that just anybody should exercise such an office. Because we are all priests of equal standing, no one must push himself forward and take it upon himself, without our consent and election, to do that for which we all have equal authority. For no one dare take upon himself what is common to all without the authority and consent of the community. And should it happen that someone chosen for such office were deposed for abuse of it, he would then be exactly what he was before. Therefore, a priest in Christendom is nothing else but an officeholder. As long as he holds office, he takes precedence; where he is deposed, he is a peasant or a townsman like anybody else. Indeed, a priest is never a priest when he is deposed. But now the Romanists have invented *characteres indelebiles* and blather that a deposed priest is nevertheless something different from a mere layman. They fancy that a priest can never be anything other than a priest, or ever become a layman.[17] All this is just contrived talk and human law.

It follows from this that there is no true, basic difference between laymen and priests, princes and bishops, or (as they say) between spiritual and secular, except that of office and work, and not that of status. For they are all of spiritual status, all are truly priests, bishops, and popes. But they do not

15. The term Luther uses here (and elsewhere) is *das geystlich recht* ("spiritual law"), a term that refers to church law as codified in the later medieval period into what is now known as the *Corpus Iuris Canonici*. Of the five collections that make up the *Corpus*, Luther referred most often to the two oldest: the *Decretum Gratiani* (c. 1140), and the *Decretals*, i.e., the *Liber Decretalium Gregorii IX* (1234). His attitude toward canon law was ambiguous. On the one hand, he hated it as the embodiment in law of papal tyranny. On the other hand, he found in it much useful evidence about the wholesome practices and teachings of the ancient church, and he became adroit at citing it to prove his contention that the "Romanists" ignored their own law when it suited their interests to do so. (On 10 December 1520 Luther burned a copy of canon law along with the papal bull of excommunication.)

16. St. Augustine, bishop of Hippo (354–430); St. Ambrose, bishop of Milan (c. 340–397); St. Cyprian, bishop of Carthage (d. 258).

17. The doctrine that ordination impresses on the soul an indelible mark that distinguishes the recipient from all those who have not received it was given authoritative formulation in the 1439 bull *Exultate Deo* of Pope Eugene IV (1383–1447); see Mirbt-Aland 484–85, no. 774, §9. Thus, a man in orders could cease functioning as a priest, but he could never again be a mere layman.

all have the same work to do, just as priests and monks do not all have exactly the same work. This is the teaching of St. Paul in Rom. 12[:4-5] and 1 Cor. 12[:12] and in 1 Pet. 2[:9], as I have said above, namely, that we are all one body of Christ the Head, and all members one of another. Christ has neither two bodies nor two kinds of body, one secular and the other spiritual. There is but one head and one body.

Therefore, just as those who are now called "spiritual," that is, priests, bishops, or popes, are neither different from other Christians nor superior to them, except that they are charged with the administration of the word of God and the sacraments, which is their work and office, so it is with secular government, which has the sword and rod in hand to punish the wicked and protect the good. A cobbler, a blacksmith, a peasant—each has the work and office of his trade, and yet they are all alike consecrated priests and bishops, and everyone should benefit and serve everyone else by means of their own work or office, so that in this way many kinds of work may be done for the bodily and spiritual welfare of the community, just as all the members of the body serve one another [1 Cor. 12:14-26].

Now consider how Christian the decree is which says that the secular power is not above the "spiritual estate" and has no right to punish it.[18] That is as much as to say that the hand should not help the eye when it suffers pain. Is it not unnatural, not to mention un-Christian, that one member should not help another and prevent its destruction? In fact, the more honorable the member, the more the others ought to help. I say therefore that since secular authority is ordained of God to punish the wicked and protect the good, it should be left free to perform its office in the whole body of Christendom without restriction and without respect to persons, whether it affects pope, bishops, priests, monks, nuns, or anyone else. If it were sufficient for the purpose of preventing secular authority from doing its work to say that among Christian offices it is inferior to that of preacher, confessor, or anyone of spiritual status, one would also have to prevent tailors, cobblers, stonemasons, carpenters, cooks, innkeepers, farmers, and the practitioners of all other secu-

18. The claim that spiritual authority was superior to all secular authority and not subject to correction by it was classically formulated in the 1302 bull *Unam sanctam* of Boniface VIII (c. 1235–1303). An important corollary of this view was the claim that clergymen had the *privilegium fori*, i.e., that they were exempt from the jurisdiction of the secular courts, even when charged with secular crimes. See nn. 21, 22 below.

lar trades from providing pope, bishops, priests, and monks with shoes, clothes, house, meat, and drink, as well as from paying them any tribute. But if these laypeople are allowed to do their proper work without restriction, what then are the Romanist scribes[19] doing with their own laws, which exempt them from the jurisdiction of secular Christian authority? It is just so that they can be free to do evil and fulfill what St. Peter said: "False teachers will rise up among you who will deceive you, and with their false and fanciful talk, they will take advantage of you" [2 Pet. 2:1-3].

For these reasons, Christian secular authority ought to exercise its office without hindrance, regardless of whether it is pope, bishop, or priest whom it affects. Whoever is guilty, let him suffer [punishment]. All that canon law has said to the contrary is the invention of Romanist presumption. For thus St. Paul says to all Christians, "Let every soul (I take that to mean the pope's soul also) be subject to governing authority, for it does not bear the sword in vain, but serves God by punishing the wicked and benefiting the good" [Rom. 13:1, 4]. St. Peter, too, says, "Be subject to all human ordinances for the sake of the Lord, who so wills it" [1 Pet. 2:13, 15]. He has also prophesied in 2 Pet. 2[:1] that such men would arise and despise secular government. This is exactly what has happened through canon law.

So I think this first paper wall is overthrown. Inasmuch as secular rule has become a part of the Christian body, it is part of the spiritual estate, even though its work is physical. Therefore, its work should extend without hindrance to all the members of the whole body, to punish and use force whenever guilt deserves or necessity demands, without regard to whether the culprit is pope, bishop, or priest. Let the Romanists hurl threats and bans as they like. That is why guilty priests, when they are handed over to secular law, are first deprived of their priestly dignities.[20] This would not be right unless the secular sword previously had had authority over these priests by divine right. Moreover, it is intolerable that in canon law so much importance is attached to the freedom, life, and property of the clergy,[21] as though the laity were not also as spiritual and as good Christians

19. An allusion to references in the Gospels to "scribes and Pharisees."

20. A clergyman found guilty of a secular crime by an ecclesiastical court was first deprived of his priestly office and then surrendered to the secular authorities for punishment.

21. In addition to the *privilegium fori* (see note 18), members of the clergy and religious orders enjoyed the *privilegium canonis*, according to which anyone who laid a hand on a clergyman or monk automatically incurred excommunication, the lifting of which was reserved to the pope. Canon law also declared that ecclesiastical persons and property were exempt from most of the general obligations (e.g., military service) and taxes required of laypeople (*privilegium immunitatis*).

as they, or did not also belong to the church. Why are your life and limb, your property and honor, so cheap and mine not, inasmuch as we are all Christians and have the same baptism, the same faith, the same Spirit, and all the rest? If a priest is murdered, the whole country is placed under interdict.[22] Why not when a peasant is murdered? How does this great difference come about between two men who are both Christians? It comes from the laws and fabrications of men.

It can, moreover, be no good spirit that has invented such exceptions and granted such license and impunity to sin. For if it is our duty to strive against the words and works of the devil and to drive him out in whatever way we can, as both Christ and his apostles command us, how have we come to the point that we have to do nothing and say nothing when the pope or his cohorts undertake devilish words and works? Ought we merely out of regard for these people allow the suppression of divine commandments and truth, which we have sworn in baptism to support with life and limb? Then we should have to answer for all the souls that would thereby be abandoned and led astray!

It must, therefore, have been the chief devil himself who said what is written in the canon law, that if the pope were so scandalously bad as to lead crowds of souls to the devil, still he could not be deposed.[23] At Rome they build on this accursed and devilish foundation, and think that we should let all the world go to the devil rather than resist their knavery. If the fact that one man is set over others were sufficient reason why he should not be punished, then no Christian could punish another, since Christ commanded that all people should esteem themselves as the lowliest and the least [Matt. 18:4].

Where sin is, there is no longer any shielding from punishment. St. Gregory writes that we are indeed all equal, but guilt makes a person inferior to others.[a] Now we see how the Romanists treat Christendom. They take away its freedom without any proof from Scripture, at their own whim. But God, as well as the apostles, made them subject to the

22. An interdict banned the administration of the sacraments and other ecclesiastical rites (e.g., Christian burial) in a given jurisdiction, even an entire kingdom (as in the case of England, placed under interdict by Pope Innocent III [c. 1160–1216] in 1208). The use of interdict was not uncommon in the Middle Ages, but by 1500 its frequent use for trifling infractions of church law or clerical privilege was a common grievance of the laity against the clergy.

23. In his *Epitome* (see p. 2, n. 1), Sylvester Prierias had quoted this provision of canon law against Luther: "An undoubtedly legitimate pope cannot be lawfully deposed or judged by either a council or the entire world, even if he be so scandalous as to lead people with him *en masse* into the possession of the devil in hell." See WA 6:336.

a Pope Gregory the Great (c. 540–604), *Regula pastoralis* 2.6.

secular sword. It is to be feared that this is a game of the Antichrist,[24] or at any rate that his forerunner has appeared.

The second wall is still more loosely built and less substantial. [The Romanists] want to be the only masters of Holy Scripture, although they never learn a thing from the Bible all their life long. They assume the sole authority for themselves, and, quite unashamed, they play about with words before our very eyes, trying to persuade us that the pope cannot err in matters of faith, regardless of whether he is righteous or wicked.[25] Yet they cannot point to a single letter.[b] This is why so many heretical and un-Christian, even unnatural, ordinances stand in the canon law. But there is no need to talk about these ordinances at present. Since these Romanists think the Holy Spirit never leaves them, no matter how ignorant and wicked they are, they become bold and decree only what they want. And if what they claim were true, why have Holy Scripture at all? Of what use is Scripture? Let us burn the Scripture and be satisfied with the unlearned gentlemen at Rome who possess the Holy Spirit! And yet the Holy Spirit can be possessed only by upright hearts. If I had not read the words with my own eyes,[c] I would not have believed it possible for the devil to have made such stupid claims at Rome, and to have won supporters for them.

But so as not to fight them with mere words, we will quote the Scriptures. St. Paul says in 1 Cor. 14[:30], "If something better is revealed to anyone, though he is already sitting and listening to another in God's word, then the one who is speaking shall hold his peace and give place." What would be the point of this commandment if we were compelled to believe only the man who does the talking, or the man who is at the top? Even Christ said in John 6[:45] that all Christians shall be taught by God. If it were to happen that the pope and his cohorts were wicked and not true Christians, were not taught by God and were without understanding, and at the same time some obscure person had a right

24. Luther and his contemporaries believed the appearance of the Antichrist was prophesied in 2 Thess. 2:3-10; 1 John 2:18, 22; 4:3; and Revelation 13. It was precisely at this time that Luther's suspicion that the papacy was the Antichrist turned to conviction and was expressed publicly in his response to the *Epitome* of Prierias; see the introduction, p. 2, n. 1 and note d.

25. Papal infallibility did not finally become official doctrine of the Catholic Church until 1870. In Luther's day, it was an opinion that had long been vigorously asserted by champions of papal authority, particularly at the Curia in Rome, but was not universally accepted. In his attack on the *95 Theses*, for example, Sylvester Prierias had argued, without citing Scripture, that "whoever does not rely on the teaching of the Roman church and the supreme pontiff as an infallible rule of faith, from which even Holy Scripture draws its vigor and authority, is a heretic" (*D. Martini Lutheri Opera Latina varii argumenti*, vol. 1: *Scripta 1515–1518* [Frankfurt/Main: Heyder & Zimmer, 1865], 347). But in the wake of Luther's excommunication in 1521, there were many in Germany and elsewhere who did not believe that he was a heretic just because the pope said so.

b I.e., to a single letter of Scripture to support their claim.

c Luther is referring to the passage quoted in n. 25.

understanding, why should the people not follow that one? Has the pope not erred many times? Who would help Christendom when the pope erred if we did not have others[d] who had the Scriptures on their side and whom we could trust more than him?

Therefore, their claim that only the pope may interpret Scripture is an outrageous fancied fable. They cannot produce a single letter [of Scripture] to maintain that the interpretation of Scripture or the confirmation of its interpretation belongs to the pope alone. They themselves have usurped this power. And although they allege that this power was given to St. Peter when the keys were given him, it is clear enough that the keys were not given to Peter alone but to the whole community.[e] Further, the keys were not ordained for doctrine or government, but only for the binding or loosing of sin. Whatever else or whatever more they arrogate to themselves on the basis of the keys is a mere fabrication. But Christ's words to Peter, "I have prayed for you that your faith fail not" [Luke 22:32], cannot be applied to the pope, since the majority of the popes have been without faith, as they must themselves confess. Besides, it is not only for Peter that Christ prayed, but also for all apostles and Christians, as he says in John 17[:9, 20], "Father, I pray for those whom thou hast given me, and not for these only, but for all who believe on me through their word." Is that not clear enough?

Just think of it! The Romanists must admit that there are among us good Christians who have the true faith, spirit, understanding, word, and mind of Christ. Why, then, should we reject the word and understanding of good Christians and follow the pope, who has neither faith nor intelligence? To follow the pope would be to deny the whole faith as well as the Christian church. Again, if the article, "I believe in one holy Christian church," is correct, then the pope cannot be the only one who is right.[f] Otherwise, we would have

d Singular in the original.

e Matt. 16:19; 18:18; and John 20:23. See *A Sermon on the Sacrament of Penance* in *The Annotated Luther*, Volume 1, pp. 195–96. For the "Keys," see *The 95 Theses* in *The Annotated Luther*, Volume 1, p. 37, n. 36.

f Citing the Nicene Creed, according to the standard German translation.

to pray, "I believe in the pope at Rome." This would reduce the Christian church to one man, and be nothing else than a devilish and hellish error.

Besides, if we are all priests, as was said above,[g] and all have one faith, one gospel, one sacrament, why should we not also have the power to test and judge what is right or wrong in matters of faith? What becomes of Paul's words in 1 Cor. 2[:15], "A spiritual person judges all things and yet is judged by no one"? And 2 Cor. 4[:13], "We all have one spirit of faith"? Why, then, should not we perceive what is consistent with faith and what is not, just as well as an unbelieving pope does?

We ought to become bold and free on the authority of all these texts, and many others. We ought not to allow the Spirit of freedom (Paul's appellation [2 Cor. 3:17]) to be frightened off by the fabrications of the popes but ought rather to march boldly forward and test all that they do or leave undone by our faithful understanding of the Scriptures. We must compel the Romanists to follow not their own interpretation but the better one. Long ago Abraham had to listen to Sarah, although she was in more complete subjection to him than we are to anyone on earth [Gen. 21:12]. And Balaam's donkey was wiser than the prophet himself [Num. 22:21-35]. If God spoke then through a donkey against a prophet, why should he not be able even now to speak through a righteous person against the pope? Similarly, St. Paul rebukes St. Peter as someone in error in Gal. 2[:11-12]. Therefore, it is the duty of every Christian to espouse the cause of the faith, to understand and defend it, and to denounce every error.

The third wall[26] falls of itself once the first two are down. For when the pope acts contrary to the Scriptures, it is our duty to stand by the Scriptures, to reprove him, and to constrain him, according to the word of Christ, Matthew 18[:15-17], "If your brother sins against you, go and tell it to him, between you and him alone; if he does not listen to you, then take one or two others with you; if he does not

26. See p. 13 (first wall) and p. 19 (second wall).

g See p. 15f.

listen to them, tell it to the church; if he does not listen to the church, consider him a heathen." Here every member is commanded to care for every other. How much more should we do this when the member that does evil is responsible for the government of the church, and by that one's evildoing is the cause of much harm and offense to the rest. But if I am to accuse such a person before the church, I must naturally call the church together.

[The Romanists] have no basis in Scripture for their claim that the pope alone has the right to call or confirm a council.[27] It is just their own law, and it is only valid as long as it is not harmful to Christendom or contrary to the laws of God. But if the pope deserves punishment, this law ceases to be valid, for it is harmful to Christendom not to punish him by authority of a council.

Thus we read in Acts 15 that it was not St. Peter who called the Apostolic Council but the apostles and elders. If then that right had belonged to St. Peter alone, the council would not have been a Christian council, but a heretical *conciliabulum*.[h] Even the Council of Nicaea, the most famous of all councils, was neither called nor confirmed by the bishop of Rome, but by the emperor Constantine.[28] Many other emperors after him have done the same, and yet these councils were the most Christian of all.[29] But if the pope alone has the right to convene councils, then these councils would all have been heretical. Further, when I examine the councils the pope did summon, I find that they did nothing of special importance.

Therefore, when necessity demands it, and the pope is an offense to Christendom, the first one who is able should, as true members of the whole body, do what can be done to bring about a truly free council. No one can do this so well as the secular authorities, especially since they are also fellow-Christians, fellow-priests, fellow-participants in spiritual authority, sharing power over all things. Whenever it is necessary or profitable, they ought to exercise the office and work that they have received from God over everyone.

27. The claim, asserted in several decrees of canon law, had been advanced against Luther by Prierias in his *Epitome*: "[W]hen there is one undisputed pontiff, it belongs to him alone to call a council." Moreover, "the decrees of councils neither bind nor constrain unless they are confirmed by the authority of the Roman pontiff" (WA 6:335).

28. The Council of Nicaea (325), the first general council, was called by Emperor Constantine (c. 272–337) to deal with the Arian Controversy.

29. Besides Nicaea, there were the councils of Constantinople (381), Ephesus (431), and Chalcedon (451). More recently, Emperor Maximilian I and King Louis XII (1462–1515) of France had convoked the Second Council of Pisa (1511), but Pope Julius II countered by summoning the Fifth Lateran Council to Rome (1512).

h I.e., a miserable little invalid gathering rather than a true council.

Would it not be unnatural if a fire broke out in a city and everybody were to stand by and let it burn on and on and consume everything that could burn because nobody had the authority of the mayor, or because, perhaps, the fire broke out in the mayor's house? In such a situation is it not the duty of every citizen to rouse and summon the rest? How much more should this be done in the spiritual city of Christ if a fire of offense breaks out, whether in the pope's government or anywhere else! The same argument holds if an enemy were to attack a city. The person who first rouses the others deserves honor and gratitude. Why, then, should that person not deserve honor who makes known the presence of the enemy from hell and rouses Christian people and calls them together?

All their boasting about an authority that dare not be opposed amounts to nothing at all. Nobody in Christendom has authority to do injury or to forbid the resisting of injury. There is no authority in the church except to foster improvement. Therefore, if the pope were to use his authority to prevent the calling of a free council, thereby preventing the improvement of the church, we should have regard neither for him nor for his authority. And if he were to hurl his bans and thunderbolts, we should despise his conduct as that of a madman, and we should instead ban him and drive him out as best we can, relying completely upon God. For his presumptuous authority is nothing, nor does he possess it. He is quickly defeated by a single text of Scripture, where Paul says to the Corinthians, "God has given us authority not to ruin Christendom, but to build it up" [2 Cor. 10:8]. Who will leap over the hurdle of this text? It is the power of the devil and of Antichrist, which resists the things that serve to build up Christendom. Such power is not to be obeyed, but rather resisted with life, property, and with all our might and main.

Statue of Emperor Constantine.

Even though a miracle were to be performed against secular authority on the pope's behalf, or if somebody were struck down by the plague—which they boast has sometimes happened—it should be considered as nothing but the work of the devil designed to destroy our faith in God.

Christ foretold this in Matt. 24[:24], "False Christs and false prophets shall come in my name, who shall perform signs and miracles in order to deceive even the elect." And Paul says in 2 Thess. 2[:9] that Antichrist shall, through the power of Satan, be mighty in false miracles.

Let us, therefore, hold fast to this: Christian authority can do nothing against Christ. As St. Paul says, "We can do nothing against Christ, only for Christ" [2 Cor. 13:8]. But if an authority does anything against Christ, then it is that of the Antichrist and the devil, even if it were to rain and hail miracles and plagues. Miracles and plagues prove nothing, especially in these evil latter days. The whole of Scripture foretells such false miracles. This is why we must cling to the word of God with firm faith, and then the devil will soon drop his miracles!

Papal coat of arms showing a triple-crowned tiara.

With this I hope that all these wicked and lying terrors, with which the Romanists have long intimidated and dulled our consciences, have been overcome and that they, just like all of us, shall be made subject to the sword. For they have no right to interpret Scripture merely on their own authority and without learning. They have no authority to prevent a council, much less at their mere whim to put it under obligation, impose conditions on it, or deprive it of its freedom. When they do such things, they are truly in the fellowship of Antichrist and the devil. They have nothing at all of Christ except the name.

Let us now look at the matters that ought to be properly dealt with in councils, matters with which popes, cardinals, bishops, and all scholars ought properly to be occupied day and night if they loved Christ and his church. But if this is not the case, let ordinary people[i] and the secular authorities take action,[j] without regard to papal bans and fulminations, for [suffering under] an unjust ban is better than ten just and proper absolutions, and [trusting] one unjust,

i Luther's word is *der hauff* (literally, "the crowd," i.e., ordinary people without ecclesiastical office).

j I.e., convoke a council and do whatever else they can to restore health to the church.

improper absolution is worse than ten just bans. Therefore, let us awake, dear Germans, and fear God more than mortals [Acts 5:29], lest we suffer the same fate of all the poor souls who are so lamentably lost through the shameless, devilish rule of the Romanists, and the devil grow stronger every day—as if it were possible that such a hellish regime could grow any worse, something that I can neither conceive nor believe.

First. It is horrible and shocking to see the head of Christendom, who boasts that he is the vicar of Christ and successor of St. Peter, going about in such a worldly and ostentatious style that neither king nor emperor can equal or approach him. He claims the title of "most holy" and "most spiritual," and yet he is worldlier than the world itself. He wears a triple crown, whereas the highest monarchs wear but one.[30] If that is like the poverty of Christ and of St. Peter, then it is a new and strange kind of likeness! When anybody says anything against it, [the Romanists] bleat, "Heresy!" They refuse to hear how un-Christian and ungodly all this is. In my opinion, if the pope were to pray to God with tears, he would have to lay aside his triple crown, for the God we worship cannot put up with pride. In fact, the pope's office should be nothing else but to weep and pray for Christendom and to set an example of utter humility.

30. The tiara or triple crown, the papal headdress on nonliturgical occasions, was first used in the fourteenth century. The symbolism of the three layers of the crown was variously interpreted, but it undoubtedly included the assertion of the pope's elevation above all secular authority as well as his headship of the church.

Be that as it may, this kind of splendor is offensive, and the pope is bound for the sake of his own salvation to set it aside. It was for this reason that St. Paul said, "Abstain from all practices which give offense" [1 Thess. 5:22], and in Rom. 12[:17], "We should do good, not only in the sight of God, but also in the sight of all people." An ordinary bishop's mitre ought to be good enough for the pope. It is in wisdom and holiness that he should be above his fellows. He ought to leave the crown of pride to Antichrist, as his predecessors did centuries ago. The Romanists say he is a lord of the earth. That is a lie! For Christ, whose vicar and vicegerent he claims to be, said to Pilate, "My kingdom is not of this world" [John 18:36]. No vicar's rule can go beyond that of his lord. Moreover, he is not the vicar of Christ glorified but of Christ crucified. As Paul says, "I was determined to know nothing among you save Christ, and him only as the crucified" [1 Cor. 2:2], and in Phil. 2[:5-7], "This is how you should regard yourselves, as you see in Christ, who emptied himself and took upon himself the form of a servant." Or again in 1 Cor. 1[:23], "We preach Christ, the crucified." Now the Romanists make the pope a vicar of the glorified Christ in heaven, and some of them have allowed the devil to rule them so completely that they have maintained that the pope is above the angels in heaven and has them at his command.[31] These are certainly the proper works of the real Antichrist.

31. Cf. LW 32:74–75. This claim was advanced by Augustinus de Ancona (known as Augustinus Triumphans [1243–1328]) in Quaestio 18 of his *Summa de potestate ecclesiastica*, 1326 (first printed at Augsburg in 1473). See Blasius Ministeri, "De vita et operibus Augustine de Ancona, O.E.S.A. (d. 1328)," *Analecta Augustiniana* 22 (1953): 115, 156.

Second. Of what use to Christendom are those people called cardinals? I shall tell you. Italy and Germany have many rich monasteries, foundations,[k] benefices, and livings. No better way has been discovered of bringing all these to Rome than by creating cardinals and giving them bishoprics, monasteries, and prelacies for their own use and so overthrowing the worship of God. You can see that Italy is now almost a wilderness: monasteries in ruins, bishoprics despoiled, the prelacies and the revenues of all the churches drawn to Rome, cities decayed, land and people ruined because services are no longer held and the word of God is not preached. And why? Because the cardinals must have the income! No Turk[32] could have devastated Italy and suppressed the worship of God so effectively!

32. Luther's term for adherents of Islam, who were familiar to sixteenth-century Europeans primarily as Muslims from the Ottoman Turkish Empire. Besides being his word for subjects of the Ottoman Turkish Empire, "Turk" was Luther's word for "Muslim." Islam was familiar to sixteenth-century Europeans primarily via their confrontation with the Ottoman Turks, who were long a military threat on the eastern borders of the Holy Roman Empire as well as in the Mediterranean.

Now that Italy is sucked dry, the Romanists are coming into Germany.[l] They have made a gentle beginning. But let us keep our eyes open! Germany shall soon be like Italy. We have some cardinals already. The "drunken Germans" are not supposed to understand what the Romanists are up to until there is not a bishopric, a monastery, a parish, a benefice, not a single penny left. Antichrist must seize the treasures of the earth, as it is prophesied [Dan. 11:39, 43]. It works like this: they skim the cream off the bishoprics, monasteries, and benefices, and because they do not yet ven-

k German: *Stift*. This refers to university foundations and the collegiate foundations of cathedrals.

l Cf. *Treatise on Good Works* in *The Annotated Luther*, Volume 1, p. 340f.

ture to put them all to shameful use, as they have done in Italy, they in the meantime practice their holy cunning and couple together ten or twenty prelacies. They then tear off a little piece each year so as to make quite a tidy sum after all. The provostship of Würzburg yields a thousand gulden; that of Bamberg also yields a sum, [as do] Mainz, Trier, and others. In this way, one thousand or ten thousand gulden may be collected, so that a cardinal could live like a wealthy monarch at Rome.

When we have gotten used to that, we shall appoint thirty or forty cardinals in one day.[33] We shall give to one of them the Münchenberg at Bamberg,[m] along with the bishopric of Würzburg, with a few rich benefices attached to them, until churches and cities are destitute, and then we shall say, "We are Christ's vicars, and shepherds of Christ's sheep. The foolish, drunken Germans will just have to put up with it."

My advice, however, is to make fewer cardinals, or to let the pope support them at his own expense. Twelve of them would be enough, and each of them might have an income of a thousand gulden.[34] How is it that we Germans must put up with such robbery and extortion of our goods at the hands of the pope? If the kingdom of France has prevented it, why do we Germans let them make such fools and apes of us?[35] We could put up with all this if they stole only our property, but they lay waste to the churches in so doing, rob Christ's sheep of their true shepherds, and debase the worship and word of God. If there were not a single cardinal, the church would not perish. The cardinals do nothing to serve Christendom. They are only interested in the money side of bishoprics and prelacies, and they wrangle about them just as any thief might do.

Third. If ninety-nine percent of the papal court were abolished and only one percent kept, it would still be large enough to give answers in matters of faith. Today, however, there is such a swarm of parasites in that place called Rome, all of them boasting that they belong to the pope, that not even Babylon saw the likes of it. There are more than three

m I.e., the Michaelsberg Abbey in Bamberg.

33. On 1 July 1517, Pope Leo X (1475–1521) named thirty-one cardinals, the largest number ever created in a single consistory until 1946. At the end of Leo's reign, the total number of cardinals was forty-eight, seventeen more than it had been at the time of his election in 1513, but only three more than it had been at the time of the election of Julius II in 1503.

34. It was a common complaint that the College of Cardinals was too large, its size fed more by the income derived from the fees charged for an appointment to it than by the needs of the church. The fifteenth-century reform councils of Constance and Basel had wanted the total number fixed at twenty-four. The actual number at this time tended to hover at around twice that (see n. 33). The idea that the cardinals should be assigned a fixed income rather than endowed with benefices was also a common suggestion in the literature for church reform. The Council of Constance recommended an income of three to four thousand gulden.

35. In 1438 King Charles VIII (1470–1498) of France presided over a synod of French clergy and nobility at Bourges that adopted the so-called

thousand papal secretaries alone. Who could count the other officials? There are so many offices that one could scarcely count them.[36] These are all the people lying in wait for the endowments and benefices of Germany as wolves lie in wait for sheep. I believe that Germany now gives much more to the pope at Rome than it used to give to the emperors in ancient times. In fact, some have estimated that more than three hundred thousand gulden a year find their way from Germany to Rome.[n] This money serves no use or purpose. We get nothing for it except scorn and contempt. And we still go on wondering why princes and nobles, cities and endowments, land and people, grow poor. We ought to marvel that we have anything left to eat!

Since we have now come to the heart of the matter, we will pause a little and let it be seen that the Germans are not quite such crass fools that they know nothing about or do not understand the sharp practices of the Romanists. I do not here complain that God's command and Christian law are despised at Rome, for things are not going so well throughout Christendom, especially in Rome, that we may complain of such exalted matters. Nor do I complain that natural law, or secular law, or even reason count for nothing. My complaint goes deeper than that. I complain that the Romanists do not keep their own fabricated canon law, even though it is in fact plain tyranny, avarice, and temporal splendor rather than genuine law. This we shall see.

In former times, German emperors and princes permitted the pope to receive annates from all the benefices of the German nation. This sum amounts to one-half of the revenue of the first year from every single benefice.[37] This permission was given, however, so that by means of these large sums of money the pope might raise funds to fight against the Turks and infidels in defense of Christendom, and, so that the burden of war might not rest too heavily upon the nobility, the clergy too should contribute something toward it. The popes have so far used the splendid and simple devotion of the German people—they have received this money for more

n See RTA 2:675, par. 11.

Pragmatic Sanction, which applied to France some of the reform decrees of the Council of Basel. In effect, the Pragmatic Sanction took control over the election of bishops, abbots, and other benefice holders in France away from the pope and bestowed it on the crown, thus severely reducing the income derived from such appointments by the pope or his nonresident appointees. The payment of annates (see n. 37) to the pope was forbidden. In 1516 Pope Leo X and King Francis I (1494–1547) concluded the Concordat of Bologna, which replaced the Pragmatic Sanction but kept many of its provisions. The right of nomination to bishoprics and other high offices was expressly reserved to the crown, the pope retaining the right to withhold confirmation from appointments that violated canonical requirements. The matter of annates, however, was passed over in complete silence, which meant that the pope was tacitly given permission to collect them again. In Germany, relations between the pope and the German church were regulated by the Concordat of Vienna, concluded by Pope Nicholas V (1397–1455) and Emperor Frederick III (1415–1493) in 1448. By its terms, the pope had much greater freedom in appointments to ecclesiastical office and in collection revenues.

36. The papal court, or Curia, consisted of all the officials engaged in conduct of papal business as well as the pope's personal "household." According to a list published at Rome in 1545, there were in that year 949 curial positions that were available for the one-time payment of a fee. This

than a hundred years and have now made it an obligatory tax and tribute, but they have not only amassed no money [for this defense], they have used it to endow many posts and positions at Rome and to provide salaries for these posts, as though annates were a fixed rent.

When they pretend that they are about to fight the Turks, they send out emissaries to raise money. They often issue an indulgence on the same pretext of fighting the Turks. They think that those half-witted Germans will always be gullible, stupid fools, and will just keep handing over money to them to satisfy their unspeakable greed. And they think this even though it is public knowledge that not a cent of the annates, or of the indulgence money, or of all the rest, is spent to fight the Turks. It all goes into their bottomless moneybag. They lie and deceive. They make laws and they make agreements with us, but they do not intend to keep a single letter of them. Yet all this is done in the holy names of Christ and St. Peter.

In this matter, the German nation, bishops and princes, should now consider that they, too, are Christians. They should govern and protect the physical and spiritual goods of the people entrusted to them and defend them against these rapacious wolves who, dressed in sheep's clothing, pretend to be shepherds and rulers.[o] And since annates have been so shockingly abused, and not even kept for their original agreed purpose, [the bishops and princes] should not allow their land and people to be so pitilessly robbed and ruined contrary to all law. By decree either of the emperor or of the whole nation[p] the annates should either be kept here at home or else abolished. Since the Romanists do not abide by their agreement, they have no right to the annates. Therefore, the bishops and princes are responsible for punishing such thievery and robbery, or even preventing it, as the law requires.

In such a matter, they ought to help the pope and strengthen his hand. Perhaps he is too weak to prevent such

o Cf. Matt. 7:15.

p That is, by decree of the imperial diet.

number did not include the members of the papal household or the officials responsible for the government of the city of Rome and the papal states. See Benrath, 88, n. 18; 95–96, n. 36.

37. *Annates* consisted of the first year's revenue of an ecclesiastical benefice (or a specified portion of that revenue) paid to the papal treasury in return for appointment to that benefice. The rate of half the annual revenue was set by Pope John XXII (1244–1334) in 1317. It was an onerous tribute and much resented. The Council of Constance (1415) limited the payment of annates to bishoprics, abbacies, and other benefices with an income of more than twenty-four gulden, a rule that was applied to Germany in the Concordat of Vienna (1448).

abuse single-handedly. Or, in those cases where he wants to defend and maintain this state of affairs, they ought to resist him and protect themselves from him as they would from a wolf or a tyrant, for he has no authority to do evil or defend it. Even if it were ever desirable to raise such funds to fight the Turks, we ought to have at least enough sense to see that the German nation could better manage these funds than the pope. The German nation itself has enough people to wage war if the money is available. It is the same with annates as it has been with many other Romanist schemes.

Then, too, the year has been so divided between the pope and the ruling bishops and chapters that the pope has six months in the year (every other month) in which to bestow the benefices that become vacant in his months. In this way, almost all the best benefices have fallen into the hands of Rome, especially the very best prebends and dignities.[38] And when they once fall into the hands of Rome, they never come out of them again, though a vacancy may never occur again in the pope's month. In this way the chapters are short-changed. This is plain robbery, and the intention is to let nothing escape. Therefore, it is high time to abolish the "papal months" altogether. Everything that has been taken to Rome in this way must be restored. The princes and nobles ought to take steps for the restitution of the stolen property, punish the thieves, and strip the privilege of those who have abused that privilege. If it is binding and valid for the pope on the day after his election to make regulations and laws in his chancellery by which our endowed chapters and livings are stolen from us—a thing he has absolutely no right to do—then it should be still more valid for Emperor Charles,[39] on the day after his coronation, to make rules and laws that not another benefice or living in all Germany should be allowed to pass into the hands of Rome by means of the "papal months." The livings that have already fallen into the hands of Rome should be restored and redeemed from these Romanist robbers. Charles V has the right to do this by virtue of his authority as ruler.

But now this Romanist See[40] of avarice and robbery has not had the patience to wait for the time when all the bene-

38. Ever since the early fourteenth century, popes had claimed the authority to reserve to themselves the right of appointment to all ecclesiastical benefices, a right that might in specific cases be graciously conceded to others (Friedberg 2:1259–61). Abolished in France, "reservations" were still valid in Germany. The Concordat of Vienna (1448) provided for the free election of bishops and abbots, subject to confirmation by the pope, who could object to persons deemed unsuitable. If the election were found to violate canon law, the pope was to provide a candidate. In the case of canonries and other benefices below those of highest rank, those that fell vacant in the even-numbered months of the year were reserved for appointment by the pope. In the odd-numbered months, local authorities exercised their right of election.

39. Charles V (1500–1558) was Holy Roman Emperor from 1519 to 1556. His empire included Spain and the Habsburg Empire that extended across Europe from Spain and the Netherlands to Austria and the Kingdom of Naples.

40. The ecclesiastical jurisdiction of the Holy Catholic Church in Rome.

fices would fall to it one by one through this device of the "papal months." Rather, urged on by its insatiable appetite to get them all in its hands as speedily as possible, the Romanist See has devised a scheme whereby, in addition to the "annates" and "papal months," the benefices and livings should fall to Rome in three ways.[q]

First, if anyone who holds a "free" living[r] should die in Rome or on a journey to Rome, his living becomes the property in perpetuity of the Romanist—I ought to say roguish—See. But the Romanists do not want to be called robbers on this account, though they are guilty of robbery of a kind never heard of or read about before.

Second, if anyone belonging to the household of the pope or cardinals holds or takes over a benefice, or if anyone who had previously held a benefice subsequently enters the household of the pope or cardinals, [his living becomes the property in perpetuity of the Romanist See]. But who can count the household of the pope and cardinals? If he only goes on a pleasure ride, the pope takes with him three or four thousand on mules, in disdain of all emperors and kings! Christ and St. Peter went on foot so that their successors might have all the more pomp and splendor. Now Avarice has cleverly thought out another scheme, and arranges it so that many even outside Rome have the name "member of the papal household" just as if they were in Rome. This is done for the sole purpose that, by the simple use of that pernicious phrase "member of the pope's household," all benefices may be brought to Rome and bound there for all time. Are not these vexatious and devilish little inventions? Let us beware! Soon Mainz, Magdeburg, and Halberstadt will quietly slip into the hands of Rome, and then the cardinalate will cost a pretty penny![41] After that they will make all the German bishops cardinals, and then there will be nothing left.

Portrait of Holy Roman Emperor, Charles V.

41. The reference is to the accumulation of bishoprics in the hands of Albrecht von Brandenburg (1490–1545), who in 1513 became archbishop of Magdeburg and administrator of the bishopric of Halberstadt, and in the following year archbishop-elector of Mainz. In 1518 he was made cardinal. The need to raise money to pay the enormous fees for the dispensations from the canonical ban on such accumulation of benefices was in part behind the sale of indulgences by Johann Tetzel (c. 1460–1519). Luther objected to this indulgence in the *95 Theses* but was unaware of Albrecht's financial dealings. See *The 95 Theses* in *The Annotated Luther*, Volume 1, p. 17f.

q Here Luther summarizes provisions of the Concordat of Vienna.

r I.e., one not previously subject to appointment by the pope.

Third, when a dispute has started at Rome over a benefice, [it reverts to Roman control]. In my opinion this is the commonest and widest road for bringing livings into the hands of Rome. Even when there is no real dispute, countless knaves will be found at Rome who will unearth one and snatch the benefices at will. Thus many a good priest must lose his living or pay a sum of money to avoid having his benefice disputed. Such a living, rightly or wrongly contested, becomes the property of the Roman See forever. It would be no wonder if God were to rain fire and brimstone from heaven and sink Rome into the abyss, as he did Sodom and Gomorrah of old [Gen. 19:24]. Why should there be a pope in Christendom if his power is used for nothing else than for such gross wickedness and to protect and practice it? O noble princes and lords, how long will you leave your lands and your people naked and exposed to such ravenous wolves?

Since even these practices were not enough, and Avarice grew impatient at the long time it took to seize all the bishoprics, my Lord Avarice devised the fiction that the bishoprics should be nominally abroad but that their origin and foundation is at Rome. Furthermore, no bishop can be confirmed unless he pays a huge sum for his pallium and binds himself with solemn oaths to the personal service of the pope.[42] That explains why no bishop dares to act against the pope. That is what the Romanists were seeking when they imposed the oath [of allegiance]. It also explains why all the richest bishoprics have fallen into debt and ruin. I am told that Mainz pays twenty thousand gulden.[s] That is the Romanists all over! To be sure, they decreed a long time ago in canon law that the pallium should be given without cost, that the number in the pope's household be reduced, disputes lessened, and the chapters and bishops allowed their liberty. But this did not bring in money. So they turned over a new leaf and have taken all authority away from the bishops and chapters. These sit there like ciphers and have neither office nor authority nor work. Everything is

42. The pallium, a woolen shoulder cape that had to be secured from Rome, was the emblem of the office of archbishop as well as a symbol of his close ties to the papacy. A newly elected archbishop was required to acquire the pallium within three months of his election. In the early history of the church, it had been granted free of charge, but by Luther's day it had long since become an extremely expensive acquisition.

s Elsewhere Luther put the price at thirty thousand; see LW 39:60 (*On the Papacy in Rome*).

controlled by those arch-villains at Rome, almost right down to the office of sexton and bell ringer. Every dispute is called to Rome, and everyone does just as he pleases, under cover of the pope's authority.

What has happened in this very year? The bishop of Strasbourg wanted to govern his chapter properly and reform it in matters of worship. With this end in view, he established certain godly and Christian regulations. But our dear friend the pope and the Holy Roman See wrecked and damned this holy and spiritual ordinance, all at the instigation of the priests.[43] This is called feeding the sheep of Christ! That is how priests are strengthened against their own bishop, and how their disobedience to divine law is protected! Antichrist himself, I hope, will not dare to shame God so openly. There is your pope for you! Just as you have always wanted! Why did the pope do this? Ah! If one church were reformed, that would be a dangerous breakthrough. Rome might have to follow suit. Therefore, it is better that no priest be allowed to get along with another and, as we have grown accustomed to seeing right up to the present day, that kings and princes should be set at odds. It is better to flood the world with Christian blood, lest the unity of Christians compel the Holy Roman See to reform itself!

So far we have been considering how they deal with benefices that become vacant and are unoccupied. But for tender-hearted Avarice the vacancies are too few. Therefore, he has kept a very close watch even on those benefices still occupied by their incumbents, so that these too can be made vacant, even though they are not now vacant. He does this in several ways.

First, Avarice lies in wait where fat prebends or bishoprics are held by an old or sick man, or even by one with an alleged disability. The Holy See then provides a coadjutor, that is, an assistant, to an incumbent of this kind. This is done without the holder's consent or permission, and for the benefit of the coadjutor, because he is a member of the pope's "household," or because he has paid for it, or has otherwise earned it by some sort of service to Rome. In this case, the free rights of the chapter or the rights of the incumbent

43. Although he became a determined opponent of the Reformation, Wilhelm III, Count of Honstein (c. 1470–1541), bishop of Strasbourg from 1506 to 1541, had a long history of failed attempts to reform the clergy of his diocese. It is not clear what particular event Luther is referring to here, but he appears to have learned of it from Georg Spalatin; see WA Br 2:130, 20.

are disregarded, and the whole thing falls into the hands of Rome.

Second, there is the little word *commenda*.[44] This means the pope puts a cardinal, or another of his underlings, in charge of a rich, prosperous monastery, just as if I were to give you a hundred gulden to keep. This does not mean to give the monastery or bestow it. Nor does it mean abolishing it or the divine service. It means quite simply to give it into his keeping. Not that he to whom it is entrusted is to care for it or build it up, but he is to drive out the incumbent, receive the goods and revenues, and install some apostate, renegade monk or another,[45] who accepts five or six gulden a year and sits all day long in the church selling pictures and images to the pilgrims, so that neither prayers nor Masses are said in that place anymore. If this were to be called destroying monasteries and abolishing the worship of God, then the pope would have to be called a destroyer of Christendom and an abolisher of divine worship. He certainly does well at it! But this would be harsh language for Rome, so they have to call it a "*commenda*," or an entrusting for taking over the charge of the monastery. The pope can make "*commenda*" of four or more of these monasteries in one year, any single one of which may have an income of more than six thousand gulden. This is how the Romanists increase the worship of God and maintain the monasteries! Even the Germans are beginning to find that out!

Third, there are some benefices they call *incompatabilia*,[46] which, according to the ordinances of canon law, cannot be held at the same time, such as two parishes, two bishoprics, and the like. In these cases, the Holy Roman See of Avarice evades canon law by making glosses to its own advantage,[47] called *unio* and *incorporatio*. This means that the pope incorporates many *incompatabilia* into one single unit, so that each is a part of every other, and all of them together are looked upon as one benefice. They are then no longer *incompatabilia*, and the holy canon law is satisfied because it is no longer binding, except upon those who do not buy these glosses from the pope or his *datarius*.[48] The *unio*, that is, the uniting, is very similar. The pope combines many such

44. To be awarded a benefice *in commendam* was to be assigned the income from it without being obligated to perform the spiritual office that went with it (which would usually be assigned to a paid deputy or curate). *Commenda* had long been used to supplement the income of students, professors, ecclesiastical diplomats, cardinals, and others. The appointment of cardinals or even laymen as abbots *in commendam* was a longstanding abuse that was not effectively dealt with until the Council of Trent.

45. A monk who had abandoned his monastery without permission was deemed "apostate." In Luther's day, such renegade monks, wandering about in their garb and exercising the rights and privileges of their order, were a common sight. They were a nuisance to the resident parish clergy and often disrupted parish life.

46. Offices that cannot be combined in the hands of one officeholder.

47. In this context, "gloss" means a specious, self-serving interpretation and application of a word or expression. Luther is not referring to the "ordinary glosses" (*glossa ordinaria*), which were the authoritative commentaries on canon law by medieval jurists (glossators).

48. The *datarius* was the head of the *Dataria apostolica*, the bureau of the

benefices like a bundle of sticks, and they are all regarded as one benefice. There is at present a certain papal courtier[t] in Rome who alone holds twenty-two parishes, seven priories, as well as forty-four benefices.[49] All these are held by the help of that masterly gloss, which declares that this is not against canon law. What the cardinals and other prelates get out of it is anybody's guess. And this is the way the Germans are to have their purses emptied and their insolence deflated.

Another of these glosses is the *administratio*. This means that a man may hold, in addition to his bishopric, some abbacy or dignity and all its emoluments, without having the title attached to it. He is simply called the "administrator."[50] At Rome it is sufficient to change a word or two but leave the actuality what it was before. It is as if I were to teach that we were now to call the brothel-keeper the mayor's wife. She still remains what she was before. This kind of Romish regime Peter foretold in 2 Pet. 2[:1, 3], "False teachers will come who will deal with you in greed and lying words for their gain."

Our worthy Roman Avarice has devised another technique. He sells and bestows benefices on the condition that the vendor or bestower retains reversionary rights to them. In that event, when the incumbent dies the benefices automatically revert to him who had sold, bestowed, or surrendered them in the first instance. In this way, they have made hereditary property out of the benefices. Nobody else can come into possession of them except the man to whom the seller is willing to dispose of them, or to whom he bequeaths his rights at death. Besides, there are many who transfer to another the mere title to a benefice, but from which the titleholder does not draw a cent. Today, too, it has become an established custom to confer a benefice on a man while reserving a portion of the annual income for oneself. This used to be called simony.[51] There are many more things of this sort than can be counted. They treat benefices more shamefully than the heathen soldiers treated Christ's clothes at the foot of the cross.

t Luther's word is *kurtisan* (from the Latin *curtisanus*), the common (pejorative) term for a member of the papal Curia, or for a clergyman who secured his appointment from the Roman Curia.

papal Curia responsible for drafting, registering, and dating (hence the name) such written decisions of the pope as dispensations, appointments to benefices, and so forth. Fees were charged for its services.

49. The papal courtier referred to by Luther has not been identified. But there is documentation for two Germans, Johannes Zink (d. c. 1527) and Johannes Ingenwinkel (1469–1535), who accumulated papal appointments in Rome. In the period 1513 to 1521, Zink received fifty-six appointments; in the years 1496 to 1521 Ingenwinkel received 106. See Aloys Schulte, *Die Fugger in Rom 1495–1523*, vol. 1 (Leipzig: Verlag von Duncker, 1904), 282–306.

50. As, for example, in the case of Albrecht von Brandenburg, who was the administrator of Halberstadt; see above, n. 41.

51. Simony (named for Simon Magus; cf. Acts 8:18-20) was the buying or selling of an ecclesiastical office for money, favors, or any kind of material reward. It was strictly against canon law but widely practiced nonetheless.

But all that has been said up till now has been going on for so long that it has become established custom at Rome. Yet Avarice has come up with something else, which I hope may be his last and choke him. The pope has a noble little device called *pectoralis reservatio*, meaning mental reservation,[u] and *proprius motus*, meaning the arbitrary exercise of his authority.[52] It goes like this. A certain man goes to Rome and succeeds in procuring a benefice. It is duly signed and sealed in the customary manner. Then another candidate comes along, who brings money or else has rendered services to the pope, which bears no mention here, and desires the same benefice of the pope. The pope then gives it to him and takes it away from the other. If anybody complains that this is not right, then the Most Holy Father has to find some excuse lest he be accused of a flagrant violation of [canon] law. He then says that he had mentally reserved that particular benefice to himself and had retained full rights of disposal over it, although he had neither given it a thought in his whole life nor even heard of it. In this way, he has now found his usual little gloss. As pope he can tell lies, deceive, and make everybody look like a fool. And all this he does openly and unashamedly. And yet he still wants to be the head of Christendom, but lets himself be ruled by the evil spirit in obvious lies.

52. From 1484 popes claimed and occasionally exercised the right to issue decrees, the content of which had been determined by the pope *motu proprio* ("of his own accord"), without consulting the cardinals or any other authorities, for reasons that he himself found sufficient.

The pope's arbitrary and deceptive reservation now creates such a state of affairs in Rome that it defies description. There is buying, selling, bartering, exchanging, trading, pretense, deceit, robbery, theft, luxury, whoring, knavery, and every sort of contempt of God. Even the rule of the Antichrist could not be more scandalous. Venice, Antwerp, and Cairo[53] have nothing on this fair at Rome and all that goes on there. In these places there is still some regard for right and reason, but in Rome the devil himself is in charge. And out of this sea the same kind of morality flows into the whole world. Is it any wonder that people like this are terrified of reformation and of a free council, and prefer rather to set all the kings and princes at enmity lest in their unity they

53. Three major ports in the commerce of the day, famed as centers of vice.

u Literally, "reservation in the breast or heart."

should call a council? Who could bear to have such villainy brought to light?

Finally, the pope has built his own emporium for all this noble commerce, that is, the house of the *datarius* in Rome.[v] All who deal in benefices and livings must go there. Here they have to buy their glosses, transact their business, and get authority to practice such arch-knavery. There was a time when Rome was still lenient. In those days, people just had to buy justice or suppress it with money. But Rome has become so expensive today that it allows no one to practice such knavery unless he has first bought the right to do so. If that is not a brothel above all imaginable brothels, then I do not know what brothels are.

If you have money in such an emporium, you can obtain all the things we have just discussed. Indeed, not just these! Here usury[54] becomes honest money; the possession of property acquired by theft or robbery is legalized. Here vows are dissolved; monks are granted freedom to leave their orders. Here marriage is on sale to the clergy. Here the children of whores can be legitimized. Here all dishonor and shame can be made to look like honor and glory. Here every kind of fault and blemish is knighted and ennobled. Here marriage within the forbidden degrees or otherwise forbidden is rendered acceptable. O what assessing and fleecing take place there! It seems as though canon law were instituted solely for the purpose of setting a great many money traps from which anyone who wants to be a Christian must purchase his freedom. In fact, here the devil becomes a saint, and a god as well. What cannot be done anywhere else in heaven or on earth, can be done in this emporium. They call these things *compositiones*! Compositions indeed! Better named confusions.[55] Compared with the exactions of this holy house the Rhine toll is a poor sum indeed.[56]

Let no one accuse me of exaggeration. It is all so open that even in Rome they have to admit that the state of affairs there is more atrocious than anyone can say. I have not yet stirred the real hellish dregs of their personal vices—nor do

54. Canon law still condemned as usury the charging by Christians of interest on loans to other Christians.

55. *Compositiones* were the fees paid for dispensations from the provisions of canon law. Luther makes a pun on *compositiones* (literally, "things in good order") and *confusiones* ("things in disorder").

56. Princes and nobles who had fortresses along the Rhine commonly exacted tolls from passing merchant ships.

v See n. 48 above.

I want to. I speak only of ordinary, well-known matters, and still cannot find adequate words for them. Bishops, priests, and above all the theologians in the universities ought to have done their duty and with common accord written against such goings-on and cried out against them. This is what they are paid to do! But the truth is found on the other side of the page.[w]

I must take leave of this subject with one final word. Since this Boundless Avarice is not satisfied with all this wealth, wealth with which three great kings would be content, he now begins to transfer this trade and sell it to the Fuggers of Augsburg.[57] The lending, trading, and buying of bishoprics and benefices, and the commerce in ecclesiastical holdings, have now come to the right place. Now spiritual and secular goods have become one. I would now like to hear of somebody clever enough to imagine what Roman Avarice could do more than what it has already done, unless perhaps Fugger were to transfer or sell this present combination of two lines of business to somebody else. I really think it has just reached the limit.

As for what they have stolen in all lands, and still steal and extort, through indulgences, bulls,[58] confessional letters,[59] butter letters,[60] and other *confessionalia*—all this is just patchwork. It is just as if one were rolled dice with a devil right into hell. Not that these things bring in little money—for a powerful king could well support himself on such proceeds—but it is not to be compared with the streams of treasure referred to above. I shall say nothing at present about where this indulgence money has gone. I shall have more to say about that later. The Campo de' Fiore and the Belvedere and certain other places probably know something about that.[61]

Since, then, such devilish rule is not only barefaced robbery, deceit, and the tyranny of the gates of hell but also ruinous to the body and soul of Christendom, it is our duty to exercise all diligence to protect Christendom from

w I.e., the opposite is the case.

57. The Fugger firm of Augsburg was the greatest international banking house of the sixteenth century. It numbered popes, bishops, emperors, kings, and princes among its clients and benefactors. The Fuggers advanced to Charles V the funds needed to secure his election as emperor. Similarly, they advanced to Albrecht von Brandenburg the monies required for the purchase from Rome of the dispensations he needed to become archbishop of Mainz (see p. 31, n. 41).

58. A bull is a solemn mandate of the pope on any subject under his authority (the definition of doctrine, the granting of privileges, etc.). The name "bull" derives from the Latin *bulla*, a term for the seal attached to an official document.

59. Certificates that entitled the bearer to choose his or her own confessor and authorized the confessor to confer absolution for offenses normally reserved to the jurisdiction of bishops or the pope.

60. *Butterbriefe* was the popular term for written dispensations to consume butter, cheese, and milk during Lent.

61. The Campo de' Fiore was a Roman marketplace that Pope Eugene IV and his successors restored and developed at great expense. The Belvedere, originally a garden house in the Vatican, was turned into an elegant banquet hall and then used by Pope Julius II to store his collection of ancient art (e.g., the Apollo Belvedere). Luther hints that indulgence money was lavished on such projects rather than used for constructing St. Peter's in Rome as advertised.

such misery and destruction. If we want to fight against the Turks, let us begin here where they are worst of all. If we are right in hanging thieves and beheading robbers, why should we let Roman Avarice go free? He is the worst thief and robber that has ever been or could ever come into the world, and all in the holy name of Christ and St. Peter! Who can put up with it a moment longer and say nothing? Almost everything Avarice possesses has been procured by theft and robbery. It has never been otherwise, as all the history books prove. The pope never purchased such extensive holdings that the income from his *officia*[x] should amount to one million ducats, over and above the gold mines we have just been discussing and the income from his lands. Nor did Christ and St. Peter bequeath it to him. Neither has anyone given or lent it to him. Neither is it his by virtue of ancient rights or usage. Tell me, then, from what source could he have obtained it? Learn a lesson from this, and watch carefully what they are after and what they say when they send out their legates to collect money to fight the Turks.

Now, although I am too insignificant a man to make concrete proposals for the improvement of this dreadful state of affairs, nevertheless I shall sing my fool's song through to the end and say, so far as I am able, what could and should be done, either by secular authority or by a general council.

1. Every prince, every noble, every city should henceforth forbid their subjects to pay annates to Rome and should abolish them entirely. The pope has broken the agreement and made the annates a robbery to the injury and shame of the whole German nation. He gives them to his friends, sells them for huge sums of money, and uses them to endow offices. In so doing he has lost his right to them and deserves punishment. Consequently, secular authority is under obligation to protect the innocent and prevent injustice, as Paul teaches in Romans 13, and St. Peter in 1 Pet. 2[:14], and even the canon law in Case 16, Question 7, [canon 31], *de filiis*.[62] From this came the basis for saying to the pope and his own

x The curial offices that could be purchased; see p. 28, n. 36.

62. The correct name of the canon is *Filiis vel nepotibus*; Friedberg 1:809. It provides that when the endowment provided for a church is misused, and appeals to the bishop and archbishop fail to correct the abuse, the heirs of the person who established the endowment may appeal to the secular courts. Luther wants this principle applied to annates as well.

[the clergy], "*Tu ora*, thou shalt pray"; to the emperor and his servants, "*Tu protege*, thou shalt protect"; to the common man, "*Tu labora*, thou shalt labor," not, however, as though each person were not to pray, protect, and labor. (For the one who performs any task diligently does nothing but pray, protect, and labor.) But to each a special work is assigned.[63]

63. Although Luther here adheres to the traditional threefold division of society into priests, rulers, and workers (or farmers), he does so in accordance with the position taken in his assault on the first wall (pp. 13-17), namely that secular rulers have the obligation to protect their subjects against secular crimes committed by the clergy.

2. Since the pope with his Romish tricks—his *commenda*, coadjutors, reservations, *gratiae expectativae*, papal months, incorporations, unions, pensions, *pallia*, chancery rules, and such knavery[y]—usurps for himself all the German foundations without authority and right and gives and sells them to foreigners at Rome who do nothing for Germany in return, and since he robs the local bishops of their rights and makes mere ciphers and dummies of them, and thereby acts contrary to his own canon law, common sense, and reason, it has finally reached the point where the livings and benefices are, out of sheer greed, sold to coarse, unlettered donkeys and ignorant knaves at Rome. Pious and learned people do not benefit from their service or skill. Consequently the poor German people must go without competent and learned prelates and be destroyed.

For this reason, the Christian nobility should set itself against the pope as against a common enemy and destroyer of Christendom for the salvation of the poor souls who perish because of this tyranny. The Christian nobility should ordain, order, and decree that henceforth no further benefice shall be drawn into the hands of Rome, and that hereafter no appointment shall be obtained there in any manner whatsoever, but that the benefices should be dragged from this tyrannical authority and kept out of his reach. The nobility should restore to the local bishops their right and responsibility to administer the benefices in the German nation to the best of their ability. And when a papal courtier comes along,[z] he should be given a strict order to keep out, to jump into the Rhine or the nearest river, and give the

y With the exception of *gratiae expectivae* (promises to bestow a benefice not yet vacant), these "tricks" were explained earlier; see above, pp. 33-37, with the explanatory notes.

z Cf. p. 35, n. 49 and note *t*.

Romish ban with all its seals and letters a nice, cold bath. If this happened, they would sit up and take notice in Rome. They would not think that the Germans are always dull and drunk but have really become Christian again. They would realize that the Germans do not intend to permit the holy name of Christ, in whose name all this knavery and destruction of souls goes on, to be scoffed at and scorned any longer, and that they have more regard for God's honor than for the authority of mortals.

3. An imperial law should be issued that no bishop's cloak [*pallium*] and no confirmation of any dignity whatsoever shall henceforth be secured from Rome, but that the ordinance of the most holy and famous Council of Nicaea be restored. This ordinance decreed that a bishop shall be confirmed by the two nearest bishops or by the archbishop.[64] If the pope breaks the statutes of this and of all other councils, what is the use of holding councils? Who has given him the authority to despise the decisions of councils and tear them to shreds like this? Perhaps we should depose all bishops, archbishops, and primates[65] and make ordinary pastors of them, with only the pope as their superior, as he now is. The pope allows no proper authority or responsibility to the bishops, archbishops, and primates. He usurps everything for himself and lets them keep only the name and the empty title. It has even gone so far that by papal exemption the monasteries, abbots, and prelates as well are removed from the regular authority of the bishops.[66] Consequently there is no longer any order in Christendom. The inevitable result of all this is what has happened already: relaxation of punishment and the license to do evil all over the world. I certainly fear that the pope may properly be called "the man of sin" [2 Thess. 2:3]. Who but the pope can be blamed for there being no discipline, no punishment, no government, no order in Christendom? By his usurpation of power he ties the prelates' hands and takes away their rod of discipline. He opens his hands to all those set under him, and gives away or sells them freedom.[a]

64. Canon 4 of the Council of Nicaea (325). Here Luther still assumes that the existing ecclesiastical hierarchy would be preserved and reformed.

65. A primate was the highest-ranking archbishop of a country; in the Empire it was the archbishop of Mainz.

66. It was common practice for monastic houses to be removed from the jurisdiction of the local bishop and placed directly under that of the pope. Indeed, it was all but universal in the case of the houses of the mendicant orders.

a I.e., freedom from the jurisdiction of the local prelate.

Lest the pope complain that he is being robbed of his authority, it should be decreed that in those cases where the primates or the archbishops are unable to settle a case, or when a dispute arises between them, then the matter should be laid before the pope, but not every little thing. It was done this way in former times, and this was the way the famous Council of Nicaea decreed.[67] Whatever can be settled without the pope, then, should be settled in such a way that his holiness is not burdened with such minor matters, but gives himself to prayer, study and the care of all Christendom. This is what he claims to do. This is what the apostles did. They said in Acts 6[:2-4], "It is not right that we should leave the Word of God and serve tables, but we will hold to preaching and prayer, and set others over that work." But now Rome stands for nothing else than the despising of the gospel and prayer, and for the serving of tables, that is, temporal things. The government of the apostles and of the pope have as much in common as Christ has with Lucifer, heaven with hell, night with day. Yet the pope is called "Vicar of Christ" and "Successor to the Apostles."

4. It should be decreed that no secular matter is to be referred to Rome, but that all such cases shall be left to secular authority, as the Romanists themselves prescribe in that canon law of theirs, which they do not observe.[68] It should be the pope's duty to be the most learned in the Scriptures and the holiest (not in name only but in fact) and to regulate matters that concern the faith and holy life of Christians. He should hold the primates and archbishops to this task, and help them in dealing with these matters and taking care of these responsibilities. This is what St. Paul teaches in 1 Cor. 6[:7], and he takes the Corinthians severely to task for their concern with worldly things. That such matters are dealt with in Rome causes unbearable grief in every land. It increases the costs, and, moreover, these judges do not know the usage, laws, and customs of these lands, so that they often do violence to the facts and base their decisions on their own laws and precedents. As a result, the contesting parties often suffer injustice.

67. This was actually a decree of the Council of Sardica (343), but it was incorporated into canon law with inaccurate attribution to the Council of Nicaea; see Friedberg 1:520.

68. The councils of Constance and Basel had both tried to put an end to the evocation of secular cases to the Roman Curia, but it remained one of the most often-repeated of the grievances of the Holy Roman Empire against Rome. See Benrath, 97–98, n. 43; RTA 2:672, par. 1.

Moreover, the horrible fleecing practiced by the officials[69] must be forbidden in every diocese, so that they no longer assume jurisdiction over anything except matters of faith and morals and leave matters of money and property, life and honor, to the secular judges. Secular judges, therefore, should not allow sentences of excommunication and banishment in cases where faith and morals are not involved. Spiritual authority should rule over matters that are spiritual, as reason teaches. Spiritual goods, however, do not consist of money or material things but rather of faith and good works.

One might, nonetheless, grant that cases concerning benefices or livings be tried before bishops, archbishops and primates. Accordingly, whenever disputes or conflicts needed to be resolved, the primate of Germany could hold a general consistory with its jurists and judges, which would have the same authority as that of the *signatura gratiae* and *signatura justitiae* in Rome.[70] Cases in Germany would, by means of appeal, be brought before it and transacted in good order. One could not be required to pay for this by occasional presents and gifts, as is the case at Rome, as a result of which they have grown accustomed to the selling of justice and injustice. This is because the pope does not pay them a salary, but lets them grow fat from gifts. For no one at Rome cares anything about what is right or wrong, only about what is money and what is not. One might, rather, pay for this [court] from the annates, or in some other way devised by those who are better informed and more experienced in these things than I am. All I seek to do is to arouse and set to thinking those who have the ability and inclination to help the German nation be free and Christian again after the wretched, heathenish, and un-Christian reign of the pope.

5. Reservations should no longer be valid,[b] and no more benefices should be seized by Rome, even if the incumbent dies or there is a dispute, or even if the incumbent is a member of the pope's household or on the staff of a cardinal. And it must be strictly forbidden and prevented for any

b See p. 30, n. 38.

69. The *officialis* was the presiding judge of a bishop's court.

70. The supreme tribunal of the church was the *Signatura*, which was divided into the *Signatura gratiae*, presided over by the pope himself, and the *Signatura justitiae*, headed by a cardinal. The latter resolved conflicts of jurisdiction among various legal entities in the Curia. The former handled the pope's responses to requests for privileges or favors and in so doing could grant exemptions from church law. The proposal to turn the honorary primacy of the archbishop of Mainz into the effective headship of a German church with extensive administrative independence of Rome was first advanced by the Alsatian humanist Jakob Wimpfeling (1450–1528) in a memorandum submitted to Emperor Maximilian I in 1510. A shortened version of the memorandum had been published in May 1520, but Luther appears to have had access to the full manuscript. See Benrath, 98, n. 45.

papal courtier[c] to contest any benefice whatsoever, to summon pious priests to court, harass them, or force them into lawsuits. If, in consequence of this prohibition, any ban or ecclesiastical pressure should come from Rome, it should be disregarded, just as though a thief were to put a man under the ban because he would not let him steal. Indeed, they should be severely punished for blasphemous misuse of the ban and the divine name to strengthen their hand at robbery, and for desiring, by means of lies and fabrications, to compel us to endure and praise such blasphemy of God's name and such abuse of Christian authority, and to be participants in their rascality in the sight of God. We are responsible before God to oppose them, as St. Paul in Rom. 1[:32] reproves as worthy of death not only those who do such things, but also those who approve and permit them to be done. Most unbearable of all is the lying *reservatio pectoralis*,[d] whereby Christendom is so scandalously and openly put to shame and scorn because its head deals with open lies and for filthy lucre unashamedly deceives and fools everybody.

6. The *casus reservati*, reserved cases,[71] should also be abolished. They are not only the means of extorting much money from the people, but by means of them the ruthless tyrants ensnare and confuse many tender consciences, intolerably injuring their faith in God. This is especially true of the ridiculous, childish cases they make such a fuss about in the bull *Coena Domini*,[72] sins which should not even be called everyday sins, much less so great that the pope cannot remit them by indulgence. Examples of these sins are hindering a pilgrim on his way to Rome, supplying weapons to the Turk, or counterfeiting papal briefs.[73] They make fools of us with such crude, silly, clumsy goings-on! Sodom and Gomorrah, and all the sins that are or may be committed against the commandments of God, are not reserved cases. But what God has never commanded and they themselves have imagined—these must be reserved cases, in order that no one be prevented from bringing money to Rome, so that

71. Those cases in which the granting of absolution was reserved to the pope.

72. Since the fourteenth century it had been the custom to publish at Rome on Maundy Thursday an updated version of the bull *In coena Domini*, a catalog of heresies and offenses punishable by excommunication, absolution for which was reserved to the pope. After his excommunication in 1521, Luther's name was added to the list of heretics.

73. A decree in the form of a letter emanating from the pope, simpler in form than a bull but of comparable authority.

c See p. 35, n. 49.

d I.e., mental reservation; see above, p. 36.

they may live in the lap of luxury, safe from the Turks and by their wanton, worthless bulls and briefs keep the world subjected to their tyranny.

Such knowledge should properly be available from all priests or be a public ordinance, namely, that no secret, undenounced sin constitutes a reserved case; and that every priest has the power to remit every sin no matter what it is.[e] Where sins are secret, neither abbot, bishop, nor pope has the power to reserve one of them to himself. If they did that, their action would be null and void. They ought even to be punished as people who without any right at all presume to make judgments in God's stead, and thereby ensnare and burden poor and ignorant consciences. In those cases, however, where open and notorious sins are committed, especially sins against God's commandments, then there are indeed grounds for reserved cases. But even then there should not be too many of them, and they should not be reserved arbitrarily and without cause. For Christ did not set tyrants in his church, but shepherds, as Peter said in the last chapter of his first epistle [1 Pet. 5:2-3].

7. The Roman See should do away with the *officia*[f] and cut down the creeping, crawling swarm of vermin at Rome, so that the pope's household can be supported out of the pope's own pocket. The pope should not allow his court to surpass the courts of all kings in pomp and extravagance, because this kind of thing not only has never been of any use to the cause of the Christian faith but also has kept the courtiers from study and prayer until they are hardly able to speak about the faith at all. This they proved quite flagrantly at this last Roman council,[74] in which, among many other childish and frivolous things, they decreed that the human soul is immortal and that every priest must say his

74. The Fifth Lateran Council (1412–1417), convened by Julius II.

e Thesis 6 (See *The 95 Theses* in *The Annotated Luther*, Volume 1, p. 35) stated, "The pope cannot remit any guilt except by declaring and confirming its remission by God or, of course, by remitting guilt in [legal] cases reserved to himself." In terms of divine grace and the removal of guilt, priests simply announced God's forgiveness. Regarding especially heinous sins, ecclesiastical absolution was restricted to the papal see.

f See p. 28, n. 36.

prayers once a month unless he wants to lose his benefice. How can the affairs of Christendom and matters of faith be settled by people who are hardened and blinded by gross avarice, wealth, and worldly splendor, and who now for the first time decree that the soul is immortal? It is no small shame to the whole of Christendom that they deal so disgracefully with the faith at Rome. If they had less wealth and pomp, they could pray better and study to be worthy and diligent in dealing with matters of faith, as was the case in former times, when bishops did not presume to be the kings of all kings.

8. The harsh and terrible oaths that the bishops are wrongfully compelled to swear to the pope should be abolished. These oaths bind the bishops like servants and are decreed in that arbitrary, stupid, worthless, and unlearned chapter, *Significasti*.[75] Is it not enough that they burden us in body, soul, and property with their countless foolish laws by which they weaken faith and waste Christendom, without also making a prisoner of the bishop both as a person as well as in his office and function? In addition, they have also assumed the investiture,[76] which in ancient times was the right of the German emperor, and in France and other countries investiture still belongs to the king. They had great wars and disputes with the emperors about this matter until finally they had the brazen effrontery to take it over, and have held it until now; just as though the Germans more than all other Christians on earth had to be the silly fools of the pope and the Romanist See and do and put up with what no one else will either put up with or do. Since this is sheer robbery and violence, hinders the regular authority of the bishop, and injures poor souls, the emperor and his nobles are duty-bound to prevent and punish such tyranny.

9. The pope should have no authority over the emperor, except the right to anoint and crown him at the altar, just as a bishop crowns a king. We should never again yield to that devilish pride which requires the emperor to kiss the pope's feet, or sit at his feet, or, as they say, hold his stirrup or the bridle of his mule when he mounts to go riding. Still less should he do homage and swear faithful allegiance to

75. It provided that no pallium (above, p. 32 n. 42) was to be bestowed on an archbishop until he had sworn an oath of allegiance to the Holy See; Friedberg 2:49–50.

76. Investiture was the ceremony of installing a bishop in office by bestowing on him the staff and ring that were the symbols of his authority. In Germany this was a matter complicated by the fact that most bishops were the secular rulers of an imperial territory (e.g., the electorate of Mainz) as well as the overseers of an ecclesiastical benefice (e.g., the archbishopric of Mainz). In the eleventh and twelfth centuries, this situation had produced a bitter struggle between pope and emperor over who controlled the investiture of bishops. The Concordat of Worms (1122) took away from the emperor the right to invest bishops with ring and staff and left him with only the right to invest them with authority as secular rulers.

the pope, as the popes brazenly demand as though they had a right to it. The chapter *Solite*,[g] which sets papal authority above imperial authority, is not worth a cent, and the same goes for all those who base their authority on it or pay any deference to it. For it does nothing else than force the holy words of God, and wrest them out of their true meaning to conform to their own fond imaginations, as I have shown in a Latin treatise.[h]

This most extreme, arrogant, and wanton presumption of the pope has been devised by the devil, who under cover of this intends to usher in the Antichrist and raise the pope above God, as many are now doing and even have already done. It is not proper for the pope to exalt himself above the secular authorities, except in spiritual offices such as preaching and giving absolution. In other matters, the pope is subject to the crown, as Paul and Peter teach in Rom. 13[:1-7] and 1 Pet. 2[:13], and as I have explained above.[i]

The pope is not a vicar of Christ in heaven but only of Christ as he walked the earth. Christ in heaven, in the form of a ruler, needs no vicar, but sits on his throne and sees everything, does everything, knows everything, and has all power. But Christ needs a vicar in the form of a servant, the form in which he went about on earth, working, preaching, suffering, and dying. Now the Romanists turn all that upside down. They take the heavenly and kingly form from Christ and give it to the pope, and leave the form of a servant to perish completely. He might almost be the Counter-Christ, whom the Scriptures call Antichrist,[j] for all his nature, work, and pretensions run counter to Christ and only blot out Christ's nature and destroy his work.

It is also ridiculous and childish for the pope, on the basis of such perverted and deluded reasoning, to claim in his decretal *Pastoralis* that he is rightful heir to the emperorship

g Friedberg 2:196.

h *Resolutio Lutheriana super propositione XIII de potestate papae* (1519) in WA 2:217-21, 8, part of the Leipzig Debate with Johann Eck in 1519.

i See pp. 8-18.

j See p. 19, n. 24.

in the event of a vacancy.[k] Who has given him this right? Was it Christ when he said, "The princes of the Gentiles are lords, but it shall not be so among you" [Luke 22:25-26]? Or did Peter bequeath it to him? It makes me angry that we have to read and learn such shameless, gross, and idiotic lies in canon law and must even hold them as Christian doctrine when they are devilish lies.

That impossible lie, the *Donation of Constantine*,[77] is the same sort of thing. It must have been some special plague from God that so many intelligent people have let themselves be talked into accepting such lies. They are so crude and clumsy that I should imagine any drunken peasant could lie more adroitly and skillfully. How can a person rule and at the same time preach, pray, study, and care for the poor? Yet these are the duties which most properly and peculiarly belong to the pope, and they were so earnestly imposed by Christ that he even forbade his disciples to take cloak or money with them [Matt. 10:9-10]. Christ commanded this because it is almost impossible for anybody to fulfill these duties if they have to look after one single household. Yet the pope would rule an empire and still remain pope. This is what those rogues have thought up, who under the cover of the pope's name would like to be lords of the world and would gladly restore the Roman Empire to its former state through the pope and in the name of Christ.

10. The pope should restrain himself, take his fingers out of the pie, and claim no title to the kingdom of Naples and Sicily.[78] He has exactly as much right to that kingdom as I have, and yet he wants to be its overlord. It is property gotten by robbery and violence, like almost all his other possessions. The emperor, therefore, should not grant him this realm, and where it has been granted, he should no longer give his consent.[79] Instead, he should draw the pope's attention to the Bible and the prayer book, that he preach and pray and leave the government of lands and people—especially those that no one has given to him—to the lords.

77. This document, the *Donation of Constantine* (Mirbt-Aland, no. 504), purported to be the testament of Emperor Constantine. It conferred on the pope temporal sovereignty in Rome, Italy, and "all the western regions" and was used to bolster not only papal claims to secular rule in Italy but also the claim that the secular authority of kings and emperors was a gracious concession from the pope, in whom supreme secular and ecclesiastical authority were united. In 1440 the Italian humanist Lorenzo Valla (c. 1407–1457) demonstrated that the *Donation* was a forgery. Shortly before writing this treatise, Luther had read the edition of Valla's treatise published by Ulrich von Hutten in 1517. For an abbreviated English version, see Henry Bettenson and Chris Maunder, eds., *Documents of the Christian Church*, 4th ed. (New York: Oxford University Press, 2011), 102–6.

78. Since 1060, popes had claimed feudal sovereignty over the kingdom of Naples and Sicily, where much land had been given to the church since late antiquity. These claims, justified on the basis of the *Donation of Constantine* (see preceding note), were hotly contested.

79. At this time the kingdom was contested between the royal houses of France and Spain. Emperor Charles V was also King Charles I of Spain.

k *Clem.* lib 2, tit. 11. cap. 2 (Friedberg 2:1151–53).

The same goes for Bologna, Imola, Vicenza, Ravenna, and all the territories in the March of Ancona, Romagna, and other lands that the pope has seized by force and possesses without right.[80] Moreover, the pope has meddled in these things against every express command of Christ and St. Paul. For as St. Paul says, "No one should be entangled in worldly affairs who should tend to being a soldier of God."[l] Now the pope should be the head and chief of these soldiers, and yet he meddles in worldly affairs more than any emperor or king. We have to pull him out of these affairs and let him tend to being a soldier. Even Christ, whose vicar the pope boasts he is, was never willing to have anything to do with secular rule. In fact, when somebody sought a judgment from him in the matter of a brother's action, he said to that man, "Who made me a judge over you?" [Luke 12:14]. But the pope rushes in without invitation and boldly takes hold of everything as if he were a god, until he no longer knows who Christ is, whose vicar he pretends to be.

11. Further, the kissing of the pope's feet should cease.[m] It is an un-Christian, indeed, an anti-Christian thing for a poor sinful man to let his feet be kissed by one who is a hundred times better than himself. If it is done in honor of his authority, why does the pope not do the same to others in honor of their holiness? Compare them with each other—Christ and the pope. Christ washed his disciples' feet and dried them, but the disciples never washed his feet [John 13:4-16]. The pope, as though he were higher than Christ, turns that about and allows his feet to be kissed as a great favor. Though properly, if anyone wanted to do so, the pope ought to use all his power to prevent it, as did St. Paul and Barnabas, who would not let the people of Lystra pay them divine honor, but said, "We are mortals like you" [Acts 14:15]. But our flatterers have gone so far as to make an idol [of the pope] for us, so that no one fears or honors God as

80. All these were components of the states of the church, the conglomeration of territories in central Italy over which the pope exercised direct secular rule. It was in large measure the result of claims to secular authority in Italy that the papacy was inextricably involved in the political and military struggles of Italy and western Europe.

l This is a free rendering of the Vulgate text of 2 Tim. 2:4.

m See above, p. 46 and below, n. 81., p. 50.

much as he fears and honors the pope. They will stand for that, but not for diminishing the pope's majesty by so much as a hairsbreadth. If they were only Christian and esteemed God's honor more than their own, the pope would never be happy to see God's honor despised and his own exalted. Nor would he let anyone honor him until he saw that God's honor was once more exalted and raised higher than his own.[81, n]

81. Both kissing the pope's feet and his being carried were depicted in *Passional Christi und Antichristi* (1521; WA 9:677–715 with the appendix), with woodcuts by Lukas Cranach Sr. (1472–1553) and comments by Philip Melanchthon and Martin Luther contrasting papal practices with Christ's passion. For depiction of this, see below, p. 277.

Another example of the same scandalous pride is that the pope is not satisfied to ride or be driven, but, although strong and in good health, has himself borne by men like an idol and with unheard-of splendor. Dear readers, how does such satanic pride compare with Christ, who went on foot, as did all his disciples? Where has there ever been a worldly monarch who went about in such worldly pomp and glory as he who wants to be the head of all those who ought to despise and flee from the pomp and vanity of this world, that is, the Christians? Not that we should bother ourselves very much about him as a person, but we certainly ought to fear the wrath of God if we flatter this sort of pride and do not show our indignation. It is enough that the pope rants and plays the fool in this way. But it is too much if we approve of it and grant it to him.

Antichristi / Anno xxi.

The pope being carried in a procession.

What Christian heart can or should take pleasure in seeing that when the pope wishes to receive communion, he sits quietly like a gracious lord and has the sacrament brought to him on a golden rod by a bowing cardinal on bended knee? As though the holy sacrament were not worthy that the pope, a poor, stinking sinner, should rise and show respect to his God, when all other Christians, who are much holier than the Most Holy Father the pope, receive it with all due reverence! Would it be a wonder if God sent down a plague upon us all

n The remainder of this section was not included in the first printing of the treatise. Along with two other passages indicated in the

because we tolerate and praise such dishonor of God by our prelates, and make ourselves participants in this damnable pride by our silence or flattery?

It is the same when the pope carries the sacrament in procession. He must be carried, but the sacrament is set before him like a jug of wine on a table. At Rome Christ counts for nothing, but the pope counts for everything. And yet the Romanists want to compel us—and even use threats—to approve, praise, and honor these sins of the Antichrist, even though they are against God and all Christian doctrine. Help us, O God, to get a free, general council, which will teach the pope that he, too, is a mortal and not more than God, as he presumes himself to be!

12. Pilgrimages to Rome should either be abolished or else no one should be allowed to make such a pilgrimage simply out of curiosity or pious devotion, unless his parish priest, his town authorities, or his overlord confirm that he has a good and sufficient reason for doing so.[82] I say this not because pilgrimages are bad, but because they are ill advised at this time. For at Rome they do not see a good example, but rather pure scandal. The Romanists themselves devised the saying, "The nearer Rome, the worse the Christians."[o] They bring back [from Rome] contempt for God and his commandments. They say the first time a man goes to Rome he seeks a rascal; the second time he finds one; the third time he brings him back home with him.[p] Now, however, they have become so accomplished that they can make three pilgrimages in one and have truly brought back to us from Rome such things that it would be better never to have seen Rome or known anything about it.

Even if this were not the case, there is still another and a better reason: simple people are led into a false estimation

82. Although there were many other popular destinations for pilgrims, like Jerusalem or Santiago de Compostela, Rome with its holy places was by far the favorite.

notes below, it was inserted into the second printing, published at Wittenberg in November 1520.

o A common proverb in German and Latin; see Wander, 3:1714, no. 21f.

p Wander, 3:1717–18, no. 72. See the remark of Ulrich von Hutten in his *Vadiscus*: "Three things there are which those who go to Rome usually bring back with them: a bad conscience, a ruined stomach, and an empty purse." See *Ulrich von Hutten Schriften*, ed. Eduard Böcking, vol. 4: *Gespräche* (Leipzig, 1860), 169.

and misconception about the divine commandments. For they think that going on a pilgrimage is a precious good work, which is not true. It is scarcely a good work—frequently a wickedly deceptive work, for God has not commanded it. But God has commanded that a man should care for his wife and children, perform the duties of a husband, and serve and help his neighbor. Today it happens that a man makes a pilgrimage to Rome, spends fifty, maybe a hundred, gulden, something that nobody commanded him to do, and leaves his wife and child, or his neighbor at any rate, to suffer want back home. And yet the silly fool thinks he can gloss over such disobedience and contempt of the divine commandment with his self-assigned pilgrimage, which is really nothing but impertinence or a delusion of the devil. By encouraging this with their false, feigned, foolish "golden years,"[83] by which the people are excited, torn away from God's commandments and drawn to the seductive papal enterprise, the popes have done the very thing they ought to have prevented. But it has brought in money and fortified their counterfeit authority. That is why it had to go on, even though it is contrary to God or the salvation of souls.

To eradicate such false, seductive faith from the minds of simple Christian people, and to restore a right understanding of good works, all pilgrimages should be abolished. For there is no good in them, no commandment and no duty, but only countless occasions for sin and disdain of God's commandments. This is why there are so many beggars who commit all kinds of mischief by going on these pilgrimages, and who learn to beg when there is no need and become accustomed to it. This accounts for vagabondage and many ills about which I shall not speak here.

Whoever wants to go on a pilgrimage today or vow to make a pilgrimage should first explain the reasons for doing so to his priest or his lord. If it turns out that he wants to do it for the sake of a good work, then let the priest or lord put his foot down firmly and put an end to the vow and the good work as a devilish delusion. Let priest and lord show him how to use the money and effort [to be expended] on the pilgrimage for God's commandments and for works a

83. "Golden" or "jubilee" years were established by Pope Boniface VIII (c. 1235–1303) in 1300. Initially, every hundredth year was to be a jubilee, but by mid-fourteenth century it had become every fifty years, and by Luther's time it was every twenty-five years. During jubilee years, plenary indulgences were offered to pilgrims to Rome who visited the churches of the apostles a specified number of times. The pope received a handsome share of the pilgrims' free offerings, and the local economy benefited from their presence. Luther was doubtless aware that a large number of Germans went on pilgrimage to Rome in 1500.

thousand times better by spending it on his own family or on his poor neighbors. If, however, he wishes to make the pilgrimage out of curiosity, to see other lands and cities, he may be allowed to do so. But if he made the vow during an illness, then that vow must be annulled and canceled. God's commandment should be emphasized, so that henceforth he will be content to keep the vow made in baptism as well as the commandments of God.[q] Nevertheless, he may be allowed to perform his foolish vow just once to quiet his conscience. Nobody wants to walk in the straight path of God's commandments common to all of us. Everybody invents new ways and vows for himself as if he had already fulfilled all of God's commandments.

[13.] Next we come to the great crowd of those who make many vows but keep few. Do not be angry, my noble lords! I really mean it for the best. It is the bittersweet truth that the further building of mendicant cloisters[84] should not be permitted. God help us, there are already too many of them. Would God they were all dissolved, or at least combined into two or three orders! Their wandering around the countryside [begging] has never done any good and never will do any good. My advice is to join together ten of these houses or as many as need be, and make them a single institution for which adequate provision is made so that begging will not be necessary. It is far more important to consider what the common people need for their salvation than what St. Francis, St. Dominic, and St. Augustine,[85] or anyone else has established as a rule, especially because things have not turned out as they planned.

The mendicants should also be relieved of preaching and hearing confession, unless they are called to do this by the bishops, parishes, congregations, or the civil authorities. Nothing but hatred and envy between priests and monks has come out of this kind of preaching and confessing, and this has become a source of great offense and hindrance to the common people. It ought to stop because it can well

84. In contrast to monks, who lived by the Benedictine rule (cf. n. 94), mendicant friars (see the following note) sustained themselves in part by begging. Many cities had designated areas where this begging was permitted.

85. Luther is referring to the three principal mendicant orders, the Franciscans (founded by Francis of Assisi [c. 1181–1226]), the Dominicans (founded by Dominic [1170–1221]), and the Augustinian Hermits (his own order, which supposedly used a rule written by Augustine, bishop of Hippo).

q In *The Babylonian Captivity* of 1520 and in Martin Luther's *Judgment against Monastic Vows* of 1521, Luther will again emphasize baptismal vows. See also *The Holy and Blessed Sacrament of Baptism* in *The Annotated Luther*, Volume 1, p. 220.

Engraving of St. Augustine, bishop of Hippo, by William Marshall (d. 1649).

be dispensed with. It looks suspiciously as though the Holy Roman See has purposely increased this army lest the priests and bishops, unable to stand the pope's tyranny any longer, some day become too powerful for him and start a reformation. That would be unbearable to his holiness.

At the same time, the manifold divisions and differences within one and the same order should be abolished. These divisions have arisen from time to time for very trivial reasons; they have been maintained for even more trivial reasons, and they quarrel with each other with unspeakable hatred and envy.[86] Nevertheless, the Christian faith, which can well exist without any of these distinctions, comes to grief because of both parties, and a good Christian life is valued and sought after only according to the standards of outward laws, works, and methods. Nothing comes of this but hypocrisy and the ruination of souls, as all can plainly see.

The pope must also be forbidden to found or approve any more of these orders; in fact, he must be ordered to abolish some and reduce the numbers of others. Inasmuch as faith in Christ, which alone is our chief possession and exists without any kind of orders, suffers no little danger in that people, confronted with so many and varied works and ways, will be easily led astray to live according to such works and ways rather than to pay heed to faith. And unless there are wise prelates in the monasteries who preach and stress faith more than the rule of the order, it is impossible for that order not to harm and mislead the simple souls who have regard only for works.

But in our day the prelates who did have faith and who founded the orders have passed away almost everywhere. It is just as it was centuries ago among the children of Israel. When the fathers who had known the wonders and the works of God had passed on, their children, ignorant of

86. This applies particularly to the Franciscans and Augustinians. By the fifteenth century, both orders were divided between the Observants, who favored strict adherence to their order's rule, and the Conventuals, who took a more flexible view. Johann von Staupitz (c. 1460–1524), the head of the Augustinian order in Germany and Luther's own confessor, tried to unite the two groups. Luther's journey to Rome in 1511 was part of the legal conflict that this attempt produced.

God's works and of faith, immediately elevated idolatry and their own human works.[r] In our day, unfortunately, these orders have no understanding of God's works or of faith, but make wretched martyrs of themselves by striving and working to keep their own rules, laws, and ways of life. Yet they never come to a right understanding of a spiritually good life. It is just as 2 Tim. 3[:5, 7] declares, "They have the appearance of a spiritual life, but there is nothing behind it: they are constantly learning, but they never come to a knowledge of what true spiritual life is." If the ruling prelate has no understanding of Christian faith, it would be better to have no monastery at all; for such a superior cannot govern an order without causing damage and destruction, and the holier and better the prelate appears to be in his external works, the more this is the case.

To my way of thinking, it would be a necessary measure, especially in our perilous times, to regulate convents and monasteries in the same way that they were regulated in the beginning, in the days of the apostles and for a long time afterward. In those days, convents and monasteries were all open for everyone to stay in them as long as they pleased. What else were the convents and monasteries but Christian schools where Scripture and the Christian life were taught, and where people were trained to rule and to preach?[87] Thus we read that St. Agnes went to school,[88] and we still see the same practice in some of the convents, like that at Quedlinburg and elsewhere. And in truth all monasteries and convents ought to be so free that God is served freely and not under compulsion. Later on, however, they became obsessed with vows and made of them an eternal prison. Consequently, these monastic vows are more highly regarded than the vows of baptism.[89] We see, hear, read, and learn more and more about the fruit of all this every day.

I can well suppose that this advice of mine will be regarded as the height of foolishness, but I am not concerned about that at the moment. I advise what seems good to me; let those who will reject it. I see for myself how the vows are

r Cf. Judg. 2:6-23.

87. This is a prominent theme in Luther's views on monasticism; see his treatise *The Judgment of Martin Luther on Monastic Vows* (1521), in LW 44:312–13, 355, 367.

88. St. Agnes of Rome, fourth-century virgin and martyr (cf. LW 45:312). According to legend, the thirteen-year-old Agnes was on her way home from school when she encountered the young man who, incensed by her rejection of his passionate advances, made the false accusations that led to her martyrdom.

89. Most medieval theologians maintained that monastic vows conveyed the same grace as baptism; see, e.g., Thomas Aquinas (1225–1274), *Summa Theologica* II.2, q. 189, a. 3 ad 3. The same theologians drew a distinction between "precepts of the gospel" (the observance of which was necessary to salvation) and "counsels of perfection" (the observance of which, especially in monastic life, enabled one to achieve salvation "better and more quickly"). See Bonaventure (1221–1274), *Breviloquium* V.9, and Aquinas, *Summa Theologica* II.2, q. 108, a. 4. Luther attacks this notion in the *Treatise on Good Works* (see *The Annotated Luther*, Volume 1, p. 267).

kept, especially the vow of chastity. This vow has become universal in these monasteries, and yet it was never commanded by Christ. On the contrary, chastity is given to very few, as he himself says [Matt. 19:11-12], as well as St. Paul [1 Cor. 7:7]. It is my heartfelt wish that everybody be helped and that Christian souls not become entangled in self-contrived human traditions and laws.

The martyrdom of St. Agnes.

14. We also see how the priesthood has fallen, and how many a poor priest is overburdened with wife and child, his conscience troubled. Yet no one does anything to help him, though he could easily be helped. Though pope and bishops may let things go on as they are and allow what is heading for ruin to go to ruin, yet I will redeem my conscience and open my mouth freely, whether it vexes pope, bishop, or anybody else. And this is what I say: according to the institution of Christ and the apostles, every city should have a priest or bishop, as St. Paul clearly says in Titus 1[:5]. And this priest should not be compelled to live without a wedded wife but should be permitted to have one, as St. Paul writes in 1 Tim. 3[:2, 4] and Titus 1[:6-7], saying, "A bishop shall be a man who is blameless, and the husband of but one wife, whose children are obedient and well behaved," etc. According to St. Paul, and also St. Jerome, a bishop and a priest are one and the same thing.[s] But of bishops as they now are the Scriptures know nothing. They have, rather, been established by an ordinance of the Christian community, so that one priest will have authority over many others.

So then, we clearly learn from the Apostle that it should be the practice in Christendom for every town to choose from among the community a learned and pious citizen,

s For St. Paul, cf. Luther's interpretation of 1 Cor. 4:1 in *Concerning the Ministry* (1523), LW 40:35. For St. Jerome (c. 347–420), see his *Commentary on Titus* (PL 26:52) and *Epistulae* 146 (PL 22:1192–95).

entrust to him the office of the ministry, and support him at the expense of the community. He should be free to marry or not. He should have several priests or deacons, also free to marry or not as they choose, to help him minister to the masses and the community with word and sacrament, as is still the practice in the Greek church. Because there was afterwards so much persecution and controversy with heretics, there were many holy fathers who voluntarily abstained from matrimony so that they might better devote themselves to study and be prepared at any moment for death and conflict.

But the Roman See has interfered and out of its own wanton wickedness turned this into a universal commandment that forbade priests to marry.[90] This was done at the bidding of the devil, as St. Paul declares in 1 Tim. 4[:1, 3], "There shall come teachers who bring the devil's teaching and forbid marriage." Unfortunately so much misery has arisen from this that tongue could never tell it. Moreover, this gave the Greek church cause to separate,[91] and discord, sin, shame, and scandal were increased to no end. But this always happens when the devil starts and carries on. What, then, shall we do about it?

My advice is to restore freedom to everybody and leave every man the free choice to marry or not to marry. But then there would have to be a very different kind of government and regulation of church property; the whole canon law would have to be demolished; and few benefices could be allowed to get into Roman hands. I fear that greed is a cause of this wretched, unchaste celibacy. As a result, everyone has wanted to become a priest and everyone wants his son to study for the priesthood, not with the idea of living in chastity, for that could be done outside the priesthood, but rather to provide themselves with temporal livelihood without work or worry, contrary to God's command in Gen. 3[:19] that "in the sweat of your face you shall eat your bread." The Romanists have artfully decorated this text to mean that their labor is to pray and say Mass.

I here take no account of popes, bishops, cathedral canons, and monks, whose offices were not instituted by God.

90. The earliest papal proscription of clerical marriage dates back to the fourth century, but a serious effort at enforcing clerical celibacy in the Western church began only in the eleventh century. It reached its apex in the twelfth century, when the first and second Lateran councils (1123 and 1139) made clerical marriage not only unlawful but invalid, which meant that all sexual relations between a priest and a woman, whether they were married or not, were classed as fornication, and their children were illegitimate. The decrees of the Lateran council were incorporated into canon law, despite which clerical concubinage remained common. See James A. Brundage, *Law, Sex, and Christian Society in Medieval Europe* (Chicago: University of Chicago Press, 1987), 214–23, 251–53, 401–5, 474–77, 536–39.

91. In the Eastern church, priests and deacons can marry before ordination (though not afterward), but bishops must remain celibate. This was a point of contention between the Eastern and Western churches, but not one of the major issues in the Great Schism (1054) between them.

They have taken these burdens upon themselves, so they themselves will have to bear them. I want to speak only of the ministry that God has instituted, which consists of presiding over a community with word and sacrament, living among them, and maintaining a household. The same should be given liberty by a Christian council to marry to avoid temptation and sin. For since God has not bound them, no one else may or should bind them, even if he were an angel from heaven,[t] let alone a pope. Everything that canon law decrees to the contrary is mere fable and blather.

Furthermore, my advice to anyone henceforth being ordained a priest or anything else is that he in no wise vow to the bishop that he will remain celibate. On the contrary, he should tell the bishop that he has no right whatsoever to require such a vow, and that it is a devilish tyranny to require it. But if anyone is compelled to say, or even wants to say, "*so far as human frailty permits*," as indeed many do, let him frankly interpret these same words in a negative manner to mean "*I do not promise chastity*." For *not human frailty* but only *the strength of angels and the power of heaven permit chaste living*.[u] In this way, a person should keep the conscience free of all vows.

I will advise neither for nor against marrying or remaining single. I leave that to a common Christian ordinance and to everyone's better judgment. I will not conceal my real opinion or withhold comfort from that pitiful band who with wives and children have fallen into disgrace and whose consciences are burdened because people call their wives priests' whores and their children priests' bastards. I say this freely by virtue of my right as court jester.[92]

92. The role in which Luther had cast himself in the introductory letter to Amsdorf; see above, pp. 9–10.

You will find many a pious priest against whom nobody has anything to say except that he is weak and has come to shame with a woman, even though from the bottom of their hearts both are of a mind to live together in lawful wedded

t Cf. Gal. 1:8.

u The italicized words are in Latin in the original and reflect Luther's ironic reference to monastic and ordination vows, always recited in Latin.

love, if they could do it with a clear conscience. But even though they both have to bear public shame, the two are certainly married in the sight of God. And I say that where they are so minded and live together, they should unburden their consciences. Let the priest take and keep her as his lawful wedded wife and live honestly with her as her husband, whether the pope likes it or not, whether it be against canon or human law. The salvation of your soul is more important than the observance of tyrannical, arbitrary, and wanton laws, which are neither necessary to salvation nor commanded by God. You should do as the children of Israel did who stole from the Egyptians the wages they had earned[v] or as a servant who steals from his wicked master the wages he has earned: steal from the pope your wedded wife and child! Let the man who has faith enough to venture this boldly follow my advice. I shall not lead him astray. Though I do not have the authority of a pope, I do have the authority of a Christian to advise and help my neighbor against sins and temptations—and that not without [good] cause or reason!

First, not every priest can do without a woman, not only because of human frailty, but much more because of keeping house. If he may have a woman [for keeping house], which the pope allows, and yet may not have her in marriage, what is that but leaving a man and a woman alone together and yet forbidding them to fall? It is just like putting straw and fire together and forbidding them to smoke or burn.

Second, the pope has as little power to command celibacy as he has to forbid eating, drinking, the natural movement of the bowels, or growing fat. Therefore, no one is bound to obey such a command, and the pope is responsible for all the sins that are committed against it, for all the souls that are lost, and for all the consciences that are confused and tortured because of it. He has strangled so many wretched souls with this devilish rope that he has long deserved to be driven out of this world. Yet it is my firm belief that God has been more gracious to many souls at their last hour than the

v Cf. Exod. 12:35-36.

pope was to them in their whole lifetime. No good has ever come nor will come out of the papacy and its laws.

Third, even though the law of the pope is against it, it is nonetheless the case that when a marriage is entered into against the pope's law, then his law is already at an end and is no longer valid. For God's commandment, which enjoins that no man shall put husband and wife asunder [Matt. 19:6], is above the pope's law. And the commandments of God must not be broken or neglected because of the pope's commandment. Nevertheless, many foolish jurists, along with the pope, have devised impediments and thereby prevented, broken, and brought confusion to the estate of matrimony, so that God's commandment concerning it has altogether disappeared.[93] Need I say more? In the entire canon law of the pope there are not even two lines that could instruct a devout Christian, and, unfortunately, there are so many mistaken and dangerous laws that nothing would be better than to make a bonfire of it.[w]

93. Because it was a sacrament, marriage was entirely a matter of church law that had to be adjudicated in ecclesiastical courts. The most common impediment to marriage was too close a degree of consanguinity (within the first four degrees), which meant, for example, that second cousins could not legally marry. Even the relationship between godparents and godchildren was defined as a forbidden degree of "spiritual consanguinity." Dispensations from these impediments were readily available to those who could pay for them.

But if you say that [clerical marriage] is scandalous, and that the pope must first grant dispensation, I reply that whatever scandal there is in it is the fault of the Roman See, which has established such laws with no right and against God. In the sight of God and the Holy Scriptures marriage of the clergy is no offense. Moreover, if the pope can grant dispensations from his greedy and tyrannical laws for money, then every Christian can grant dispensations from these very same laws for God's sake and for the salvation of souls. For Christ has set us free from all humanly devised laws, especially when they are opposed to God and the salvation of souls, as St. Paul teaches in Gal. 5[:1] and 1 Cor. 10[:23].

15. Nor must I forget the poor monasteries.[94] The evil spirit, who has now confused all the estates of life and made them unbearable through human laws, has taken possession of some abbots, abbesses, and prelates. As a result, they govern their brothers and sisters in such a way that they quickly go to hell and lead a wretched existence here and now, as do all the devil's martyrs. That is to say, these supe-

94. Having dealt with the mendicant friars above (pp. 53–54), Luther now turns to monks and nuns, such as Benedictines and Cistercians, who lived by the Rule of St. Benedict.

w This is exactly what Luther did; see p. 15, n. 15.

riors have reserved to themselves in confession all, or at least some, of the mortal sins that are secret, so that no brother can absolve another, on pain of excommunication. Now then, we do not find angels at all times and in all places, but also flesh and blood, which would rather undergo all excommunications and threats rather than confess secret sins to prelates and appointed confessors. Thus these people go to the sacrament with such consciences that they become irregulars and even worse.[95] O blind shepherds! O mad prelates! O ravenous wolves!

To this I say: if a sin is public or notorious, then it is proper for the prelate alone to punish it, and it is only these sins and no others that he may reserve and select for himself. He has no authority over secret sins, even if they were the worst sins that ever are or can be found. If the prelate reserves them, then he is a tyrant. He has no such right and is trespassing upon the prerogative of God's judgment.

And so I advise these children, brothers and sisters: if your superiors are unwilling to permit you to confess your secret sins to whomever you choose, then take them to your brother or sister, whomever you like, and be absolved and comforted. Then go and do what you want and ought to do. Only believe firmly that you are absolved, and nothing more is needed. And do not be distressed or driven mad by threats of excommunication, being made irregular, or whatever else they threaten. These [penalties] are valid only in the case of public or notorious sins that no one will confess. They do not apply to you. What are you trying to do, you blind prelates, prevent secret sins by threats? Relinquish what you obviously cannot hold on to so that God's judgment and grace may work in the people under your care! He has not given them so entirely into your hands as to let them go entirely out of his own! In fact, you have the smaller part under you. Let your statutes be merely statutes. Do not exalt them to heaven or give them the weight of divine judgments!

16. It is also necessary to abolish completely the celebration of anniversary Masses for the dead,[96] or at least to reduce their number, since we plainly see that they have become

95. Irregulars were monks who had violated the *regula* (rule) of their order and were no longer members in good standing.

96. I.e., Masses said for the repose of the souls of one or more persons on the anniversary (or appointed day of remembrance) of their deaths. Endowments were commonly provided for this purpose.

97. Endowed Masses for departed members were particularly popular with religious fraternities, and Luther had already voiced criticism of the immoderate eating and drinking that accompanied their celebration; see *Sermon on the Blessed Sacrament* in *The Annotated Luther*, Volume 1, pp. 249–53.

98. Vigils were preparatory observances (prayers, Scripture readings, etc.) on the eve (or the entire day) before a major church festival, or they were prayers or observances said throughout the night as a special religious discipline, which is the sense in which Luther is using the word.

nothing but a mockery. God is deeply angered by these, and their only purpose is money-grubbing, gluttony, and drunkenness.[97] What pleasure can God take in wretched vigils and Masses that are so miserably rattled off and neither read nor prayed.[98] And if they were prayed, it would not be for God's sake and out of love, but for the sake of money and of getting the job done. But it is impossible for a work that is not done out of unconstrained love to please God or secure anything from him. So it is altogether Christian to abolish, or at least to diminish, everything we see that is becoming an abuse and that angers God rather than appeases him. I would rather—in fact, it would be more pleasing to God and much better—that a chapter, church, or monastery combine all its anniversary Masses and vigils and on one day, with sincerity of heart, reverence, and faith, hold one true vigil and Mass on behalf of all its benefactors, than hold thousands every year for each individual benefactor without reverence and faith. O dear Christians, God does not care for much praying but for true praying. In fact, he condemns long and repetitious prayers, and says in Matt. 6[:7; 23:14], "They will only earn the more punishment thereby." But Avarice, which cannot put its trust in God, brings such things to pass, for it fears that it will die of hunger.

17. Certain penalties or punishments of canon law should be abolished, too, especially the interdict,[x] which without any doubt was invented by the evil spirit. Is it not a devilish work to correct one sin through many and great sins? It is actually a greater sin to silence or suppress the word and worship of God than if one had strangled twenty popes at one time, to say nothing of a priest, or had appropriated church property. This is another of the tender virtues taught in canon law. One of the reasons this law is called "spiritual" is that it comes from "the spirit": not from the Holy Spirit but from the evil spirit.

Excommunication must never be used except where the Scriptures prescribe its use, that is, against those who do not

x See above, p. 18, n. 22.

hold the true faith or who live in open sin, but not for material advantage. But today it is the other way around. Everybody believes and lives as he pleases, especially those who use excommunication to fleece and defame other people. All the excommunications are for material advantage, for which we have nobody to thank but the holy canon law of unrighteousness. I have said more about this in an earlier discourse.[y]

The other punishments and penalties—suspension, irregularity, aggravation, reaggravation, deposition,[99] lightning, thundering, cursings, damnings, and the rest of these devices—should be buried ten fathoms deep in the earth so that their name and memory not be left on earth. The evil spirit unleashed by canon law has brought such a terrible plague and misery into the heavenly kingdom of holy Christendom, having done nothing but destroy and hinder souls by canon law, that the words of Christ in Matt. 23[:13] may well be understood as applying to them, "Woe to you scribes! You have taken upon yourselves the authority to teach and have closed the kingdom of heaven to the people, for you do not enter and you stand in the way of those who go in."

99. For "irregularity," see above, n. 95. "Aggravation" was the threat of excommunication; "reaggravation" was the excommunication itself. "Deposition" was permanent dismissal from clerical office, as opposed to temporary "suspension."

18. All festivals should be abolished, and Sunday alone retained. If it were desired, however, to retain the festivals of Our Lady and of the major saints, they should be transferred to [the nearest] Sunday, or observed only by a morning Mass, after which all the rest of the day should be a working day. Here is the reason: since the feast days are abused by drinking, gambling, loafing, and all manner of sin, we anger God more on holy days than we do on other days.[z] Things are so topsy-turvy that holy days are not holy, but working days are. Nor is any service rendered God and his saints by so many saints' days. On the contrary, they are dishonored;

y In the *Sermon on the Power of Excommunication*, published in Latin in 1518 (WA 1:638–43), and in the *Sermon on the Ban*, preached in German in December 1519 and published early in 1520 (LW 39:5–22).

z Cf. Luther's similar observations concerning the excessive number and riotous celebration of saints' days in the *Treatise on Good Works* in *The Annotated Luther*, Volume 1, p. 321.

although some foolish prelates think that they have done a good work if each, following the promptings of his own blind devotion, celebrates a festival in honor of St. Otilie or St. Barbara.[100] But they would be doing something far better if they honored the saint by turning the saint's day into a working day.

100. Otilie (Odilia), feast day 13 December (c. 662–c. 720), was the patron saint of Alsace, and her shrine at Odilienberg was a well-known place of pilgrimage. The much more widely known and venerated St. Barbara (feast day 4 December) was the patron saint of gunners, miners, and others who work with explosives. See the *Treatise on Good Works* (*The Annotated Luther*, Volume 1, p. 317, n. 82).

Over and above the spiritual injury, the average man incurs two material disadvantages from this practice. First, he neglects his work and spends more money that he would otherwise spend. Second, he weakens his body and makes it less fit. We see this every day, yet nobody thinks of correcting the situation. In such cases, we ought not to consider whether or not the pope has instituted the feasts, or whether we must have a dispensation or permission [to omit them]. Every community, town council, or government not only has the right, without the knowledge and consent of the pope or bishop, to abolish what is opposed to God and injurious to men's bodies and souls, but indeed is bound, at the risk of the salvation of its souls to abolish it, even though popes and bishops, who ought to be the first to do so, do not consent.

Above all, we ought to abolish completely all church anniversary celebrations, since they have become nothing but taverns, fairs, and gambling places, and only increase the dishonoring of God and foster the damnation of souls.[101] It does not help matters to boast that these festivals had a good beginning and are a good work. Did not God set aside his own law, which he had given from heaven, when it was perverted and abused? And does he not daily overturn what he has set up and destroy what he has made because of the same perversion and abuse? As it is written of him in Ps. 18[:26], "You show yourself perverse with the perverted."

101. The anniversary of the consecration of a church, to which often a special indulgence was attached, was a feast day in that parish. The frequently raucous and disorderly celebration of these local feast days was a common topic of complaint from clerical reformers and public officials. See the *Explanations of the 95 Theses* (1518), LW 31:198.

19. The grades or degrees within which marriage is forbidden, such as those affecting godparents or the third and fourth degree of kinship,[a] should be changed. If the pope in Rome can grant dispensations and scandalously sell them for money, then every priest may give the same dispensations

a See above, n. 93.

without charge and for the salvation of souls. Would God that every priest were able to do and remit without payment all those things we have to pay for at Rome, such as indulgences, letters of indulgence, butter letters, Mass letters, and all the rest of the *confessionalia* and skullduggery at Rome[102] and free us from that golden noose, canon law, by which the poor people are deceived and cheated of their money! If the pope has the right to sell his noose of gold and his spiritual snares (I ought to say "law")[b] for money, then a priest certainly has more right to tear these nooses and snares apart, and for God's sake tread them underfoot. But if the priest does not have this right, neither does the pope have the right to sell them at his disgraceful fair.

Furthermore, fasts should be left to individual choice and every kind of food made optional, as the gospel makes them.[c] Even those gentlemen at Rome scoff at the fasts and leave us commoners to eat the fat they would not deign to use to grease their shoes, and then afterward they sell us the liberty to eat butter and all sorts of other things. The holy Apostle says that we already have freedom in all these things through the gospel.[d] But they have bound us with their canon law and robbed us of our rights so that we have to buy them back again with money. In so doing they have made our consciences so timid and fearful that it is no longer easy to preach about liberty of this kind because the common people take offense at it and think that eating butter is a greater sin than lying, swearing, or even living unchastely. Do with it what you will, it is still a human work decreed by human beings, and nothing good will ever come of it.

20. The chapels in forests and the churches in fields,[103] such as Wilsnack,[104] Sternberg,[105] Trier,[106] the Grimmenthal,[107] and now Regensburg[108] and a goodly number of others that recently have become the goal of pilgrimages, must be leveled. Oh, what a terrible and heavy reckoning

b Luther makes an untranslatable pun on *geistliche netz* ("spiritual snares") and *geistlich recht* ("spiritual law" = canon law).

c Cf. Matt. 15:11.

d 1 Cor. 10:23; Col. 2:16.

102. For indulgences and butter letters, see above, p. 38, n. 60 [Butterbriefe]. Mass letters (*messbriefe*) were certificates entitling the bearer to the benefits of Masses celebrated by confraternities. See *Sermon on the Blessed Sacrament* in *The Annotated Luther*, Volume 1, p. 229, n. 3.

103. Chapels built in the countryside as goals of pilgrimage, not as parish churches.

104. Bad Wilsnack in Brandenburg became a pilgrimage site after 1384, when three consecrated hosts (communion wafers) reportedly survived a fire undamaged and with a drop of Christ's blood in each.

105. From 1491 the Augustinian monastery at Sternberg in Mecklenberg was a popular goal of pilgrims because of a "bleeding host" (consecrated bread) displayed there.

106. The cathedral at Trier possessed one of the many cloaks claiming to be the seamless robe of Christ for which his executioners had cast lots (John 19:23-24).

107. Grimmenthal (near Meiningen) had a pilgrimage church (rebuilt and expanded 1499–1507) with a statue of the Virgin Mary that was said to effect miraculous cures.

108. In 1519, when the Jews were expelled from Regensburg, the synagogue was torn down and replaced with a chapel dedicated to the Virgin Mary. "The Fair Virgin of Regensburg," a painting in the chapel, quickly became an object of veneration and pilgrimage.

The pilgrimage shrine of St. Mary's in Regensburg, built on the site of a recently destroyed synagogue. Woodcut by Michael Ostendorfer (c. 1490–1559).

those bishops will have to give who permit this devilish deceit and profit by it. They should be the first to prevent it, and yet they regard it all as a godly and holy thing. They do not see that the devil is behind it all, to strengthen greed, to create a false and fictitious faith, to weaken the parish churches, to multiply taverns and whoring, to lose money and working time to no purpose, and to lead ordinary people by the nose. If they had read Scripture as well as the damnable canon law, they would know how to deal with this matter!

The miracles that happen in these places prove nothing, for the evil spirit can also work miracles, as Christ has told us in Matt. 24[:24]. If they took the matter seriously and forbade this sort of thing, the miracles would quickly come to an end. But if the thing were of God, their prohibition would not hinder it.[e] And if there were no other evidence that it is not of God, the fact that people come running to them like herds of cattle, as if they had lost all reason, would be proof enough. This could not be possible if it were of God. Further, since God never gave any command about all this, there is neither obedience nor merit in doing it. Therefore one should step in boldly and protect the people. For whatever has not been commanded and is done beyond what God commands is certainly the devil's doing. It also works to the disadvantage of parish churches, because they are held in less respect. In short, these things are signs of great unbelief among the people, for if they really had faith they would find all they need in their own parish churches, to which they are commanded to go.

e Acts 5:39.

But what shall I say now? Every bishop thinks only of how he can set up and maintain such a place of pilgrimage in his diocese. He is not at all concerned that the people believe and live aright. The rulers are just like the people. The blind lead the blind [Luke 6:39]. In fact, where pilgrimages do not catch on, they set to work to canonize saints, not to honor the saints, who would be honored enough without being canonized, but to draw the crowds and bring in the money. At this point, pope and bishops lend their aid. There is a deluge of indulgences. There is always money enough for these. But nobody worries about what God has commanded. Nobody runs after these things; nobody has money for them. How blind we are! We not only give the devil free rein for his mischief, but we even strengthen and multiply his mischief. I would rather the dear saints were left in peace and the simple people not led astray! What spirit gave the pope authority to canonize saints? Who tells him whether they are saints or not? Are there not enough sins on earth already without tempting God, without interfering in his judgment and setting up the dear saints as decoys to get money?

My advice is to let the saints canonize themselves. Indeed, it is God alone who should canonize them. And let all stay in their own parishes, where they will find more than in all the shrines even if they were all rolled into one. In one's own parish one finds baptism, the sacrament, preaching, and one's neighbor, and these things are greater than all the saints in heaven, for all of them were made "saints" by God's word and sacrament. As long as we esteem such wonderful things so little, God is just in his wrathful condemnation in allowing the devil to lead us where he likes, to conduct pilgrimages, found churches and chapels, canonize saints, and do other such fool's works, so that we depart from true faith into a novel and wrong kind of belief. This is what the devil did in ancient times to the people of Israel, when he led them away from the temple at Jerusalem to countless other places. Yet he did it all in the name of God and under the pretense of holiness. All the prophets preached against it, and they were martyred for doing so. But today nobody preaches against it. If somebody were to preach against it all, perhaps bishop, pope, priest, and monk would possibly martyr him, too. St. Antoninus of Florence[109] and certain others must now be made saints and canonized in this way, so that their holiness, which would otherwise have served only for the glory of God and set a good example, may be used to bring fame and money.

Although the canonization of saints may have been a good thing in former days, it is certainly never good practice now, just as many other things that were good in former times—feast days, church treasures and ornaments—are now scandalous and offensive. For it is evident that through the canonization of saints neither God's glory nor the improvement of Christians is sought, but only money and reputation. One church wants to have the advantage over the other and would not like to see another church enjoy that advantage in common. In these last evil days spiritual treasures have even been misused to gain temporal goods, so that everything, even God himself, has been forced into the service of Avarice. This only promotes schisms, sects, and pride. A church that has advantages over others looks down on them and exalts itself. Yet all divine treasures are common to all and serve all and ought to further the cause of unity. But the pope likes things as they are. He would not like it if all Christians were equal and one with each other.

It is fitting to say here that all church privileges, bulls, and whatever else the pope sells in that skinning house of his in Rome should be abolished, disregarded, or extended to all. But if he sells or gives indults,[110] privileges, indulgences, graces, advantages, and faculties[111] to Wittenberg, Halle, Venice, and above all to his own city of Rome, why does he not give these things to all churches in general? Is it not his duty to do everything in his power for all Christians, freely and for God's sake, even to shed his blood for them? Tell me, then, why does he give or sell to one church and not to another? Or must the accursed money make so great a difference in the eyes of His Holiness among Christians, who all have the same baptism, word, faith, Christ, God, and all else?[f] Do the Romanists want us to be so blind to all these things, though we have eyes to see, and be such fools, though

109. Antoninus (1389–1459), archbishop of Florence, achieved renown as reformer of the Dominican order. When Luther wrote this treatise, the procedure of canonizing Antoninus (completed in 1523) was already under way.

110. An indult is a permission or a privilege, awarded to an individual or group by competent ecclesiastical authority (the pope or a bishop), granting exemption from a particular norm of canon law.

111. "Faculties" were extraordinary powers to grant indulgences and absolution in reserved cases. They were usually bestowed on papal legates or commissioners but could be bestowed on local church officials.

we have a perfectly good faculty of reason, that we worship such greed, skullduggery, and pretense?[g] The pope is your shepherd, but only so long as you have money and no longer. And still the Romanists are not ashamed of this rascality of leading us hither and thither with their bulls. They are concerned only about the accursed money and nothing else!

My advice is this: If such fool's work is not abolished, then all upright Christians[h] should open their eyes and not permit themselves to be led astray by the Romanist bulls and seals and all their glittering show. Let them stay at home in their own parish church and let their baptism, their gospel, faith, Christ, and God, who is the same God everywhere, be what is best to them. Let the pope remain a blind leader of the blind.[i] Neither an angel nor a pope can give you as much as God gives you in your parish church. Indeed, the pope leads you away from God's gifts, which are yours for free, to his gifts, for which you have to pay. He gives you lead for gold, hide for meat, the string for the purse, wax for honey, words for goods, the letter for the spirit.[112] You see all this before your very eyes, but you refuse to take notice. If you intend to ride to heaven on his wax and parchment, this chariot will soon break down and you will fall into hell, and not in God's name![j]

112. The imagery here is that of a papal bull, which was written on parchment (animal hide) and to which was attached with wax a cord from which the seal hung. For "letter and spirit," see 2 Cor. 3:6.

Let this be your one sure rule. Whatever you have to buy from the pope is neither good nor from God. For what God gives is not only given without charge, but the whole world is punished and damned for not being willing to receive it as a free gift. I am talking about the gospel and God's work. We have deserved God's letting us be so led astray because we have despised his holy word and the grace of baptism. It is as St. Paul says, "God shall send a strong delusion upon all those who have not received the truth to their salvation, so

f Cf. Eph. 4:4-6.

g German: *Spiegelfechten*, literally, "standing in front of a mirror and pretending to fight"; in other words, being pretentious, hypocritical, or phony.

h Singular in the original.

i Cf. Matt. 15:14.

j Echoing 2 Kgs. 2:1-12.

that they believe and follow lies and knavery" [2 Thess. 2:11], as they deserve.

21. One of the greatest necessities is the abolition of all begging in all of Christendom. Nobody ought to go begging among Christians. It would indeed be a very simple matter to make a law to the effect that every city should look after its own poor, if only we had the courage and the intention to do so.[113] No beggar from outside should be allowed into the city, whether he call himself pilgrim or mendicant monk. Every city should support its own poor, and if it was too small, the people in the surrounding villages should also be urged to contribute, since in any case they have to feed so many vagabonds and evil rogues who call themselves mendicants. In this way, too, it could be known who was really poor and who was not.

There would have to be an overseer or warden who knows all the poor and informs the city council or the clergy what they needed. Or some other better arrangement might be made. As I see it, there is no other business in which so much skullduggery and deceit are practiced as in begging, and yet it could all be easily abolished. Moreover, this unrestricted universal begging is harmful to the common people. I have figured out that each of the five or six mendicant orders[k] visits the same place more than six or seven times every year. In addition to these, there are the common beggars, the ambassador beggars,[114] and the pilgrims. This adds up to sixty times a year that a town is laid under tribute. This is over and above what the secular authorities demand in the way of taxes and assessments. All this the Romanist See steals in return for its wares and consumes for no purpose. To me it is one of God's greatest miracles that we can still go on existing and find the wherewithal to support ourselves.

To be sure, some think that if these proposals were adopted the poor would not be so well provided for, that fewer great stone houses and monasteries would be built, and fewer so well furnished. I can well believe all this. But none of it is necessary. Whoever has chosen poverty ought

k Franciscans, Dominicans, Augustinians, Carmelites, Servites.

113. Luther is breaking with the medieval tradition, in which begging was a respectable activity for those who had fallen into poverty or for those who, like mendicant friars and pilgrims, chose to support themselves in that fashion. By the early sixteenth century, urban populations increasingly viewed the large numbers of beggars as a threat to good order. While Catholic authorities sought to regulate begging, Protestant authorities outlawed it and established laws and institutions for the care of the poor. By 1522, for example, Wittenberg had outlawed begging and established a Poor Chest Ordinance. In the following year, Luther provided a preface for the *Ordinance of a Common Chest* enacted by the Saxon town of Leisnig (LW 45:161–94).

114. Luther's word is *botschafften* ("messengers" or "ambassadors"). The reference is to the so-called *stationarii* (*stationirer* in German), members of religious orders who exploited the gullibility of peasants and villagers by enrolling them, in return for an annual fee, on lists of beneficiaries of the intercession of the saint whose messenger they claimed to be (e.g., St. Valentine). The supposed benefit derived was freedom from certain diseases (epilepsy in the case of Valentine). See Benrath, 105–6, n. 79, and cf. p. 73, note *m*.

not be rich. If he wants to be rich, let him put his hand to the plow and seek his fortune from the land. It is enough if the poor are decently cared for so that they do not die of hunger or cold. It is not fitting that one person should live in idleness on another's labor, or be rich and live comfortably at the cost of another's hardship, as it is according to the present perverted custom. St. Paul says, "Whoever will not work shall not eat" [2 Thess. 3:10]. God has not decreed that anyone shall live off the property of another, save only the clergy who preach and have a parish to care for, and they should, as St. Paul says in 1 Corinthians 9[:14], on account of their spiritual labor. And also as Christ says to the apostles, "Every laborer is worthy of his wage" [Luke 10:7].

22. It is also to be feared that the many Masses that have been endowed in ecclesiastical foundations[115] and monasteries are not only of little use, but arouse the great wrath of God. It would therefore be beneficial to endow no more of such Masses, but rather to abolish the many that are already endowed. It is obvious that these Masses are regarded only as sacrifices and good works, even though they are sacraments just like baptism and penance, which profit only those who receive them and no one else. But now the custom of saying Masses for the living and the dead has crept in, and all things are based on them. This is why so many Masses are endowed, and why the state of affairs that we see has developed out of it.

But this is perhaps a too bold and an unheard-of proposal, especially for those who are concerned that they would lose their job and means of livelihood if such Masses were discontinued. I must refrain from saying more about it until we arrive again at a proper understanding of what the Mass is and what it is for. Unfortunately, for many years now it has been a job, a way to earn a living. Therefore, from now on I will advise a person to become a shepherd or some sort of workman rather than a priest or a monk, unless he knows well in advance what this celebrating of Masses is all about.

I am not speaking, however, of the old collegiate foundations and cathedral chapters, which were doubtless established for the sake of the children of the nobility. According

115. For example, in 1519 the All Saints' Foundation at Wittenberg's Castle Church, consisting of sixteen foundation canons, some of whom were teachers at the University of Wittenberg, recited over six thousand private Masses for the dead (mostly deceased members of the Saxon elector's family).

to German custom, not every one of a nobleman's children can become a landowner or a ruler. It was intended that these children should be looked after in such foundations, and there be free to serve God, to study, to become educated people, and to educate others. I am speaking now of the new foundations that have been established just for the saying of prayers and Masses, and because of their example the older foundations are being burdened with the same sort of praying and Mass celebrating, so that even these old foundations serve little or no purpose. And it is by the grace of God that they finally hit the bottom, as they deserve. That is to say, they have been reduced to choir singing, howling organs, and the reading of cold, indifferent Masses to get and consume the income from the endowments. Pope, bishops, and university scholars ought to be looking into these things and writing about them, and yet they are precisely the ones who do the most to promote them. Whatever brings in money they let go on and on. The blind lead the blind [Luke 6:39]. This is what greed and canon law accomplish.

It should no longer be permissible for one person to hold more than one canonry or benefice. Each must be content with a modest position so that someone else may also have something. This would do away with the excuses of those who say that they must hold more than one such office to maintain their proper station [in life]. A proper station could be interpreted in such broad terms that an entire country would not be enough to maintain it. But greed and a mistrust of God go hand in hand in this matter, so that what is alleged to be the needs of a proper station is nothing but greed and mistrust.

23. Brotherhoods,[116] and for that matter, indulgences, letters of indulgence, butter letters, Mass letters, dispensations, and everything of that kind,[l] should be snuffed out and brought to an end. There is nothing good about them. If the pope has the authority to grant you a dispensation to eat butter, to absent yourself from Mass and the like, then he ought also to be able to delegate this authority to priests,

116. Brotherhoods (*bruderschaften*)—also known as fraternities, sodalities, religious guilds, and (most often in English) confraternities—were associations of laymen created for the purpose of promoting the religious life of their members. Any town of any size had several; in 1520 Wittenberg had twenty. Frequently certain indulgences were attached to membership and attendance at Masses or other rituals at appointed times. Great importance was attached to the endowment of Masses for the souls of departed members. Although brotherhoods could become deeply involved in the charitable and cultural as well as the religious life of their communities, they were often criticized, in Germany at any rate, as drinking clubs whose members missed no opportunity for gluttony and drunkenness. Luther's jaundiced view of them is more fully expressed in his *Sermon on the Blessed Sacrament* in *The Annotated Luther*, Volume 1, pp. 249–53. Cf. Benrath, 105–6, n. 79.

l See nn. 55, 59, 60, and 102.

from whom he had no right to take it in the first place. I am speaking especially of those brotherhoods in which indulgences, Masses, and good works are apportioned. My dear friend, in your baptism you have entered into a brotherhood with Christ, with all the angels, with the saints, and with all Christians on earth. Hold fast to these and do right by them, and you will have brotherhoods enough. Let the others glitter as they will, compared with the true brotherhood in Christ those brotherhoods are like a penny compared with a gulden. But if there were a brotherhood that raised money to feed the poor or to help the needy, that would be a good idea. It would find its indulgences and its merits in heaven. But today nothing comes of these groups except gluttony and drunkenness.

Above all, we should drive out of German territory the papal legates[m] with their faculties,[n] which they sell to us for large sums of money. This traffic is nothing but skullduggery. For example, for the payment of money they make unrighteousness into righteousness, and they dissolve oaths, vows, and agreements, thereby destroying and teaching us to destroy the faith and fealty that have been pledged. They assert that the pope has authority to do this. It is the devil who tells them to say these things. They sell us doctrine so satanic, and take money for it, that they are teaching us sin and leading us to hell.

If there were no other base trickery to prove that the pope is the true Antichrist, this one would be enough to prove it. Hear this, O pope, not of all men the holiest but of all men the most sinful! O that God from heaven would soon destroy your throne and sink it in the abyss of hell! Who has given you authority to exalt yourself above your God, to violate and "loosen"[117] what he has commanded, and teach Christians, especially the German nation, praised throughout history for its nobility, constancy, and fidelity, to be inconstant, perjurers, traitors, profligates, and faithless?

117. A play on the power to bind and loose sins, first given to Peter (Matt. 16:19) and claimed by later popes as their exclusive right.

m The word again is *botschafften*, but here it appears to mean not the *stationarii* of n. 114 but, rather, actual papal commissioners.

n See n. 111.

God has commanded us to keep word and faith even with an enemy, but you have taken it upon yourself to loosen his commandment and have ordained in your heretical, anti-Christian decretals that you have his power. Thus through your voice and pen the wicked Satan lies as he has never lied before. You force and twist the Scriptures to suit your fancy. O Christ, my Lord, look down; let the day of your judgment burst forth and destroy this nest of devils at Rome. There sits the man of whom St. Paul said, "He shall exalt himself above you, sit in your church, and set himself up as God, that man of sin, the son of perdition" [2 Thess. 2:3-5]. What else is papal power but simply the teaching and increasing of sin and wickedness? Papal power serves only to lead souls into damnation in your name and, to all outward appearances, with your approval!

In ancient times the children of Israel had to keep the oath that they had unwittingly been deceived into giving to their enemies, the Gibeonites [Josh. 9:3-21]. And King Zedekiah was miserably lost along with all his people because he broke his oath to the king of Babylon [2 Kgs. 24:20—25:7]. In our own history, a hundred years ago, that fine king of Hungary and Poland, Ladislaus, was tragically slain by the Turk along with a great many of his people because he allowed himself to be led astray by the papal legate and cardinal and broke the good and advantageous treaty and solemn agreement he had made with the Turk.[118] The pious Emperor Sigismund had no more success after the Council of Constance when he allowed those scoundrels to break the oath that had been given to John Hus and Jerome.[119] All the trouble between the Bohemians and us stems from this. Even in our own times—God help us!—how much Christian blood has been shed because of the oath and the alliance which Pope Julius made between Emperor Maximilian and King Louis of France, and afterward broke![120] How could I tell all the trouble the popes have stirred up by their devilish presumption with which they annul oaths and vows made between powerful princes, making a mockery of these things, and taking money for it? I hope that the judgment day is at hand. Things could not possibly be worse than the state of

118. In 1443 Vladislaus III, king of Poland (1424–1444) and (as Uladislaus I) king of Hungary, signed at Szeged a ten-year truce with the Turks. In the following year, Vladislaus allowed himself to be persuaded by the papal legate, Cardinal Cesarini (1398–1444), that the truce was invalid because the Turks could not be trusted to keep their word. So he renewed the war, as a result of which both he and the legate were killed at the battle of Varna on 10 November 1444.

119. Like Luther after him, the Bohemian reformer Jan Hus (1372–1415), lecturer at the University of Prague and popular preacher in the Bethlehem Chapel in Prague, rejected papal authority, demanded free preaching of the gospel, insisted on the right of the laity to receive communion in both kinds, and denounced clerical vices such as simony and the sale of indulgences. He was excommunicated in 1410, and when his supporters in Prague took to the streets in his defense, the city was placed under interdict (1412). Summoned to appear at the Council of Constance, Hus did so under a safe-conduct granted by Emperor Sigismund (1368–1437). But the council decreed that, according to divine and human law, no promise made to a heretic was binding. Hus was arrested, imprisoned, put on trial, and on 6 July 1415 burned at the stake. Luther is mistaken in assuming that Hus's colleague Jerome of Prague (1379–1416), who journeyed to Constance to support Hus, was also given a safe-conduct. Like Hus, he was arrested and burned at the stake.

Portrait of Jan Hus (c. 1369–1415). Engraved by Hendrik Hondius (1573–1650), whose initial is at the upper right.

affairs the Romanist See is promoting. The pope suppresses God's commandment and exalts his own. If he is not the Antichrist, then somebody tell me who is. But more of this another time.[o]

24. It is high time we took up the Bohemian question and dealt seriously and honestly with it.[121] We should come to an understanding with them so that the terrible slander,

o Luther may have been referring to his recently published tract (26 June 1520), *On the Papacy in Rome, against the Most Celebrated Romanist in Leipzig* (LW 39:49–104).

120. In 1508, Pope Julius II, King Louis XII of France, Emperor Maximilian I, and King Ferdinand of Aragon (1452–1516) formed the League of Cambrai against Venice. After the defeat of Venice at the hands of the French in 1509, Julius abandoned the League and in 1510 concluded with Ferdinand of Aragon, Emperor Maximilian, Henry VIII of England (1491–1547), and the Swiss a new alliance, the Holy League, aimed at expelling the French from Italy. This aim had been largely achieved by the death of Louis XII in 1515, but only temporarily. The Italian wars—essentially a dynastic power-struggle between the Valois of France (Francis I) and the Habsburgs of Spain and Burgundy (Charles V)—would continue, with brief periods of respite, until 1559, with frequently disastrous consequences for the papacy and the Italian states, especially with the sack of Rome in 1527 by the troops of Charles V.

121. Following the burning of Hus at Constance, the Hussite nobles and cities in Bohemia rallied to the defense of their reform movement. This led to a Hussite revolution, which five "crusades" mounted by Sigismund, Holy Roman Emperor and king of Bohemia, could not put down (1419–1431). In 1436, a peace treaty between the Council of Basel, Emperor Sigismund, and the Hussites was concluded, guaranteeing the continued existence of the Hussite communities and the right of Hussites to hold public office. Rome never officially accepted this agreement, but it remained in force in Bohemia nonetheless. This meant that there were two confessions in one Christian country: Hussites (predominantly Czech speaking) and Catholics (German speaking).

hatred, and envy on both sides comes to an end. As befits my folly, I shall be the first to submit an opinion on this subject, with due deference to everyone who may understand the case better than I.

First, we must honestly confess the truth and stop justifying ourselves. We must admit to the Bohemians that John Hus and Jerome of Prague were burned at Constance against the papal, Christian, imperial oath, and promise of safe-conduct. This happened contrary to God's commandment and gave the Bohemians ample cause for bitterness. And although they should have acted as perfect Christians and suffered this grave injustice and disobedience to God by these people, nevertheless, they were not obliged to condone such conduct and acknowledge it as just. To this day they would rather give up life and limb than admit that it is right to break and deal contrarily with an imperial, papal, and Christian oath. So then, although it is the impatience of the Bohemians that is at fault, yet the pope and his crowd are still more to blame for all the misery, error, and the loss of souls which have followed that council.

I will not pass judgment here on the articles of John Hus, or defend his errors, although I have not yet found any errors in his writings according to my way of thinking.[122] I firmly believe that those who violated a Christian safe-conduct and a commandment of God with their faithless betrayal gave neither a fair judgment nor an honest condemnation. Without doubt they were possessed more by the evil spirit than by the Holy Spirit. Nobody will doubt that the Holy Spirit does not act contrary to the commandment of God, and nobody is so ignorant as not to know that the violation of good faith and of a promise of safe-conduct is contrary to the commandment of God, even though they had been promised to the devil himself, to say nothing of a mere heretic. It is also quite evident that such a promise was made to John Hus and the Bohemians and was not kept, and that he was burnt at the stake as a result. I do not wish, however, to make John Hus a saint or a martyr, as some of the Bohemians do. But at the same time I do acknowledge that an injustice was done

122. Because Luther denied that the pope ruled the church by divine right, his enemies had accused him of teaching "the Bohemian heresy" of Hus, a charge made by Johann Eck (1486–1543) at the Leipzig Debate in 1519. On that occasion, as here, Luther insisted that Hus had been erroneously and unjustly condemned as a heretic. See Brecht 1:319–21 and LW 31:314.

to him, and that his books and doctrines were unjustly condemned. For the judgments of God are secret and terrible, and no one save God alone should undertake to reveal or utter them.

I only want to say this. John Hus may have been as bad a heretic as it is possible to be, but he was burned unjustly and in violation of the commandment of God. Further, the Bohemians should not be forced to approve of such conduct, or else we shall never achieve any unity. Not obstinacy, but the open admission of the truth must make us one. It is useless to pretend, as was done at the time, that the oath of safe-conduct given to a heretic need not be kept. That is as much as to say that God's commandments need not be kept so that God's commandments may be kept. The devil made the Romanists insane and foolish so that they did not know what they had said and done. God has commanded that a promise of safe-conduct ought to be kept. We should keep such a commandment though the whole world collapses. How much more, then, when it is only a question of freeing a heretic! We should overcome heretics with books, not with fire, as the ancient fathers did. If it were wisdom to vanquish heretics with fire, then public hangmen would be the most learned scholars on earth. We would no longer need to study books, for he who overcomes another by force would have the right to burn him at the stake.

Second, the emperor and princes should send a few really upright and sensible bishops and scholars [to the Bohemians]. On no account should they send a cardinal or a papal legate or an inquisitor, for such people are most unversed in Christian things. They do not seek the salvation of souls, but, like all the pope's henchmen, only their own power, profit, and prestige. In fact, these very people were the chief actors in this miserable business at Constance. The people sent into Bohemia should find out from the Bohemians how things stand in regard to their faith, and whether it is possible to unite all their sects.[123] In this case, the pope ought, for the sake of saving souls, relinquish his power [of appointment] for a time and, in accordance with the decree of the

123. After the death of Hus, his followers divided into two groups. The more moderate group was known as the Utraquists or the Calixtines because of their demand for communion in both kinds (*sub utraque*), i.e., that the cup (*calix*) be administered to the laity. Otherwise they were essentially Catholic in doctrine. The other group, know as Taborites (after Mount Tabor, their fortified stronghold near Prague) were socially and theologically more radical and sought to extend the kingdom of God by force of arms. In the 1420s they split into two groups, the more moderate joining the Utraquists, the radicals surviving only to be annihilated on the battlefield in 1434. In the 1460s a radical group of Utraquists broke away to form the Bohemian Brethren (also known as the Unity of the Brotherhood), who rejected private property, oaths and all other civic obligations, and sought to live simple Christian lives away from urban centers. In the 1470s the Utraquists again began to splinter in two directions. A conservative faction sought to reestablish their connections with Rome, while the more radical faction, now called the New Utraquists, deliberately distanced themselves from Rome. By 1519 leaders of this group were in communication with Martin Luther. See *Oxford Encyclopedia of the Reformation*, ed. Hans Hillebrandt, 4 vols. (New York & Oxford: Oxford University Press, 1996), 1:185–86 s.v. "Bohemian Brethren"; 2:278–80, s.v. "Hussites"; and 4:206–8, s.v. "Utraquists."

truly Christian Council of Nicaea,[p] allow the Bohemians to choose an archbishop of Prague from among their number and let him be confirmed by the bishop of Olmütz in Moravia, or the bishop of Gran in Hungary, or the bishop of Gnesen in Poland, or the bishop of Magdeburg in Germany. It would be enough if he is confirmed by one or two of these, as was the custom in the time of St. Cyprian.[q] The pope has no right to oppose such an arrangement, and if he does oppose it, he will be acting like a wolf and a tyrant; no one ought to obey him, and his ban should be met with a counterban.

If, however, in deference to the chair of Peter, it were desired to do this with the pope's consent, then let it be done this way—provided that it does not cost the Bohemians a single penny and provided that the pope does not put them under the slightest obligation or bind them with his tyrannical oaths and vows as he does all other bishops, contrary to God and right. If he is not satisfied with the honor of being asked for consent, then let them not bother anymore about the pope or his vows and his rights, his laws and his tyrannies. Let the election suffice, and let the blood of all the souls endangered by this state of affairs cry out against him. No one ought to consent to what is wrong. It is enough to have shown courtesy to tyranny. If it cannot be otherwise, then an election and the approval of the common people can even now be quite as valid as confirmation by a tyrant, though I hope this will not be necessary. Someday some of the Romanists or some of the good bishops and scholars will take notice of the pope's tyranny and repudiate it.

I would also advise against compelling the Bohemians to abolish both kinds in the sacrament, since that practice is neither un-Christian nor heretical. If they want to, I would let them go on in the way they have been doing. Yet the new bishop should be careful that no discord arises because of such a practice. He should kindly instruct them that neither practice is wrong,[124] just as it ought not to cause dissension that the clergy differ from the laity in manner of life and

124. Luther defends communion in both bread and wine for the laity in *The Babylonian Captivity of the Church* (1520), LW 36:19–28, but still permitted communion in one kind, a position maintained (for the sake of the weak) in his *Invocavit* sermons, preached upon his return from Wartburg in March 1522 (LW 51:90–91) and in the *Instruction by the Visitors for the Parish Pastors of Saxony* from 1528 (LW 40:288–92).

p See p. 41, n. 64. q See p. 15, n. 16.

r Cf. 1 Cor. 7:23; Gal. 5:1.

dress. By the same token, if they were unwilling to receive Roman canon law, they should not be forced to so do, but rather the prime concern should be that they live sincerely in faith and in accordance with Holy Scripture. For Christian faith and life can well exist without the intolerable laws of the pope. In fact, faith cannot properly exist unless there are fewer or none of these Romanist laws. In baptism we have become free and have been made subject only to God's word. Why should we become bound by the word of any man? As St. Paul says, "You have become free; do not become a bond-servant of mortals,"[r] that is, of those who rule by human laws.

If I knew that the Pickards[125] held no other error regarding the sacrament of the altar except believing that the bread and wine are present in their true nature, but that the body and blood of Christ are truly present under them, then I would not condemn them but would let them come under the bishop of Prague. For it is not an article of faith that bread and wine are not present in the sacrament in their own essence and nature, but this is an opinion of St. Thomas and the pope.[126] On the other hand, it is an article of faith that the true natural body and blood of Christ are present in the natural bread and wine. So then, we should tolerate the opinions of both sides until they come to an agreement, because there is no danger in believing that the bread is there or that it is not.[s] We have to endure all sorts of practices and ordinances that are not harmful to faith. On the other hand, if they held heterodox beliefs, I would rather think of them as outside [the church], although I would teach them the truth.

Whatever other errors and schisms are discovered in Bohemia should be tolerated until the archbishop has been restored and has gradually brought all the people together again in one common doctrine. They will certainly never be united by force, defiance, or by haste. Patience and gentleness

125. Strictly speaking, the word *Pickards*, a corruption of *Beghards*, applies to the communities of pious laymen (members of corresponding sisterhoods were known as Beguines) that arose, chiefly in the Low Countries, in the twelfth and thirteenth centuries and were suspected of heresy by the ecclesiastical hierarchy. But, as here, the name was often applied to Hussites in Bohemia.

126. Since the Fourth Lateran Council of 1215, it has been official Catholic doctrine that in the Eucharist the whole substance of the bread and wine are transubstantiated into the whole substance of the body and blood of Christ, only the accidents (i.e., the outward appearances of bread and wine) remaining. The doctrine received its classical formulation from St. Thomas Aquinas, who employed the categories of substance and accidents found in Aristotelian metaphysics.

s Luther's views were more fully developed in *The Babylonian Capitivity of the Church* (1520) in LW 36:28–35.

t I.e., the *Liber Decretalium Gregorii IX* (1234); see p. 15, n. 15. It was an

are needed here. Did not even Christ have to tarry with his disciples and bear with their unbelief for a long time until they believed his resurrection? If only the Bohemians had a regular bishop and church administration again, without Romanist tyranny, I am sure that things would soon be better.

The restoration of the temporal goods that formerly belonged to the church should not be too strictly demanded, but since we are Christians and each is bound to help the rest, we have full power to give them these things for the sake of unity and allow them to retain them in the sight of God and before the eyes of the world. For Christ says, "Where two are in agreement with one another on earth, there am I in the midst of them" [Matt. 18:19-20]. Would God that on both sides we were working toward this unity, extending to each other the hand of brotherhood and humility. Love is greater and is more needed than the papacy at Rome, which is without love. Love can exist apart from the papacy.

With this counsel I shall have done what I could. If the pope or his supporters hinder it, they shall have to render an account for having sought their own advantage rather than their neighbor's, contrary to the love of God. The pope ought to give up his papacy and all his possessions and honors, if thereby he could save one soul. But today he would rather let the whole world perish than yield one hair's-breadth of his presumptuous authority. And yet he wants to be the holiest of all! Herewith I am excused.

25. The universities, too, need a good, thorough reformation. I must say this, no matter whom it annoys. Everything the papacy has instituted and ordered serves only to increase sin and error. What else are the universities, unless they are utterly changed from what they have been hitherto, than what the book of Maccabees calls *gymnasia epheborum et graecae gloriae*?[127] What are they but places where loose living is practiced, where little is taught of the Holy Scriptures and Christian faith, and where only the blind, heathen teacher Aristotle rules far more than Christ?[128] In this regard my advice would be that Aristotle's *Physics*, *Metaphysics*, *Concerning the Soul*, and *Ethics*, which hitherto have been thought to

127. I.e., schools in which young men were taught the Greek way of life, including the worship of other gods, rather than Jewish law. Cf. 2 Macc. 4:7-17.

128. Although Luther greatly appreciated the value of Aristotle's works for the discipline of logical reasoning, he agreed with Erasmus and other humanists (not to mention some medieval scholars) that Aristotle had had a baneful influence on Scholastic theology. He took particular exception to Aristotle's teaching that human beings become good by doing good, which, in his judgment, encouraged the mistaken attribution of efficacy to human effort, apart from grace, in the process of justification.

be his best books, should be completely discarded along with all the rest of his books that boast about nature, although nothing can be learned from them either about nature or the Spirit. Moreover, nobody has yet understood him, and many souls have been burdened with fruitless labor and study, at the cost of much precious time. I dare say that any potter has more knowledge of nature than is written in these books. It grieves me to the quick that this damned, arrogant, villainous heathen has deluded and made fools of so many of the best Christians with his misleading writings. God has sent him as a plague upon us on account of our sins.

Scottish philosopher and theologian Duns Scotus (c. 1266–1308), also known as Doctor Subtilis (the subtle doctor). Painting by Justus Van Ghent (1410–1480).

This wretched fellow in his best book, *Concerning the Soul*, even teaches that the soul dies with the body, although many have tried without success to save his reputation. As though we did not have the Holy Scriptures, in which we are fully instructed about all things, things about which Aristotle has not the faintest clue! And yet this dead heathen has conquered, obstructed, and almost succeeded in suppressing the books of the living God. When I think of this miserable business, I can only believe that the evil spirit has introduced the study [of Aristotle].

For the same reasons his *Ethics* is the worst of all books. It flatly opposes divine grace and all Christian virtues, and yet it is considered one of his best works. Away with such books! Keep them away from Christians. No one can accuse me of overstating the case, or of condemning what I do not understand. Dear friend, I know what I am talking about. I know my Aristotle as well as you or the likes of you. I have lectured on him and have been lectured at on him,[129] and I understand him better than St. Thomas or Duns Scotus did.[130] I can boast about this without arrogance, and if necessary, I can prove it. It makes no difference to me that so many great minds have devoted their labor to him for so many centuries.

129. During his first year in Wittenberg (1508–1509), Luther gave lectures on Aristotle's *Nichomachean Ethics.* He had been required to study Aristotle during his student years. See *Heidelberg Disputation* in *The Annotated Luther*, Volume 1, pp. 76–78.

130. Duns Scotus (c. 1266–1308), as thoroughgoing an Aristotelian as Thomas Aquinas, was the latter's chief rival for first place among medieval theologians.

Such objections do not disturb me as once they did, for it is plain as day that other errors have remained for even more centuries in the world and in the universities.

I would gladly agree to keeping Aristotle's books *Logic, Rhetoric,* and *Poetics,* or at least keeping and using them in an abridged form, as useful in training young people to speak and to preach properly. But the commentaries and notes must be abolished,[131] and as Cicero's *Rhetoric* is read without commentaries and notes, so Aristotle's *Logic* should be read as it is without all these commentaries. But today nobody learns how to speak or how to preach from it. The whole thing has become nothing but a matter for wearying disputation.

In addition to all this, there are, of course, the Latin, Greek, and Hebrew languages, as well as the mathematical disciplines and history.[132] But all this I commend to the experts. In fact, reform would come readily if only we devoted ourselves seriously to it. Actually a great deal depends on it, for it is here in the universities that the Christian youth and our nobility, with whom the future of Christendom lies, will be educated and trained. Therefore, I believe that there is no work more worthy of pope or emperor than a thorough reform of the universities. And on the other hand, nothing could be more devilish or disastrous than unreformed universities.

I leave it to the physicians to reform their own faculties; I take the jurists and theologians for myself.[133] I say first that it would be a good thing if canon law were completely blotted out, from the first letter to the last, especially the Decretals.[t] More than enough is written in the Bible about how we should behave in all circumstances. The study of canon law only hinders the study of the Holy Scriptures. Moreover, the greater part smacks of nothing but greed and pride. Even if there were much in it that was good, it should still be destroyed, for the pope has the whole canon law imprisoned in the chamber of his heart,[134] so that hence-

131. I.e., the commentaries by the Scholastics. By this time, the curriculum at Wittenberg had all but discarded medieval commentators in rhetoric and logic in favor of Philipp Melanchthon's humanist work (published in 1519 and 1521 [on rhetoric] and 1520 [on logic]).

132. These subjects, with the exception of history, were part of the curriculum in Wittenberg since 1518.

133. In addition to the basic arts faculty, discussed in the previous paragraph, there were three higher faculties at all medieval universities: medicine, law, and theology.

134. German: *in seynis hertzen kasten,* which is Luther's rendering of the Latin *in scrinio pectoris* (further on in

important subject in the faculty of theology.

forth any study of it is just a waste of time and a farce. These days canon law is not what is written in the books of law, but whatever the pope and his flatterers want. Your cause may be thoroughly established in canon law, but the pope always has his "chamber of the heart" in the matter, and all law, and with it the whole world, has to be guided by that. Now it is often a villain, and even the devil himself who controls the chamber, and they proudly boast that it is the Holy Spirit who controls it! Thus they deal with Christ's poor people. They impose many laws upon them but obey none themselves. They compel others to obey these laws or buy their way out with money.

Since then the pope and his followers have suspended the whole canon law as far as they themselves are concerned, and since they pay it no heed but give thought only to their own wanton will, we should do as they do and discard these volumes. Why should we waste our time studying them? We could never fathom the arbitrary will of the pope, which is all that canon law has become. Let canon law perish in God's name, for it arose in the devil's name. Let there be no more "doctors of the Decretals" in the world, but only "doctors of the papal chamber [of his heart]" that is, the pope's flatterers. It is said that there is no better secular government anywhere than among the Turks,[135] who have neither canon law nor secular law but only their Koran. But we must admit that there is no more shameful rule than ours with its canon and secular law, which has resulted in nobody living according to common sense, much less according to Holy Scripture anymore.

Secular law—God help us—has become a wilderness.[136] Though it is much better, wiser, and more honest than the spiritual law,[u] which has nothing good about it except its name, there is nevertheless far too much of it. Surely, wise rulers, along with Holy Scripture, would be more than enough law. As St. Paul says in 1 Cor. 6[:5-6], "Is there no one among you who can judge his neighbor's cause, that you must go to law before heathen courts?" It seems just

u I.e., canon law.

this paragraph and in the one that follows, he uses the Latin phrase), traditionally translated into English as "shrine of the heart." A *scrinium* was a chest or box for the storage of books and papers and, later, relics. According to Pope Boniface VIII, the pope had all laws in his *scrinium pectoris* (literally, "in the storage box of his heart") and was the final judge of its meaning and application. See Friedberg 2:937; LW 31:385 (*Why the Books of the Pope and His Disciples Were Burned*, 1520); and *Smalcald Articles*, III.8.4, in BC, 322.

135. See p. 26, n. 32.

136. By "secular law" Luther means primarily Roman law as codified in the *Corpus Iuris Civilis*, which, together with the *Corpus Iuris Canonici,* constituted the "common law" (*ius commune*) of the Holy Roman Empire (i.e., the law that applied to all cases not governed by a recognized local law, custom, or privilege). In addition, there were various versions of Germanic law that

to me that territorial laws and customs should take precedence over general imperial laws, and that the imperial laws be used only in case of necessity. Would God that every land were ruled by its own brief laws suitable to its gifts and peculiar character. This is how these lands were ruled before these imperial laws were designed, and as many lands are still ruled without them! Rambling and farfetched laws are only a burden to the people, and they hinder cases more than they help them. But I hope that others have already given more thought and attention to this matter than I am able to do.[137]

My dear theologians have saved themselves worry and work. They just leave the Bible alone and lecture on the *Sentences*.[138] I should have thought that the *Sentences* ought to be the first study for young students of theology, and the Bible left to the doctors. But today it is the other way round. The Bible comes first and is then put aside when the baccalaureate is received. The *Sentences* come last, and they occupy a doctor as long as he lives.[139] There is such a solemn obligation attached to these *Sentences* that a person who is not a priest may well lecture on the Bible, but the sentences must be lectured on by someone who is a priest. As I see it, a married man may well be a Doctor of the Bible, but under no circumstances could he be a Doctor of the *Sentences*.[140] How can we prosper when we behave so wrongly and give the Bible, the holy word of God, a back seat? To make things worse, the pope commands in the strongest language that his words are to be studied in the schools and used in the courts, but very little is thought of the gospel. Consequently, the gospel lies neglected in the schools and in the courts. It is pushed aside under the bench and gathers dust so that the scandalous laws of the pope alone may have full sway.

If we bear the name and title of teachers of Holy Scripture, then by this criterion we ought to be compelled to teach the Holy Scripture and nothing else, although we all know that this high and mighty title is much too exalted for a person to take pride in it and allow being designated a Doctor of Holy Scripture. Yet that title might be permitted if the work justified the name. But nowadays, the *Sentences* alone domi-

were in the process of being replaced by Roman law or integrated into it, to the advantage of centralizing governments and the disadvantage of local customs and privileges. See Gerald Strauss, *Law, Resistance, and the State: The Opposition to Roman Law in Reformation Germany* (Princeton: Princeton University Press, 1986), ch. 3.

137. By 1530 Luther would have arrived at a far more positive attitude toward Roman law, deeming it the epitome of God-given wisdom in the secular realm, and a correspondingly harsher attitude toward Germanic law, which he found barbarous in its severity and frequently unfair in its application. See James Estes, "Luther's Attitude toward the Legal Traditions of His Time," *Luther-Jahrbuch* 76 (2009): 87–88, 96–99.

138. That is, on the *Four Books of Sentences* (*Sententiarum libri quatuor*) in which the twelfth-century theologian Peter Lombard (c. 1096–1164), who was known as "the Master of the *Sentences*," collected and briefly explained the opinions (*sententiae*) of ancient church fathers on a wide range of theological subjects. As part of their progress toward doctorates, theologians (including Luther) had to lecture on the *Sentences*, which in Luther's day was still the basic textbook for theological instruction.

139. The first degree granted to a candidate in theology was that of bachelor of the Bible (*baccalaureus biblicus*), which qualified the recipient to lecture on the Bible. The next

nate in such a way that we find among the theologians more pagan and human darkness than holy and certain doctrine of Scripture. What are we to do about it? I know of nothing else to do than to pray humbly to God to give us such real doctors of theology as we have in mind. Pope, emperor, and universities may make doctors of arts, of medicine, of laws, of the *Sentences*; but be assured that no one can make a doctor of Holy Scripture except the Holy Spirit from heaven. As Christ says in John 6[:45], "They must all be taught by God himself." Now the Holy Spirit does not care about red or brown birettas[141] or other decorations. Nor does he ask whether a person is young or old, lay or cleric, monk or secular, unmarried or married. In fact, in ancient times he actually spoke through a donkey against the prophet who was riding it [Num. 22:28]. Would God that we were worthy to have such doctors given to us, regardless of whether they were lay or cleric, married or single! They now try to force the Holy Spirit into pope, bishops, and doctors, although there is not the slightest sign or indication whatever that he is in them.

The number of books on theology must be reduced and only the best ones published. It is not many books that make people learned or even much reading. It is, rather, a good book frequently read, no matter how small it is, that makes a person learned in the Scriptures and upright. Indeed, the writings of all the holy Fathers should be read only for a time so that through them we may be led into the Scriptures. As it is, however, we only read them these days to avoid going any further and getting into the Bible. We are like people who read the signposts and never travel the road they indicate. Our dear Fathers wanted to lead us to the Scriptures by their writings, but we use their works to get away from the Scriptures. Nevertheless, the Scripture alone is our vineyard in which we must all labor and toil.[142]

Above all, the foremost reading for everybody, both in the universities and in the schools, should be Holy Scripture—and for the younger boys, the Gospels. And would God that every town had a girls' school as well, where the girls would be taught the gospel for an hour every day either in German

degree was that of bachelor of the sentences (*baccalaureus sententiarius*), which obligated the recipient to lecture on Lombard's *Sentences*. After mastering the first two of the four books of the *Sentences*, the candidate became a *baccalaureus sententiarius formatus* or licentiate, which obliged him to participate in disputations and other academic functions. Then came the doctorate. For Luther's (unusually rapid) traversal of these stages of promotion, see Brecht 1:125–27.

140. At Wittenberg, this pattern was reversed in the case of Philip Melanchthon, who received his bachelor of Bible in 1519 under Luther's direction but never lectured on the *Sentences*. Instead, he was married (in 1520) and developed a new kind of lecture on main topics of Christian doctrine, derived especially from Paul's letter to the Romans, which were published in 1521 as the *Loci communes theologici* ("Theological Common Places").

141. A red biretta was the headdress of a doctor of theology; a brown or russett (*braunrot*) one was that of a master in the arts faculty.

142. Cf. the much later painting by Lucas Cranach Jr. (1515–1586), in the Wittenberg City Church, "The Vineyard of the Lord," which depicted the reformers as vinedressers.

or in Latin.[v] But real schools! Monasteries and nunneries began long ago with that end in view,[w] and it was a praiseworthy and Christian purpose, as we learn from the story of St. Agnes and of other saints.[x] Those were the days of holy virgins and martyrs when all was well with Christendom. But today these monasteries and nunneries have come to nothing but praying and singing. Is it not only right that every Christian know the entire holy gospel by the age of nine or ten? Does not each person derive name and life from the gospel? A spinner or a seamstress teaches her daughter her craft in her early years. But today even the great, learned prelates and the very bishops do not know the gospel.

Oh, how irresponsibly we deal with these poor young people who are committed to us for training and instruction. We shall have to render a solemn account of our neglect to set the word of God before them. Their lot is as described by Jeremiah in Lam. 2[:11-12], "My eyes are grown weary with weeping, my bowels are terrified, my heart is poured out upon the ground because of the destruction of the daughter of my people, for the youth and the children perish in all the streets of the entire city. They said to their mothers, 'Where is bread and wine?' as they fainted like wounded men in the streets of the city and gave up the ghost on their mothers' bosom." We do not see this pitiful evil, how today the young people of Christendom languish and perish miserably in our midst for want of the gospel, in which we ought to be giving them constant instruction and training.

Moreover, even if the universities were diligent in [the teaching of] Holy Scripture, we should not send everybody there as we do now, where their only concern is numbers and where everybody wants a doctor's degree. We should send only the most highly qualified students who have been well trained in the lower schools. Every prince or city coun-

v On this, including the need of schools for girls, see Luther's *To the Councilmen of All Cities in Germany, That They Establish and Maintain Christian Schools* (1524), LW 45:339–78.

w See p. 55, n. 87.

x See p. 55, n. 88.

cil should see to this, and permit only the well qualified to be sent. I would advise no one to send his child where the Holy Scriptures are not supreme. Everything that does not unceasingly pursue the study of God's word must corrupt, and because of this we can see what kind of people there are and will be in the universities. Nobody is to blame for this except the pope, the bishops, and the prelates, for it is they who are charged with the welfare of young people. The universities only ought to turn out people who are experts in the Holy Scriptures, who can become bishops and priests, and can stand in the front line against heretics, the devil, and the whole world. But where do you find that? I greatly fear that the universities, unless they teach the Holy Scriptures diligently and impress them on the young students, are wide gates of hell.

26.[y] I know full well that the gang in Rome will allege and trumpet mightily that the pope took the Holy Roman Empire from the Greek emperor and bestowed it upon the Germans, for which honor and benevolence he is said to have justly deserved and obtained submission, thanks, and all good things from the Germans.[143] For this reason they will, perhaps, undertake to throw all attempts to reform themselves to the four winds and will not allow us to think about anything but the bestowal of the Roman Empire. For this cause they have persecuted and oppressed many a worthy emperor so willfully and arrogantly that it is a shame even to mention it.[z] And with the same adroitness they have made themselves overlords of every secular power and authority, contrary to the holy gospel. I must therefore speak of this, too.

There is no doubt that the true Roman Empire, which the writings of the prophets foretold in Num. 24[:17-24] and Dan. 2[:36-45], has long since been overthrown and come

143. Through a series of military conquests, Charles the Great (a.k.a. Charlemagne, c. 742–814), king of the Franks, managed to unite most of western Europe under one rule for the first time since the collapse of the western Roman Empire in the fifth century. In the year 800 Charles had himself crowned "Emperor of the Romans" by Pope Leo III (750–816) in St. Peter's Basilica, an act that nullified any claim by the Byzantine emperors in Constantinople to authority in what had been the western Empire. Thereafter Charlemagne and his successors as German kings were known as Roman emperors. In later struggles with the German emperors over who possessed the highest jurisdiction, medieval popes interpreted Charlemagne's coronation by Leo as the act of someone who, by virtue of his supreme jurisdiction in both secular and spiritual matters, had the authority to take imperial power from the Greek emperor and bestow it on the Frankish king. The pope's confirmation was deemed necessary for the election of the German king/Roman emperor to be deemed valid, and that confirmation could be withheld or withdrawn.

y This entire section is missing from the first printing of the treatise; Luther added it to the second printing; see p. 50, note *n*.

z See p. 11, n. 9.

to an end,[144] as Balaam clearly prophesied in Num. 24[:24] when he said, "The Romans shall come and overthrow the Jews, and afterward they also shall be destroyed."[145] That happened under the Goths,[146] but more particularly when the empire of the Turks began almost a thousand years ago. Then eventually Asia and Africa fell away, and in time France and Spain, and finally Venice broke away, and nothing was left to Rome of its former power.

When, then, the pope could not subdue to his arrogant will the Greeks and the emperor at Constantinople, who was the hereditary Roman emperor, he invented a little device to rob this emperor of his empire and his title and to turn it over to the Germans, who at that time were warlike and of good repute. In so doing, [the Romanists] brought the power of the Roman Empire under their control so that it had to be held as a fief from them. And this is just what happened. [Imperial authority] was taken away from the emperor at Constantinople, and its name and title given to us Germans, and thereby we became servants of the pope. There is now a second Roman Empire, built by the pope upon the Germans, for the former one, as I said earlier, has long since fallen.

So, then, the Roman See now gets its own way. It has taken possession of Rome, driven out the German emperor, and bound him by oaths not to dwell at Rome.[a] He is supposed to be Roman emperor, and yet he is not to have possession of Rome; and besides, he is to be dependent on and move within the limits of the good pleasure of the pope and his supporters. We have the title, but they have the land and the city. They have always abused our simplicity to serve their own arrogant and tyrannical designs. They call us crazy Germans for letting them make fools and monkeys of us as they please.

Now then, it is a small thing for God to toss empires and principalities to and fro. He is so gentle with them that once in a while he gives a kingdom to a scoundrel and takes one from a good man, sometimes by the treachery of wicked,

a According to the *Donation of Constantine* (cf. n. 110); see Mirbt-Aland, 255, no. 504, §§17–19.

144. Luther here dissociates himself in part from the conception of "world history" that had prevailed in western Europe in the Middle Ages. It was based on the prophecy in Daniel 2 (repeated in variant form in Daniel 7) of the rise and fall of the four great empires of "gold," "silver," "bronze," and "iron" (with the latter to be divided into empires of "iron" and "clay") that would precede the apocalypse and the establishment of Christ's kingdom. Medieval exegetes identified the four empires as Babylon, Persia, Greece (Macedonia), and Rome. For as long as the apocalypse had not occurred, it remained necessary to argue that the Roman Empire still existed. Hence, theologians argued that the collapse of the western Roman Empire in 476 left imperial authority intact in the eastern Empire (Byzantium) and that the papal coronation of Charlemagne in 800 effected a transfer of imperial rule from the Greeks to the Germans (*translatio imperii a Graecis ad Germanos*). See above, n. 143.

faithless men, and sometimes by inheritance. This is what we read about the kingdoms of Persia and Greece, and about almost all kingdoms. It says in Dan. 2[:21] and 4[:34-35], "He who rules over all things dwells in heaven, and it is he alone who overthrows kingdoms, tosses them to and fro, and establishes them." Since no one, particularly a Christian, can think it a very great thing to receive a kingdom, we Germans, too, need not lose our heads because a new Roman Empire is bestowed on us. For in God's eyes it is but a trifling gift, one that he often gives to the most unworthy, as it says in Dan. 4[:35], "All who dwell on earth are as nothing in his eyes, and he has the power in all the kingdoms of men to give them to whom he will."

But although the pope used violence and unjust means to rob the true emperor of his Roman Empire, or of the title of his Roman Empire, and gave it to us Germans, yet it is nevertheless certain that God has used the pope's wickedness to give such an empire to the German nation, and after the fall of the first Roman Empire, to set up another, the one that now exists. And although we had nothing to do with this wickedness of the popes, and although we did not understand their false aims and purposes, we have nevertheless paid tragically and far too dearly for such an empire with incalculable bloodshed, with the suppression of our liberty, the occupation and theft of all our possessions, especially of our churches and benefices, and with the suffering of unspeakable deception and insult. We carry the title of empire, but it is the pope who has our wealth, honor, body, life, soul, and all that we possess. This is how they deceive the Germans and cheat them with tricks.[b] What the popes have sought was to be emperors themselves, and though they could not achieve this, they nonetheless succeeded in setting themselves over the emperors.

Since the Empire has been given us by the providence of God as well as by the plotting of evil men, without any guilt

145. NRSV: "But ships shall come from Kittim and shall afflict Asshur and Eber." Luther follows the Vulgate, which translates "They will come in ships from Italy and be over the Assyrians and destroy the Hebrews," In the 1523 translation into German, Luther leaves the Hebrew Kittim in the text and in a marginal note insists that it applies rather to Macedonia (Greece) and Alexander the Great (356-323 BCE). In his lectures on Genesis from 1537, Luther associates Kittim primarily with Greece but also with the coasts of Italy and France (LW 2:191). In the 1545 edition of the German Bible, he explains that Kittim refers to both Alexander the Great and the Romans, whose kingdoms will collapse, leaving only Israel (WA DB 8:514-15).

146. The Visigoths sacked Rome in the year 410.

b *Szo sol man die Deutschen teuschen und mit teuschen teuschen*, a pun on *Deutchen* ("Germans"), *teuschen* ("deceive," "cheat"), and *teuschen* ("tricks," "deceptions") that cannot be duplicated in English.

on our part, I shall not advise that we give it up, but rather that we rule it wisely and in the fear of God, as long as it pleases him for us to rule it. For, as has been said already, it does not matter to him where an empire comes from; his will is that it be governed regardless. Though the popes were dishonest in taking it from others, we were not dishonest in receiving it. It has been given us through evil people by the will of God, for which we have more regard that for the fraudulent intention to be emperors themselves, and indeed more than emperors, and only to mock and ridicule us with the title. The king of Babylon also seized his kingdom by robbery and violence. Yet it was God's will that that kingdom be ruled by the holy princes Daniel, Hananiah, Azariah, and Mishael.[c] Much more, then, is it God's will that this empire should be ruled by the Christian princes of Germany, no matter whether the pope stole it, got it by force, or established it anew. It is all God's ordering, which came to pass before we knew about it.

Therefore, the pope and his followers have no right to boast that they have done the German nation a great favor by giving us the Roman Empire. In the first place, they did not mean it for our good. Rather, they took advantage of our simplicity when they did it in order to strengthen their proud designs against the real Roman emperor at Constantinople, from whom the pope took his empire against God and right, which he had no authority to do. In the second place, the pope's intention was not to give us the Empire, but to get it for himself, so that he might bring all our power, our freedom, our wealth, our souls, and our bodies into subjection to himself, and through us (had God not prevented it) to subdue all the world. He clearly says so himself in his Decretals,[d] and has attempted to do so by means of many wicked wiles with a number of the German emperors. Thus have we Germans been beautifully neatly taught our

c Dan. 1:6-7; 2:48; 5:29. The latter three are renamed in Dan. 1:7—Shadrach, Meshach, and Abednego.

d See, e.g., the decretal *Venerabilem fratrem* (1202). See Mirbt-Aland 307, no. 596; Friedberg 2:80.

German.[e] While we supposed we were going to be lords, we became in fact servants of the most deceitful tyrants of all time. We have the name, the title, and the insignia of empire, but the pope has its treasures, authority, rights, and liberties. The pope gobbles the kernel while we are left playing with the husk.

Now may God, who (as I said) tossed this empire into our lap by the wiles of tyrants and has charged us with its rule, help us to live up to the name, title, and insignia and to retrieve our liberty. Let the Romanists see once and for all what it is that we have received from God through them. If they boast that they have bestowed an empire on us, let them. If that is true, then let the pope give us back Rome and all that he has gotten from the Empire; let him free our land from his intolerable taxing and fleecing; let him give us back our liberty, our rights, our honor, our body and soul; and let the Empire be what an empire should be, so that the pope's words and pretensions might be fulfilled.

If he will not do that, then what is he playing at with his false, fabricated words and his deceptions? Has there not for so many centuries now been enough of his ceaseless and uncouth leading of this noble nation around by the nose? It does not follow that the pope must be above the emperor because he crowns or appoints him. The prophet St. Samuel anointed and crowned the kings Saul and David at God's command, and yet he was their subject.[f] The prophet Nathan anointed King Solomon,[g] but he was not set over the king on that account. Similarly, St. Elisha had one of his servants anoint Jehu king of Israel, but they still remained obedient and subject to the king.[h] It has never happened in all the history of the world that he who consecrated or crowned the king was over the king, except in this single instance of the pope.

e Probably a pun similar to note *b*, p. 89, meaning "We Germans have been tricked [by the popes]."

f 1 Sam. 10:1; 16:13.

g 1 Kgs. 1:39. It was in fact Zadok the priest who anointed Solomon.

h 2 Kgs. 9:6.

The pope permits himself to be crowned by three cardinals who are beneath him, but he is nonetheless their superior. Why should he then go against his own example, against universal practice, and against the teaching of Scripture by exalting himself above secular authority or imperial majesty simply because he crowns or consecrates the emperor? It is quite enough that he is the emperor's superior in the things of God, that is, in preaching, teaching, and the administration of the sacraments. In these respects, any bishop and any priest is over everybody else, just as St. Ambrose in his diocese was over the emperor Theodosius,[147] the prophet Nathan over David, and Samuel over Saul. Therefore, let the German emperor be really and truly emperor. Let neither his authority nor his power be suppressed by such sham pretensions of these papist deceivers as though they were to be excepted from his authority and were themselves to rule in all things.

147. In the year 390, St. Ambrose, bishop of Milan, refused to admit Emperor Theodosius I (347–395) to communion until after he had done public penance for having ordered the indiscriminate slaughter of seven thousand inhabitants of Thessalonica following the murder there of the Roman governor by rioters.

27.[i] Enough has now been said about the failings of the clergy, though you may and will find more if you look in the right place. Let us now take a look at some of those of the secular realm.

In the first place, there is a great need for a general law and decree in the German nation against boundlessly excessive and costly dress, because of which so many nobles and rich people are impoverished.[j] God has certainly given us, as he has to other countries, enough wool, flax, linen, and everything else necessary for the seemly and honorable dress of every class. We do not need to waste fantastic sums for silk, velvet, golden ornaments, and foreign wares. I believe that even if the pope had not robbed us with his intolerable fleecing, we would still have more than enough of these home-grown robbers, the traders in silk and velvet. We see that now everybody wants to be like everybody else, and pride and envy are thereby aroused and increased among us, as we deserve. All this misery and much more besides would

i In the first printing of the treatise, this section followed immediately after section 25 and was numbered 26.

j Such a law (part of a larger *Polizeiordunung*) was proposed at the Diet of Worms in 1521; see RTA 2:335–41.

probably be avoided if only our ardor [for such things] would let us be thankfully content with the good things God has already given us.

It is also necessary to restrict the traffic in spices, which is another of the great ships in which money is carried out of the German lands. By the grace of God, more things to eat and drink grow here than in any other country, and they are just as tasty and good. Perhaps my proposals seem foolish, impractical, and give the impression that I want to ruin the greatest of all trades, that of commerce. But I am doing my best, and if there is no general improvement in these matters, then let him who will try his hand at improving them. I do not see that many good morals have ever come to a country through commerce, and in ancient times God made his people Israel dwell away from the sea because of this and did not let them engage in much commerce.[k]

But the greatest misfortune of the German nation is certainly the *zynskauf*.[148] If that did not exist, many people[l] would have to leave unpurchased their silks, velvets, golden ornaments, spices, and display of every kind. This traffic has not existed much longer than a hundred years, and it has already brought almost all princes, endowed institutions, cities, nobles, and their heirs to poverty, misery, and ruin. If it goes on for another hundred years, Germany will not have a penny left, and the chances are we shall have to eat one another. The devil invented the practice, and by confirming it the pope has brought woe upon the whole world.

Therefore, I beg and pray at this point that everyone open their eyes and see the ruin of their children and heirs. Ruin is not just at the door, it is already in the house. I pray and beseech emperor, princes, lords, and city councilors to condemn this trade as speedily as possible and prevent it from now on, regardless of whether the pope with all his unjust justice objects, or whether benefices or monasteries are based upon it. It is better for a city to have one benefice supported by honest legacies or revenue than to have a hundred

k See Ezek. 27:3, 8; and Isa. 23:1, 8, where Tyre is described, in contrast to Israel, as having merchant ships and being engaged in commerce.

l Singular in the original.

148. *Zinskauf* in modern German, a synonym for *Rentenkauf*, i.e., the purchase of an annuity (a yearly rent) in return for the use of a sum of money or a piece of property. Because the buyer was theoretically purchasing something and could not recall the sum paid, the annual payments could not be called interest. In this way the biblical and canon-law prohibitions of lending at interest to other Christians (usury) was circumvented. Luther, who was more conservative on the subject of charging interest than were his Catholic opponents, like Johann Eck, insisted that the *Zinskauf* was indeed usurious unless rigorous standards of fairness (e.g., equal risk on the part of both buyer and seller) were met. See his *Treatise on Good Works* (*The Annotated Luther*, Volume 1, p. 346, n. 118), and his *Long Sermon on Usury* (early 1520); LW 45:233–43 (helpful introduction), 273–95 (text); and Brecht 1:356–57.

benefices supported by *zynskauf.* Indeed, a benefice supported by a *zynskauf* is more grievous and oppressive than twenty supported by legacies. In fact, the *zynskauf* must be a sign and proof that the world has been sold to the devil because of its grievous sins and that at the same time we are losing both temporal and spiritual possessions. And yet we do not even notice it.

In this connection, we must put a bit in the mouth of the Fuggers and similar companies.[m] How is it possible in the lifetime of one person to accumulate such great possessions, worthy of a king, legally and according to God's will? I don't know. But what I really cannot understand is how a person with one hundred gulden can make a profit of twenty in one year. Nor, for that matter, can I understand how a person with one gulden can make another—and make it not from tilling the soil or raising cattle, where the increase of wealth depends not on human wit but on God's blessing. I leave this to people who understand the ways of the world.[149] As a theologian I have no further reproof to make on this subject except that it has an evil and offending appearance, about which St. Paul says, "Avoid every appearance or show of evil" [1 Thess. 5:22]. I know full well that it would be a far godlier thing to increase agriculture and decrease commerce. I also know that those who work on the land and seek their livelihood from it according to the Scriptures do far better. All this was said to us and to everybody else in the story of Adam, "Cursed be the ground when you work it; it shall bear you thistles and thorns, and in the sweat of your face you shall eat your bread" [Gen. 3:17-19]. There is still a lot of land lying fallow and neglected.

Next comes the abuse of eating and drinking, which gives us Germans a bad reputation in foreign lands, as though it were a special vice of ours. Preaching cannot stop it so deeply is it rooted and so firmly has it got the upper hand. The waste of money would be insignificant were it not for all the vices that accompany it—murder, adultery, stealing, blasphemy, and every other form of immorality. Govern-

149. Luther here reflects the Aristotelian economic principle that money is simply an object like a chair or table and thus incapable of making money.

m See p. 38, n. 57.

ment can do something to prevent it; otherwise, what Christ says will come to pass, that the last day shall come like a secret snare, when they shall be eating and drinking, marrying and wooing, building and planting, buying and selling.[n] It is so much like what is now going on that I sincerely hope the Judgment Day is at hand, although very few people give it any thought.

Finally, is it not lamentable that we Christians tolerate open and common brothels in our midst, when all of us are baptized unto chastity?[o] I know perfectly well what some say to this, that is, that it is not a custom peculiar to one nation, that it would be difficult to put a stop to it, and, moreover, that it is better to keep such a house than that married women, or girls, or others of still more honorable estate should be molested. Nevertheless, should not secular and Christian governments consider that one ought not to counteract these things in such a heathen manner? If the children of Israel could exist without such impropriety, why cannot Christians do as much? In fact, how do so many cities, country towns, market towns, and villages do without such houses? Why can't large cities do without them as well?

In this matter and in the other matters previously mentioned, I have tried to point out how many good works secular government could do, and what the duty of every government should be, so that everyone may learn what an awful responsibility it is to rule and sit in high places. What use would it be if a ruler were himself as holy as St. Peter, if he did not diligently try to help his subjects in these matters? His very authority would condemn him. It is the duty of governing authority to seek the best for its subjects. But if the authorities were to give some thought to how young people might be brought together in marriage, the hope of married life would greatly help every one of them to endure and resist temptation.

But today everybody is attracted to the priesthood or the monastic life, and among them, I am sorry to say, there is

n Cf. Luke 21:34; 12:45, and Matt. 24:36-44.

o See *Treatise on Good Works* in *The Annotated Luther*, Volume 1, p. 347.

not one in a hundred who has any other reason than that he seeks a living and doubts that he will ever be able to support himself in married life. Therefore, they live wildly enough beforehand, and wish, as they say, to get it out of their system, but experience shows that it is only more deeply embedded in them. I find the proverb true, "Despair makes most monks and priests."[p] That is what happens and that is how it is, as we see.

I will, however, sincerely advise that to avoid the many sins that spread so shamelessly, neither youths nor maidens should bind themselves to chastity or clerical life before the age of thirty. Chastity, as St. Paul says, is a special gift [1 Cor. 7:7]. Therefore, I would advise those upon whom God has not conferred his special gift to abstain from clerical life and making vows. I say further that if you trust God so little that you fear you won't be able to support yourself as a married man, and you wish to become a cleric only because of this distrust, then I beg you for your own soul's sake not to become a cleric at all, but rather a farmer or anything you like. For where a single measure of faith in God is needed to earn your daily bread, there must be ten times that amount of faith to remain a cleric. If you do not trust God to provide for you in temporal things, how will you trust him to support you in spiritual things? Alas, unbelief and distrust spoil everything and lead us into all kinds of misery, as we see in all walks of life.

Much more could be said of this pitiful state of affairs. Young people have nobody to watch over them. They all do as they please, and the government is as much use to them as if it did not exist. And yet the care of young people ought to be the chief concern of the pope, bishops, rulers, and councils. They want to exercise authority far and wide, and yet they help nobody. For just this reason a lord and ruler will be a rare sight in heaven, even though he build a hundred churches for God and raise up all the dead!

Let this suffice for the moment. [I think I have said enough in my little book *Treatise on Good Works*[q] about what

p Wander, 4:1625.

the secular authorities and the nobility ought to do. There is certainly room for improvement in their lives and in their rule, yet the abuses of the temporal power are not to be compared with those of the spiritual power, as I have shown in that book.][r]

I know full well that I have sung rather grandly. I have made many suggestions that will be considered impractical. I have attacked many things too severely. But how else ought I to do it? I am duty-bound to speak. These are the things I would do if I were able. I would rather have the wrath of the world upon me than the wrath of God. The world can do no more to me than take my life. In the past I have made frequent overtures of peace to my enemies, but as I see, God has compelled me through them to open my mouth ever wider and to give them enough to say, bellow, shout, and write because they have nothing else to do. Well, I know another little song about Rome and the Romanists. If their ears are itching to hear it, I will sing that one to them, too—and pitch it in the highest key! You understand what I mean, dear Rome.[150]

Moreover, I have many times offered my writings for investigation and hearing, but to no avail because, as I too know full well, if my cause is just, it must be condemned on earth and be justified by Christ alone in heaven. For all the Scriptures bear witness that the cause of Christians and of Christendom must be judged by God alone, and no cause has ever yet been justified on earth by human effort because the opposition has always been too great and too strong. It is still my greatest concern and anxiety that my cause may not be condemned, by which I would know for certain that it is not yet pleasing to God. Therefore, just let them go hard at it, pope, bishop, priest, monk, or scholar. They are just the ones to persecute the truth, as they have always done. May God give us all a Christian mind and grant to the Christian nobility of the German nation in particular true spiritual courage to do the best they can for the poor church. Amen.

Wittenberg, in the year 1520.

150. The "little song" is *The Babylonian Captivity of the Church* (LW 36:3–126), which was also written in 1520, shortly after this treatise was published.

q See *Treatise on Good Works* in *The Annotated Luther*, Volume 1, pp. 342–47.

r The bracketed passage was inserted into the second edition of the treatise. See above, p. 50f., note *n*.

DE CAPTIVITATE
BABYLONICA
ECCLESIAE,
Præludium Martini
Lutheri.

Vuittembergæ.

Title page of Luther's *The Babylonian Captivity of the Church [De Captivitate Babylonica Ecclesiae]*, published in Wittenberg by Melchior Lotter the Younger (1520).

The Babylonian Captivity of the Church

1520

ERIK H. HERRMANN

INTRODUCTION

At the end of his German treatise *Address to the Christian Nobility* (*An den christlichen Adel deutscher Nation*), Luther dropped a hint of what was coming next: "I know another little song about Rome and the Romanists. If their ears are itching to hear it, I will sing that one to them, too—and pitch it in the highest key!" This "little song" Luther would call a "prelude" on the captivity of the Roman church—or the *Babylonian Captivity of the Church*, published just a few months later in October of 1520. A polemical treatise, it was truly "pitched high," with Luther hiding little of his dissatisfaction with the prevalent sacramental practices sanctioned by Rome. Although he fully expected the work to elicit a cacophony of criticisms from his opponents, Luther's positive aim was to set forth a reconsideration of the sacramental Christian life that centered on the Word. His thesis is that the papacy had distorted the sacraments with its own traditions and regulations, transforming them into a system of control and coercion. The evangelical liberty of the sacramental promises had been replaced by a papal absolutism that, like a feudal lordship, claimed its own jurisdictional liberties and privileges over the totality of Christian life through a sacramental system that spanned birth to death. Yet Luther does not replace one tyranny for another; his argument for a return to the biblical understanding of the sacraments is moderated by a consideration of traditions and external practices in relation to their effects on the individual conscience and faith.

On the one hand, Luther's treatise is shaped by some of the specific arguments of his opponents. There are two treatises in particular to which Luther reacts. The first is by an Italian Dominican, Isidoro Isolani (c. 1480–1528), who wrote a tract calling for Luther's recantation, *Revocatio Martini Lutheri Augustiniani ad sanctam sedem* (1519). The second writing, appearing in July of 1520, was by the Leipzig theologian Augustinus Alveld (c. 1480–1535), who argued against Luther on the topic of communion in "both kinds." In some sense, the *Babylonian Captivity* serves as Luther's reply.

But Luther's ideas on the sacraments had been in development for some time before. His early personal struggles with penance and the Mass are well known and were the context for much of his *Anfechtungen*[1] and spiritual trials in the monastery. Likewise, his subsequent clarity on the teaching of justification and faith quickly reshaped his thinking on the sacramental life. By 1519, he had decided that only three of the seven sacraments could be defined as such on the basis of Scripture, publishing a series of sermons that year on the sacraments of penance, baptism, and the Lord's Supper.[a] In 1520, he wrote another, more extensive treatise on the Lord's Supper, a *Treatise on the New Testament*. In all of these works, the sacrament chiefly consists in the divine promise and the faith which grasps it. So it is in the *Babylonian Captivity*, where the correlative of faith and promise is the *leitmotif* that runs through the entire work.

As Luther discusses each of the sacraments, he exhibits a remarkable combination of detailed, penetrating biblical interpretation and pastoral sensitivity for the common person. In fact, it is precisely the perceived lack of attention to Scripture and to pastoral care that drives Luther's ire and polemic. Christians are being fleeced, coerced, and misled by those who should be guiding and caring for consciences. The errors of Rome are

1. *Anfechtung(en)* embraces several concepts and is not readily translated into a single English word. It can be simply understood as "temptation" or "trial" (Lat. *tentatio*) and is employed in this manner by Luther in his German translation of the Bible. But even these examples do not give a single picture on the nature of the temptation and from whence it comes. In some places *Anfechtung* is a struggle within—a conflict with flesh and spirit (e.g., Matt. 26:41); in other places the trial seems to come from the outside—from enemies and persecuters of the church (Luke 8:13 and James 1:12). In Luther's writings, he adds to the complexity of the term as he reflects both upon his own personal experiences of *Anfechtung* and the theological implications attached to them. At the basic level, they are experienced as a contradiction of God's love and protection, a perceived antagonism and hostility to the security of one's salvation. Satan's accusations, self-doubt and the weakness of the flesh, and God's wrath are all various aspects of this experience. Yet for Luther, such trials are ultimately to be received as a blessing from God, a tool of his fatherly love to refine faith and strengthen one's confidence in God's Word and promises. Thus, he describes *Anfechtung* as one of the necessary experiences for the making of a Christian theologian: "This is the touchstone which teaches you not only to know and understand, but also to experience how right, how true, how sweet, how lovely, how mighty, how comforting God's Word is, wisdom beyond all wisdom" (*Preface to the Wittenberg Edition of Luther's German Writings*, TAL 4:475–88).

a *The Sacrament of Penance* (LW 35:9–23; WA 2:714–23); *The Holy and Blessed Sacrament of Baptism* (LW 35:29–45; WA 2:727–37); *The Blessed Sacrament of the Holy and True Body of Christ and the Brotherhoods* (LW 35:49–73; WA 2:742–58). All are included in TAL 1.

intolerable because they are so injurious to faith. The most egregious for Luther was how the Eucharist was understood and practiced. Here he identifies three "captivities" of the Mass by which the papacy imprisons the Christian church: the reservation of the cup, the doctrine of transubstantiation, and the use of the Mass as a sacrifice and work to gain divine favor. In all three of these areas, Luther focuses on the pastoral implications of Rome's misuse and tyranny.

The *Babylonian Captivity* is written in Latin, attesting to the technical nature of the topic and to the education of Luther's audience. It is clear that he assumes for his reader at least a broad knowledge of Scholastic theology and, for his humanist readership, a facility with classical allusions which, relative to Luther's other writings, are not infrequent. The reception of the work was a mixed one. Georg Spalatin (1484–1545), the elector's secretary,[2] was worried about the effects the tone would have. Erasmus[3] believed (perhaps rightly) that the breach was now irreparable. Johannes Bugenhagen (1485–1558) was appalled upon his first reading, but upon closer study became convinced that Luther was in the right, and soon became Luther's trusted colleague, co-reformer, and friend. Henry VIII of England (1491–1547) even entered into the fray, writing his own refutation of Luther, a *Defense of the Seven Sacraments*, for which he received the title *Fidei defensor* from the pope. The papal bull[4] threatening Luther with excommunication was already on its way, so in some sense Luther hardly felt he could make matters worse. But in the end, the *Babylonian Captivity* had the effect of galvanizing both opponents and supporters. It became the central work for which Luther had to answer at the Diet of Worms in 1521.

Some of Luther's expressed positions—though provocative at the time—became less agreeable to his followers later on. In particular, Luther seemed ambivalent regarding the role of laws in civil affairs, suggesting that the gospel was a better guide for rulers. Luther himself deemed this position deficient when faced with the Peasants' War in 1525. Likewise, when discussing marriage, Luther was inclined to dismiss the manifold laws and regulations that had grown around the institution and rely only on biblical mandates and examples. This led to some of his more controversial remarks regarding the permissibility of bigamy. After the marital scandal of Philip of Hesse,[5] which ensued in part from following Luther's advice, these remarks were deemed

2. Spalatin served Elector Frederick III the Wise (b. 1463) from 1509 till Frederick's death in 1525.

3. Erasmus of Rotterdam (1466–1536) was a Dutch humanist whose works in moral philosophy and editions of the church fathers and the Greek New Testament made him famous throughout Europe.

4. Pope Leo X (1475–1521) issued the papal bull *Exsurge domine* calling for Luther's excommunication in 1520.

5. Philip I, landgrave of Hesse (1504–1567), was a supporter of the Reformation and used his political authority to encourage Protestantism in Hesse. Soon after he married Christine of Saxony in 1523, he engaged in an adulterous affair, and by 1526 was considering how to make bigamy permissible. Luther counseled Philip against this, advising Christians to avoid bigamous marriage, except in extreme circumstances.

A portrait of Philip I, Landgrave of Hesse, and his wife Christine of Saxony, painted by Jost V. Hoff.

unacceptable. When Luther's works were first collected and published in Jena and Wittenberg, the publishers excised these portions from Luther's treatise. These sections are indicated in the annotations of this edition.

THE BABYLONIAN CAPTIVITY OF THE CHURCH[6]

A PRELUDE OF MARTIN LUTHER ON THE BABYLONIAN CAPTIVITY OF THE CHURCH

Jesus

MARTIN LUTHER, AUGUSTINIAN, to his friend, Hermann Tulich,[7] greeting.

Whether I wish it or not, I am compelled to become more learned every day, with so many and such able masters eagerly driving me on and making me work. Some two years ago I wrote on indulgences, but in such a way that I now deeply regret having published that little book.[8] At that time I still clung with a mighty superstition to the tyranny of Rome, and so I held that indulgences should not be altogether rejected, seeing that they were approved by the common consent of so many. No wonder, for at the time it was only I rolling this boulder by myself.[9] Afterwards, thanks to Sylvester,[10] and aided by those friars who so strenuously defended indulgences, I saw that they were nothing but impostures of the Roman flatterers, by which they rob people of their money and their faith in God. Would that I could prevail upon the booksellers and persuade all who have read them to burn the whole of my booklets on indulgences,[b] and instead of all that I have written on this subject adopt this proposition: INDULGENCES ARE WICKED DEVICES OF THE FLATTERERS OF ROME.

b In addition to the *Ninety-Five Theses*, WA 1:233–38; LW 31:17–33; TAL 1:13–46, these include: *Explanations of the Ninety-Five Theses*, WA 1:525–628; *A Sermon on Indulgences and Grace*, WA 1:243–56; *The Freedom of the "Sermon on Papal Indulgences and Grace" of Doctor Martin Luther against the "Refutation," Being Completely Fabricated to Insult That Very Sermon*, WA 1:380–93.

6. The English translation for this edition is a revision of that which is found in vol. 36 of *Luther's Works* (Philadelphia: Muhlenberg Press, 1959), 3–126. The revisions are based on WA 6:497–573, and *Martin Luther: Studien Ausgabe*, vol. 2 (Leipzig: Evangelische Verlagsanstalt, 1982), 168–259. Annotations and footnotes are the work of the editors but are also informed by notes included in previous critical editions.

7. Hermann Tulich was born at Steinheim (c. 1488), near Paderborn, in Westphalia. He studied in Wittenberg in 1508 and in 1512 matriculated at the University of Leipzig where he was a proofreader in Melchior Lotter's printing house. He returned to Wittenberg in 1519 and received the doctorate in 1520 and became professor of poetry. He was a devoted supporter of Luther. Eventually he became rector of the Johanneum gymnasium at Lüneberg from 1532 until his death on 28 July 1540.

8. Luther apparently is referring to the *Explanations of the Ninety-Five Theses* (1518), WA 1:522f.; LW 31:83–252; but compare also *A Sermon on Indulgences and Grace* (1518), WA 1:243–56, written around the same time. There he noted that indulgences were not necessary, yet he deemed them permissible for "lazy Christians." See also TAL 1:57–66.

9. A reference to the Greek myth of Sisyphus rather than, as some have suggested, to the proverb from Erasmus's *Adagia* (2, 4, 40): *Saxum volutum non obducitur musco*—"a rolling stone gathers no moss."

10. Sylvester Prierias (i.e., Mazzolini), from Prierio in Piedmont (1456–1523), was a Dominican prior. As an official court theologian for Pope Leo X

Next, Eck and Emser and their fellow conspirators undertook to instruct me concerning the primacy of the pope.[11] Here too, not to prove ungrateful to such learned men, I acknowledge that I have profited much from their labors. For while I denied the divine authority of the papacy, I still admitted its human authority.[12] But after hearing and reading the super-subtle

Johann Eck (1486–1543)

(*magistri sacri palati*, "Master of the Sacred Palace"), Prierias was ordered to provide theological critique of Luther's *Ninety-Five Theses*. In 1518, Prierias wrote his *Dialogus de potestate papae* ("Dialogue on the Power of the Pope"), which set out a general critique of Luther's arguments against the theology behind indulgences. Like Luther's other opponents (the Dominicans Johann Tetzel [1475–1521] and Jacob van Hoogstraaten (c. 1460–1527), as well as Johann Eck), Prierias shifted the debate toward church authority rather than focusing solely on the question of indulgences.

11. Johann Eck (born Maier; 1486–1543), from the Swabian village of Eck, became professor at Ingolstadt in Bavaria in 1510. His opposition to Luther began with his criticism of the *Ninety-Five Theses* in his *Obelisci*, which led to heated exchanges with Luther and his colleague Andreas Bodenstein von Karlstadt (1486–1541) and culminated with the Leipzig Disputation in 1519. Hieronymus Emser (1477–1527), the secretary and chaplain of Duke George of Saxony (1471–1539), had been a humanist professor at Erfurt in the days that Luther attended. Emser published several works against Luther after the Leipzig debate. See David V. N. Bagchi, *Luther's Earliest Opponents: Catholic Controversialists, 1518–1525* (Minneapolis: Fortress Press, 1991).

12. Only a few months before, Luther expressed this opinion in his treatise *On the Papacy in Rome against the Most Celebrated Romanist in Leipzig*, LW 39:49–104. Cf. *Resolutio Lutheriana super propositione sua decima tertia de potestate papae* (1519), WA 2:180–240.

subtleties of these showoffs,[c] with which they so adroitly prop up their idol (for my mind is not altogether unteachable in these matters), I now know for certain that the papacy is the kingdom of Babylon and the power of Nimrod, the mighty hunter.[13] Once more, therefore, that all may turn out to my friends' advantage, I beg both the booksellers and my readers that after burning what I have published on this subject they hold to this proposition: THE PAPACY IS THE MIGHTY HUNT OF THE BISHOP OF ROME. This is proved by the arguments of Eck, Emser, and the Leipzig lecturer on the Scriptures.[14]

[Communion in Both Kinds]

Now they are making a game of schooling me concerning communion in both kinds[15] and other weighty subjects: this is the task[d] lest I listen in vain to these self-serving teachers of mine.[16] A certain Italian friar of Cremona has written a "Recantation of Martin Luther before the Holy See," which is not that I revoke anything, as the words declare, but that he revokes me.[17] This is

c The original Latin here is *Trossulorum*, a reference to Roman knights who conquered the city of Trossulum in Etruria (central Italy) without the aid of foot soldiers (*Pliny* 32, 2; *Seneca*, ep. 87). Later the term was used in a derogatory sense of a conceited dandy.

d This phrase is perhaps a reference to Virgil's *Aeneid* 6, 129: ". . . *Hoc opus, hic labor est*" ("that is the work, that is the task"), wherein the Sibyl warns Aeneas that his desire to enter Hades is simple; it is *leaving* hell that is the difficult task.

13. A reference to Gen. 10:8-9: "Cush fathered Nimrod; he was the first on earth to be a mighty man. He was a mighty hunter before the LORD. Therefore it is said, 'Like Nimrod a mighty hunter before the LORD.'" Luther here voices the criticism that the pope was seeking power rather than being a good pastor. So he describes the pope as a "mighty hunter" and his use of authority as a "mighty hunt" rather than describing him as a shepherd tending the sheep.

14. Augustinus Alveld was a Franciscan professor at Leipzig who wrote a treatise against Luther in April of 1520, *Concerning the Apostolic See, Whether It Is a Divine Law or Not*, which sparked Luther's response *On the Papacy in Rome* (see n.8 above).

15. In June 1520, Alveld wrote a treatise against Luther on communion in both kinds, *Tractatus de communione sub utraque specie*. Luther already proposed restoring the cup to the laity in two earlier treatises: *The Blessed Sacrament of the Holy and True Body of Christ, and the Brotherhoods* (1519), LW 35:50; TAL 1:225-56; and *Treatise on the New Testament, That Is, the Holy Mass* (1520), LW 35:106-7.

16. The original Latin here is *Cratippos meos*, a reference to Cratippus of Pergamon (first century BCE), a philosopher who taught in Athens. Because he was an instructor of Cicero's son, Cratippus gained the famed orator's favor, thereby gaining Roman citizenship. The reference is consistent with Luther's opinion of his opponents as flatterers and sycophants.

17. Isidoro Isolani, a Dominican from Milan, published *Revocatio Martini Lutheri Augustiniani ad sanctam sedem* on 22 November 1519 in Cremona.

the kind of Latin the Italians are beginning to write nowadays.[18] Another friar, a German of Leipzig, that same lecturer, as you know, on the whole canon of Scripture[e] has written against me concerning the sacrament in both kinds and is about to perform, as I understand, still greater and more marvelous things. The Italian[f] was canny enough to conceal his name, fearing perhaps the fate of Cajetan[19] and Sylvester.[20] The man of Leipzig, on the other hand, as becomes a fierce and vigorous German, boasts on his ample title page of his name, his life, his sanctity, his learning, his office, his fame, his honor, almost his very clogs.[21] From him I shall doubtless learn a great deal, since he writes his dedicatory epistle to the Son of God himself: so familiar are these saints with Christ who reigns in heaven! Here it seems three magpies are addressing me, the first in good Latin, the second in better Greek, the third in the best Hebrew.[22] What do you think, my dear Hermann, I should do, but prick up my ears?[g] The matter is being dealt with at Leipzig by the "Observance" of the Holy Cross.[23]

18. A barb that would certainly delight his humanist readers.

19. Tomasso de Vio (Cardinal) Cajetan (1469–1534), vicar general of the Dominican order and influential Aquinas scholar, interviewed Luther at Augsburg in 1518 as papal legate in order to acquire a recantation. His three-day debate with Luther on indulgences, Aquinas, canon law, and church authority was recounted and critically reviewed by Luther in his published *Proceedings at Augsburg* (1518), LW 31:253–92; TAL 1:121–66.

20. Luther's response to Sylvester Prierias, *Ad dialogum Silvestri Prieratis de potestate papae responsio*, was published in 1518.

21. The title page of Alveld's treatise contained twenty-six lines. The "clogs" (*calopodia = calcipodium*) that Luther mentioned were the wooden-soled sandals worn by the Observant Franciscans.

22. Luther is referring to the unusual spelling, IHSVH, for Jesus that Alveld tries to justify by arguments which involve an admixture of the three languages.

23. Alveld belonged to the stricter part of the Franciscan order, known as the Observantines. Luther is playing on this word.

Cajetan (at the table, far left) and Luther (standing right) at Augsburg. Colored woodcut from Ludwig Rabus, *Historien der Heyligen Ausserwählten Gottes Zeugen* (Straßburg, 1557).

e I.e., Alveld.

f I.e., Isolani.

Fool that I was, I had hitherto thought that it would be a good thing if a general council were to decide that the sacrament should be administered to the laity in both kinds.[h] This view our more-than-learned friar would correct, declaring that neither Christ nor the apostles had either commanded or advised that both kinds be administered to the laity; it was therefore left to the judgment of the church what to do or not to do in this matter, and the church must be obeyed. These are his words.

You will perhaps ask, what madness has entered into the man, or against whom is he writing? For I have not condemned the use of one kind, but have left the decision about the use of both kinds to the judgment of the church. This is the very thing he attempts to assert, in order to attack me with this same argument. My answer is that this sort of argument is common to all who write against Luther: either they assert the very things they assail, or they set up a man of straw whom they may attack. This is the way of Sylvester and Eck and Emser, and of the men of Cologne and Louvain,[24] and if this friar had not been one of their kind, he would never have written against Luther.

This man turned out to be more fortunate than his fellows, however, for in his effort to prove that the use of both kinds was neither commanded nor advised, but left to the judgment of the church, he brings forward the Scriptures to prove that the use of one kind for the laity was ordained by the command of Christ.[i] So it is true, according to this new interpreter of the Scriptures, that the use of one kind was not commanded and at the same time was commanded by Christ! This novel kind of argument is, as you know, the one which these dialecticians[25] of Leipzig are especially fond of using. Does not Emser profess to speak fairly of me in his earlier book,[26] and then, after I had convicted him of the foulest envy and shameful lies, confess, when about to confute me in his later book,[j] that both were true, and that he has written in both a friendly and an unfriendly spirit? A fine fellow, indeed, as you know!

g "*Aures arrigam*," a common classical turn of phrase, cf. Terence, *Andria* 5, 4, 30; Virgil, *Aeneid* 1, 152; Erasmus, *Adagia* 3, 2, 56.

h See *The Blessed Sacrament of the Holy and True Body of Christ, and the Brotherhoods* (1519), LW 35:45–74; TAL 1:225–56. Cf. *Treatise on the New Testament, That Is, the Holy Mass* (1520), LW 35:106–7.

i See below where Luther details Alveld's interpretation of John 6.

j *A venatione Luteriana aegocerotis assertio* (1519).

24. In February of 1520, the theological faculties of Louvain and Cologne published a condemnation of Luther's doctrine based on his collected Latin writings as printed by the Basel printer Johann Froben in 1518.

25. A name derived from the discipline of dialectic, or logic, which was one of the three basic disciplines of medieval education, along with grammar and rhetoric.

26. Emser first published a report of the Leipzig debate between Luther and Eck with his interpretation of it, *De disputatione Lipsicensi, quantum ad Boemos obiter deflexa est* (1519).

But listen to our distinguished distinguisher of "kinds," to whom the decision of the church and the command of Christ are the same thing, and again the command of Christ and no command of Christ are the same thing. With such dexterity he proves that only one kind should be given to the laity, by the command of Christ, that is, by the decision of the church. He puts it in capital letters, thus: THE INFALLIBLE FOUNDATION. Then he treats John 6[:35, 41] with incredible wisdom, where Christ speaks of the bread of heaven and the bread of life, which is he himself. The most learned fellow not only refers these words to the Sacrament of the Altar, but because Christ says: "I am the living bread" [John 6:51] and not "I am the living cup," he actually concludes that we have in this passage the institution of the sacrament in only one kind for the laity. But here follow the words: "For my flesh is food indeed, and my blood is drink indeed" [John 6:55] and, "Unless you eat the flesh of the Son of Man and drink his blood" [John 6:53]. When it dawned upon the good friar that these words speak undeniably for both kinds and against one kind—presto! how happily and learnedly he slips out of the quandary by asserting that in these words Christ means to say only that whoever receives the sacrament in one kind receives therein both flesh and blood. This he lays down as his "infallible foundation" of a structure so worthy of the holy and heavenly "Observance."

I pray you now to learn along with me from this that in John 6 Christ commands the administration of the sacrament in one kind, yet in such a way that his commanding means leaving it to the decision of the church; and further that Christ is speaking in this same chapter only of the laity and not of the priests. For to the latter the living bread of heaven, that is the sacrament in one kind, does not belong, but perhaps the bread of death from hell! But what is to be done with the deacons and subdeacons,[27] who are neither laymen nor priests? According to this distinguished writer they ought to use neither the one kind nor both kinds! You see, my dear Tulich, what a novel and "Observant" method of treating Scripture this is.

But learn this too: In John 6 Christ is speaking of the Sacrament of the Altar, although he himself teaches us that he is speaking of faith in the incarnate Word, for he says: "This is the work of God, that you believe in him whom he has sent" [John 6:29]. But we'll have to give him credit: this Leipzig professor

27. Subdeacons and deacons are the fifth and sixth of the seven offices through which clergy advanced to the priesthood. Theologians debated whether these middle offices participated in the sacrament of Holy Orders until the Council of Trent decided that they did. For a discussion of the seven offices, see Martin Chemnitz, *Examination of the Council of Trent*, II:9:2 (St. Louis: Concordia, 1978).

of the Bible can prove anything he pleases from any passage of Scripture he pleases. For he is an Anaxagorian,[28] or rather an Aristotelian, theologian for whom nouns and verbs when interchanged mean the same thing and any thing.[29] Throughout the whole of his book he so fits together the testimony of the Scriptures that if he set out to prove that Christ is in the sacrament he would not hesitate to begin thus: "The lesson is from the book of the Revelation of St. John the Apostle." All his quotations are as apt as this one would be, and the wiseacre imagines he is adorning his drivel with the multitude of his quotations. The rest I will pass over, lest I smother you with the filth of this vile-smelling sewer.[k]

In conclusion, he brings forward 1 Cor. 11[:23], where Paul says that he received from the Lord and delivered to the Corinthians the use of both the bread and the cup. Here again our distinguisher of kinds, treating the Scriptures with his usual brilliance, teaches that Paul permitted, but did not deliver, the use of both kinds. Do you ask where he gets his proof? Out of his own head, as he did in the case of John 6. For it does not behoove this lecturer to give a reason for his assertions; he belongs to that order whose members prove and teach everything by their visions.[30] Accordingly we are here taught that in this passage the apostle did not write to the whole Corinthian congregation, but to the laity alone—and therefore gave no "permission" at all to the clergy, but deprived them of the sacrament altogether! Further, according to a new kind of grammar, "I have received from the Lord" means the same as "it is permitted by the Lord," and "I have delivered to you" is the same as "I have permitted to you." I pray you, mark this well. For by this method not only the church, but any worthless fellow, will be at liberty, according to this master, to turn all the universal commands, institutions, and ordinances of Christ and the apostles into mere "permission."

I perceive therefore that this man is driven by a messenger of Satan[l] and that he and his partners are seeking to make a name for themselves in the world through me, as men who are worthy to cross swords with Luther. But their hopes shall be dashed. In my contempt for them I shall never even mention their names, but content myself with this one reply to all their books. If they

k *Cloaca.*

l 2 Cor. 12:7.

28. Anaxagoras (c. 510–428 BCE) was a pre-Socratic philosopher charged with impiety for his novel interpretations of myths that he adapted to fit his naturalistic explanations of physical phenomena. Luther is using the comparison to highlight Alveld's forced interpretations of Scripture.

29. The philosophy of Aristotle (384–322 BCE) was an essential feature of Scholastic theology. Aristotle's categories, method, and scientific and ethical theories were often incorporated into the explanation of theological topics and the interpretation of Scripture. Such extensive and uncritical use of Aristotle in theology was quite controversial from the outset and a central point of Luther's early critique of Scholastic theology. Here Luther probably has in mind Aristotle's study of language, "On Interpretation," in his collection of logical treatises, the *Organon*.

30. Franciscans. St. Francis (c. 1182–1226) was known for his various visions, including the call to rebuild the ruined chapel of San Damiano that marked the beginning of his mendicant life and his vision at the end of his life on Mt. Verna which bestowed on him the *stigmata*, the five wounds of Christ.

are worthy of it, I pray that Christ in his mercy may bring them back to a sound mind. If they are not worthy, I pray that they may never leave off writing such books, and that the enemies of truth may never deserve to read any others. There is a true and popular saying:

> "This I know for certain—whenever I fight with filth,
> victor or vanquished, I am sure to be defiled."[31]

31. Luther used the common saying later in his edition of *Aesop's Fables* (1530). There he used it as the moral to the fable of the ass and the lion. See Carl P. E. Springer, *Luther's Aesop*, Early Modern Studies, vol. 8 (Kirksville, MO: Truman State University Press, 2011).

And since I see that they have an abundance of leisure and writing paper, I shall furnish them with ample matter to write about. For I shall keep ahead of them, so that while they are triumphantly celebrating a glorious victory over one of my heresies (as it seems to them), I shall meanwhile be devising a new one. I too am desirous of seeing these illustrious leaders in battle decorated with many honors. Therefore, while they murmur that I approve of communion in both kinds, and are most happily engrossed with this important and worthy subject, I shall go one step further and undertake to show that all who deny communion in both kinds to the laity are wicked men. To do this more conveniently I shall compose *a prelude on the captivity of the Roman church*. In due time, when the most learned papists have disposed of this book I shall offer more.

I take this course, lest any pious reader who may chance upon this book, should be offended by the filthy matter with which I deal and should justly complain that he finds nothing in it which cultivates or instructs his mind or which furnishes any food for learned reflection. For you know how impatient my friends are that I waste my time on the sordid fictions of these men. They say that the mere reading of them is ample confutation; they look for better things from me, which Satan seeks to hinder through these men. I have finally resolved to follow the advice of my friends and to leave to those hornets the business of wrangling and hurling invectives.

Of that Italian friar of Cremona[m] I shall say nothing. He is an unlearned man and a simpleton, who attempts with a few rhetorical passages to recall me to the Holy See, from which I am not as yet aware of having departed, nor has anyone proved that

m Isidoro Isolani; see n. 17, p. 105 above.

I have. His chief argument in those silly passages[n] is that I ought to be moved by my monastic vows and by the fact that the empire has been transferred to the Germans. Thus he does not seem to have wanted to write my "recantation" so much as the praise of the French people and the Roman pontiff.[32] Let him attest his allegiance in this little book, such as it is. He does not deserve to be harshly treated, for he seems to have been prompted by no malice; nor does he deserve to be learnedly refuted, since all his chatter is sheer ignorance and inexperience.

[Central Premise]

To begin with, I must deny that there are seven sacraments, and for the present maintain that there are but three: baptism, penance, and the bread.[33] All three have been subjected to a miserable captivity by the Roman curia, and the church has been robbed of all her liberty. Yet, if I were to speak according to the usage of the Scriptures, I should have only one single sacrament,[34] but with three sacramental signs, of which I shall treat more fully at the proper time.

[The Sacrament of the Lord's Supper]

Now concerning the sacrament of the bread first of all.

I shall tell you now what progress I have made as a result of my studies on the administration of this sacrament. For at the time when I was publishing my treatise on the Eucharist,[35] I adhered to the common custom and did not concern myself at all with the question of whether the pope was right or wrong. But now that I have been challenged and attacked, no, forcibly thrust into this arena, I shall freely speak my mind, whether all the papists laugh or weep together.

In the first place the sixth chapter of John must be entirely excluded from this discussion, since it does not refer to the sacrament in a single syllable. Not only because the sacrament was not yet instituted, but even more because the passage itself and

n I.e., *Revocatio Martini Lutheri Augustiniani ad sanctam sedem*; cf. n. 15.

32. On Christmas day, 800, the Frankish ruler, Charlemagne (c. 747–814), was crowned by Pope Leo III as the "Emperor of the Romans" (*Imperator Romanorum*), and since that time Germanic kings claimed continuity with the ancient Roman Empire (*translatio imperii*), even though in the East the empire continued on with its own succession of emperors in Constantinople. More specifically, Luther is here referring to the most recent election of Charles V (1500–1558) in 1519 who, though only partly German, was certainly more so than Francis I of France, the pope's preferred candidate.

33. The common designation for the Lord's Supper, especially since the cup was withheld from the laity. By the end of the treatise Luther will conclude that there are only two sacraments; see p. 217.

34. 1 Tim. 3:16: "Without any doubt, the mystery of our religion is great: He was revealed in flesh, vindicated in spirit, seen by angels, proclaimed among Gentiles, believed in throughout the world, taken up in glory." In the Latin Bible, the word *mystery* is translated with *sacramentum*. See below, n. 210, p. 188. Cf. also thesis 18 of Luther's *Disputatio fide infusa et acquisita* ("Disputation Concerning Infused and Acquired Faith"), WA 6:85–86.

35. *The Blessed Sacrament of the Holy and True Body of Christ, and the Brotherhoods* (1519), LW 35:45–74; TAL 1:225–56.

the sentences following plainly show, as I have already stated, that Christ is speaking of faith in the incarnate Word. For he says: "My words are spirit and life" [John 6:63], which shows that he was speaking of a spiritual eating, by which he who eats has life; whereas the Jews understood him to mean a bodily eating and therefore disputed with him. But no eating can give life except that which is by faith, for that is truly a spiritual and living eating. As Augustine also says: "Why do you make ready your teeth and your stomach? Believe, and you have eaten."[36] For the sacramental eating does not give life, since many eat unworthily. Hence Christ cannot be understood in this passage to be speaking about the sacrament.

Some persons, to be sure, have misapplied these words in their teaching concerning the sacrament, as in the decretal *Dudum*[37] and many others. But it is one thing to misapply the Scriptures and another to understand them in their proper sense. Otherwise, if in this passage Christ were enjoining a sacramental eating, when he says: "Unless you eat my flesh and drink my blood, you have no life in you" [John 6:53], he would be condemning all infants, all the sick, and all those absent or in any way hindered from the sacramental eating, however strong their faith might be. Thus Augustine, in his *Contra Julianum*, Book II,[o] proves from Innocent[38] that even infants eat the flesh and drink the blood of Christ without the sacrament; that is, they partake of them through the faith of the church.[39] Let this then be accepted as proved: John 6 does not belong here. For this reason I have written elsewhere[p] that the Bohemians[40] cannot properly rely on this passage in support of the sacrament in both kinds.

Now there are two passages that do bear very clearly upon this matter: the Gospel narratives of the Lord's Supper and Paul in 1 Cor. 11[:23-25]. Let us examine these. Matt. [26:26-28], Mark [14:22-24], and Luke [22:19f.] agree that Christ gave the whole sacrament to all his disciples. That Paul delivered both kinds is so certain that no one has ever had the temerity to say otherwise. Add to this that Matt. [26:27] reports that Christ did not say of the bread, "eat of it, all of you," but of the cup, "drink of it, all of you." Mark [14:23] likewise does not say, "they all ate of it," but

36. Augustine (354–430), bishop of Hippo in North Africa, was the most influential church father in Western Christianity and remained particularly important for Luther. He is quoting from Augustine's *Sermo* 112, 5.

37. *Dudum* is the incorrect decretal. The correct reference is *Quum Marthae*, in the Decretals of Gregory IX (r. 1227–1241), lib. 3, tit. 41: *de celebratione missarum, et sacramento eucharistiae et divinis officiis*, CIC 2:636–39.

38. Pope Innocent I (d. 417).

39. Innocent's argument can be found in the letters of Augustine, *Ep.* 182, 5; CSEL 44:720.

40. Luther is referring to the followers of Jan Hus (1369–1415). After the condemnation and burning of Hus at the Council of Constance (1414–18), his successor, Jacobellus von Mies (c. 1372–1429), argued for the necessity of communion in both kinds—the bread and the cup—for salvation on the basis of John 6:54. The Bohemians were granted the use of the cup by the Council of Basel in 1433, but this was revoked by Pope Pius II (r. 1458–1464) in 1462.

o *Against Julian* II, 36; CSEL 85¹:183f.

p *Verklärung etlicher Artikel in einem Sermon vom heiligen Sakrament* (1520), WA 6:80.

"they all drank of it." Both attach the note of universality to the cup, not to the bread, as though the Spirit foresaw this schism, by which some would be forbidden to partake of the cup, which Christ desired should be common to all. How furiously, do you suppose, would they rave against us, if they had found the word "all" attached to the bread instead of to the cup? They would certainly leave us no loophole to escape. They would cry out and brand us as heretics and damn us as schismatics. But now, when the Scripture is on our side and against them, they will not allow themselves to be bound by any force of logic. Men of the most free will they are, even in the things that are God's; they change and change again, and throw everything into confusion.

But imagine me standing over against them and interrogating my lords, the papists. In the Lord's Supper, the whole sacrament, or communion in both kinds, is given either to the priests alone or else it is at the same time given to the laity. If it is given only to the priests (as they would have it),[41] then it is not right to give it to the laity in either kind. For it must not be given rashly to any to whom Christ did not give it when he instituted the sacrament. Otherwise, if we permit one institution of Christ to be changed, we make all of his laws invalid, and any man may make bold to say that he is not bound by any other law or institution of Christ. For a single exception, especially in the Scriptures, invalidates the whole.[q] But if it is given also to the laity, it inevitably follows that it ought not to be withheld from them in either form. And if any do withhold it from them when they ask for it they are acting impiously and contrary to the act, example, and institution of Christ.

I acknowledge that I am conquered by this argument, which to me is irrefutable. I have neither read nor heard nor found anything to say against it. For here the word and example of Christ stand unshaken when he says, not by way of permission, but of command: "Drink of it, all of you" [Matt. 26:27]. For if all are to drink of it, and the words cannot be understood as addressed to the priests alone, then it is certainly an impious act to withhold the cup from the laymen when they desire it, even though an angel from heaven were to do it.[r] For when they say that the distribution of both kinds is left to the decision of the church,

41. Gabriel Biel's (c. 1420–1495) *Exposition of the Canon of the Mass* (Lect. 84), which Luther studied extensively, makes the argument that Christ's words, "do this in remembrance of me," were directed to the disciples and their successors, the priests. Thus the cup can be withheld from the laity in order to distinguish them from the clergy.

q Perhaps a reference to James 2:10.

r Cf. Gal. 1:8.

they make this assertion without reason and put it forth without authority. It can be ignored just as readily as it can be proved. It is of no avail against an opponent who confronts us with the word and work of Christ; he must be refuted with the word of Christ, but this we[42] do not possess.

If, however, either kind may be withheld from the laity, then with equal right and reason a part of baptism or penance might also be taken away from them by this same authority of the church. Therefore, just as baptism and absolution must be administered in their entirety, so the sacrament of the bread must be given in its entirety to all laymen, if they desire it. I am much amazed, however, by their assertion that the priests may never receive only one kind in the Mass under pain of mortal sin; and that for no other reason except (as they unanimously say) that the two kinds constitute one complete sacrament, which may not be divided.[43] I ask them, therefore, to tell me why it is lawful to divide it in the case of the laity, and why they are the only ones to whom the entire sacrament is not given? Do they not acknowledge, by their own testimony, either that both kinds are to be given to the laity or that the sacrament is not valid when only one kind is given to them? How can it be that the sacrament in one kind is not complete in the case of the priests, yet in the case of the laity it is complete? Why do they flaunt the authority of the church and the power of the pope in my face? These do not annul the words of God and the testimony of the truth.

It follows, further, that if the church can withhold from the laity one kind, the wine, it can also withhold from them the other, the bread. It could therefore withhold the entire Sacrament of the Altar from the laity and completely annul Christ's institution as far as they are concerned. By what authority, I ask. If the church cannot withhold the bread, or both kinds, neither can it withhold the wine. This cannot possibly be disputed; for the church's power must be the same over either kind as it is over both kinds, and if it has no power over both kinds, it has none over either kind. I am curious to hear what the flatterers of Rome will have to say to this.

But what carries most weight with me, however, and is quite decisive for me is that Christ says: "This is my blood, which is poured out for you and for many for the forgiveness of sins."[44] Here you see very clearly that the blood is given to all those for whose sins it was poured out. But who will dare to say that it

42. Luther is speaking in the person of his opponents.

43. Thomas Aquinas (1225–1274), a Dominican theologian at the University of Paris, maintained that though there are several signs in the sacrament, namely, the bread and wine, this does not constitute two but only one complete sacrament. Both are necessary for the spiritual refreshment offered; *STh* III, q. 73, a. 2: "The bread and wine are materially several signs, yet formally and perfectively one, inasmuch as one refreshment is prepared therefrom." Regarding the communion of priests, in canon 5 of the Twelfth Council of Toledo (681 CE) it is required that the celebrating priest must receive both the body and blood of Christ. Likewise, there is a prohibition against dividing the sacrament in the twelfth-century *Decretum Gratiani*, pt. III, *de Consecratione*, d. 2, chap. 12: "Let them either receive the sacraments entire or be excluded from the entire sacraments, for a division of one and the same sacrament cannot be made without great sacrilege." Aquinas, aware of both, makes the same point in *STh* III, q. 82, a. 4.

44. The words of Christ in the *Canon of the Mass* harmonized the reading of Matt. 26:28, "poured out for many" (which is very possibly a reference to Isa. 53:12, "yet he bore the sin of many"), and Luke 22:20, "poured for you."

was not poured out for the laity? And do you not see whom he addresses when he gives the cup? Does he not give it to all? Does he not say that it is poured out for all? "For you" [Luke 22:20], he says—let this refer to the priests. "And for many" [Matt. 26:28], however, cannot possibly refer to the priests. Yet he says: "Drink of it, all of you" [Matt. 26:27]. I too could easily trifle here and with my words make a mockery of Christ's words, as my dear trifler[s] does. But those who rely on the Scriptures in opposing us must be refuted by the Scriptures.

This is what has prevented me from condemning the Bohemians,[t] who, whether they are wicked men or good, certainly have the word and act of Christ on their side, while we have neither, but only that inane remark of men: "The church has so ordained." It was not the church which ordained these things, but the tyrants of the churches, without the consent of the church, which is the people of God.

But now I ask, where is the necessity, where is the religious duty, where is the practical use of denying both kinds, that is, the visible sign, to the laity, when everyone concedes to them the grace of the sacrament without the sign?[u] If they concede the grace, which is the greater, why not the sign, which is the lesser? For in every sacrament the sign as such is incomparably less than the thing signified. What then, I ask, is to prevent them from conceding the lesser, when they concede the greater? Unless indeed, as it seems to me, it has come about by the permission of an angry God in order to give occasion for a schism in the church, to bring home to us how, having long ago lost the grace of the sacrament, we contend for the sign, which is the lesser, against that which is the most important and the chief thing; just as some men for the sake of ceremonies contend against love.[v] This monstrous perversion seems to date from the time

s Alveld, cf. n. 14, p. 105.

t See n. 40, p. 112.

u E.g., Augustine, *Sermo* 272; Peter Lombard, *Sentences* 4, d. 1, c. 2-4; Aquinas, *STh* III, q. 80, a. 1; Gabriel Biel, *Sentences* 4, d. 1, q.1, a.1, n. 1; Cf. *STh* III, q. 79, a. 4: "Two things may be considered in this sacrament, namely, the sacrament itself (*ipsum sacramentum*), and the reality of the sacrament (*res sacramenti*) . . . the reality of this sacrament is charity (*res autem huius sacramenti est caritas*)."

v Perhaps a reference to Matt. 15:1-9.

when we began to rage against Christian love for the sake of the riches of this world. Thus God would show us, by this terrible sign, how we esteem signs more than the things they signify. How preposterous it would be to admit that the faith of baptism is granted to the candidate for baptism, and yet to deny him the sign of this very faith, namely, the water!

Finally, Paul stands invincible and stops the mouth of everyone when he says in 1 Cor. 11[:23]: "For I received from the Lord what I also delivered to you." He does not say: "I permitted to you," as this friar[45] of ours lyingly asserts out of his own head. Nor is it true that Paul delivered both kinds on account of the contention among the Corinthians. In the first place, the text shows that their contention was not about the reception of both kinds, but about the contempt and envy between rich and poor. The text clearly states: "One is hungry and another is drunk, and you humiliate those who have nothing" [1 Cor. 11:21-22]. Moreover, Paul is not speaking of the time when he first delivered the sacrament to them, for he does not say "I receive from the Lord" and "I give to you," but "I received" and "I delivered"—namely, when he first began to preach among them, a long while before this contention. This shows that he delivered both kinds to them, for "delivered" means the same as "commanded," for elsewhere he uses the word in this sense.[46] Consequently there is nothing in the friar's fuming about permission; he has raked it together without Scripture, without reason, without sense. His opponents do not ask what he has dreamed, but what the Scriptures decree in the matter, and out of the Scriptures he cannot adduce one jot or tittle in support of his dreams, while they can produce mighty thunderbolts in support of their faith.

Rise up then, you popish flatterers, one and all! Get busy and defend yourselves against the charges of impiety, tyranny, and treason[w] against the gospel, and of the crime of slandering your brethren. You decry as heretics those who refuse to contravene such plain and powerful words of Scripture in order to acknowledge the mere dreams of your brains! If any are to be called heretics and schismatics, it is not the Bohemians or the Greeks,[47] for they take their stand upon the Gospels. It is you Romans who are the heretics and godless schismatics, for you presume upon

45. Luther is still dealing with Alveld's argument.

46. 1 Cor. 11:1 in the Vulgate reads, "but I praise you brothers that you remember me in everything and keep my *commandments* just as I *delivered* them to you" (*laudo autem vos fratres quod omnia mei memores estis et sicut tradidi vobis praecepta mea tenetis*).

47. That is, the Eastern Orthodox Church, which split from the Western church in 1054. In the Eastern Rite, both kinds in the sacrament are administered to the faithful with the eucharistic spoon.

w Or "lèse-majesté," from the Latin, *laesa maiestate*; literally, "having caused injury to the sovereignty," in this case of the gospel.

your figments alone against the clear Scriptures of God. Wash yourself of that, men!

But what could be more ridiculous and more worthy of this friar's brains than his saying that the Apostle wrote these words and gave this permission, not to the church universal, but to a particular church, that is, the Corinthian? Where does he get his proof? Out of one storehouse, his own impious head. If the church universal receives, reads, and follows this epistle as written for itself in all other respects, why should it not do the same with this portion also? If we admit that any epistle, or any part of any epistle, of Paul does not apply to the church universal, then the whole authority of Paul falls to the ground. Then the Corinthians will say that what he teaches about faith in the Epistle to the Romans does not apply to them. What greater blasphemy and madness can be imagined than this! God forbid that there should be one jot or tittle in all of Paul which the whole church universal is not bound to follow and keep! The fathers never held an opinion like this, not even down to these perilous times of which Paul was speaking when he foretold that there would be blasphemers and blind, insensate men.[x] This friar is one of them, perhaps even the chief.

However, suppose we grant the truth of this intolerable madness. If Paul gave his permission to a particular church, then, even from your own point of view, the Greeks and Bohemians are in the right, for they are particular churches. Hence it is sufficient that they do not act contrary to Paul, who at least gave permission. Moreover, Paul could not permit anything contrary to Christ's institution. Therefore, O Rome, I cast in your teeth, and in the teeth of all your flatterers, these sayings of Christ and Paul, on behalf of the Greeks and the Bohemians. I defy you to prove that you have been given any authority to change these things by as much as one hair, much less to accuse others of heresy because they disregard your arrogance. It is rather you who deserve to be charged with the crime of godlessness and despotism.

Concerning this point we may read Cyprian,[48] who alone is strong enough to refute all the Romanists. In the fifth book of his treatise *On the Lapsed,* he testifies that it was the widespread

48. Cyprian (c. 200–258) was bishop of Carthage during the Decian persecution (250–251). In dealing with the lapsed Christians who desired readmittance, Cyprian tried to steer a middle course between laxist and rigorist positions. The treatise *De lapsis* ("On the Lapsed") was written c. 251–252. Cyprian was martyred during the Valerian persecution on 14 September 258.

x 2 Tim. 3:1-9.

custom in that church [at Carthage] to administer both kinds to the laity, even to children, indeed, to give the body of the Lord into their hands. And of this he gives many examples. Among other things, he reproves some of the people as follows: "The sacrilegious man is angered at the priests because he does not immediately receive the body of the Lord with unclean hands, or drink the blood of the Lord with unclean lips." He is speaking here, you see, of irreverent laymen who desired to receive the body and the blood from the priests. Do you find anything to snarl at here, wretched flatterer? Will you say that this holy martyr, a doctor of the church endowed with the apostolic spirit, was a heretic, and that he used this permission in a particular church?

In the same place Cyprian narrates an incident that came under his own observation. He describes at length how a deacon was administering the cup to a little girl,[49] and when she drew away from him he poured the blood of the Lord into her mouth.[y] We read the same of St. Donatus, and how trivially does this wretched flatterer dispose of his broken chalice![50] "I read of a broken chalice," he says, "but I do not read that the blood was administered."[51] No wonder! He that finds what he pleases in the Holy Scriptures will also read what he pleases in the histories. But can the authority of the church be established, or the heretics be refuted, in this way?

But enough on this subject! I did not undertake this work for the purpose of answering one who is not worthy of a reply, but to bring the truth of the matter to light.

I conclude, then, that it is wicked and despotic to deny both kinds to the laity, and that this is not within the power of any angel, much less of any pope or council. Nor does the Council of Constance give me pause, for if its authority is valid, why not that of the Council of Basel as well, which decreed to the contrary that the Bohemians should be permitted to receive the sacrament in both kinds?[52] That decision was reached only after considerable discussion, as the extant records and documents of the Council show. And to this Council the ignorant flatterer refers in support of his dream; with such wisdom does he handle the whole matter.

49. The Latin, *infanti*, indicates a child under the age of seven.

50. Donatus (d. c. 372), not to be confused with the schismatic bishop of Carthage, was bishop of Arezzo. According to one legend, Donatus was celebrating the Eucharist with a glass chalice when, during a sudden attack by pagan intruders, the chalice was shattered. Miraculously, Donatus was able to reassemble the chalice immediately and even with a missing piece continue the celebration.

51. Alveld uses the story in his *Tractatus* to argue against the cup being administered to the laity.

52. The Council of Constance (1414–1418) adjudicated the case of Jan Hus and the Bohemian practice of communion in both kinds. The Council upheld the practice of withholding the cup and condemned Hus, burning him at the stake as a heretic. Alveld cited the decrees of the council in his *Tractatus*. On the other hand, the Council of Basel granted the Bohemians special privilege for the administration of the sacrament in both kinds in 1433.

y *De lapsis* 25; CSEL 31, 255. Augustine also mentions the story in a letter: *Ep.* 98,4; CSEL 34 II, 524–26.

[The First Captivity: Withholding the Cup]

In this polyptych (1320) by Pietro Lorenzetti (1280–1348), St. Donatus is pictured (far left) at the Church of Santa Maria della Pieve in Arezzo, Tuscany.

The first captivity of this sacrament, therefore, concerns its substance or completeness, which the tyranny of Rome has wrested from us. Not that those who use only one kind sin against Christ, for Christ did not command the use of either kind, but left it to the choice of each individual, when he said: "As often as you do this, do it in remembrance of me" [1 Cor. 11:25]. But they are the sinners, who forbid the giving of both kinds to those who wish to exercise this choice. The fault lies not with the laity, but with the priests. The sacrament does not belong to the priests, but to everyone. The priests are not lords but servants whose duty is to administer both kinds to those who desire them, as often as they desire them. If they wrest this right from the laity and deny it to them by force, they are tyrants; but the laity are without fault, whether they lack one kind or both kinds. In the meantime they must be preserved by their faith and by their desire for the complete sacrament.[53] These same servants are likewise bound to administer baptism and absolution to everyone who seeks them, because he has a right to them; but if they do not administer them, the seeker has the full merit of his faith, while they will be accused before Christ as wicked servants. Thus the holy fathers of old in the desert did not receive the sacrament in any form for many years at a time.[z]

Therefore I do not urge that both kinds be seized upon by force, as if we were bound to this form by a rigorous command, but I instruct men's consciences so that they may endure

53. Cf. Aquinas, *STh* III, q. 80, a.1: "the effect of the sacrament can be secured by every man if he receive it in desire, though not in reality. Consequently, just as some are baptized with the baptism of desire, through their desire of baptism, before being baptized in the baptism of water; so likewise some eat this sacrament spiritually ere they receive it sacramentally. Now this happens in two ways. First of all, from desire of receiving the sacrament itself, and thus are said to be baptized, and to eat spiritually, and not sacramentally,

z Cf. Luther's *A Treatise Concerning the Ban*, LW 39:3–22.

the Roman tyranny, knowing well that they have been forcibly deprived of their rightful share in the sacrament because of their own sin. This only do I desire—that no one should justify the tyranny of Rome, as if it were doing right in forbidding one kind to the laity. We ought rather to abhor it, withhold our consent, and endure it just as we should do if we were held captive by the Turk and not permitted to use either kind. This is what I meant by saying that it would be a good thing, in my opinion, if this captivity were ended by the decree of a general council,[a] our Christian liberty restored to us out of the hands of the Roman tyrant, and everyone left free to seek and receive this sacrament, just as we are free to receive baptism and penance. But now we are compelled by the same tyranny to receive the one kind year after year, so utterly lost is the liberty which Christ has given us. This is the due reward of our godless ingratitude.

[The Second Captivity: Transubstantiation]

The second captivity of this sacrament is less grievous as far as the conscience is concerned, yet the gravest of dangers threatens the person who would attack it, to say nothing of condemning it. Here I shall be called a Wycliffite[54] and a heretic by six hundred names. But what of it? Since the Roman bishop has ceased to be a bishop and has become a tyrant, I fear none of his decrees; for I know that it is not within his power, nor that of any general council, to make new articles of faith.[b]

Some time ago, when I was drinking in scholastic theology, the learned Cardinal of Cambrai[55] gave me food for thought in his comments on the fourth book of the *Sentences*.[56] He argues with great acumen that to hold that real bread and real wine, and not merely their accidents,[57] are present on the altar, would be much more probable and require fewer superfluous miracles—if only the church had not decreed otherwise. When I learned later

a See n. 52, p. 118.

b See Luther's *On the Councils and the Church* in *The Annotated Luther*, Volume 3, pp. 317–443.

c The Latin saying is *inter sacrum et saxum*—literally, "between the sacred thing (i.e., sacrificial victim) and the stone knife." The meaning here is that when in such a position, hesitation due to uncertainty is extremely dangerous. Cf. Erasmus, *Adagia* 1, 1, 15.

they who desire to receive these sacraments since they have been instituted. Secondly, by a figure: thus the Apostle says (1 Corinthians 10:2), that the fathers of old were 'baptized in the cloud and in the sea,' and that 'they did eat . . . spiritual food, and . . . drank . . . spiritual drink.' Nevertheless, sacramental eating is not without avail, because the actual receiving of the sacrament produces more fully the effect of the sacrament than does the desire thereof, as stated above of baptism."

54. John Wycliffe (c. 1331–1384), an English Scholastic theologian and philosopher at Oxford, was an early critic of the doctrine of transubstantiation. For this and a variety of other positions, Wycliffe was posthumously declared a heretic at the Council of Constance on 4 May 1415. Later, in 1428, his body was exhumed and burned.

55. Pierre d'Ailly (1350–1420), chancellor of the University of Paris and cardinal of Cambrai, was an influential Scholastic theologian in the Occamist tradition. Luther studied his *Questiones quarti libri sententiarum* in his early career as a student of theology in Erfurt.

56. The *Sentences* of Peter Lombard (c. 1096–1160) was the standard text for medieval Scholastic theology. Prominent theologians would often publish their own commentaries on Lombard's *Sentences*, which then became the focus of subsequent study and comment.

57. "Accident" refers to the property or quality of a thing that does not touch upon its essential nature or substance. This is an Aristotelian distinction that attained common usage in medieval

what church it was that had decreed this, namely, the Thomistic[58]—that is, the Aristotelian church—I grew bolder, and having lingered "between knife and sacrifice,"[c] I at last found rest for my conscience in the above view, namely, that it is real bread and real wine, in which Christ's real flesh and real blood are present in no other way and to no less a degree than the others assert them to be under their accidents. I reached this conclusion because I saw that the opinions of the Thomists, whether approved by pope or by council,[59] remain only opinions, and would not become articles of faith even if an angel from heaven were to decree otherwise.[60] For what is asserted without the Scriptures or proven revelation may be held as an opinion, but need not be believed. But this opinion of Thomas hangs so completely in the air without support of Scripture or reason that it seems to me he knows neither his philosophy nor his logic. For Aristotle speaks of subject and accidents so very differently from St. Thomas that it seems to me this great man is to be pitied not only for attempting to draw his opinions in matters of faith from Aristotle, but also for attempting to base them upon a man whom he did not understand, thus building an unfortunate superstructure upon an unfortunate foundation.[61]

Image of John Wycliffe, English theologian, translator, and reformist, originally published in Bale's *Scriptor Majoris Britanniae* (1548).

theology; see for example Lombard, *Sentences* 4, d. 12, c. 1. In the doctrine of transubstantiation, the "accidents" of the bread and wine—i.e., their appearance, smell, and taste—are said to remain while the "substance" is miraculously changed into Christ's body and blood through consecration. Luther is probably referring to d'Ailly's comments in *Sentences* 4, qu. 6 J; however, see Leif Grane, "Luthers Kritik an Thomas von Aquin in 'De captivate Babylonica,'" *Zeitschrift für Kirchengeschichte* (1969): 3 n.7.

58. Thomas Aquinas (see n. 43 above) was known for his reliance on Aristotle in his attempt to demonstrate a synthesis between philosophy and theology. His articulation of the doctrine of transubstantiation came to be the most influential in the medieval church. See *STh* III, q. 75.

59. In 1215, the Fourth Lateran Council referred to the bread and wine as "transubstantiated" into the body and blood of Christ. Pope Innocent III presided over this council. An official decree on the doctrine of transubstantiation was not arrived at until the Council of Trent in 1551.

60. See Gal. 1:8: "But even if we or an angel from heaven should preach to you a gospel contrary to the one we preached to you, let him be accursed."

61. Aristotle did not conceive of accidental qualities existing apart from the substance; they are de facto a quality of a prior substance. Aquinas is aware of this difficulty; citing Aristotle, however, he appeals to divine providence and the power of God to dispense with this logical problem. Nonetheless, this is precisely the problem for Luther: Why insist on using Aristotle as an aid to theology if one must dispense with it precisely in the moment of theological difficulty?

Therefore I permit everyone to hold either of these opinions, as he or she chooses. My one concern at present is to remove all scruples of conscience, so that they need not fear being called heretics if they believe that real bread and real wine are present on the altar,[d] and that everyone may feel at liberty to ponder, hold, and believe either one view or the other without endangering one's salvation. However, I shall now set forth my own view.

In the first place, I do not intend to listen or attach the least importance to those who will cry out that this teaching of mine is Wycliffite, Hussite, heretical, and contrary to the decree of the church. No one will do this except those very persons whom I have convicted of manifold heresies in the matter of indulgences, freedom of the will and the grace of God, good works and sins, etc.[62] If Wycliffe was once a heretic, they are heretics ten times over; and it is a pleasure to be blamed and accused by heretics and perverse sophists, since to please them would be the height of impiety. Besides, the only way in which they can prove their opinions and disprove contrary ones is by saying: "That is Wycliffite, Hussite, heretical!" They carry this feeble argument always on the tip of their tongues, and they have nothing else. If you ask for scriptural proof, they say: "This is our opinion, and the church (that is, we ourselves) has decided thus." To such an extent these men, who are reprobate concerning the faith[63] and untrustworthy, have the effrontery to set their own fancies before us in the name of the church as articles of faith.

But there are good grounds for my view, and this above all—no violence is to be done to the words of God, whether by human or angel.[e] They are to be retained in their simplest meaning as far as possible. Unless the context manifestly compels it, they are not to be understood apart from their grammatical and proper

62. Some of Luther's most important writings on these topics since 1517: *Disputation Against Scholastic Theology* (1517); *[Ninety-Five Theses or] Disputation for Clarifying the Power of Indulgences* (1517); *A Sermon on Indulgences and Grace* (1518); *The Heidelberg Disputation* (1518); *Treatise on Good Works* (1520). See TAL, vol. 1.

63. See 2 Tim. 3:8: "As Jannes and Jambres opposed Moses, so these people, of corrupt mind and counterfeit faith [*reprobi circa fidem*], also oppose the truth."

64. Origen (c. 184–253) was a theologian who taught in the catechetical school in Alexandria. He was a prolific interpreter of the Scriptures and perhaps the most influential biblical commentator in the Western church. He helped shape principles for recognizing multiple spiritual meanings in the biblical text, commonly referred to as the allegorical approach to the Bible. While this approach was not without controversy, questions of orthodoxy focused primarily on Origen's theological speculation regarding the origin of the soul and the equality of the Son with the Father. He was posthumously condemned of heresy in the sixth century.

d The original of this part of the sentence is singular.

e Gal. 1:8.

sense, lest we give our adversaries occasion to make a mockery of all the Scriptures. Thus Origen was rightly repudiated long ago because, ignoring the grammatical sense, he turned the trees and everything else written concerning Paradise into allegories, from which one could have inferred that trees were not created by God.[64] Even so here, when the Evangelists plainly write that Christ took bread [Matt. 26:26; Mark 14:22; Luke 22:19] and blessed it, and when the Book of Acts and the Apostle Paul in turn call it bread [Acts 2:46; 20:7; 1 Cor. 10:16; 11:23, 26-28], we have to think of real bread and real wine, just as we do of a real cup (for even they do not say that the cup was transubstantiated). Since it is not necessary, therefore, to assume a transubstantiation effected by divine power, it must be regarded as a figment of the human mind, for it rests neither on the Scriptures nor on reason, as we shall see.

Therefore it is an absurd and unheard-of juggling with words to understand "bread" to mean "the form or accidents of bread," and "wine" to mean "the form or accidents of wine."[65] Why do they not also understand all other things to mean their "forms or accidents"? And even if this might be done with all other things, it would still not be right to enfeeble the words of God in this way, and by depriving them of their meaning to cause so much harm.

Moreover, the church kept the true faith for more than twelve hundred years, during which time the holy fathers never, at any time or place, mentioned this transubstantiation (an unnatural[f] word and a dream), until the pseudo philosophy of Aristotle began to make its inroads into the church in these last three hundred years.[66] During this time many things have been wrongly defined, as, for example, that the divine essence is neither begotten nor begets;[67] that the soul is the substantial form of the

f *Portentoso.* This word could also be translated "monstrous."

65. E.g., Aquinas, *STh* III, q. 75, a. 5: "It is evident to sense that all the accidents of the bread and wine remain after the consecration. And this is reasonably done by divine providence. . . . Christ's flesh and blood are set before us to be partaken of under the species of those things which are the more commonly used by men, namely, bread and wine." See also n. 74, p. 125 ["accident"].

66. The prominence of Aristotle in medieval theology came from several tributaries. The use of dialectic for resolving contradictory statements from various theological authorities became increasingly necessary during the Carolingian period. What was already known of Aristotle was prized for this endeavor as can be seen in such early theological logicians as Peter Abelard (1079–1142). In a relatively short period of time, however, a vast corpus of Aristotle's writings were discovered, coming into the Latin church via the Crusades, the reconquest of Muslim Spain, and various scholarly interactions in the Mediterranean provinces of Venice and Sicily. The result was a widespread effort to bring Aristotle's method and conclusions into conformation with theological doctrine in order to help clarify and defend Christian truth.

67. Lombard, *Sentences* 1, d. 5, c. 1: "In consensus with Catholic expounders, we say regarding this that neither did the Father generate a divine essence, nor did a divine essence generate the Son, nor did a divine essence generate an essence. And here by the term 'essence' we understand the divine nature, which is common to the three persons and is whole in each of them."

Aristotle portrayed in the 1493 *Nuremberg Chronicle* as a scholar of the fifteenth century.

human body.[68] These and like assertions are made without any reason or cause, as the Cardinal of Cambrai himself admits.[69]

Perhaps they will say that the danger of idolatry demands that the bread and wine should not be really present.[70] How ridiculous! The laymen have never become familiar with their subtle philosophy of substance and accidents, and could not grasp it if it were taught to them. Besides, there is the same danger in the accidents which remain and which they see, as in the case of the substance which they do not see. If they do not worship the accidents, but the Christ hidden under them, why should they worship the substance of the bread, which they do not see?

68. Aquinas, *STh* I, q. 76, a. 1: "Therefore this principle by which we primarily understand, whether it be called the intellect or the intellectual soul, is the form of the body. This is the demonstration used by Aristotle (*De anima* ii, 2)."

69. Pierre d'Ailly, *Sentences* 1, q. 5 E: "[The church] is not able to clearly conclude [these ideas on divine generation] from the canonical Scriptures. But if God wanted such truths [about divine generation] to be believed by catholics, then he himself would reveal [them] to the church and through [such a revelation] define [them]. Thus sometimes definitions of the church do not always proceed through obvious conclusions drawn from the Scriptures, but by a special revelation given to catholics."

70. Aquinas, *STh* III, q. 75, a. 2: "Some have held that the substance of the bread and wine remains in this sacrament after the consecration. But this opinion cannot stand . . . because it would be opposed to the veneration of this sacrament, if any substance were there, which could not be adored with adoration of *latria*."

And why could not Christ include his body in the substance of the bread just as well as in the accidents? In red-hot iron, for instance, the two substances, fire and iron, are so mingled that every part is both iron and fire.[71] Why is it not even more possible that the body of Christ be contained in every part of the substance of the bread?

What will they reply? Christ is believed to have been born from the inviolate womb of his mother.[72] Let them say here too that the flesh of the Virgin was meanwhile annihilated, or as they would more aptly say, transubstantiated, so that Christ, after being enfolded in its accidents, finally came forth through the accidents! The same thing will have to be said of the shut door[g] and of the closed mouth of the sepulcher,[h] through which he went in and out without disturbing them.

Out of this has arisen that Babel of a philosophy of a constant quantity distinct from the substance,[73] until it has come to such a pass that they themselves no longer know what are accidents and what is substance. For who has ever proved beyond the shadow of a doubt that heat, color, cold, light, weight, or shape are mere accidents? Finally, they have been driven to pretend that a new substance is created by God for those accidents on the altar, all on account of Aristotle, who says: "It is the nature of an accident to be in something,"[74] and endless other monstrosities. They would be rid of all these if they simply permitted real bread to be present. I rejoice greatly that the simple faith of this sacrament is still to be found, at least among the common people. For as they do not understand, neither do they dispute whether accidents are present without substance, but believe with a simple faith that Christ's body and blood are truly contained there, and leave to those who have nothing else to do the argument about what contains them.

But perhaps they will say: "Aristotle teaches that in an affirmative proposition subject and predicate must be identical," or (to quote the wild beast's own words in the sixth book of his *Metaphysics*): "An affirmative proposition requires the agreement

g John 10:19, 26.

h Matt. 28:2-6.

71. The analogy of fire and iron was not uncommon to describe a variety of consubstantial relationships in theology; for example, Origen when describing the possibility of the incarnation in *Concerning First Principles* 2, 6, 6: "the metal iron is capable of cold and heat. If, then, a mass of iron be kept constantly in the fire, receiving the heat through all its pores and veins, and the fire being continuous and the iron never removed from it."

72. The view that not only Christ's conception but also his birth occurred with his mother's virginity intact can already be found in the second-century *Protoevangelium of James*. Many others also speak of Mary as "ever-Virgin," including Origen, Hilary of Poitiers (c. 300–c. 368), Athanasius (c. 296–373), Epiphanius of Salamis (c. 310–403), Jerome (c. 347–420), Didymus the Blind (c. 313–398), and Augustine. Likewise, Luther would continue to use the title "the ever-Virgin Mary."

73. Because in the doctrine of transubstantiation the accidents of the bread and wine remain without the substance, one must now posit the accidental property of quantity purely in relation to other accidental properties. Accidental properties (e.g., quantity) without essential properties (e.g., substance) would be an absurdity according to the *Categories* of Aristotle.

74. Aristotle, *Metaphysics* 4, 30, 1: "'Accident' means that which attaches to something and can be truly predicated, but neither of necessity nor usually." See also Aquinas, *STh* I, q. 28, a. 2: "For the essence of an accident is to inhere [in something]."

of the subject and the predicate."[75] They interpret agreement to mean identity. Hence, when I say: "This is my body," the subject cannot be identical with the bread, but must be identical with the body of Christ.

What shall we say when Aristotle and these human doctrines are made to be the arbiters of such lofty and divine matters? Why do we not put aside such curiosity and cling simply to the words of Christ, willing to remain in ignorance of what takes place here and content that the real body of Christ is present by virtue of the words? Or is it necessary to comprehend the manner of the divine working in every detail?

But what do they say when Aristotle admits that all of the categories of accidents[76] are themselves a subject—although he grants that substance is the chief subject? Hence for him "this white," "this large," "this something" are all subjects, of which something is predicated.[77] If that is correct, I ask: If a "transubstantiation" must be assumed in order that Christ's body may not be identified with the bread, why not also a "transaccidentation," in order that the body of Christ may not be identified with the accidents?[78] For the same danger remains if one understands the subject to be "this white or this round is my body."[79] And for the same reason that a "transubstantiation" must be assumed, a "transaccidentation" must also be assumed, because of this identity of subject and predicate.

If, however, merely by an act of the intellect, you can do away with the accident, so that it will not be regarded as the subject when you say, "this is my body," why not with equal ease transcend the substance of the bread, if you do not want it to be regarded either as the subject, so that "this my body" is no less in the substance than in the accident? After all, this is a divine work performed by God's almighty power, which can operate just as much and just as well in the accident as it can in the substance.

Let us not dabble too much in philosophy, however. Does not Christ appear to have anticipated this curiosity admirably by saying of the wine, not *Hoc est sanguis meus*, but *Hic est sanguis meus*? [Mark 14:24]. He speaks even more clearly when he brings in the word "cup" and says: "This cup [*Hic calix*] is the new testament in my blood" [Luke 22:20; 1 Cor. 11:25].[80] Does it not seem as though he desired to keep us in a simple faith, sufficient for us to believe that his blood was in the cup? For my part, if I cannot fathom how the bread is the body of Christ, yet I will take my

75. It is not Aristotle's *Metaphysics* but his *Organon*; namely, the sixth book of *Concerning Interpretation* which contains this proposition.

76. Aristotle identifies nine categories of accidents: quantity, quality, relation, place, time, position, state, action, and affection.

77. Aristotle, *Metaphysics* 7, 3: "The word 'substance' is applied, if not in more senses, still at least in four ways; for the essence and the universal and the genus are thought to be the substance of each thing, and fourthly the subject. Now the subject is that of which everything else is predicated, while it is itself not predicated of anything else."

78. Luther is pointing out how relying simply on logical categories and the rules of philosophical language will not bring one nearer to Christian truth. By positing "transaccidentation," Luther shows how the requirements of logic can remain intact even while setting forth absurd theological statements.

79. That is, the accidental properties of the eucharistic host: white and round.

80. Luther is here appealing to the grammatical agreement between the demonstrative pronoun, *hic* ("this"), and *calix* ("cup"), which are both masculine. With the correlation of cup and blood with the demonstrative pronoun, Luther seems to be saying that the continued presence of the wine is indicated in the very words of Christ.

reason captive to the obedience of Christ,[i] and clinging simply to his words, firmly believe not only that the body of Christ is in the bread, but that the bread is the body of Christ. My warrant for this is the words which say: "He took bread, and when he had given thanks, he broke it and said, 'Take, eat, this (that is, this bread, which he had taken and broken) is my body'" [1 Cor. 11:23-24]. And Paul says: "The bread which we break, is it not a participation in the body of Christ?" [1 Cor. 10:16]. He does not say "in the bread there is," but "the bread itself is the participation in the body of Christ." What does it matter if philosophy cannot fathom this? The Holy Spirit is greater than Aristotle. Does philosophy fathom their transubstantiation? Why, they themselves admit that here all philosophy breaks down.[81] That the pronoun "this," in both Greek and Latin, is referred to "body" is due to the fact that in both of these languages the two words are of the same gender. In Hebrew, however, which has no neuter gender, "this" is referred to "bread," so that it would be proper to say *Hic* [bread] *est corpus meum*. Actually, the idiom of the language and common sense both prove that the subject ["this"] obviously points to the bread and not to the body, when he says: *Hoc est corpus meum—das ist meyn leyp*—that is, "This very bread here [*iste panis*] is my body."

Thus, what is true in regard to Christ is also true in regard to the sacrament. In order for the divine nature to dwell in him bodily [Col. 2:9], it is not necessary for the human nature to be transubstantiated and the divine nature contained under the accidents of the human nature. Both natures are simply there in their entirety, and it is truly said: "This man is God; this God is man." Even though philosophy cannot grasp this, faith grasps it nonetheless. And the authority of God's Word is greater than the capacity of our intellect to grasp it. In like manner, it is not necessary in the sacrament that the bread and wine be transubstantiated and that Christ be contained under their accidents in order that the real body and real blood may be present. But both remain there at the same time, and it is truly said: "This bread is my body; this wine is my blood," and vice versa. Thus I will understand it for the time being to the honor of the holy words of God, to which I will allow no violence to be done by

81. E.g., Gabriel Biel, *Sentences* 4, d. 11, q. 1, a. 3, dub. 6 N: "Because this cessation [of the substance of the bread] is supernatural and miraculous, one does not have a concept to impose from philosophy, but is able to speak about the cessation of the thing according to the whole."

i 2 Cor. 10:5.

petty human arguments, nor will I allow them to be twisted into meanings which are foreign to them. At the same time, I permit other men to follow the other opinion, which is laid down in the decree *Firmiter*,[82] only let them not press us to accept their opinions as articles of faith (as I have said above).

[The Third Captivity: The Mass as a Sacrifice]

The third captivity of this sacrament is by far the most wicked abuse of all, in consequence of which there is no opinion more generally held or more firmly believed in the church today than this, that the Mass is a good work and a sacrifice. And this abuse has brought an endless host of other abuses in its train, so that the faith of this sacrament has become utterly extinct and the holy sacrament has been turned into mere merchandise, a market, and a profit-making business. Hence participations,[83] brotherhoods,[84] intercessions, merits, anniversaries,[85] memorial days,[86] and similar goods are bought and sold, traded and bartered, in the church. On these the priests and monks depend for their entire livelihood.

I am attacking a difficult matter, an abuse perhaps impossible to uproot, since through century-long custom and the common consent of men it has become so firmly entrenched that it would be necessary to abolish most of the books now in vogue, and to alter almost the entire external form of the churches[87] and introduce, or rather reintroduce, totally different kinds of ceremonies. But my Christ lives, and we must be careful to give more heed to the Word of God than to all the thoughts of human beings and of angels. I will perform the duties of my office[88] and bring to light the facts in the case. As I have received the truth freely,[j] I will impart it without malice. For the rest let all look to their own salvation; I will do my part faithfully so that none may be able to cast on me the blame for their lack of faith and their ignorance of the truth when we appear before the judgment seat of Christ.[k]

In the first place, in order that we might safely and happily attain to a true and free knowledge of this sacrament, we must be particularly careful to put aside whatever has been added to

j Matt. 10:8.

k 2 Cor. 5:10.

82. Luther is referring to the first canon of the Fourth Lateran Council (1215), which uses the term *transubstantiation*: "His body and blood are truly contained in the sacrament of the altar under the forms of bread and wine, the bread and wine having been changed in substance (*transubstantiatis*), by God's power, into his body and blood, so that in order to achieve this mystery of unity we receive from God what he received from us." *Firmiter, Decretalium Gregorii IX, lib. I, tit I: de summa trinitate et fide catholica,* cap. 1, sec 3.

83. A "participation" was the notion that one could, without being present, obtain spiritual benefits from the saying of Masses. For example, such was possible with the regular Masses said in monasteries.

84. Confraternities that paid to have Masses said for them alongside other devotional practices for the purpose of gaining merit. The benefits accrued by one member through his devotion and attendance at Masses was then made available to all other members. See Luther's critique of this practice in his treatise *The Blessed Sacrament of the Holy and True Body of Christ, and the Brotherhoods* (1519), LW 35:45–74; TAL 1:225–56.

85. "Anniversaries" can refer to a year of daily Masses said on behalf of the soul of a deceased person or to Masses said every year on the anniversary of one's death.

86. Masses for the dead said on memorial days.

87. Medieval church architecture

its original simple institution by human zeal and devotion: such things as vestments, ornaments, chants, prayers, organs, candles, and the whole pageantry of outward things. We must turn our eyes and hearts simply to the institution of Christ and this alone,[89] and set nothing before us but the very word of Christ by which he instituted the sacrament, made it perfect, and committed it to us. For in that word, and in that word alone, reside the power, the nature, and the whole substance of the Mass. All the rest is the work of human beings, added to the word of Christ, and the Mass can be held and remain a Mass just as well without them. Now the words of Christ, in which he instituted this sacrament, are these:

"Now as they were eating, Jesus took bread, and blessed, and broke it, and gave it to his disciples and said, 'Take, eat; this is my body, which is given for you.' And he took a cup, and when he had given thanks he gave it to them, saying, 'Drink of it, all of you; for this cup is the new testament in my blood, which is poured out for you and for many for the forgiveness of sins. Do this in remembrance of me.'"[90]

Albrecht Dürer's woodcut illustration of the Lord's Supper (completed 1510).

facilitated these sacramental practices, from high altars for feast-day Masses to side altars and apsidiole chapels for private Masses, alcoves for the reservation and adoration of consecrated hosts, and screens dividing celebrants from the congregation.

88. As a sworn doctor of Holy Scripture (1512), Luther vowed to uphold the teachings of the Scripture and defend the faith from false doctrine.

89. Luther's examination of the biblical words of institution as the primary interpretation of the sacrament's meaning, benefit, and practice was first set forth a few months earlier in his *Treatise on the New Testament* (1520), LW 35:79–112.

90. Luther follows the canon of the Mass in conflating the various accounts of the words of institution from Matt. 26:26-28; Mark 14:22-24; Luke 22:19-20; and 1 Cor. 11:23-25, but excludes ornamental phrases in the canon not found explicitly in Scripture.

These words the Apostle also delivers and more fully expounds in 1 Cor. 11[:23-26]. On them we must rest; on them we must build as on a firm rock, if we would not be carried about with every wind of doctrine,[l] as we have till now been carried about by the wicked doctrines of men who reject the truth.[m] For in these words nothing is omitted that pertains to the completeness, the use, and the blessing of this sacrament; and nothing is included that is superfluous and not necessary for us to know. Whoever sets aside these words and meditates or teaches concerning the Mass will teach monstrous and wicked doctrines, as they have done who have made of the sacrament an *opus operatum*[91] and a sacrifice.

Let this stand, therefore, as our first and infallible proposition—the Mass or Sacrament of the Altar is Christ's testament, which he left behind him at his death to be distributed among his believers. For that is the meaning of his words, "This cup is the new testament in my blood" [Luke 22:20; 1 Cor. 11:25]. Let this truth stand, I say, as the immovable foundation on which we shall base all that we have to say. For, as you will see, we are going to overthrow all the godless opinions of men which have been imported into this most precious sacrament. Christ, who is the truth, truly says that this is the new testament in his blood, poured out for us. Not without reason do I dwell on this sentence; the matter is of no small moment, and must be most deeply impressed on our minds.

Thus, if we enquire what a testament is, we shall learn at the same time what the Mass is, what its right use and blessing, and what its wrong use.

A testament, as everyone knows, is a promise made by one about to die, in which he designates his bequest and appoints his heirs. A testament, therefore, involves first, the death of the testator, and second, the promise of an inheritance and the naming of the heir. Thus Paul discusses at length the nature of a testament in Rom. 4[:13f.], Gal. 3[:15-17] and 4[:1-7], and Heb. 9[:15-18].[92] We see the same thing clearly also in these words of Christ. Christ testifies concerning his death when he says: "This is my body, which is given, this is my blood, which is poured out" [Luke 22:19-20]. He names and designates the bequest when he

l Eph. 4:14.

m Titus 1:14.

91. The Scholastic notion of the sacrament as an *opus operatum* is the doctrine that the priestly act intrinsically offers grace without reference to the disposition or faith of the recipient. Luther first challenges this understanding of the sacrament's efficacy in his *Sermon on the Blessed Sacrament of the Holy and True Body and Blood of Christ* (1519), LW 35:45-74; TAL 1:225-56.

92. Luther still held the traditional view that Paul was the author of the epistle to the Hebrews. He would change his mind on this by the time of his 1522 translation of the New Testament so that his preface to the epistle reads: ". . . Hebrews is not an epistle of St. Paul, or any other apostle . . . who wrote it is not known, and will probably not be known for a while; it makes no difference." He was probably influenced by Erasmus, who first questioned the Pauline authorship in his annotations to the New Testament. Earlier that year, in a sermon on Heb. 1:1-4, Luther suggested that Apollos might be the actual author.

says "for the forgiveness of sins" [Matt. 26:28]. But he appoints the heirs when he says, "For you [Luke 22:19-20; 1 Cor. 11:24] and for many" [Matt. 26:28; Mark 14:24], that is, for those who accept and believe the promise of the testator. For here it is faith that makes us heirs, as we shall see.

You see, therefore, that what we call the Mass is a promise of the forgiveness of sins made to us by God, and such a promise as has been confirmed by the death of the Son of God. For the only difference between a promise and a testament is that the testament involves the death of the one who makes it. A testator is a promiser who is about to die, while a promiser (if I may put it thus) is a testator who is not about to die. This testament of Christ is foreshadowed in all the promises of God from the beginning of the world; indeed, whatever value those ancient promises possessed was altogether derived from this new promise that was to come in Christ. Hence the words "compact," "covenant," and "testament of the Lord"[93] occur so frequently in the Scriptures. These words signified that God would one day die. "For where there is a testament, the death of the testator must of necessity occur" (Heb. 9[:16]). Now God made a testament; therefore, it was necessary that God should die. But God could not die unless God became human. Thus the incarnation and the death of Christ are both comprehended most concisely in this one word, "testament."

From the above it will at once be seen what is the right and what is the wrong use of the Mass, and what is the worthy and what the unworthy preparation for it. If the Mass is a promise, as has been said, then access to it is to be gained, not with any works, or powers, or merits of one's own, but by faith alone. For where there is the word of the promising God, there must necessarily be the faith of the accepting person. It is plain, therefore, that the beginning of our salvation is a faith which clings to the word of the promising God, who, without any effort on our part, in free and unmerited mercy takes the initiative and offers us the word of his promise. "He sent forth his Word, and thus healed them," not: "He accepted our work, and thus healed us."[94] First of all there is God's Word. After it follows faith; after faith, love; then love does every good work, for it does no wrong; indeed, it is the fulfilling of the law.[95] In no other way can a person come to God or deal with God than through faith. That is to say, that the author of salvation is not human beings, by any works of their

93. The Latin for these three words are, respectively: *pactum*, *foedus*, *testamentum*. All three words are used interchangeably in the Latin Vulgate to translate the Hebrew *berith* in the Old Testament and the Greek *diathēkē* in the Septuagint or New Testament, rendered by most English translations as "covenant." E.g., Exod. 24:8: "Moses took the blood and dashed it on the people, and said, 'See the blood of the covenant [*sanguis foederis*] that the Lord has made with you in accordance with all these words'"; Gen. 9:8-9: "Then God said to Noah and to his sons with him, 'As for me, I am establishing my covenant [*pactum meum*] with you and your descendants after you . . .'"; Ps. 25:10: "All the paths of the Lord are steadfast love and faithfulness, for those who keep his covenant [*testamentum eius*] and his decrees."

94. Ps. 107:20. Luther inserted "thus" (*sic*) in his interpretation of the verse.

95. Rom. 13:10: "Love does no wrong to a neighbor; therefore love is the fulfilling of the law."

own,[n] but God, through his promise; and that all things depend on, and are upheld and preserved by, the word of his power,[96] through which he brought us forth, to be a kind of first fruits of his creatures.[97]

Thus, in order to raise up Adam after the fall, God gave him this promise when he said to the serpent: "I will put enmity between you and the woman, and between your seed and her seed; he shall bruise your head, and you shall bruise his heel" [Gen. 3:15]. In this word of promise Adam, together with his descendants, was carried as it were in God's bosom, and by faith in it he was preserved, waiting patiently for the woman who should bruise the serpent's head, as God had promised. And in that faith and expectation he died, not knowing when or who she would be, yet never doubting that she would come. For such a promise, being the truth of God, preserves even in hell[98] those who believe it and wait for it. After this came another promise, made to Noah—to last until the time of Abraham—when a bow was set in the clouds as a sign of the covenant,[o] by faith in which Noah and his descendants found God gracious. After that, he promised Abraham that all the nations should be blessed in his seed.[p] And this is Abraham's bosom,[q] into which his descendants have been received.[99] Then to Moses and the children of Israel,[r] especially to David,[s] he gave the plainest promise of Christ, and thereby at last made clear what the promise to the people of old really was.

And so it finally came to the most perfect promise of all, that of the new testament, in which, with plain words, life and salvation are freely promised, and actually granted to those who believe the promise. And he distinguishes this testament from the old one by a particular mark when he calls it the "new testament." For the old testament given through Moses was not a promise of forgiveness of sins or of eternal things, but of temporal things, namely, of the land of Canaan, by which no one was renewed in spirit to lay hold on the heavenly inheritance.

n The original here is singular.

o Gen. 9:12-17.

p Gen. 22:18.

q Luke 16:22.

r Deut. 18:18.

s 2 Sam. 7:12-16.

96. Heb. 1:3: "He is the radiance of the glory of God and the exact imprint of his nature, and he upholds the universe by the word of his power."

97. James 1:8: "Of his own will he brought us forth by the word of truth, that we should be a kind of firstfruits of his creatures."

98. Luther's reference to "hell" (*inferno*) here corresponds to the concept of *hades* or the Hebrew *Sheol* and the notion that, before Christ, the patriarchs remained imprisoned in this place of the dead until he would release them after his resurrection. Ephesians 4:7-10 and 1 Peter 3:19-20 were often interpreted as biblical allusions to this, and the view was relatively common in the early church. The medieval view was deeply influenced by the detailed account in the fourth-century apocryphal text *The Gospel of Nicodemus*. Dante (1265–1321) refers to this as the first circle of hell or "limbo." There the patriarchs of old were held until the "Mighty One," i.e., Christ, came and released them; cf. *Inferno*, Canto 4.52–63.

99. Hippolytus of Rome (170–235) referred to the place of the Old Testament righteous souls as the "Bosom of Abraham."

Wherefore also it was necessary that, as a figure of Christ, a dumb beast should be slain, in whose blood the same testament might be confirmed, as the blood corresponded to the testament and the sacrifice corresponded to the promise. But here Christ says "the new testament in my blood" [Luke 22:20; 1 Cor. 11:25], not somebody else's, but his own, by which grace is promised through the Spirit for the forgiveness of sins, that we may obtain the inheritance.

According to its substance, therefore, the Mass is nothing but the aforesaid words of Christ: "Take and eat, etc." [Matt. 26:26], as if he were saying: "Behold, O sinful and condemned human, out of the pure and unmerited love with which I love you, and by the will of the Father of mercies,[t] apart from any merit or desire of yours, I promise you in these words the forgiveness of all your sins and life everlasting. And that you may be absolutely certain of this irrevocable promise of mine, I shall give my body and pour out my blood, confirming this promise by my very death, and leaving you my body and blood as a sign and memorial of this same promise. As often as you partake of them, remember me, proclaim and praise my love and bounty toward you, and give thanks."

From this you will see that nothing else is needed for a worthy holding of Mass than a faith that relies confidently on this promise, believes Christ to be true in these words of his, and does not doubt that these infinite blessings have been bestowed upon it. Hard on this faith there follows, of itself, a most sweet stirring of the heart, whereby the human spirit is enlarged and enriched (that is love, given by the Holy Spirit through faith in Christ), so that a person is drawn to Christ, that gracious and bounteous testator, and made a thoroughly new and different person. Who would not shed tears of gladness, indeed, almost faint for joy in Christ, if he believed with unshaken faith that this inestimable promise of Christ belonged to him? How could he help but love so great a benefactor, who of his own accord offers, promises, and grants such great riches and this eternal inheritance to one who is unworthy and deserving of something far different?

Therefore it is our one and only misfortune that we have many Masses in the world, and yet none, or very few of us, recognize, consider, and receive these promises and riches that are

t 2 Cor. 1:3.

offered to us. Actually, during the Mass, we should do nothing with greater zeal (indeed, it demands all our zeal) than to set before our eyes, meditate upon, and ponder these words, these promises of Christ—for they truly constitute the Mass itself—in order to exercise, nourish, increase, and strengthen our faith in them by this daily remembrance. For this is what he commands, when he says: "Do this in remembrance of me" [Luke 22:19; 1 Cor. 11:24]. This should be done by the preachers of the gospel in order to impress this promise faithfully upon the people, to commend it to them, and to awaken their faith in it.

But how many are there today who know that the Mass is the promise of Christ? I will say nothing of those godless preachers of fables, who teach human ordinances instead of this great promise. And even if they teach these words of Christ, they do not teach them as a promise or testament, neither therefore as a means of obtaining faith.

What we deplore in this captivity is that nowadays they take every precaution that no layperson should hear these words of Christ, as if they were too sacred to be delivered to the common people. So mad are we priests that we arrogate to ourselves alone the so-called words of consecration, to be said secretly,[100] yet in such a way that they do not profit even us, for we too fail to regard them as promises or as a testament for the strengthening of the faith. Instead of believing them, we reverence them with I know not what superstitious and godless fancies. What else is Satan trying to do to us through this misfortune of ours but to let nothing of the Mass remain in the church, though he is meanwhile at work filling every corner of the globe with Masses, that is, with abuses and mockeries of God's testament—burdening the world more and more heavily with most grievous sins of idolatry, to its deeper condemnation?[101] For what more sinful idolatry can there be than to abuse God's promises with perverse opinions and to neglect or extinguish faith in them?

For God does not deal, nor has God ever dealt, with people otherwise than through a word of promise, as I have said. We in turn cannot deal with God otherwise than through faith in the Word of his promise. God does not desire works, nor has God need of them; rather we deal with other people and with ourselves on the basis of works. But God has need of this: that we consider God faithful in God's promises,[102] and patiently persist in this belief, and thus worship God with faith, hope, and love.

100. In the early Middle Ages, softly spoken prayers, called *secreta*, occurred before the canon of the Mass (see also n. 170 below) because the offertory psalm was being sung by the choir simultaneously. Later (probably around the eighth century), the canon of the Mass began also to be prayed quietly, after the singing of the Preface and *Sanctus*. The reason for this is probably a combination of priestly piety and a pastoral concern for profane usage by the common people. Cf. Durandus, *Rationale divinorum officiorum* 4, 35, 2. Luther attacked this practice of the *Stillmesse* in a later treatise, *The Abomination of the Secret Mass* (1525), LW 36:311–28.

101. Luther means here that nothing remains in the church of the Mass as it should be understood and celebrated, even as more and more Masses are celebrated in the wrong way and for the wrong purpose.

102. Heb. 10:23: "Let us hold fast to the confession of our hope without wavering, for he who has promised is faithful."

It is in this way that God obtains glory among us, since it is not of ourselves who run, but of God who shows mercy, promises, and gives, that we have and hold all good things.[103] Behold, this is that true worship and service of God which we ought to perform in the Mass. But if the words of promise are not delivered, what exercise of faith can there be? And without faith, who can have hope or love? Without faith, hope, and love, what service of God can there be? There is no doubt, therefore, that in our day all priests and monks, together with their bishops and all their superiors, are idolators, living in a most perilous state by reason of this ignorance, abuse, and mockery of the Mass, or sacrament, or promise of God.

For anyone can easily see that these two, promise and faith, must necessarily go together. For without the promise there is nothing to be believed; while without faith the promise is useless, since it is established and fulfilled through faith. From this everyone will readily gather that the Mass, since it is nothing but promise, can be approached and observed only in faith. Without this faith, whatever else is brought to it by way of prayers, preparations, works, signs, or gestures are incitements to impiety rather than exercises of piety. It usually happens that those who are thus prepared imagine themselves legitimately entitled to approach the altar, when in reality they are less prepared than at any other time or by any other work, by reason of the unbelief which they bring with them. How many celebrants you can see everywhere, every day, who imagine they—wretched men—have committed criminal offenses when they make some petty mistake, such as wearing the wrong vestment, or forgetting to wash their hands, or stumbling over their prayers! But the fact that they have no regard for or faith in the Mass itself, namely, the divine promise, causes them not the slightest qualms of conscience. O worthless religion of this age of ours, the most godless and thankless of all ages!

Hence the only worthy preparation and proper observance is faith, the faith by which we believe in the Mass, that is, in the divine promise. Those, therefore, who desire to approach the altar or receive the sacrament, let them beware lest they appear empty-handed before the face of the Lord God.[104] But they will be empty-handed unless they have faith in the Mass, or this new testament. By what godless work could they sin more grievously against the truth of God, than by this unbelief of theirs? By it,

103. Rom. 9:16: "So it depends not on human will or exertion, but on God who shows mercy."

104. Cf. Exod. 23:15: "You shall observe the festival of unleavened bread. . . . No one shall appear before me empty-handed"; Deut. 16:16: "Three times a year all your males shall appear before the LORD your God at the place that he will choose: at the festival of unleavened bread, at the festival of weeks, and at the festival of booths. They shall not appear before the LORD empty-handed."

as much as in their lies, they convict God of being a liar and a maker of empty promises.[105,u] The safest course, therefore, will be to go to the Mass in the same spirit in which you would go to hear any other promise of God, that is, prepared not to do or contribute much yourself, but to believe and accept all that is promised you there, or proclaimed as promises through the ministry of the priest. If you do not come in this spirit, beware of attending at all, for you will surely be going to your judgment.[106]

I was right then in saying that the whole power of the Mass consists in the words of Christ, in which he testifies that forgiveness of sins is bestowed on all those who believe that his body is given and his blood poured out for them. This is why nothing is more important for those who go to hear Mass than to ponder these words diligently and in full faith. Unless they do this, all else that they do is in vain. This is surely true, that to every promise of his, God usually adds some sign as a memorial or remembrance of the promise, so that thereby we may serve him the more diligently and he may admonish us the more effectually.[107] Thus, when he promised Noah that he would not again destroy the world by a flood, he added his bow in the clouds, to show that he would be mindful of his covenant [Gen. 9:8-17]. And after promising Abraham the inheritance in his seed, he gave him circumcision as a mark of his justification by faith [Gen. 17:3-11]. Thus he granted to Gideon the dry and the wet fleece to confirm his promise of victory over the Midianites [Judg. 6:36-40]. And through Isaiah he offered to Ahaz a sign that he would conquer the king of Syria and Samaria, to confirm in him his faith in the promise [Isa. 7:10-17]. And we read of many such signs of the promises of God in the Scriptures.

So in the Mass also, the foremost promise of all, he adds as a memorial sign of such a great promise his own body and his own blood in the bread and wine, when he says: "Do this in remembrance of me" [Luke 22:19; 1 Cor. 11:24-25]. And so in baptism, to the words of promise he adds the sign of immersion in water. We may learn from this that in every promise of God two things are presented to us, the word and the sign, so that we are to understand the word to be the testament, but the sign to be the sacrament. Thus, in the Mass, the word of Christ is the testament, and the bread and wine are the sacrament. And as

u The original of these sentences is singular.

105. This definition of unbelief can be found consistently through the earliest writings of Luther, especially as it touches on Rom. 3:4 and its citation of Pss. 116:11 and 51:4, "Although everyone is a liar, let God be proved true, as it is written, 'So that you may be justified in your words, and prevail in your judging.'"

106. Perhaps a reference to the consequences of unworthy eating that Paul mentions in 1 Cor. 11:29.

107. Luther gives many of the same examples in his earlier *Treatise on the New Testament* (1520), LW 35:86.

there is greater power in the word than in the sign, so there is greater power in the testament than in the sacrament; for a man can have and use the word or testament apart from the sign or sacrament. "Believe," says Augustine, "and you have eaten."[v] But what does one believe, other than the word of the one who promises? Therefore I can hold Mass every day, indeed, every hour, for I can set the words of Christ before me and with them feed and strengthen my faith as often as I choose. This is a truly spiritual eating and drinking.[108]

Here you may see what great things our theologians of the *Sentences*[109] have produced in this matter. In the first place, not one of them treats of that which is first and foremost, namely, the testament and the word of promise. And thus they make us forget faith and the whole power of the Mass. In addition, they discuss exclusively the second part of the Mass, namely, the sign or sacrament; yet in such a way that here too they do not teach faith, but their preparations and *opera operata*,[w] participations[x] and fruits of the Mass.[110] They come then to the profundities, babble of transubstantiation, and endless other metaphysical trivialities, destroy the proper understanding and use of both sacrament and testament together with faith as such, and cause Christ's people to forget their God—as the prophet says, days without number [Jer. 2:32]. Let the others tabulate the various benefits of hearing Mass; you just apply your mind to this, that you may say and believe with the prophet that God has here prepared a table before you in the presence of your enemies [Ps. 23:5], at which your faith may feed and grow fat. But your faith is fed only with the word of divine promise, for "One does not live by bread alone, but by every word that proceeds from the mouth of God" [Deut. 8:3; Matt. 4:4]. Hence, in the Mass you must pay closest heed above all to the word of promise, as to a most lavish banquet—your utterly green pastures and sacred still waters [Ps. 23:2]—in order that you might esteem this word above everything else, trust in it supremely, and cling to it most firmly, even through death and all sins. If you do this, you will obtain not merely those tiny drops and crumbs of "fruits of the

108. For a Scholastic understanding of spiritual eating in the sacrament, cf. Aquinas, *STh* III, q. 80, a. 2: "there are two ways of eating spiritually. First, . . . the angels eat Christ spiritually inasmuch as they are united with Him in the enjoyment of perfect charity, and in clear vision. . . . In another way one may eat Christ spiritually, . . . as a man believes in Christ, while desiring to receive this sacrament."

109. That is, commentators on the *Sentences* of Peter Lombard. See n. 56, p. 120.

110. "Fruits of the Mass" (*fructus missae*) has to do with the character and extent of benefits received in the celebration of the Mass, especially the relationship between the infinite benefits procured by Christ and present *ex opere operato* and the limited benefits correlative to the intensity of the devotion of those who participate.

v Cf. Augustine, *Sermo* 112, 5.

w See n. 91, p. 130.

x See n. 83, p. 128.

Mass" which some have superstitiously invented, but the very fountainhead of life, namely, that faith in the Word out of which every good thing flows, as is said in John 4:[111] "He who believes in me, 'Out of his heart shall flow rivers of living water.'" And again, "Whoever drinks of the water that I shall give him, it will become in him a spring of water welling up to eternal life" [John 4:14].

Now there are two things that are constantly assailing us, so that we fail to gather the fruits of the Mass. The first is that we are sinners, and unworthy of such great things because of our utter worthlessness. The second is that, even if we were worthy, these things are so high that our timid nature does not dare to aspire to them or hope for them. For who would not simply stand awe-struck before the forgiveness of sins and life everlasting rather than seek after them, once he had weighed properly the magnitude of the blessings which come through them, namely, to have God as father, to be God's child and heir of all God's goods! Against this twofold timidness of ours we must lay hold on the word of Christ, and fix our gaze much more steadfastly on it than on these thoughts of our own weakness. For "great are the works of the LORD, studied by all who have pleasure in them" [Ps. 111:2], who is able to give "more abundantly than all that we ask or think" [Eph. 3:20]. If they did not surpass our worthiness, our grasp, and all our thoughts, they would not be divine. Thus Christ also encourages us when he says: "Fear not, little flock, for it is your Father's good pleasure to give you the kingdom" [Luke 12:32]. For it is just this incomprehensible overflowing of God's goodness, showered upon us through Christ, that moves us above all to love God most ardently in return, to be drawn to God with fullest confidence, and, despising all else, be ready to suffer all things for God. Wherefore this sacrament is rightly called "a fountain of love."[112]

Let us take an illustration of this from human experience.[113] If a very rich lord were to bequeath a thousand gold coins[114] to a beggar or to an unworthy and wicked servant, it is certain that he would boldly claim and accept them without regard to his unworthiness and the greatness of the bequest. And if anyone should seek to oppose him on the grounds of his unworthiness and the large amount of the legacy, what do you suppose the man would say? He would likely say: "What is that to you? What I accept, I accept not on my merits or by any right that I may personally have to it. I know that I am receiving more than

111. John 7:38. Luther was looking ahead to the next verse cited from John 4.

112. While the phrase "fount of love" (*fons dilectionis*) is more commonly applied to the Blessed Virgin Mary in the Middle Ages, love is clearly the central benefit of the sacrament according to Scholastic theology, yet in such a way that love is infused in the recipient as a virtue meriting divine favor. See, for example, Lombard, *Sentences* 4, d. 12, c. 6: "For this Sacrament was instituted for two reasons: for the increase of virtue, namely love, and as medicine for our daily infirmity."

113. Luther used the following illustration in his earlier *Treatise on the New Testament* (1520), LW 35:89f.

114. *Guldens,* gold coins of the time, perhaps of the Holy Roman Empire.

a worthless one like me deserves; indeed, I have deserved the very opposite. But I claim what I claim by the right of a bequest and of another's goodness. If to Christ it was not an unworthy thing to bequeath so great a sum to an unworthy person, why should I refuse to accept it because of my unworthiness? Indeed, it is for this very reason that I cherish all the more his unmerited gift—because I am unworthy!" With that same thought all people[y] ought to fortify their consciences against all qualms and scruples, so that they may lay hold on the promise of Christ with unwavering faith, and take the greatest care to approach the sacrament not trusting in confession, prayer, and preparation, but rather, despairing of all these, with firm confidence in Christ who gives the promise. For, as we have said often enough, the word of promise must reign alone here in pure faith; such faith is the one and only sufficient preparation.

Hence we see how great is God's wrath with us, in that God has permitted godless teachers to conceal the words of this testament from us, and thereby to extinguish this same faith, as far as they could. It is already easy to see what is the inevitable result of this extinguishing of the faith, namely, the most godless superstition of works. For where faith dies and the word of faith is silent, there works and the prescribing of works immediately crowd into their place. By them we have been carried away out of our own land, as into a Babylonian captivity, and despoiled of all our precious possessions. This has been the fate of the Mass; it has been converted by the teaching of godless people into a good work. They themselves call it an *opus operatum*,[z] and by it they presume themselves to be all-powerful with God. Next they proceed to the very height of madness, and after inventing the lie that the Mass is effective simply by virtue of the act having been performed, they add another one to the effect that the Mass is none the less profitable to others even if it is harmful to some wicked priest who may be celebrating it.[115] On such a foundation of sand they base their applications, participations, brotherhoods, anniversaries,[a] and numberless other lucrative and profitable schemes of that kind.

y This sentence is singular in the original.

z See n. 91, p. 130.

a See n. 82, 83, and 85, p. 128.

115. Cf. Aquinas, *STh* III, q. 82, a. 6: "By reason of the power of the Holy Spirit, who communicates to each one the blessings of Christ's members on account of their being united in charity, the private blessing in the Mass of a good priest is fruitful to others. But the private evil of one man cannot hurt another, except the latter, in some way, consent." Luther refers here to the prayers of the Mass as an offering to God and not to the sacrament itself, which is God's work regardless of the worthiness of the priest. See below, p. 149.

These fraudulent disguises are so powerful, so numerous, and so firmly entrenched that you can scarcely prevail against them unless you exercise unremitting care and bear well in mind what the Mass is and what has been said above. You have seen that the Mass is nothing else than the divine promise or testament of Christ, sealed with the sacrament of his body and blood. If that is true, you will understand that it cannot possibly be in any way a work; nobody can possibly do any thing in it, neither can it be dealt with in any other way than by faith alone. However, faith is not a work, but the lord and life of all works.[b] Who in the world is so foolish as to regard a promise received by him, or a testament given to him, as a good work, which he renders to the testator by his acceptance of it? What heir will imagine that he is doing his departed father a kindness by accepting the terms of the will and the inheritance it bequeaths to him? What godless audacity is it, therefore, when we who are to receive the testament of God come as those who would perform a good work for God! This ignorance of the testament, this captivity of so great a sacrament—are they not too sad for tears? When we ought to be grateful for benefits received, we come arrogantly to give that which we ought to take. With unheard-of perversity we mock the mercy of the giver by giving as a work the thing we receive as a gift, so that the testator, instead of being a dispenser of his own goods, becomes the recipient of ours. Woe to such sacrilege!

Who has ever been so mad as to regard baptism as a good work, or what candidate for baptism has believed that he was performing a work which he might offer to God on behalf of himself and communicate to others? If, then, there is no good work that can be communicated to others in this one sacrament and testament, neither will there be any in the Mass, since it too is nothing else than a testament and sacrament. Hence it is a manifest and wicked error to offer or apply the Mass for sins, for satisfactions, for the dead, or for any needs whatsoever of one's own or of others.[116] You will readily see the obvious truth of this if you firmly hold that the Mass is a divine promise, which can benefit no one, be applied to no one, intercede for no one, and be communicated to no one, except only to one who believes with a

116. Luther is speaking against the so-called votive Mass, a Mass said with an intention other than the usual celebration of the day's divine office—often as an intercession for the sake of some need, e.g., the sick, the dead, the penitent, etc. It was a common practice throughout the Middle Ages, and became increasingly common due to the acceptance of money in exchange for such a Mass.

b On the relationship between faith and works, see Luther's *Treatise on Good Works* (1520), LW 44:15–114; TAL 1:257–368.

faith of one's own. Who can receive or apply, in behalf of another, the promise of God, which demands the personal faith of each one individually? Can I give to another the promise of God, even if that person does not believe? Can I believe for another, or cause another to believe? But this is what must happen if I am able to apply and communicate the Mass to others; for there are but two things in the Mass, the divine promise and the human faith, the latter accepting what the former promises. But if it is true that I can do this, then I can also hear and believe the gospel for another, I can be baptized for another, I can be absolved from sins for another, I can also partake of the Sacrament of the Altar for another, and—to go through the list of their sacraments also—I can marry a wife for another, get ordained for another, be confirmed for another, and receive extreme unction for another!

In short, why did not Abraham believe for all the Jews? Why was faith in the promise made to Abraham demanded of every individual Jew?[c]

Therefore, let this irrefutable truth stand fast: Where there is a divine promise, there everyone must stand on his own feet; his own personal faith is demanded, he will give an account for himself and bear his own load;[d] as it is said in the last chapter of Mark [16:16]: "He who believes and is baptized will be saved; but he who does not believe will be condemned." Even so each one can derive personal benefit from the Mass only by one's own personal faith. It is absolutely impossible to commune on behalf of anyone else. Just as the priest is unable to administer the sacrament to anyone on behalf of another, but administers the same sacrament to each one individually by himself. For in consecrating and administering, the priests are our servants. Through them we are not offering a good work or communicating something in an active sense. Rather, we are receiving through them the promises and the sign; we are being communicated unto in the passive sense. This is the view that has persisted with respect to the laity right up to the present day, for of them it is said not that they do something good but that they receive it. But the priests have strayed into godless ways; out of the sacrament and testament of God, which ought to be a good gift received, they

c Cf. Gen. 12:1f.; 15:5f.

d Gal. 6:5.

have made for themselves a good deed performed, which they then give to others and offer up to God.

But you will say: What is this? Will you not overturn the practice and teaching of all the churches and monasteries, by virtue of which they have flourished all these centuries? For the Mass is the foundation of their anniversaries, intercessions, applications, communications, etc., that is to say, of their fat income. I answer: This is the very thing that has constrained me to write of the captivity of the church.[117] For it is in this manner that the sacred testament of God has been forced into the service of a most impious traffic. It has come through the opinions and ordinances of wicked men, who, passing over the Word of God, have dished up to us the thoughts of their own hearts and led the whole world astray. What do I care about the number and influence of those who are in this error? The truth is mightier than all of them. If you are able to refute Christ, who teaches that the Mass is a testament and a sacrament, then I will admit that they are in the right. Or, if you can bring yourself to say that that man is doing a good work who receives the benefit of the testament, or to that end uses this sacrament of promise, then I will gladly condemn my teachings. But since you can do neither, why do you hesitate to turn your back on the multitude who go after evil? Why do you hesitate to give God the glory and to confess God's truth—that all priests today are perversely mistaken who regard the Mass as a work by which they may relieve their own needs and those of others, whether dead or alive? I am uttering unheard of and startling things, but if you will consider what the Mass is, you will realize that I have spoken the truth. The fault lies with our false sense of security, which blinds us to the wrath of God that is raging against us.

I am ready to admit, however, that the prayers which we pour out before God when we are gathered together to partake of the Mass are good works or benefits, which we impart, apply, and communicate to one another, and which we offer for one another.[118] Thus James [5:16] teaches us to pray for one another that we may be healed, and Paul in 1 Tim. 2[:1-2] commands "that supplications, prayers, and intercessions be made for all men, for kings and all who are in high positions." Now these are not the Mass, but works of the Mass—if the prayers of heart and lips may be called works—for they flow from the faith that is kindled or increased in the sacrament. For the Mass, or the

117. The transposition of the divine generosity and promise of the sacrament into a human work, the justification of this practice by human opinion and tradition rather than the Scriptures, and the consequent enlargement of papal power and riches are, for Luther, the fundamental abuses of the church. Much of his early theological critique can be summarized here: (1) the gospel is not to be turned into a law; (2) the word of God is the final theological authority, not human opinion; and (3) the church should shepherd the flock with practices and doctrine that strengthen faith in Christ, not fleece the sheep for its own gain.

118. In his early writings (e.g., *First Lectures on the Psalms*, 1513–1515), Luther can talk about the Mass as a sacrifice but limits the language to sacrifices of praise and thanksgiving (*sacrificium confessionis . . . laudis*). In his 1520 *Treatise on the New Testament*, Luther further develops this line of interpretation for the eucharistic sacrifice: "To be sure

promise of God, is not fulfilled by praying, but only by believing. However, as believers we pray and perform every good work. But what priest offers up the sacrifice in this sense, that he believes he is offering up only the prayers? They all imagine that they are offering up Christ himself to God the Father as an all-sufficient sacrifice, and performing a good work for all those whom they intend to benefit, for they put their trust in the work which the Mass accomplishes, and they do not ascribe this work to prayer. In this way the error has gradually grown, until they have come to ascribe to the sacrament what belongs to the prayers, and to offer to God what should be received as a benefit.

We must therefore sharply distinguish the testament and sacrament itself from the prayers that we offer at the same time. Not only this, but we must also bear in mind that the prayers avail utterly nothing, either to him who offers them or to those for whom they are offered, unless the testament is first received in faith, so that it will be faith that offers the prayers; for faith alone is heard, as James teaches in his first chapter.[119] There is therefore a great difference between prayer and the Mass. Prayer may be extended to as many persons as one desires, while the Mass is received only by the persons who believe for themselves, and only to the extent that they believe. It cannot be given either to God or to human beings. Rather it is God alone who through the ministration of the priest gives it to people, and people receive it by faith alone without any works or merits. Nor would anyone dare to be so foolish as to assert that a ragged beggar does a good work when he comes to receive a gift from a rich man. But the Mass (as I have said) is the gift of the divine promise, proffered to all people by the hand of the priest.

It is certain, therefore, that the Mass is not a work which may be communicated to others, but the object of faith (as has been said), for the strengthening and nourishing of each one's own faith.

Now there is yet a second stumbling block that must be removed, and this is much greater and the most dangerous of all. It is the common belief that the Mass is a sacrifice, which is offered to God. Even the words of the canon[120] seem to imply this, when they speak of "these gifts, these presents, these holy sacrifices," and further on "this offering." Prayer is also made, in so many words, "that the sacrifice may be accepted even as the sacrifice of Abel," etc. Hence Christ is termed "the sacrifice

this sacrifice of prayer, praise, and thanksgiving, and of ourselves as well, we are not to present before God in our own person. But we are to lay it upon Christ and let him present it for us as St. Paul teaches in Hebrews 13:15, 'Let us continually offer up a sacrifice of praise to God, that is, the fruit of lips that confess him and praise him,' and all this 'through Christ.' For this is why he is also a priest. . . . From these words we learn that we do not offer Christ as a sacrifice, but that Christ offers us. And in this way it is permissible, yea profitable, to call the Mass a sacrifice . . ." (LW 35:98–99).

119. James 1:5-8: "If any of you is lacking in wisdom, ask God, who gives to all generously and ungrudgingly, and it will be given you. But ask in faith, never doubting, for the one who doubts is like a wave of the sea, driven and tossed by the wind; for the doubter, being double-minded and unstable in every way, must not expect to receive anything from the Lord."

120. The canon of the Mass consisted of a series of prayers and collects that included the words of institution for the consecration of the bread and wine. In other words, the entire form of the liturgy around the consecration puts the celebration of the sacrament into the context of a priestly sacrifice and work spoken on behalf of the people, even as other prayers are such.

of the altar." Added to these are the sayings of the holy fathers, the great number of examples, and the widespread practice uniformly observed throughout the world.

Over against all these things, firmly entrenched as they are, we must resolutely set the words and example of Christ. For unless we firmly hold that the Mass is the promise or testament of Christ, as the words clearly say, we shall lose the whole gospel and all its comfort. Let us permit nothing to prevail against these words—even though an angel from heaven should teach otherwise [Gal. 1:8]—for they contain nothing about a work or a sacrifice. Moreover, we also have the example of Christ on our side. When he instituted this sacrament and established this testament at the Last Supper, Christ did not offer himself to God the Father, nor did he perform a good work on behalf of others, but, sitting at the table, he set this same testament before each one and proffered to him the sign. Now, the more closely our Mass resembles that first Mass of all, which Christ performed at the Last Supper, the more Christian it will be. But Christ's Mass was most simple, without any display of vestments, gestures, chants, or other ceremonies, so that if it had been necessary to offer the Mass as a sacrifice, then Christ's institution of it was not complete.

Not that anyone should revile the church universal for embellishing and amplifying the Mass with many additional rites and ceremonies. But what we contend for is this: No one should be deceived by the glamor of the ceremonies and entangled in the multitude of pompous forms, and thus lose the simplicity of the Mass itself, and indeed practice a sort of transubstantiation by losing sight of the simple "substance" of the Mass and clinging to the manifold "accidents" of outward pomp.[121] For whatever has been added to the word and example of Christ is an "accident" of the Mass, and ought to be regarded just as we regard the so-called monstrances[122] and corporal cloths[123] in which the host itself is contained.

Therefore, just as distributing a testament or accepting a promise differs diametrically from offering a sacrifice, so it is a contradiction in terms to call the Mass a sacrifice, for the former is something that we receive and the latter is something that we give. The same thing cannot be received and offered at the same time, nor can it be both given and accepted by the same person, any more than our prayer can be the same thing as that which

121. Luther's ironic use of the Scholastic language of transubstantiation is to illustrate that the papal Mass has focused on incidentals and ignored the essence or chief aspect of the sacrament.

122. The monstrance (from the Latin, *monstrare*, "to show") is a vessel designed to display the consecrated host for the veneration of the faithful, especially in the context of a liturgical procession like that of Palm Sunday or Corpus Christi. The practice of displaying and processing the consecrated host grew quickly out of the practice of the elevation of the host for the purpose of adoration. The elevation was introduced into the eucharistic liturgy in Paris in the thirteenth century, probably as a response to those who argued that the host was not the body of Christ until the wine was also consecrated. Evidence for the use of a monstrance can be identified from the fourteenth century.

123. Also called a "pall" (Lat. *palla*), which at the time was the cloth upon which the chalice and host rested. The corporal cloth was then often kept with the consecrated host.

In this sixteenth-century design for a monstrance by Daniel Hopfer (c. 1470–1535) the host is to be displayed in the center supported by angels. The twelve disciples occupy the niches above.

our prayer obtains, or the act of praying be the same thing as the act of receiving that for which we pray.

What shall we say then of the canon of the Mass and the patristic authorities? First of all, I would answer: If there were nothing at all to be said against them, it would be safer to reject them all than admit that the Mass is a work or a sacrifice, lest we deny the word of Christ and destroy faith together with the Mass. Nevertheless, in order to retain them, we shall say that we are instructed by the Apostle in 1 Cor. 11 that it was customary for Christ's believers, when they came together for Mass, to bring with them food and drink.[124] These they called "collections," and they distributed them among all who were in want, after the example of the apostles in Acts 4.[125] From this store was taken the portion of the bread and wine that was consecrated in

124. 1 Cor. 11:21, 33-34: "For when the time comes to eat, each of you goes ahead with your own supper, and one goes hungry and another becomes drunk. . . . So then, my brothers and sisters, when you come together to eat, wait for one another. If you are hungry, eat at home, so that when you come together, it will not be for your condemnation."

125. Acts 4:34-35: "There was not a needy person among them, for as many as owned lands or houses sold them and brought the proceeds of what was sold. They laid it at the apostles' feet, and it was distributed to each as any had need."

126. See, for example, Hippolytus, *The Apostolic Tradition*, chs. 5–6, where it speaks about the bringing of oil, olives, milk, and cheese in addition to the bread and wine that is consecrated.

127. 1 Tim. 4:4-5: "For everything created by God is good, and nothing is to be rejected, provided it is received with thanksgiving; for it is sanctified by God's word and by prayer."

128. Lev. 8:27: "He placed all these on the palms of Aaron and on the palms of his sons, and raised them as an elevation offering before the Lord."

129. Luther supposes that the history of the elevation of the host is connected to the language of the Old Testament offering, giving the origin of the practice the benefit of the doubt. However, see n. 133 below.

130. Isa. 37:4: "It may be that the Lord your God heard the words of the Rabshakeh, whom his master the king of Assyria has sent to mock the living God, and will rebuke the words that the Lord your God has heard; therefore lift up your prayer for the remnant that is left."

131. Philip Melanchthon (1497–1560) sets forth an argument similar to Luther's in the *Apology of the Augsburg Confession*, XXIV, BC, 258–277.

132. Referring to a holy presentation made to God. Here, the offering of bread and wine.

133. This is an example of Luther's conservative approach to reform. While he distinguishes sharply between the essence of the sacrament as it centers on the words of Christ from the ceremonies and prayers that surround this, Luther is still willing to retain

the sacrament.[126] And since all this store was consecrated by the word and prayer,[127] by being "lifted up" according to the Hebrew rite of which we read in Moses,[128] the words and rite of this lifting up or offering have come down to us, although the custom of bringing along and collecting that which was offered or lifted up has long since fallen into disuse.[129] Thus, in Isa. 37 Hezekiah commanded Isaiah to lift up his prayer in the sight of God for the remnant.[130] In the Psalms we read: "Lift up your hands to the holy place" [Ps. 134:2]. And again: "To you I will lift up my hands" [Ps. 63:4]. And in 1 Tim. 2[:8]: "In every place lifting holy hands." For this reason the words "sacrifice" and "offering" must be taken to refer not to the sacrament and testament, but to the collections themselves.[131] From this source also the word *collect* has come down to us for the prayers said in the Mass.

The same thing happens when the priest elevates the bread and the cup immediately after consecrating them. By this he does not show that he is offering anything to God, for he does not say a single word here about a victim or an offering. But this elevation is either a survival of that Hebrew rite of lifting up what was received with thanksgiving and returned to God, or else it is an admonition to us to provoke us to faith in this testament which the priest has set forth and exhibited in the words of Christ, so that now he also shows us the sign of the testament. Thus the oblation[132] of the bread properly accompanies the demonstrative "this" in the words, "this is my body," and by the sign the priest addresses us gathered about him; and in a like manner the oblation of the cup properly accompanies the demonstrative "this" in the words, "this cup is the new testament, etc." For it is faith that the priest ought to awaken in us by this act of elevation.[133] And would to God that as he elevates the sign, or sacrament, openly before our eyes, he might also sound in our ears the word, or testament, in a loud, clear voice, and in the language of the people,[134] whatever it may be, in order that faith may be the more effectively awakened. For why may Mass be said in Greek and Latin and Hebrew, but not in German or any other language?[e]

Therefore, let the priests who offer the sacrifice of the Mass in these corrupt and most perilous times take heed, first, that they do not refer to the sacrament the words of the greater and lesser canon,[135] together with the collects, because they smack

e See *The Annotated Luther*, Volume 3, p. 130 for an image of the cover of Luther's *Deutsche Messe*.

too strongly of sacrifice. They should refer them instead to the bread and the wine to be consecrated, or to their own prayers. For the bread and wine are offered beforehand for blessing in order that they may be sanctified by the word and by prayer,[f] but after they have been blessed and consecrated they are no longer offered, but received as a gift from God. And in this rite let the priest bear in mind that the gospel is to be set above all canons and collects devised by men, and that the gospel does not sanction the idea that the Mass is a sacrifice, as has been shown.

Further, when a priest celebrates public Mass, he should determine to do nothing else than to commune himself and others by means of the Mass. At the same time, however, he may offer prayers for himself and others, but he must beware lest he presume to offer the Mass. But let him that holds private Masses determine to commune himself.[136] The private Mass does not differ in the least from the ordinary communion which any person receives at the hand of the priest, and has no greater effect. The difference is in the prayers, and in the fact that the priest consecrates the elements for himself and administers them to himself. As far as the blessing of the Mass and sacrament is concerned we are all equals, whether we are priests or lay.

If a priest is requested by others to celebrate so-called votive Masses,[g] let him beware of accepting a fee for the Mass, or of presuming to offer any votive sacrifice. Rather, he should take pains to refer all this to the prayers which he offers for the dead or the living, saying to himself: "Lo, I will go and receive the sacrament for myself alone, and while doing so I will pray for this one and that one." Thus he will receive his fee for the prayers, not for the Mass, and can buy food and clothing with it.[137] Let him not be disturbed because all the world holds and practices the contrary. You have the utmost certainty of the gospel, and by relying on it, you may well disregard the belief and opinions of others. But if you disregard me and insist upon offering the Mass and not the prayers alone, remember that I have faithfully warned you, and that I will be without blame on the day of judgment; you will have to bear your sin alone.[h] I have said what I was bound to say to you as brother to brother for your salvation; yours will be

f 1 Tim. 4:5.

g See n. 116, p. 140.

h Cf. Ezek. 3:19; 33:9.

traditional rites as long as they support the original biblical intention of the sacrament, namely, to awaken faith in the gospel.

134. Luther's pastoral desire to have the Mass in the vernacular is realized in his later efforts at liturgical reform, especially in his *Deutsche Messe und Ordnung des Gottesdiensts—The German Mass and Order of Service* (1526), LW 53:51–90; also pp. 131–61 in *The Annotated Luther*, Volume 3. He also reformed the Latin Mass along the lines indicated here so that the benefit of sacrament as testament rather than sacrifice is clear; see his *Formula missae et communionis pro ecclesia Vuittembergensi* (*An Order of Mass and Communion for the Church at Wittenberg*) (1523), LW 53:15–40.

135. The offering until the conclusion of the communion distribution was considered the "canon" of the Mass. However, a distinction was made between the prayers following the prefatory dialogue (e.g., *Sursum corda*), and then the prayers leading to consecration that followed the *Sanctus*, the former being the "lesser canon" (*canon minor*) and the latter, the "greater canon" (*canon maior*).

136. The private Mass (*missa privata*) was just as it sounds, a Mass celebrated by a priest without a congregation. Luther's concern here is that someone actually commune to make it clear that the Mass is not intended only as a sacrifice. He would later reject the practice altogether; see *The Misuse of the Mass* (1521), LW 36:127–230.

137. Again, Luther is quite conservative in his approach. Focusing solely on preserving the gracious character of the sacrament, Luther allows prayers for the dead and even the fees exacted to continue as long as they are distinguished from the Mass itself.

the gain if you observe it, yours the loss if you neglect it. And if some should even condemn what I have said, I will reply in the words of Paul: "But evil men and impostors will go on from bad to worse, deceiving and being deceived" [2 Tim 3:13].

From the above everyone will readily understand the often quoted saying of Gregory:[138] "A Mass celebrated by a wicked priest is not to be considered of less effect than one celebrated by a good priest. Neither would a Mass of St. Peter have been better than that of Judas the traitor, if they had offered the sacrifice of the Mass."[139] This saying has served many as a cloak to cover their godless doings, and because of it they have invented the distinction between the *opus operatum* and the *opus operantis*, so as to be free to lead wicked lives themselves and yet benefit others.[140] Gregory speaks the truth, only they misunderstand his words. For it is true beyond a question that the testament or sacrament is given and received through the ministration of wicked priests no less completely than through the ministration of the most saintly. For who has any doubt that the gospel is preached by the ungodly? Now the Mass is part of the gospel; indeed, it is the sum and substance of it. For what is the whole gospel but the good tidings of the forgiveness of sins? Whatever can be said about forgiveness of sins and the mercy of God in the broadest and richest sense is all briefly comprehended in the word of this testament. For this reason popular sermons ought to be nothing else than expositions of the Mass, or explanations of the divine promise of this testament; this would be to teach the faith and truly to edify the church. But in our day the expounders of the Mass make mockery and jest with allegorical explanations of human ceremonies.

Therefore, just as a wicked priest may baptize, that is, apply the word of promise and the sign of water to the candidate for baptism, so he may also set forth the promise of this sacrament and administer it to those who partake, and even partake himself, as did Judas the traitor at the supper of the Lord.[i] It still remains the same sacrament and testament, which works its own work in the believer but an "alien work" in the unbeliever.[141] But when it comes to offering a sacrifice the case is quite different. For not the Mass but the prayers are offered to God, and therefore it is as plain as day that the offerings of a wicked priest avail

i Matt. 26:23-25.

138. Gregory I, "the Great" (b. 540), was pope from 590 to 604.

139. This precise quotation from Gregory cannot be identified, but the idea that the efficacy of the Mass is not dependent on the piety of the priest is prominent since Augustine's writings against the Donatists. Cf. *Augsburg Confession*, VII, BC, 42–43.

140. While the Scholastic distinction of *opus operatum* and *opus operantis* may have been used to excuse wicked behavior, the original intention of the distinction was to differentiate between the efficacy of the sacrifices of the Old Testament and that of the New. Since the sacrifices proscribed in the Mosiac law were merely signs pointing ahead to the death of Christ, their power to impart grace was not intrinsic but dependent on the faith and disposition of those performing the sacrifice (*opus operantis*). On the other hand, since the Eucharist was not a sign but the true sacrificial blood of Christ, its efficacy was intrinsic regardless of the faith or piety of the celebrant or recipient (*opus operatum*). See Artur Michael Landgraf, "Die Gnadenökonomie des Alten Bundes nach der Lehre der Frühscholastik," "Die Wirkungen der Beschneidung," and "Beiträge der Frühscholastik zur Terminologie der allgemeinen Sakramentenlehre," in *Dogmengeschichte der Frühscholastik*, 3/1 (Regensburg: Friedrich Pustet, 1954), 19–168.

nothing, but, as Gregory says again: When an unworthy person is sent as the intercessor, the heart of the judge is only turned to greater disfavor.[142] Therefore these two things—Mass and prayer, sacrament and work, testament and sacrifice—must not be confused; for the one comes from God to us through the ministration of the priest and demands our faith, the other proceeds from our faith to God through the priest and demands his hearing. The former descends, the latter ascends. The former, therefore, does not necessarily require a worthy and godly minister, but the latter does indeed require such a one, for "God does not listen to sinners" [John 9:31]. He knows how to do good through evil people, but he does not accept the work of any evil person; as he showed in the case of Cain,[143] and as is said in Prov. 15[:8]: "The sacrifice of the wicked is an abomination to the LORD," and in Rom. 14[:23]: "Whatever does not proceed from faith is sin."

But let us bring this first part to an end, though I am ready to go on with the argument if an opponent should arise. From all that has been said we conclude that the Mass was provided only for those who have a sad, afflicted, disturbed, perplexed, and erring conscience, and that they alone commune worthily. For, since the word of divine promise in this sacrament sets forth the forgiveness of sins, let all draw near fearlessly, whoever they may be, who are troubled by their sins, whether by remorse or by temptation. For this testament of Christ is the one remedy against sins, past, present, and future, if you but cling to it with unwavering faith and believe that what the words of the testament declare is freely granted to you. But if you do not believe this, you will never, anywhere, by any works or efforts of your own, be able to find peace of conscience. For faith alone means peace of conscience, while unbelief means only distress of conscience.

The Sacrament of Baptism

Blessed be God and the Father of our Lord Jesus Christ, who according to the riches of his mercy [Eph. 1:3, 7] has preserved in his church this sacrament at least, untouched and untainted by human ordinances, and has made it free to all nations and classes of people, and has not permitted it to be oppressed by the filth and great impiety of greed and superstitions. For he desired

141. The distinction of God's "alien" and "proper" work (*opus alienum—opus proprium*), derived from Isa. 28:21 ("For the LORD will rise up . . . to work his work—alien is his work"), can be found already in Luther's sermons in 1516 (e.g., WA 1:111-14). There he can speak of God's work as double (*duplex*) so that the gospel according to its proper function and intention is forgiveness and grace. Yet unbelief necessarily places one under its judgment, so that the gospel effects the opposite of its intended purpose, i.e., an alien work. Later Luther finds it clearer to correlate the language of alien and proper work with the distinction of law and gospel.

142. Gregory the Great, *Regula pastoralis* 1, 10: "For we all know well that, when one who is in disfavor is sent to intercede with an incensed person, the mind of the latter is provoked to greater severity." Cf. Gabriel Biel, *Canonis misse expositio*, lect. 27 C.

143. Gen. 4:5: "but for Cain and his offering he had no regard. So Cain was very angry, and his countenance fell."

that by it little children, who were incapable of greed and superstition, might be initiated and sanctified in the simple faith of his Word; even today baptism has its chief blessing for them. But if the intention had been to give this sacrament to adults and older people, I do not believe that it could possibly have retained its power and its glory against the tyranny of greed and superstition which has overthrown all things divine among us. Here too the wisdom of the flesh would doubtless have devised its preparations and dignities, its reservations, restrictions, and other like snares for catching money, until water brought as high a price as parchment[144] does now.

But Satan, though he could not quench the power of baptism in little children, nevertheless succeeded in quenching it in all adults, so that now there are scarcely any who call to mind their own baptism, and still fewer who glory in it; so many other ways have been discovered for remitting sins and getting to heaven. The source of these false opinions is that dangerous saying of St. Jerome—either unhappily phrased or wrongly interpreted—in which he terms penance "the second plank after shipwreck," as if baptism were not penance.[145] Hence, when people have fallen into sin, they despair of the "first plank," which is the ship, as if it had gone under, and begin to put all their trust and faith in the second plank, which is penance.[146] This has given rise to those endless burdens of vows, religious orders, works, satisfactions, pilgrimages, indulgences, and monastic sects,[147] and from them in turn has arisen that flood of books, questions, opinions, and man-made ordinances which the whole world cannot contain. Thus the church of God is incomparably worse off under this tyranny than the synagogue or any other nation under heaven ever was.

It was the duty of the pontiffs to remove all these evils and to put forth every effort to recall Christians to the purity of baptism, so that they might understand what it means to be Christians and what Christians ought to do. But instead of this, their only work today is to lead the people as far astray as possible from their baptism, to immerse all people in the flood of their tyranny, and to cause the people of Christ (as the prophet says) to forget him days without number.[148] How unregenerate are all who bear the name of pontiff today! For they neither know nor do what is becoming to pontiffs, but they are ignorant of what they ought to know and do. They fulfill what Isa. 56[:10, 11] says:

Infant baptism as depicted in *Catechismus* by Johannes Brenz (1499–1570).

144. I.e., letters of indulgence.

145. Jerome's quote, from *Ep.* 130, 9, "Let us know nothing of penitence, lest the thought of it lead us into sin. It is a plank for those who have had the misfortune to be shipwrecked," echoes the earlier saying of Tertullian (c. 155–240) in his treatise *De poenitentia*: "That repentance, O sinner, like myself . . . do you so hasten to, so embrace, as a shipwrecked man the protection of some plank. This will draw you forth when sunk in the waves of sins, and will bear you forward into the port of the divine clemency." See also Lombard, *Sentences* 4, d. 14, c. 1: "As Jerome says, it is 'the second plank after shipwreck,' because, if anyone has corrupted by sin the clothing of innocence which he received at baptism, he may repair it by the remedy of penance. . . . Those who have fallen after baptism can

"His watchmen are blind, they are all without knowledge; the shepherds also have no understanding; they have all turned to their own way, each to his own gain, etc."

[The First Part of Baptism: The Divine Promise]

Now, the first thing to be considered about baptism is the divine promise, which says: "The one who believes and is baptized will be saved" [Mark 16:16]. This promise must be set far above all the glitter of works, vows, religious orders, and whatever else human beings have introduced, for on it all our salvation depends. But we must so consider it as to exercise our faith in it, and have no doubt whatever that, once we have been baptized, we are saved. For unless faith is present or is conferred in baptism, baptism will profit us nothing; indeed, it will become a hindrance to us, not only at the moment when it is received, but throughout the rest of our lives. That kind of unbelief accuses God's promise of being a lie, and this is the greatest of all sins.[j] If we set ourselves to this exercise of faith, we shall at once perceive how difficult it is to believe this promise of God. For our human weakness, conscious of its sins, finds nothing more difficult to believe than that it is saved or will be saved; and yet, unless it does believe this, it cannot be saved, because it does not believe the truth of God that promises salvation.

This message should have been impressed upon the people untiringly, and this promise should have been dinned into their ears without ceasing. Their baptism should have been called to their minds again and again, and their faith constantly awakened and nourished. For just as the truth of this divine promise, once pronounced over us, continues until death, so our faith in it ought never to cease, but to be nourished and strengthened until death by the continual remembrance of this promise made to us in baptism. Therefore, when we rise from our sins or repent, we are merely returning to the power and the faith of baptism from which we fell, and finding our way back to the promise then made to us, which we deserted when we sinned. For the truth of the promise once made remains steadfast, always ready to receive us back with open arms when we return. And this, if I mistake not, is what they mean when they say, though obscurely,

j See n. 105, p. 136.

be renewed by penance, but not by baptism; it is lawful for someone to repent several times, but not to be baptized several times."

146. This notion of penance as an emergency rescue stems from questions regarding the possibility and consequences of postbaptismal sin. A rigorist position is demonstrable throughout the early church, possibly already reflected in Heb. 6:4f., but definitively set forth by the second-century Christian text, *Shepherd of Hermes*. The angel in the *Shepherd* admits that though one who is baptized should live a life of purity (Mandate IV, 1:8-9; 2:1; 3:1), God has mercifully introduced a single means of restoration. "'But I tell you,' said he, 'after that great and holy calling, if a man be tempted by the devil and sin, he has *one repentance*, but if he sin and repent repeatedly it is unprofitable for such a man, for scarcely shall he live'" (Mandate IV, 3:4-6). Incidentally, Luther's question over the apostolic authorship of Hebrews focuses especially on Heb. 6:4f.

147. The loss of baptism as the rhythm and shape of the daily Christian forgiveness has, according to Luther, left a vacuum that was then filled by every effort to bring security and satisfaction. This list represents many of the false *Geistlichkeiten* that Luther wished to abolish or reform, i.e., spiritual/devotional practices common throughout the Middle Ages to deal with postbaptismal sin.

148. Jer. 2:32: "Can a girl forget her ornaments, or a bride her attire? Yet my people have forgotten me, days without number."

that baptism is the first sacrament and the foundation of all the others, without which none of the others can be received.[149]

149. Lombard, *Sentences* 4, d. 2, c. 2: "Now let us examine the sacrament of baptism, which is the first among the sacraments of the new grace." Also Pope Eugene IV (1383–1447) issued a bull at the Council of Florence (1439), *Exultate Deo*: "Holy baptism, which is the gateway to the spiritual life, holds the first place among all the sacraments; through it we are made members of Christ and of the body of the Church." Cf. also Biel, *Sentences* 4, d. 2, q. 1, a. 1, n. 1 A: "just as faith is the first and foundation of the rest of the virtues, so baptism is the chief of sacraments and their doorway."

It will therefore be no small gain to penitents to remember above all their baptism, and, confidently calling to mind the divine promise which they have forsaken, acknowledge that promise before their Lord, rejoicing that they are still within the fortress of salvation because they have been baptized, and abhorring their wicked ingratitude in falling away from its faith and truth. Their hearts will find wonderful comfort and will be encouraged to hope for mercy when they consider that the promise which God made to them, which cannot possibly lie, is still unbroken and unchanged, and indeed, cannot be changed by sins, as Paul says (2 Tim. 2[:13]): "If we are faithless, he remains faithful—for he cannot deny himself." This truth of God, I say, will sustain them, so that if all else should fail, this truth, if they believe in it, will not fail them. In it the penitents have a shield against all assaults of the scornful enemy, an answer to the sins that disturb their conscience, an antidote for the dread of death and judgment, and a comfort in every temptation—namely, this one truth—when they say: "God is faithful in his promises, and I received his sign in baptism. If God is for me, who is against me?"[k,l]

The children of Israel, whenever they turned to repentance, remembered above all their exodus from Egypt, and remembering turned back to God who had brought them out. Moses impressed this memory and this protection upon them many times, and David afterwards did the same.[m] How much more ought we to remember our exodus from Egypt, and by this remembrance turn back to him who led us through the washing of regeneration,[n] remembrance of which is commended to us for this very reason! This can be done most fittingly in the sacrament of bread and wine. Indeed, in former times these three sacraments—penance, baptism, and the bread—were all celebrated at the same service, and each one supplemented the other. We

k Rom. 8:31.

l The original text of this paragraph is singular.

m Cf. Deut. 5:15; 6:12, 21; 8:14; Pss. 78:12f.; 80:8; 106:7f.; Jer. 2:5f.; Dan. 9:15.

n Titus 3:5.

also read of a certain holy virgin who in every time of temptation made baptism her sole defense, saying simply, "I am a Christian"; and immediately the enemy recognized the power of baptism and of her faith, which clung to the truth of a promising God, and fled from her.[150]

Thus you see how rich a Christian is, that is, one who has been baptized! Even if those who have been baptized would, they could not lose their salvation, however much they sinned, unless they refused to believe. For no sin can condemn them save unbelief alone.[o] All other sins, so long as the faith in God's promise made in baptism returns or remains, are immediately blotted out through that same faith, or rather through the truth of God, because he cannot deny himself if you confess him and faithfully cling to him in his promise. But as for contrition, confession of sins, and satisfaction,[151] along with all those carefully devised human exercises: if you rely on them and neglect this truth of God, they will suddenly fail you and leave you more wretched than before. For whatever is done without faith in God's truth is vanity of vanities and vexation of spirit.[p]

You will likewise see how perilous, indeed, how false it is to suppose that penance is "the second plank after shipwreck," and how pernicious an error it is to believe that the power of baptism is broken, and the ship dashed to pieces, because of sin.[q] The ship remains one, solid, and invincible; it will never be broken up into separate "planks." In it are carried all those who are brought to the harbor of salvation, for it is the truth of God giving us its promise in the sacraments. Of course, it often happens that many rashly leap overboard into the sea and perish; these are those who abandon faith in the promise and plunge into sin. But the ship itself remains intact and holds its course unimpaired. If anyone is able somehow by grace to return to the ship, it is not on any plank, but in the solid ship itself that that person is carried to life. Such a person is the one who returns through faith to the abiding and enduring promise of God. Therefore Peter, in 1 Pet. 1, rebukes those who sin, because they have forgotten that

150. St. Blandina was martyred in 177 CE in Lyon under the reign of Marcus Aurelius (121–180). The account of her death comes from a letter reproduced by Eusebius (c. 265–c. 340) in his *Church History*; see *Hist. Eccl.* 5, 1, 19.

151. On these three parts of sacramental penance see Lombard, *Sentences* 4, d. 16, c. 1: "In the performance of penance, three things are to be considered, namely compunction of heart, confession of the mouth, satisfaction in deed. . . . Just as we offend God in three ways, namely by heart, mouth, hand, so also let us make satisfaction in three ways."

o The original text of this section is singular.

p Eccles. 1:2f.

q See n. 145, p. 150.

they were cleansed from their old sins, and he clearly rebukes their wicked unbelief and their ingratitude for the baptism they had received.[152]

What is the good, then, of writing so much about baptism and yet not teaching this faith in the promise? All the sacraments were instituted to nourish faith. Yet these godless men pass over it so completely as even to assert that a Christian dare not be certain of the forgiveness of sins or the grace of the sacraments.[153] With such wicked teaching they delude the world, and not only take captive, but altogether destroy, the sacrament of baptism, in which the chief glory of our conscience consists. Meanwhile they madly rage against the miserable souls of human beings with their contritions, anxious confessions, circumstances,[154] satisfactions, works, and endless other such absurdities. Therefore read with great caution the "Master of the *Sentences*" in his fourth book;[r] better yet, despise him with all his commentators, who at their best write only of the "matter" and "form" of the sacraments;[155] that is, they treat of the dead and death-dealing letter[156] of the sacraments, but leave untouched the spirit, life, and use, that is, the truth of the divine promise and our faith.

Beware, therefore, that the external pomp of works and the deceits of man-made ordinances do not deceive you, lest you wrong the divine truth and your faith. If you would be saved, you must begin with the faith of the sacraments, without any works whatever. The works will follow faith, but do not think too lightly of faith, for it is the most excellent and difficult of all works. Through it alone you will be saved, even if you should be compelled to do without any other works. For faith is a work of God, not of man, as Paul teaches.[157] The other works he works

152. Probably a reference to 2 Pet. 1:5-9, "For this very reason, you must make every effort to support your faith with goodness, and goodness with knowledge, and knowledge with self-control, and self-control with endurance, and endurance with godliness, and godliness with mutual affection, and mutual affection with love. For if these things are yours and are increasing among you, they keep you from being ineffective and unfruitful in the knowledge of our Lord Jesus Christ. For anyone who lacks these things is short-sighted and blind, and is forgetful of the cleansing of past sins."

153. Aquinas, *STh* I-II, q. 112, a. 5: ". . . man cannot judge with certainty whether he has grace." However, see the posthumous supplement *STh* III Suppl., q. 10, a. 4. For a helpful discussion of the difference between Luther and Aquinas on the certainty of salvation, see Otto H. Pesch, "Existential and Sapiential Theology—the Theological Confrontation between Luther and Thomas Aquinas," in Jared Wicks, S.J., ed., *Catholic Scholars Dialogue with Luther* (Chicago: Loyola University Press, 1970), 61–81.

154. In the effort to confess the entirety of one's sins, the penitent must also divulge the circumstances, that is, the related conditions that accompany the action, so that the priest may determine the nature of the sin committed and degree of guilt. Circumstances may turn a venial sin into a mortal sin.

155. The early Scholastic use of the terms *matter* and *form* was more general than the technical use in Aristotle. The "matter" of the sacrament is the elements of the sign (e.g., baptism = water) and the "form" is the words used in its sacramental use (e.g., baptism =

r Peter Lombard. Book 4 of the *Sentences* is dedicated to questions "On the Doctrine of Signs" (*De Doctrina Signorum*), i.e., the sacraments; see n. 56, p. 120 and n. 149, p. 152.

through us and with our help, but this one alone he works in us and without our help.

From this we can clearly see that in baptizing there is a difference between the human minister and God the author. For the man baptizes, and yet does not baptize. He baptizes in that he performs the work of immersing the person to be baptized; he does not baptize, because in so doing he acts not on his own authority but in God's stead. Hence we ought to receive baptism at human hands just as if Christ himself, indeed, God himself, were baptizing us with his own hands. For it is not man's baptism, but Christ's and God's baptism, which we receive by the hand of a man, just as everything else that we have through the hand of somebody else is God's alone. Therefore beware of making any distinction in baptism by ascribing the outward part to man and the inward part to God. Ascribe both to God alone, and look upon the person administering it as simply the vicarious instrument of God, by which the Lord sitting in heaven thrusts you under the water with his own hands, and promises you forgiveness of your sins, speaking to you upon earth with a human voice by the mouth of his minister.

This the words themselves indicate, when the minister says: "I baptize you in the name of the Father, and of the Son, and of the Holy Ghost. Amen," and not: "I baptize you in my own name." It is as though he said: "What I do, I do not by my own authority, but in the name and stead of God, so that you should regard it just as if our Lord himself had done it in a visible manner. The doer and the minister are different persons, but the work of both is the same work, or rather, it is the work of the doer alone, through my ministry." For I hold that "in the name of"[158] refers to the person of the doer, so that the name of the Lord is not only to be uttered and invoked while the work is being done; but the work itself is to be done as something not one's own—in the name and stead of another. In this sense Christ says in Matt. 24[:5], "Many will come in my name," and Rom. 1[:5] says, "Through whom we have received grace and apostleship to bring about obedience for his name among all the nations."

This view I heartily endorse, for there is great comfort and a mighty aid to faith in the knowledge that one has been baptized, not by man, but by the Triune God himself, through a man acting among us in his name. This will put an end to that idle dispute about the "form" of baptism, as they term the words which

"I baptize you in the name . . . ," etc.). See, for example, Lombard, *Sentences* 4, d. 3, c. 2: "On the Form of Baptism: But what is that word, at whose addition to the element the sacrament is brought about?—Truth teaches it to you, who, laying down the form of this sacrament, said to the disciples: 'Go, teach all nations, baptizing them in the name . . .'"; Thomas Aquinas, adopted the earlier terminology but began interpreting it in a more precise Aristotelian manner, e.g., *STh* III, q. 60, a. 7: "As stated above, in the sacraments the words are as the form, and sensible things are as the matter. Now in all things composed of matter and form, the determining principle is on the part of the form, which is as it were the end and terminus of the matter. Consequently, for the being of a thing the need of a determinate form is prior to the need of determinate matter: for determinate matter is needed that it may be adapted to the determinate form. Since, therefore, in the sacraments determinate sensible things are required, which are as the sacramental matter, much more is there need in them of a determinate form of words."

156. 2 Cor. 3:6: "for the letter kills, but the Spirit gives life." Luther can use the language of this text to indicate the external and superficial versus the inner and essential, or he can use it in the Augustinian sense of the law versus grace.

157. Eph. 2:8: "For by grace you have been saved through faith, and this is not your own doing; it is the gift of God."

158. The Latin *in nomine* can certainly have the meaning "by the authority of"; however, the Greek of Matthew 28 from which the baptismal formula is

are used. The Greeks say: "May the servant of Christ be baptized," while the Latins say: "I baptize."[159] Others again, adhering rigidly to their pedantry, condemn the use of the words, "I baptize you in the name of Jesus Christ,"[160] although it is certain the apostles used this formula in baptizing, as we read in the Acts of the Apostles;[s] they would allow no other form to be valid than this: "I baptize you in the name of the Father, and of the Son, and of the Holy Ghost. Amen." But their contention is in vain, for they bring no proof, but merely assert their own dreams. Baptism truly saves in whatever way it is administered, if only it is administered not in the name of man, but in the name of the Lord. Indeed, I have no doubt that if anyone receives baptism in the name of the Lord, even if the wicked minister should not give it in the name of the Lord, he would yet be truly baptized in the name of the Lord. For the power of baptism depends not so much on the faith or use of the one who confers it as on the faith or use of the one who receives it. We have an example of this in the story of a certain actor who was baptized in jest.[161] These and similar perplexing disputes and questions are raised for us by those who ascribe nothing to faith and everything to works and rituals, whereas we owe everything to faith alone and nothing to rituals. Faith makes us free in spirit from all those doubts and mere opinions.

[The Second Part of Baptism: The Sign]

The second part of baptism is the sign, or sacrament, which is that immersion in water from which it derives its name, for the Greek *baptizō* means "I immerse," and *baptisma* means "immersion." For, as has been said, along with the divine promises signs have also been given to picture that which the words signify, or as they now say, that which the sacrament "effectively signifies." We shall see how much truth there is in this.

A great majority have supposed that there is some hidden spiritual power in the word and water, which works the grace of God in the soul of the recipient.[162] Others deny this and hold that there is no power in the sacraments, but that grace is given by God alone, who according to his covenant is present in the

s E.g., Acts 2:38; 8:16; 10:48; 19:5.

derived—*eis to onoma*—may also have the sense of "into the name." In this case, the meaning would be similar to Rom. 6:3, "baptized into Christ . . . into his death."

159. See the bull *Exultate Deo* (1439), from the Council of Florence: "The form is: 'I baptize you in the name of the Father and of the Son and of the Holy Spirit.' But we do not deny that true baptism is conferred by the following words: 'May this servant of Christ be baptized in the name of the Father and of the Son and of the Holy Spirit'; or, 'This person is baptized by my hands in the name of the Father and of the Son and of the Holy Spirit.' Since the Holy Trinity is the principle cause from which baptism has its power and the minister is the instrumental cause who exteriorly bestows the sacrament, the sacrament is conferred if the action is performed by the minister with the invocation of the Holy Trinity."

160. Alexander of Hales (1185–1245) denied the validity of a baptism performed "in the name of Jesus"; however, see Lombard, *Sentences* 4, d. 3, c. 3: "the apostles baptized in the name of Christ. But in this name [i.e., of Christ], as Ambrose explains, the whole Trinity is understood."

161. St. Genesius was a popular legendary saint, supposedly martyred under Emperor Diocletian (245–311). According to the legend, Genesius received a mock baptism on stage in ridicule of Christianity, but the effect was his sudden conversion.

162. Representatives of this view include Hugh of St. Victor (c. 1096–1141), *On the Sacraments of the Christian Faith* 1, 1, 1: "a sacrament, through its being sanctified, contains an invisible grace"; and Aquinas, *STh* III, q. 62, a. 4: "there

sacraments which he has instituted.[163] Yet all are agreed that the sacraments are "effective signs" of grace, and they reach this conclusion by this one argument: if the sacraments of the New Law were mere signs, there would be no apparent reason why they should surpass those of the Old Law.[164] Hence they have been driven to attribute such great powers to the sacraments of the New Law that they think the sacraments benefit even those who are in mortal sin; neither faith nor grace are required—it is sufficient that no obstacle be set in the way, that is, no actual intention to sin again.[165]

Such views, however, must be carefully avoided and shunned, because they are godless and infidel, contrary to faith and inconsistent with the nature of the sacraments. For it is an error to hold that the sacraments of the New Law differ from those of the Old Law in the effectiveness of their signs. For in this respect they are the same. The same God who now saves us by baptism and the bread saved Abel by his sacrifice,[t] Noah by the rainbow,[u] Abraham by circumcision,[v] and all the others by their respective signs. So far as the signs are concerned, there is no difference between a sacrament of the Old Law and one of the New, provided that by the Old Law you mean that which God did among the patriarchs and other fathers in the days of the Law. But those signs which were given to the patriarchs and fathers must be clearly distinguished from the legal symbols which Moses instituted in his law, such as the priestly usages concerning vestments, vessels, foods, houses, and the like. For these are vastly different, not only from the sacraments of the New Law, but also from those signs which God occasionally gave to the fathers living under the law, such as the sign of Gideon's fleece,[w] Manoah's sacrifice,[x] or that which Isaiah offered to Ahaz in Isa. 7.[y] In each of these alike some promise was given which required faith in God.

t Gen. 4:4.

u Gen. 6:13-22.

v Gen. 17:10f.

w Judg. 6:36-40.

x Judg. 13:16-23.

y Isa. 7:10-16.

is nothing to hinder an instrumental spiritual power from being in a body; in so far as a body can be moved by a particular spiritual substance so as to produce a particular spiritual effect . . . it is in this way that a spiritual power is in the sacraments, inasmuch as they are ordained by God unto the production of a spiritual effect."

163. Aquinas, though in disagreement, correctly describes this alternate position held by theologians such as Bonaventure (1221-1274) and Duns Scotus (c. 1266-1308), in *STh* III, q. 62, a. 4: "Those who hold that the sacraments do not cause grace save by a certain coincidence, deny the sacraments any power that is itself productive of the sacramental effect, and hold that the Divine power assists the sacraments and produces their effect." See also Gabriel Biel, *Sentences* 4, d. 1, q. 1, a. 1, c. 1, in which the sacraments are not effective intrinsically (*ex natura rei*) but because of the will and covenant of God (*ex voluntate Dei*).

164. Cf. Lombard, *Sentences* 4, d. 1, 3: "Observances of the Old Law are better called signs than sacraments. For those things which were instituted only for the sake of signifying are merely signs, and not sacraments; such were the carnal sacrifices and the ceremonial observances of the Old Law, which could never justify those who offered them." Aquinas, *STh* III, q. 62, a. 6: "it is therefore clear that the sacraments of the New Law do reasonably derive the power of justification from Christ's Passion, which is the cause of man's righteousness; whereas the sacraments of the Old Law did not."

165. The Scholastic doctrine that the sacraments of the New Testament intrinsically confer grace (*ex opere operato*) was conditioned by the absence of any spiritual obstacle. For example, if one receives the sacrament under false pretenses, the substance of the sacrament would still be received but the grace would not benefit the recipient (cf. Lombard, *Sentences* 4, d. 4, c. 2; Aquinas, *STh* III, q. 69, a. 9). Gabriel Biel identifies a mortal sin as an obstacle, *Sentences* 4, d. 1, q. 3, n. 2 B: "unless one impedes by an obstacle of mortal sin, grace is conferred."

The difference, then, between the legal symbols and the new and old signs is that the legal symbols do not have attached to them any word of promise requiring faith. Hence they are not signs of justification, for they are not sacraments of the faith that alone justifies, but only sacraments of works. Their whole power and nature consisted in works, not in faith. Those who performed them fulfilled them, even if they did it without faith. But our signs or sacraments, as well as those of the fathers, have attached to them a word of promise which requires faith, and they cannot be fulfilled by any other work. Hence they are signs or sacraments of justification, for they are sacraments of justifying faith and not of works. Their whole efficacy, therefore, consists in faith itself, not in the doing of a work. Those who believe them, fulfill them, even if they should not do a single work. This is the origin of the saying: "Not the sacrament, but the faith of the sacrament, justifies." Thus circumcision did not justify Abraham and his seed, and yet the Apostle calls it the seal of the righteousness by faith,[z] because faith in the promise, to which circumcision was added, justified him and fulfilled what the circumcision signified. For faith was the spiritual circumcision of the foreskin of the heart,[a] which was symbolized by the literal circumcision of the flesh. In the same way it was obviously not Abel's sacrifice that justified him, but it was his faith[b] by which he offered himself wholly to God, and this was symbolized by the outward sacrifice.

Thus it is not baptism that justifies or benefits anyone, but it is faith in that word of promise to which baptism is added. This faith justifies, and fulfills that which baptism signifies. For faith is the submersion of the old person and the emerging of the new.[c] Therefore the new sacraments cannot differ from the old sacraments, for both alike have the divine promises and the same spirit of faith, although they do differ vastly from the old symbols—on account of the word of promise, which is the sole effective means of distinguishing them. Even so, today, the outward show of vestments, holy places, foods, and all the endless

z Rom. 4:11.

a Deut. 10:16; Jer. 4:4.

b Heb. 11:4.

c Cf. Eph. 4:22-24; Col. 3:9-10.

ceremonies doubtless symbolize excellent things to be fulfilled in the spirit, yet, because there is no word of divine promise attached to these things, they can in no way be compared with the signs of baptism and the bread. Neither do they justify, nor benefit one in any way, since they are fulfilled in their very observance, even in their observance apart from faith. For while they are taking place, or being performed, they are being fulfilled, as the Apostle says of them in Col. 2[:22]: "Which all perish as they are used, according to human precepts and doctrines." The sacraments, on the contrary, are not fulfilled when they are taking place, but when they are being believed.

It cannot be true, therefore, that there is contained in the sacraments a power efficacious for justification, or that they are "effective signs" of grace. All such things are said to the detriment of faith, and out of ignorance of the divine promise. Unless you should call them "effective" in the sense that they certainly and effectively impart grace where faith is unmistakably present. But it is not in this sense that efficacy is now ascribed to them; as witness the fact that they are said to benefit all people, even the wicked and unbelieving, provided they do not set an obstacle in the way[d]—as if such unbelief were not in itself the most obstinate and hostile of all obstacles to grace. To such an extent have they exerted themselves to turn the sacrament into a command and faith into a work. For if the sacrament confers grace on me because I receive it, then indeed I receive grace by virtue of my work, and not by faith; and I gain not the promise in the sacrament but only the sign instituted and commanded by God. Thus you see clearly how completely the sacraments have been misunderstood by the theologians of the *Sentences*.[e] In their discussions of the sacraments they have taken no account either of faith or of promise. They cling only to the sign and the use of the sign, and draw us away from faith to the work, away from the word to the sign. Thus, as I have said, they have not only taken the sacraments captive, but have completely destroyed them, as far as they were able.

d See n. 165, pp. 157–58.

e See n. 56, p. 120.

Therefore let us open our eyes and learn to pay heed more to the word than to the sign, more to faith than to the work or use of the sign. We know that wherever there is a divine promise, there faith is required, and that these two are so necessary to each other that neither can be effective apart from the other. For it is not possible to believe unless there is a promise, and the promise is not established unless it is believed. But where these two meet, they give a real and most certain efficacy to the sacraments. Hence, to seek the efficacy of the sacrament apart from the promise and apart from the faith is to labor in vain and to find condemnation. Thus Christ says: "The one who believes and is baptized will be saved; but the one who does not believe will be condemned" [Mark 16:16]. He shows us in this word that faith is such a necessary part of the sacrament that it can save even without the sacrament, and for this reason he did not add: "The one who does not believe, and is not baptized."

[Baptism Signifies Death and Resurrection]

Baptism, then, signifies two things—death and resurrection,[f] that is, full and complete justification. When the minister immerses the child in the water it signifies death, and when he draws it forth again it signifies life. Thus Paul expounds it in Rom. 6[:4]: "Therefore we have been buried with [Christ] by baptism into death, so that just as Christ was raised from the dead by the glory of the Father, so we too might walk in newness of life." This death and resurrection we call the new creation, regeneration, and spiritual birth.[g] This should not be understood only allegorically as the death of sin and the life of grace, as many understand it, but as actual death and resurrection. For baptism is not a false sign. Neither does sin completely die, nor grace completely rise, until the sinful body that we carry about in this life is destroyed, as the Apostle says in the same passage.[166] For as long as we are in the flesh, the desires of the flesh stir and are stirred. For this reason, as soon as we begin to believe, we also begin to die to this world and live to God in the life to come; so

166. Rom. 6:6-7: "We know that our old self was crucified with him so that the body of sin might be destroyed, and we might no longer be enslaved to sin. For whoever has died is freed from sin."

f Cf. *The Holy Sacrament of Baptism* (1519), LW 35:30f.

g Cf. 2 Cor. 5:17; Titus 3:5; John 3:6.

that faith is truly a death and a resurrection, that is, it is that spiritual baptism into which we are submerged and from which we rise.

It is therefore indeed correct to say that baptism is a washing away of sins, but the expression is too mild and weak to bring out the full significance of baptism, which is rather a symbol of death and resurrection. For this reason, I would have those who are to be baptized completely immersed in the water, as the word says and as the mystery indicates.[h] Not because I deem this necessary, but because it would be well to give to a thing so perfect and complete a sign that is also complete and perfect. And this is doubtless the way in which it was instituted by Christ. The sinner does not so much need to be washed as he needs to die, in order to be wholly renewed and made another creature, and to be conformed to the death and resurrection of Christ, with whom he dies and rises again through baptism.[i] Although you may say that when Christ died and rose again he was washed clean of mortality, that is a less forceful way of putting it than if you said that he was completely changed and renewed. Similarly it is far more forceful to say that baptism signifies that we die in every way and rise to eternal life, than to say that it signifies merely that we are washed clean of sins.

Here again you see that the sacrament of baptism, even with respect to its sign, is not a matter of the moment, but something permanent. Although the ceremony itself is soon over the thing it signifies continues until we die, yes, even until we rise on the last day. For as long as we live we are continually doing that which baptism signifies, that is, we die and rise again. We die, not only mentally and spiritually by renouncing the sins and vanities of this world, but in very truth we begin to leave this bodily life and to lay hold on the life to come, so that there is, as they say, a "real" and bodily passing out of this world unto the Father.

We must therefore beware of those who have reduced the power of baptism to such small and slender dimensions that, while they say that by it grace is indeed poured in, they maintain that afterwards it is poured out again through sin, and

h Cf. *The Holy Sacrament of Baptism* (1519), LW 35:30f.

i Cf. Rom. 6:8.

that then one must reach heaven by another way, as if baptism had now become entirely useless.[j] Do not hold such a view, but understand that this is the significance of baptism, that through it you die and live again. Therefore, whether by penance or by any other way, you can only return to the power of your baptism, and do again that which you were baptized to do and which your baptism signified. Baptism never becomes useless, unless you despair and refuse to return to its salvation. You may indeed wander away from the sign for a time, but the sign is not therefore useless. Thus, you have been once baptized in the sacrament, but you need continually to be baptized by faith, continually to die and continually to live. Baptism swallowed up your whole body and gave it forth again; in the same way that which baptism signifies should swallow up your whole life, body and soul, and give it forth again at the last day, clad in the robe of glory and immortality. We are therefore never without the sign of baptism nor without the thing it signifies. Indeed, we need continually to be baptized more and more, until we fulfill the sign perfectly at the last day.

You will understand, therefore, that whatever we do in this life which mortifies the flesh or quickens the spirit has to do with our baptism. The sooner we depart this life, the more speedily we fulfill our baptism;[k] and the more cruelly we suffer, the more successfully do we conform to our baptism. Hence the church was at its best at the time when martyrs were being put to death every day and accounted as sheep for the slaughter,[l] for then the power of baptism reigned supreme in the church, whereas today we have lost sight of this power amid the multitude of human works and doctrines. For our whole life should be baptism, and the fulfilling of the sign or sacrament of baptism, since we have been set free from all else and given over to baptism alone, that is, to death and resurrection.

This glorious liberty of ours and this understanding of baptism have been taken captive in our day, and to whom can we give the blame except the Roman pontiff with his despotism? More than all others, as chief shepherd it was his first duty to proclaim this doctrine and defend this liberty, as Paul says in 1 Cor. 4[:1]:

j See n. 146, p. 151.

k Cf. *The Holy Sacrament of Baptism* (1519), LW 35:30f.

l Ps. 44:22; Rom. 8:36.

"This is how one should regard us, as servants of Christ and stewards of the mysteries, or sacraments, of God." Instead he seeks only to oppress us with his decrees and laws, and to ensnare us as captives to his tyrannical power. By what right, I ask you, does the pope impose his laws upon us (to say nothing of his wicked and damnable neglect to teach us these mysteries)? Who gave him power to deprive us of this liberty of ours, granted to us in baptism? One thing only, as I have said, has been enjoined upon us to do all the days of our lives—to be baptized, that is, to be put to death and to live again through faith in Christ. This and this alone should have been taught, especially by the chief shepherd. But now faith is passed over in silence, and the church is smothered with endless laws concerning works and ceremonies; the power and understanding of baptism are set aside, and faith in Christ is obstructed.

Therefore I say: Neither pope nor bishop nor any other person has the right to impose a single syllable of law upon Christians without their[m] consent; if anyone does, it is done in the spirit of tyranny. Therefore the prayers, fasts, donations, and whatever else the pope ordains and demands in all of his decrees, as numerous as they are iniquitous, he demands and ordains without any right whatever; and he sins against the liberty of the church whenever he attempts any such thing. Hence it has come to pass that the churchmen of our day are such vigorous guardians of "ecclesiastical liberty"—that is, of wood and stone, of lands and rents[167] (for to such an extent has "ecclesiastical" today come to mean the same as "spiritual"!). Yet with such verbal fictions they not only take captive the true liberty of the church; they utterly destroy it, even worse than the Turk, and in opposition to the word of the Apostle: "Do not become slaves of men" [1 Cor. 7:23]. For to be subjected to their statutes and tyrannical laws is indeed to become slaves of men.

This impious and desperate tyranny is fostered by the pope's disciples, who here twist and pervert that saying of Christ: "He who hears you hears me" [Luke 10:16]. With puffed cheeks they inflate this saying to a great size in support of their own ordinances. Though Christ spoke this word to the apostles when they

167. The word *liberty* (Lat. *libertas*) gained a new meaning and usage in the Middle Ages, especially in the context of feudal society. Whereas Christian liberty was expressed as freedom from the bondage of sin and death in order to be a servant of Christ (e.g., Rom. 6.6f.; Gal. 5:1; 1 Cor. 7:22f.), liberty in the feudal system indicated one's possession of power and jurisdiction—usually over property—without external coercion or limits. Thus, granting a liberty was to grant a privilege. Clergy already began receiving such liberties in the age of Constantine, but as the church participated in the emerging feudal system as a landowner, the notion of "ecclesiastical liberty" had more to do with political and economic jurisdiction than liberty in a spiritual or theological sense. Luther is exploiting this irony in his comments here. Luther would set forth a very different sense of "freedom" in his subsequent treatise, *The Freedom of the Christian* (1520). For more on "liberty" in the Middle Ages and its impact on the church, see Gerd Tellenbach, *Church, State and Christian Society at the Time of the Investiture Controversy* (Oxford: Oxford University Press, 1938).

m Singular in the original.

went forth to preach the gospel, and though it should apply only to the gospel, they pass over the gospel and apply it only to their fables. For he says in John 10[:27, 5]: "My sheep hear my voice, but the voice of a stranger they do not hear." He left us the gospel so that the pontiffs might sound the voice of Christ. Instead they sound their own voices, and yet hope to be heard. Moreover, the Apostle says that he was not sent to baptize, but to preach the gospel.[n] Therefore, no one is obliged to obey the ordinances of the pope, or required to listen to him, except when he teaches the gospel and Christ. And the pope should teach nothing but faith without any restrictions. But since Christ says, "He who hears you [plural] hears me" [Luke 10:16], why does not the pope also hear others? Christ does not say to Peter alone, "He who hears you" [singular]. In short, where there is true faith, there the word of faith must of necessity be also. Why then does not an unbelieving pope now and then hear a believing servant of his, who has the word of faith? Blindness, sheer blindness, reigns among the pontiffs.

Others, even more shameless, arrogantly ascribe to the pope the power to make laws, on the basis of Matt. 16[:19], "Whatever you bind, etc.," although Christ in this passage treats of binding and loosing sins, not of taking the whole church captive and oppressing it with laws. So this tyranny treats everything with its own lying words and violently twists and perverts the words of God. I admit indeed that Christians ought to bear this accursed tyranny just as they would bear any other violence of this world, according to Christ's word: "If any one strikes you on the right cheek, turn to him the other also" [Matt. 5:39]. But this is my complaint: that the godless pontiffs boastfully claim to do this by right, that they pretend to be seeking the church's welfare with this Babylon of theirs, and that they foist this fiction upon all people. For if they did these things and we suffered their violence, both sides being well aware that it was godlessness and tyranny, then we might easily number it among those things that contribute to the mortifying of this life and the fulfilling of our baptism, and might with a good conscience glory in the inflicted injury. But now they seek to deprive us of this consciousness of

n 1 Cor. 1:17.

our liberty, and would have us believe that what they do is well done, and must not be censured or complained of as wrongdoing. Being wolves, they masquerade as shepherds, and being Antichrists, they wish to be honored as Christ.

I lift my voice simply on behalf of liberty and conscience, and I confidently cry: No law, whether of men or of angels, may rightfully be imposed upon Christians without their consent, for we are free of all laws. And if any laws are imposed upon us, we must bear them in such a way as to preserve that sense of freedom which knows and affirms with certainty that an injustice is being done to it, even though it glories in bearing this injustice—so taking care neither to justify the tyrant nor to murmur against his tyranny. "Now who is there to harm you," says Peter, "if you are zealous for what is right?" [1 Pet. 3:13]. "All things work together for good to them that are the elect" [Rom. 8:28].

Nevertheless, since but few know this glory of baptism and the blessedness of Christian liberty, and cannot know them because of the tyranny of the pope, I for one will disengage myself, and keep my conscience free by bringing this charge against the pope and all his papists: Unless they will abolish their laws and ordinances, and restore to Christ's churches their liberty and have it taught among them, they are guilty of all the souls that perish under this miserable captivity, and the papacy is truly the kingdom of Babylon and of the very Antichrist.[168] For who is "the man of sin" and "the son of perdition" [2 Thess. 2:3] but he who with his doctrines and his laws increases the sins and perdition of souls in the church, while sitting in the church as if he were God?[169] All this the papal tyranny has fulfilled, and more than fulfilled, these many centuries. It has extinguished faith, obscured the sacraments and oppressed the gospel; but its own laws, which are not only impious and sacrilegious, but even barbarous and foolish, it has decreed and multiplied without end.

Behold, then, our miserable captivity. "How lonely sits the city that was full of people! How like a widow has she become, she that was great among the nations! She that was a princess among the cities has become a vassal. She has none to comfort her; all her friends have dealt treacherously with her, etc." [Lam. 1:1-2]. There are so many ordinances, so many rites, so many sects,[170] so many vows, so many exertions, and so many works in which Christians are engaged today, that they lose sight of their baptism. Because of this swarm of locusts, palmerworms, and

168. Calling the pope the Antichrist was not uncommon rhetoric, especially since the Western Schism (1378–1417). However, Luther's designation is more than rhetoric. He first privately floated the idea in a letter to a friend, Wenceslas Link (1482–1547), after his encounter with the papal legate, Cardinal Cajetan, in 1518, WA Br 1:270. With the threat of excommunication and no indication that the papacy would change its course, Luther finally put the epithet in print in his 1520 treatise against Augustinus von Alveld (see n. 14, p. 105), *On the Papacy in Rome, Against the Most Celebrated Romanist in Leipzig*, LW 39:49–104. For a helpful overview on the question, see Robert Rosin, "The Papacy in Perspective: Luther's Reform and Rome," in *Concordia Journal* 29 (October 2003): 407–26.

169. 2 Thess. 2:3-4: "Let no one deceive you in any way; for that day will not come unless the rebellion comes first and the lawless one is revealed, the one destined for destruction. He opposes and exalts himself above every so-called god or object of worship, so that he takes his seat in the temple of God, declaring himself to be God."

170. "Sects" here is taken to mean the various rival monastic orders and divisions within Scholastic theology.

cankerworms,[o] no one is able to remember that he is baptized, or what blessings baptism has brought him. We should be even as little children, when they are newly baptized, who engage in no efforts or works, but are free in every way, secure and saved solely through the glory of their baptism. For we are indeed little children, continually baptized anew in Christ.

In contradiction to what has been said, some might cite the baptism of infants who do not comprehend the promise of God and cannot have the faith of baptism; so that therefore either faith is not necessary or else infant baptism is without effect. Here I say what all say: Infants are aided by the faith of others, namely, those who bring them for baptism.[171] For the Word of God is powerful enough, when uttered, to change even a godless heart, which is no less unresponsive and helpless than any infant. So through the prayer of the believing church which presents it, a prayer to which all things are possible,[p] the infant is changed, cleansed, and renewed by the pouring in of faith [*fide infusa*].[172] Nor should I doubt that even a godless adult could be changed, in any of the sacraments, if the same church prayed for and presented him, as we read of the paralytic in the Gospel, who was healed through the faith of others.[q] I should be ready to admit that in this sense the sacraments of the New Law are efficacious in conferring grace, not only to those who do not,

o Cf. Joel 1:4.

p Cf. Mark 9:23.

q Cf. Mark 2:3-12.

171. Cf. Augustine, *Against Two Letters of the Pelagians*, I, 40: "in the Church of the Savior, infants believe by means of other people, even as they have derived those sins which are remitted them in baptism from other people"; Lombard, *Sentences* 4, d. 4, c. 2: "remission is not given in baptism to children without someone else's faith, since they are unable to have their own"; Aquinas, *STh* III, d. 68, a. 9: "Just as a child, when he is being baptized, believes not by himself but by others, so is he examined not by himself but through others, and these in answer confess the Church's faith in the child's stead, who is aggregated to this faith by the sacrament of faith."

172. Luther's point is somewhat different from the traditional understanding of the *fides aliena*, i.e., grace given through the faith of another. The faith of the church or of the sponsors does not stand in as proxy for the child's faith; rather, it is faith that acts in prayer and thus intercedes on behalf of the child. As an answer to this prayer, God grants the child the personal faith necessary to receive baptism. Luther would make the same point later when advising one on how to comfort a mother of a stillborn or miscarriage: "God accomplishes much through the faith and longing of another, even a stranger, even though there is still no personal faith. But this is given through the channel of another's intercession, as in the Gospel Christ raised the widow's son at Nain because of the prayers of his mother apart from the faith of the son" (LW 43:250).

Luther's use of the term *fides infusa* ("the pouring in of faith") is also different from the Scholastic usage which, following Aristotelian ethics, approximates the gift of the theological virtues (faith, hope, and love) to the

but even to those who do most obstinately present an obstacle.[173] What obstacle cannot be removed by the faith of the church and the prayer of faith? Do we not believe that Stephen converted Paul the Apostle by this power?[174] But then the sacraments do what they do not by their own power, but by the power of faith, without which they do nothing at all, as I have said.

The question remains whether an unborn infant, with only a hand or a foot projecting from the womb, can be baptized. Here I will confess my ignorance and make no hasty decision. I am not sure whether the reason they give is sufficient—that in any part of the body whatsoever the entire soul resides. For it is not the soul but the body that is externally baptized with water. But neither do I share the view of those who insist that he who is not yet born cannot be born again (even though it has considerable force).[175] I leave these things to the teaching of the Spirit, and "meanwhile allow everyone to enjoy his own opinion" [Rom. 14:5].

[Religious Vows Versus Baptism]

One thing I will add—and I wish that I could persuade everyone to do it—namely, that all vows should be completely abolished and avoided, whether of religious orders, or about pilgrimages or about any works whatsoever, that we may remain in that which is

acquisition of other virtues, namely, through the acquiring of a habit (*habitus*). But Luther is only stressing that faith is a divine gift with this phrase. Luther's critical engagement with the Scholastic teaching occurs also in 1520: *Disputatio de fide infusa et acquisita*, WA 6:85f. See also Reinhard Schwarz, *Fides, spes und caritas beim jungen Luther: unter besonderer Berücksichtigung der mittelalterlichen Tradition* (Berlin: Walter de Gruyter, 1962). The question of the possibility of faith in an infant is taken up by Luther more thoroughly in his treatise *Concerning Rebaptism: A Letter to Two Pastors* (1528), LW 40:225–62.

173. For the notion of setting an "obstacle" against the reception of grace, see n. 165, pp. 157–58.

174. Acts 7:58—8:1: "Then they dragged him out of the city and began to stone him; and the witnesses laid their coats at the feet of a young man named Saul. While they were stoning Stephen, he prayed, 'Lord Jesus, receive my spirit.' Then he knelt down and cried out in a loud voice, 'Lord, do not hold this sin against them.' When he had said this, he died. And Saul approved of their killing him." Augustine makes this point in a sermon on the birthday of St. Stephen, *Sermo* 382, 4, 4: "For if the martyr Stephen did not pray as he did, the church would not have Paul today."

175. Augustine held this opinion; cf. *Ep.* 187, 9: "No one can be reborn before being born." This opinion was carried on into much of the Scholastic tradition, for example, Lombard, *Sentences* 4, d. 6, c. 3. Aquinas holds an interesting middle position, *STh* III, q. 68, a. 11: "If, however, the head, wherein the senses are rooted, appear first, it should be baptized, in cases of danger: nor should it be baptized

supremely religious and most rich in works—the freedom of baptism.[176] It is impossible to say how much that most widespread delusion of vows detracts from baptism and obscures the knowledge of Christian liberty, to say nothing now of the unspeakable and infinite peril of souls which that mania for making vows and that ill-advised rashness daily increase. O most godless pontiffs and unregenerate pastors, who slumber on unheeding and indulge in your evil lusts, without pity for this most dreadful and perilous "ruin of Joseph"! [Amos 6:4-6].

Vows should either be abolished by a general edict, especially those taken for life, and all people recalled to the vows of baptism, or else everyone should be diligently warned not to take a vow rashly. No one should be encouraged to do so; indeed, permission should be given only with difficulty and reluctance. For we have vowed enough in baptism, more than we can ever fulfill; if we give ourselves to the keeping of this one vow, we shall have all we can do. But now we traverse sea and land to make many proselytes;[r] we fill the world with priests, monks, and nuns, and imprison them all in lifelong vows. You will find those who argue and decree that a work done in fulfillment of a vow ranks higher than one done without a vow, and in heaven is to be rewarded above others with I know not what great rewards. Blind and godless Pharisees, who measure righteousness and holiness by the greatness, number, or other quality of the works! But God measures them by faith alone, and with him there is no difference among works, except insofar as there is a difference in faith.

With such bombast wicked men by their inventions puff up human opinion and human works, in order to lure on the unthinking Masses who are almost always led by the glitter of works to make shipwreck of their faith, to forget their baptism, and to injure their Christian liberty. For a vow is a kind of law or requirement. When vows are multiplied, laws and works are necessarily multiplied, and when these are multiplied, faith is extinguished and the liberty of baptism is taken captive. Others, not content with these wicked allurements, assert in addition that entrance into a religious order is like a new baptism, which may afterward be repeated as often as the purpose to live

r Matt. 23:15.

again, if perfect birth should ensue. And seemingly the same should be done in cases of danger no matter what part of the body appears first. But as none of the exterior parts of the body belong to its integrity in the same degree as the head, some hold that since the matter is doubtful, whenever any other part of the body has been baptized, the child, when perfect birth has taken place, should be baptized with the form: 'If you are not baptized, I baptize you,' etc."

176. Luther's concern is with the view that religious and monastic vows have set up a spiritual standard above and beyond the sacrament of baptism. In the late-medieval context, members of the monastic life and, by derivation, the clerical office, were regarded as belonging to a higher spiritual class than ordinary lay Christians. After martyrdom, monasticism was long regarded as the religious ideal of Christianity. In an attempt to embody the sacrificial, radical tenets in the Gospels, the monastic distinguished himself from the ordinary Christian by his vows of poverty, chastity, and obedience. The Ten Commandments were important, but "if you would be perfect," said the Lord, "sell all you have, give it to the poor, and come follow me." Pursuing the path the "perfect" those who took up monastic vows could even regard them as a kind of second baptism. But in Luther's earlier treatise, *The Address to the Christian Nobility* (1520), he argued that all ordinary Christians were truly spiritual and religious. Only faith made one spiritual, and the life of the laity was a true religious sacrifice and worship when lived out from that faith. Likewise the priesthood—it was not ordination but baptism that made one priests (1 Pet. 2:9). See TAL 1:382.

the monastic life is renewed. Thus these votaries have appropriated to themselves all righteousness, salvation, and glory, and left to those who are merely baptized nothing to compare with them. Now the Roman pontiff, that fountain and source of all superstitions, confirms, approves, and adorns this mode of life with high-sounding bulls[177] and dispensations, while no one deems baptism worthy of even a thought. And with such glittering pomp, as I have said, they drive the pliable people of Christ into the "Clashing Rocks,"[178] so that in their ingratitude toward baptism they presume to achieve greater things by their works than others achieve by their faith.

177. A "bull" (*bulla*) is an official papal decree. The name is derived from the seal on the document that guaranteed its authenticity.

178. The Latin has *Symplegades*—the name of the rocks at the Bosphorus, the entrance to the Black Sea, which, according to the Greek myth of Jason and the Argonauts, would leave their moorings and crush all who attempted to pass through. The sense here is that monastic vows are put forth as a greater sense of security than mere faith, but like the Symplegades they are deceptively dangerous.

This fresco, painted by Fra Angelico (c. 1395–1455), shows a monk with Roman tonsure, in which the top of the head is shaved as a sign of religious devotion.

Therefore, God again is "perverse with the crooked" [Ps. 18:26], and to punish the makers of vows for their ingratitude and pride, God brings it about that they break their vows, or keep them only with prodigious labor, and remain sunk in them, never knowing the grace of faith and of baptism; that they continue in their hypocrisy to the end, since their spirit is not approved of God; and that at last they become a laughing-stock to the whole world, ever pursuing righteousness and never attaining righteousness, so that they fulfill the word of Isa. 2[:8]: "Their land is filled with idols."

I am indeed far from forbidding or discouraging anyone who may desire to vow something privately and of his own free choice; for I would not altogether despise and condemn vows. But I would most strongly advise against setting up and sanctioning the making of vows as a public mode of life. It is enough that every one should have the private right to take a vow at his own peril; but to commend the vowing of vows as a public mode of life—this I hold to be most pernicious to the church and to simple souls. First, because it runs directly counter to the Christian life, for a vow is a kind of ceremonial law and a human ordinance or presumption, from which the church has been set free through baptism; for a Christian is subject to no law but the law of God. Second, because there is no instance in Scripture of such a vow, especially of lifelong chastity, obedience, or poverty.[179] But whatever is without warrant of Scripture is most hazardous and should by no means be urged upon anyone, much less established as a common and public mode of life, even if it be permitted to somebody who wishes to make the venture at his own peril. For certain works are wrought by the Spirit in a few people, but they must not be made an example or a mode of life for all.

Moreover, I greatly fear that these votive modes of life of the religious orders belong to those things which the Apostle foretold: "They will be teaching lies in hypocrisy, forbidding marriage, and enjoining abstinence from foods which God created to be received with thanksgiving" [1 Tim. 4:2-3]. Let no one retort by pointing to SS. Bernard, Francis, Dominic,[180] and others, who founded or fostered monastic orders. Terrible and marvelous is God in his counsels toward the sons of men. He could keep Daniel, Hananiah, Azariah, and Mishael holy at the court of the king of Babylon (that is, in the midst of godlessness);[s] why could God not sanctify those men also in their perilous mode of living

179. The common threefold vow of the monastic life.

180. Bernard of Clairvaux (1090–1153) was the leading figure of the Cistercian reforms and established 163 monasteries throughout Europe. Francis of Assisi (1182–1226) founded the *Ordo Fratrum Minorum* (Order of Little Brothers), dedicated to a life of absolute poverty in order to live in conformity with Christ and his apostles. Dominic de Guzman (c. 1170–1221) was a Spanish priest who founded the *Ordo Praedicatorum* (Order of Preachers), also known as the Dominicans. A mendicant order like the Franciscans, the Dominicans were originally dedicated to the evangelization and combating heresy.

or guide them by the special operation of his Spirit, yet without desiring it to be an example to others? Besides, it is certain that none of them was saved through his vows and his religious[181] life; they were saved through faith alone, by which all people are saved, and to which that showy subservience to vows is more diametrically opposed than anything else.

But everyone may hold his or her[t] own view on this. I will return to my argument. Speaking now in behalf of the church's liberty and the glory of baptism, I feel myself in duty bound to set forth publicly the counsel I have learned under the Spirit's guidance. I therefore counsel those in high places in the churches, first of all, to abolish all those vows and religious orders, or at least not to approve and extol them. If they will not do this, then I counsel all men who would be assured of their salvation to abstain from all vows, above all from the major and lifelong vows. I give this counsel especially to teenagers and young people. This I do, first, because this manner of life has no witness or warrant in the Scriptures, as I have said, but is puffed up solely by the bulls (and they truly are "bulls"[182]) of human popes. Second, because it greatly tends to hypocrisy, by reason of its outward show and unusual character, which engender conceit and a contempt of the common Christian life. And if there were no other reason for abolishing these vows, this one would be reason enough, namely, that through them faith and baptism are slighted and works are exalted, which cannot be done without harmful results. For in the religious orders there is scarcely one in many thousands who is not more concerned about his works than about faith, and on the basis of this madness, they claim superiority over each other, as being "stricter" or "laxer," as they call it.[183]

Therefore I advise no one to enter any religious order or the priesthood; indeed, I advise everyone against it—unless he is forearmed with this knowledge and understands that the works of monks and priests, however holy and arduous they may be, do not differ one whit in the sight of God from the works of the rustic laborer in the field or the woman going about her household tasks, but that all works are measured before God by faith alone, as Jer. 5[:3] says: "O Lord, do not your eyes look for faith?"

s Cf. Dan. 1:6-21.

t Feminine added.

181. The designation "religious" is technical, referring to those having formally taken monastic vows.

182. The wordplay is on *bulla*, which can also mean "bubble."

183. Monastic orders had a history of debates regarding the proper interpretation of their particular rule. Often this led to divisions within their order with stricter "observants" separating from the more lax. The most famous conflict was among the Franciscans after the death of their founder, with the stricter "Spiritualists" set in opposition to the "Conventuals." Luther himself belonged to the stricter observant branch of the Augustinians.

and Sir. 32[:23]: "In all your works believe with faith in thy heart, for this is to keep the commandments of God." Indeed, the menial housework of a manservant or maidservant is often more acceptable to God than all the fastings and other works of a monk or priest, because the monk or priest lacks faith. Since, therefore, vows nowadays seem to tend only to the glorification of works and to pride, it is to be feared that there is nowhere less of faith and of the church than among the priests, monks, and bishops. These men are in truth heathen or hypocrites. They imagine themselves to be the church, or the heart of the church, the "spiritual" estate and the leaders of the church, when they are everything else but that. This is indeed "the people of the captivity," among whom all things freely given to us in baptism are held captive, while the few poor "people of the earth" who are left behind,[184] such as the married folk, appear vile in their eyes.

From what has been said we recognize two glaring errors of the Roman pontiff.

In the first place, he grants dispensation from vows,[185] and does it as if he alone of all Christians possessed this authority; so great is the temerity and audacity of wicked men. If it is possible to grant a dispensation from a vow, then any brother may grant one to his neighbor, or even to himself. But if one's neighbor cannot grant a dispensation, neither has the pope any right to do so. For where does he get this authority? From the power of the keys? But the keys belong to all, and avail only for sins, Matthew 18.[186] Now they themselves claim that vows are "of divine right." Why then does the pope deceive and destroy the poor souls of people by granting dispensations in matters of divine right, in which no dispensations can be granted? In the section, "Of vows and their redemption,"[187] he babbles indeed of having the power to change vows, just as in the law the firstborn of an ass was changed for a sheep[188] as if the firstborn of an ass, and the vow he commands to be offered everywhere and always, were one and the same thing; or as if when the Lord decrees in the law that a sheep shall be changed for an ass, the pope, a mere man, may straightway claim the same power, not in his own law, but in God's! It was not a pope, but an ass changed for a pope, that made this decretal;[189] it is so egregiously senseless and godless.

The second error is this: The pope decrees, on the other hand, that a marriage is dissolved if one party enters a monastery without the consent of the other, provided that the marriage has not

184. Luther is referring to the Babylonian exile in the Old Testament. When King Nebuchadnezzar initiated the first deportation, he led out the upper class and aristocracy of the nation. These are the "people of captivity"—an expression taken from the Latin title to Psalm 65 (*populo transmigrationis*). Those left behind—the common folk—are the "people of the earth" (*populi terrae*); 2 Kgs. 24:14, "He carried away all Jerusalem, . . . no one remained, except the poorest people of the land."

185. E.g., Aquinas, *STh* II-II, q. 88, a. 10: "if it be decided absolutely that a particular vow is not to be observed, this is called a 'dispensation' from that vow; but if some other obligation be imposed in lieu of that which was to have been observed, the vow is said to be 'commuted.' Hence it is less to commute a vow than to dispense from a vow: both, however, are in the power of the Church."

186. Matt. 18:15-18: "If another member of the church sins against you, go and point out the fault when the two of you are alone. If the member listens to you, you have regained that one. But if you are not listened to, take one or two others along with you, so that every word may be confirmed by the evidence of two or three witnesses. If the member refuses to listen to them, tell it to the church; and if the offender refuses to listen even to the church, let such a one be to you as a Gentile and a tax collector. Truly I tell you, whatever you bind on earth will be bound in heaven, and whatever you loose on earth will be loosed in heaven."

187. Luther is referring to canon law, *Decretalium Gregorii IX*, lib. 3, tit. 34, *de*

yet been consummated.[190] Now I ask you, what devil puts such monstrous things into the pope's mind? God commands people to keep faith and not break their word to one another, and again, to do good with that which is their own, for God hates "robbery with a burnt offering," as is spoken by the mouth of Isaiah.[191] But spouses[u] are bound by the marriage contract to keep faith with one another, and they are not for themselves alone. They cannot break this faith by any right, and whatever they do with themselves alone is robbery, if it is done without the other's consent. Why does not those who are burdened with debt follow this same rule and obtain admission into a religious order, so as to be released from their debts and be free to break their word? O blind, blind people! Which is greater, the fidelity commanded by God or a vow devised and chosen by human beings? Are you a shepherd of souls, O pope? And you who teach these things, are you doctors of sacred theology? Why then do you teach them? No doubt because you have decked out your vow as a better work than marriage; you do not exalt faith, which alone exalts all things, but works, which are nothing in the sight of God, or which are all alike as far as merit is concerned.

I am sure, therefore, that neither human beings nor angels can grant a dispensation from vows, if they are proper vows. But I am not fully clear in my own mind whether all the things that people vow nowadays come under the head of vows. For instance, it is simply foolish and stupid for parents to dedicate their children, before birth or in infancy, to the "religious life," or to perpetual chastity;[192] indeed, it is certain that this can by no means be termed a vow. It seems to be a kind of mockery of God for them to vow things which are not at all in their power. As to the triple vow[193] of the monastic orders, the longer I consider it, the less I comprehend it, and I wonder where the custom of exacting this vow arose. Still less do I understand at what age vows may be taken in order to be legal and valid. I am pleased to find unanimous agreement that vows taken before the age of puberty are not valid.[194] Nevertheless, they deceive many young children who are ignorant both of their age and of what they are vowing. They do not observe the age of puberty in receiving such children; but the children, after making their profession, are held captive and

u This sentence and what follows were singular in the original.

voto et voti redemptione, c. 7 (hereafter *Decr. Greg. IX*).

188. Cf. Exod. 13:13: "But every firstborn donkey you shall redeem with a sheep; if you do not redeem it, you must break its neck."

189. "Decretal" refers to papal and conciliar decrees that made up most of church law. In the broadest sense, the decretals include all official letters of the pope in which a specific decision or decree is contained. More specifically, the term refers to various collections of such decrees.

190. *Decr. Greg. IX*, lib. 3, tit. 32, *de conversione coniugatorum*, c. 2: "before the marriage is consummated one of the spouses can enter a religious order, even if the other is unwilling."

191. Isa. 61:8: "For I the Lord love justice, I hate robbery and wrongdoing [*or* with a burnt offering]."

192. The child dedicated to the religious life by his parents is called an "oblate." Provisions for this practice were already present in the Rule of Benedict of Nursia (c. 480–571): "let parents draw up the petition which we have mentioned above; and at the oblation let them wrap the petition and the boy's hand in the altar cloth and so offer him [to God]." Rabanus Maurus (780–856) wrote a treatise on the practice, *De oblatione puerorum*, arguing on the basis of biblical precedent with the redemption of the firstborn, the dedication of the Levites, and the vow of Hannah to give Samuel.

193. Poverty, chastity, and obedience.

194. According to canon law the earliest one can take a vow is age fourteen for boys and twelve for girls;

Decr. Greg. IX, lib. 3, tit. 31, *de regularibus et transeuntibus ad religionem*, c. 8.

consumed by a troubled conscience as though they had afterward given their consent. As if a vow which was invalid could finally become valid with the passing of the years!

It seems absurd to me that the effective date of a legitimate vow should be predetermined for others by people who cannot predetermine it for themselves. Nor do I see why a vow taken at eighteen years of age should be valid, but not one taken at ten or twelve years. It will not do to say that at eighteen a man feels his carnal desires. What if he scarcely feels them at twenty or thirty, or feels them more keenly at thirty than at twenty? Why not also set a certain age limit for the vows of poverty and obedience? But what age will you set, by which a man should feel his greed and pride, when even the most spiritual persons hardly become aware of these emotions? Therefore, no vow will ever become binding and valid until we have become spiritual, and no longer have any need of vows. You see that these are uncertain and most perilous matters, and it would therefore be a wholesome counsel to keep such lofty modes of living free of vows, and leave them to the Spirit alone as they were of old, and never in any way to change them into a mode of life which is perpetually binding.

However, let this be sufficient for the present concerning baptism and its liberty. In due time I shall perhaps discuss vows at greater length,[195] and truly there is an urgent need for this.

195. Luther would, in fact, dedicate an entire treatise to this topic in 1521 while at the Wartburg, namely, *On Monastic Vows*, LW 44:243–400.

The Sacrament of Penance

In the third place, we are to discuss the sacrament of penance. On this subject I have already given no little offense to many people by the treatises and disputations already published, in which I have amply set forth my views.[v] These I must now briefly repeat in order to unmask the tyranny that is rampant here no less than in the sacrament of the bread. For, because these two

v The *Ninety-Five Theses against Indulgences* (1517), LW 31:25–33; TAL 1:13–46; *Ein Sermon von Ablaß und Gnade* (*A Sermon on Indulgences and Grace* [1517]), WA 1:239–46; TAL 1:57–66; *The Sacrament of Penance* (1519), LW 35:3–22; TAL 1:181–202; *Explanations of the Ninety-Five Theses* (1518), LW 31:83–252; *A Discussion on How Confession Should Be Made* (1520), LW 39:23–47.

sacraments furnish opportunity for gain and profit, the greed of the shepherds has raged in them with incredible zeal against the flock of Christ, although, as we have just seen in our discussion of vows, baptism too has sadly declined among adults and become the servant of greed.

In this woodcut by Albrecht Dürer (1471–1528), a man, perhaps King David, is depicted doing penance (1510).

The first and chief abuse of this sacrament is that they have completely abolished it. Not a vestige of the sacrament remains. For this sacrament, like the other two, consists in the word of divine promise and our faith, and they have undermined both of them. For they have adapted to their own tyranny the word of promise which Christ speaks in Matt. 16[:19] and 18[:18]: "Whatever you bind, etc.," and in the last chapter of John [20:23]: "If you forgive the sins of any, they are forgiven, etc." By these words the faith of penitents is aroused for obtaining the forgiveness of sins. But in all their writing, teaching, and preaching, their sole concern has been, not to teach what is promised to Christians in these words, or what they ought to believe, and what great consolation they might find in them, but only through force and violence to extend their own tyranny far, wide, and deep. It has finally come to such a pass that some of them have begun to command the very angels in heaven,[196] and to boast in incredible, mad wickedness that in these words they have obtained the right to rule in heaven and earth, and possess the power to bind even in heaven. Thus they say nothing of faith which is the salvation of the people, but babble only of the despotic power of the pontiffs, whereas Christ says nothing at all of power, but speaks only of faith.

196. The reference here is to a spurious bull of Pope Clement VI, *Ad memoriam*, promulgated during the Jubilee year of 1350. Many pilgrims traveling to Rome died from the plague that was widespread throughout Europe, and the bull responds by saying, "We command the angels of paradise that their souls be taken directly to the bliss of paradise, as being fully absolved from purgatory." Luther seems to be referring to this event again in his *Defense and Explanation of All the Articles* (1521), LW 32:74-75: "This is what happened in the days of John Hus. In those days the pope commanded the angels in heaven to lead to heaven the souls of those pilgrims who died on the way to Rome. John Hus objected to this horrible blasphemy and more than diabolic presumption. This protest cost him his life, but he at least caused the pope to change his tune and embarrassed by this sacrilege, to refrain from such proclamation."

For Christ has not ordained authorities or powers or lordships in his church, but ministries, as we learn from the Apostle, who says: "This is how one should regard us, as ministers of Christ and stewards of the mysteries of God" [1 Cor. 4:1]. Just as, when he said: "He who believes and is baptized will be saved" [Mark 16:16], he was calling forth the faith of those who were to be baptized, so that by this word of promise a person might be certain of salvation if baptized in faith. There was no conferring of any power there, but only the instituting of the ministry of those who baptize. Similarly, here where he says, "Whatever you bind, etc." [Matt. 16:19; 18:18], he is calling forth the faith of the penitent, so that by this word of promise we[w] might be certain that if we are absolved in faith, we are truly absolved in heaven. Here there is no mention at all of power, but only of the ministry of the one who absolves. One cannot but wonder what happened to these blind and overbearing men that they did not arrogate to themselves a despotic power from the promise of baptism; or, if they did not do it there, why they presumed to do it from the promise of penance? For in both there is a like ministry, a similar promise, and the same kind of sacrament. It cannot be denied: if baptism does not belong to Peter alone, then it is a wicked usurpation of power to claim the power of the keys for the pope alone.

Again, when Christ says: "Take, this is my body, which is given for you. This is the cup in my blood, etc." [1 Cor. 11:24-25], he is calling forth the faith of those who eat, so that when their conscience has been strengthened by these words they might be certain through faith that they receive the forgiveness of sins when they have eaten. Here too, nothing is said of power, but only of the ministry.

So the promise of baptism remains to some extent, at least for infants; but the promise of the bread and the cup has been destroyed and made subservient to greed, faith has become a work, and the testament has become a sacrifice. The promise of penance, however, has been transformed into the most oppressive despotism, being used to establish a sovereignty which is more than merely temporal.

Not content with these things, *this Babylon of ours has so completely extinguished faith* that it insolently *denies its necessity in this*

w The singular pronoun is replaced with the plural in this sentence.

sacrament. Indeed, with the wickedness of Antichrist it brands it as heresy for anyone to assert that faith is necessary.[x] What more could this tyranny do than it has done? Truly, "by the waters of Babylon we sit down and weep, when we remember thee, O Zion. On the willows there we hang up our lyres" [Ps. 137:1-2]. May the Lord curse the barren willows of those streams! Amen.

Now that promise and faith have been thus blotted out and overthrown, let us see what they have put in their place. *They have divided penance into three parts—contrition, confession, and satisfaction;*[y] but in such a way that they have removed whatever was good in each of them, and have established in each of them their caprice and tyranny.

[Contrition]

In the first place, they teach that contrition takes precedence over, and is far superior to, faith in the promise, as if contrition were not a work of faith, but a merit; indeed, they do not mention faith at all. They stick so closely to works and to those passages of Scripture where we read of many who obtained pardon by reason of their contrition and humility of heart; but they take no account of the faith which effected this contrition and sorrow of heart, as is written of the men of Nineveh in Jon. 3[:5]: "And the people of Nineveh believed God; they proclaimed a fast, etc." Others again, more bold and wicked, have invented a so-called attrition, which is converted into contrition by the power of the keys, of which they know nothing.[197] This attrition they grant to the wicked and unbelieving, and thus abolish contrition altogether. O the intolerable wrath of God, that such things should be taught in the church of Christ! Thus, with both faith and its work destroyed, we go on secure in the doctrines and opinions of men, or rather we perish in them. A contrite heart is a precious thing, but it is found only where there is an ardent faith in the promises and threats of God. Such faith, intent on the immutable truth of God, makes the conscience

197. "Attrition" is imperfect contrition, i.e., sorrow for sin for reasons less than altruistic, such as fear of punishment or love of reward. True or perfect contrition is sorrow for sin out of love for God. It is related to the traditional distinction of two kinds of "fear of God" (*timor Dei*), i.e., servile fear and filial fear. In late medieval theology, attrition was connected to the distinction of congruent merit (*meritum de congruo*—merit inadequate vis-à-vis its reward) and condign merit (*meritum de condigno*—merit intrinsically "worth" its reward). Though attrition did not fulfill the full requirements of contrition in the sacrament of penance, through the priest, God would mercifully consider it sufficient to merit grace (*meritum de congruo*), since God will not deny grace to those who do what is in them (*facere quod in se est*).

x Cf. Luther's dispute with Cajetan on the role of faith, *The Proceedings at Augsburg*, LW 31:271; also TAL 1:141–42.

y See n. 151, p. 153.

tremble, terrifies it and bruises it; and afterwards, when it is contrite, raises it up, consoles it, and preserves it. Thus the truth of God's threat is the cause of contrition, and the truth of his promise the cause of consolation, if it is believed. By such faith a man "merits" the forgiveness of sins. Therefore faith should be taught and aroused before all else. Once faith is obtained, contrition and consolation will follow inevitably of themselves.

Therefore, although there is some truth in their teaching that contrition is to be attained by the enumeration and contemplation (as they call it) of their sins,[198] yet their teaching is perilous and perverse so long as they do not teach first of all the beginnings and causes of contrition—the immutable truth of God's threat and promise which calls forth faith—so that men may learn to pay more heed to the truth of God, by which they are cast down and lifted up, than to the multitude of their sins. If their sins are regarded apart from the truth of God, they will excite afresh and increase the desire for sin rather than lead to contrition. I will say nothing now of the insurmountable task which they have imposed upon us, namely, that we are to frame a contrition for every sin. That is impossible. We can know only the smaller part of our sins; and even our good works are found to be sins, according to Ps. 143[:2]: "Enter not into judgment with your servant; for no one living is righteous before you." It is enough if we lament the sins which distress our conscience at the present moment, as well as those which we can readily call to mind. Whoever is in this frame of mind is without doubt ready to grieve and fear for all his sins, and will grieve and fear whenever they are brought to his knowledge in the future.

Beware, then, of putting your trust in your own contrition and of ascribing the forgiveness of sins to your own remorse. God does not look on you with favor because of that, but because of the faith by which you have believed God's threats and promises, and which has effected such sorrow within you. Thus we owe whatever good there may be in our penance, not to our scrupulous enumeration of sins, but to the truth of God and to our faith. All other things are the works and fruits which follow of their own accord. They do not make a person good, but are done by the one who is already made good through faith in the truth of God. Even so, "smoke goes up in his wrath; because he is angry he shakes the mountains and sets them on fire," as it is said in Ps. 18[:8, 7]). First comes the terror of this threatening, which sets

198. Cf. Aquinas, *STh* III Suppl., q. 9, a. 2: "In prescribing medicine for the body, the physician should know not only the disease for which he is prescribing, but also the general constitution of the sick person, since one disease is aggravated by the addition of another, and a medicine which would be adapted to one disease, would be harmful to another. The same is to be said in regard to sins, . . . hence it is necessary for confession that man confess all the sins that he calls to mind, and if he fails to do this, it is not a confession, but a pretense of confession."

the wicked on fire; then faith, accepting this, sends up smoke-clouds of contrition, etc.

But the trouble is not so much that contrition has been exposed to tyranny and avarice, as that it has been given over completely to wickedness and pestilent teaching. It is confession and satisfaction that have become the chief workshops of greed and power.

[Confession]

Let us first take up *confession*. There is no doubt that confession of sins is necessary and commanded of God, in Matt. 3[:6]: "They were baptized by John in the River Jordan, confessing their sins," and in 1 John 1[:9-10]: "If we confess our sins, he is faithful and just, and will forgive our sins. If we say we have not sinned, we make him a liar, and his word is not in us." If the saints may not deny their sin, how much more ought those who are guilty of great and public sins to make confession! But the institution of confession is proved most effectively of all by Matt. 18,[199] where Christ teaches that those[z] who sin should be told of their faults, brought before the church, accused, and if they will not hear, be excommunicated. They "hear" if they heed the rebuke and acknowledge and confess their sins.

As to the current practice of private confession, I am heartily in favor of it, even though it cannot be proved from the Scriptures. It is useful, even necessary, and I would not have it abolished. Indeed, I rejoice that it exists in the church of Christ, for it is a cure without equal for distressed consciences. For when we have laid bare our conscience to another Christian and privately made known to the evil that lurked within, we receive from that person's lips the word of comfort [as if] spoken by God. And, if we accept this in faith, we find peace in the mercy of God speaking to us through our brother or sister. There is just one thing about it that I abominate, and that is the fact that this kind of confession has been subjected to the despotism and extortion of the pontiffs. They reserve to themselves even the secret sins,[200] and command that they be made known to confessors named by them, only to trouble the consciences of people. They merely

z Plural substituted for singular in this and the next sentence.

199. Matt. 18:15-17: "If another member of the church sins against you, go and point out the fault when the two of you are alone. If the member listens to you, you have regained that one. But if you are not listened to, take one or two others along with you, so that every word may be confirmed by the evidence of two or three witnesses. If the member refuses to listen to them, tell it to the church; and if the offender refuses to listen even to the church, let such a one be to you as a Gentile and a tax collector."

200. The notion of "reserved cases" in which the pope claimed exclusive jurisdiction to grant remission and satisfaction (*casus papales*) developed gradually as bishops would refer certain grave transgressions to the Holy See, for example, violence done to clerics and the burning of church buildings being the most common early on. Official lists of cases reserved for the pope were enumerated in the bull *In coena domini*, which was published annually against heretics since 1364. This list, however, grew with papal discretion and continued to be a contentious conflict of jurisdiction over the bishops who had claimed the right to absolve a similar list of "secret" (*casus occultus*) as well as "public" sins. In 1414, the Council of Constance tried, though unsuccessfully, to curtail these cases and leave them at the discretion of the bishop. Even the Council of Trent in 1563 would try to limit papal cases only to certain public sins, leaving the secret sins in the hands of the bishops (*Sess.* 24, *de Reform*, c. 8 and c. 20), but this, too, was often overturned by the publication of *Coena domini*.

play the pontiff, while they utterly despise the true duties of pontiffs, which are to preach the gospel and to care for the poor. Indeed, the godless despots leave the great sins to the common priests, and reserve to themselves only those sins which are of less consequence, such as those ridiculous and fictitious things in the bull *Coena domini*. To make the wickedness of their error even more apparent, they not only fail to reserve, but actually teach and approve things which are against the service of God, against faith and the chief commandments—such as their running about on pilgrimages, the perverse worship of the saints, the lying saints' legends, the various ways of trusting in works and ceremonies and practicing them. Yet in all of these faith in God is extinguished and idolatry fostered, as we see in our day. As a result we have the same kind of priests today as Jeroboam ordained of old in Dan and Beersheba, ministers of the golden calves,[a] men who are ignorant of the law of God, of faith, and of whatever pertains to the feeding of Christ's sheep. They inculcate in the people nothing but their own inventions with fear and violence.

Although I urge that this outrage of reserved cases should be borne patiently, even as Christ bids us bear all human tyranny, and teaches us that we should obey these extortioners; nevertheless, I deny that they have the right to make such reservations, and I do not believe that they can bring one jot or tittle of proof that they have it. But I am going to prove the contrary. In the first place, Christ speaks in Matt. 18 of public sins and says that if our brother hears us, when we tell him his fault, we have saved the soul of our brother, and that he is to be brought before the church only if he refuses to hear us, so that his sin can be corrected among brethren.[b] How much more will it be true of secret sins, that they are forgiven if one brother freely makes confession to another? So it is not necessary to tell it to the church, that is, as these babblers interpret it, to the prelate or priest. On this matter we have further authority from Christ, where he says in the same chapter: "Whatever you bind on earth shall be bound in heaven, and whatever you loose on earth shall be loosed in heaven" [Matt. 18:18]. For this is said to each and every Christian. Again, he says in the same place: "Again I say to you, if two

a 1 Kgs. 12:26-32.

b Matt. 18:15-17.

of you agree on earth about anything they ask, it will be done for them by my father in heaven" [Matt. 18:19]. Now, the one who lays secret sins before another believer and craves pardon, certainly agrees with this brother or sister on earth, in the truth which is Christ. Of this Christ says even more clearly, confirming his preceding words: "For truly, I say to you, where two or three are gathered in my name, there am I in the midst of them" [Matt. 18:20].

Hence, I have no doubt but that we are absolved from our secret sins when we have made confession, privately before any brother or sister, either of our own accord or after being rebuked, and have sought pardon and amended our ways, no matter how much the violence of the pontiffs may rage against it. For Christ has given to every one of his believers the power to absolve even open sins. Add yet this little point: If any reservation of secret sins were valid, so that one could not be saved unless they were forgiven, then one's salvation would be prevented most of all by those aforementioned good works and idolatries that are taught by the popes nowadays. But if these most grievous sins do not prevent one's salvation, how foolish it is to reserve those lighter sins! In truth, it is the foolishness and blindness of the shepherds that produce these monstrous things in the church. Therefore I would admonish those princes of Babylon and bishops of Beth-aven[201] to refrain from reserving any cases whatsoever. Let them, moreover, permit all brothers and sisters most freely to hear the confession of secret sins, so that the sinner may make his sins known to whomever he will and seek pardon and comfort, that is, the word of Christ, by the mouth of his neighbor. For with these presumptions of theirs they only ensnare the consciences of the weak without necessity, establish their wicked despotism, and fatten their avarice on the sins and ruin of their brethren. Thus they stain their hands with the blood of souls; sons are devoured by their parents. Ephraim devours Judah, and Syria Israel, with an open mouth, as Isaiah says.[202]

To these evils they have added the "circumstances,"[c] and also the mothers, daughters, sisters, sisters-in-law, branches and fruits of sins; since these most astute and idle men have worked out, if you please, a kind of family tree of relationships and

201. Hos. 4:15; 10:5. "Beth-aven" was the new name given to Bethel by the prophet in response to Israel's idolatry. Rather than "house of God," it was "house of nothingness."

202. Isa. 9:20-22: "They gorged on the right, but still were hungry, and they devoured on the left, but were not satisfied; they devoured the flesh of their own kindred; Manasseh devoured Ephraim, and Ephraim Manasseh, and together they were against Judah. For all this his anger has not turned away; his hand is stretched out still."

c See n. 154, p. 154.

affinities even among sins—so prolific is wickedness coupled with ignorance. For this conception, whatever rogue may be its author, has become a public law, like many others. Thus do the shepherds keep watch over the church of Christ: whatever new work or superstition those most stupid devotees may have dreamed of, they immediately drag to the light of day, deck out with indulgences, and fortify with bulls. So far are they from suppressing such things and preserving for God's people true faith and liberty. For what has our liberty to do with the tyranny of Babylon?

My advice would be to ignore all "circumstances" whatsoever. With Christians there is only one circumstance—that a fellow Christian[d] has sinned. For there is no person to be compared with a fellow Christian. And the observance of places, times, days, persons, and all other rank superstition only magnifies the things that are nothing, to the injury of the things which are everything; as if anything could be of greater weight or importance than the glory of Christian fellowship! Thus they bind us to places, days, and persons, so that the name of [Christian] "brother" [or "sister"] loses its value, and we serve in bondage instead of being free—we, to whom all days, places, persons, and all external things are one and the same.

[Satisfaction]

How unworthily they have dealt with *satisfaction,* I have abundantly shown in the controversies concerning indulgences.[e] They have grossly abused it, to the ruin of Christians in body and soul. To begin with, they have taught it in such a manner that the people have never had the slightest understanding what satisfaction really is, namely, the renewal of one's life. Then, they so continually harp on it and emphasize its necessity, that they leave no room for faith in Christ. With these scruples they torture poor consciences to death; and one runs to Rome, one to this place, another to that; this one to Chartreuse,[203] that one to some other place; one scourges himself with rods, another mortifies his body with fasts and vigils; and all cry with the same

203. The founding cloister of the Carthusian order, founded by Bruno of Cologne (1030–1101) in 1084.

d *Brother* in the German.

e Cf. *A Sermon on Indulgence and Grace* (1518), WA 1:243–46; TAL 1:56–65; *Resolutiones* (1518), concl. 5., WA 1:538,1–35.

mad zeal: "Lo, here is Christ! Lo, there!" believing that the kingdom of Christ, which is within us, will come with observation.[204]

This image by an unknown artist depicts flagellants doing penance.

For these monstrous things we are indebted to you, O Roman See, and to your murderous laws and ceremonies, with which you have corrupted all humankind, so that they believe they can with works make satisfaction for sin to God, when God can be satisfied only by the faith of a contrite heart! Not only do you keep this faith silent with this uproar of yours, but you even oppress it, only so that your insatiable bloodsucker may have those to whom it may say, "Give, give!" [Prov. 30:15] and may traffic in sins.

Some have gone even further and have constructed those instruments for driving souls to despair, their decrees that the penitents must rehearse all sins anew for which they neglected to make the imposed satisfaction. What would they not venture to do, these men who were born for the sole purpose of carrying all things into a tenfold captivity?

Moreover, how many, I ask, are possessed with the notion that they are in a saved state and are making satisfaction for their sins, if they only mumble over, word for word, the prayers imposed by the priest, even though meanwhile they never give a thought to the amending of their way of life! They believe that their life is changed in the one moment of contrition and confession, and there remains only to make satisfaction for their past sins. How should they know better if they have not been taught otherwise? No thought is given here to the mortifying of the flesh, no value is attached to the example of Christ, who, when he absolved the woman caught in adultery, said: "Go, and do not sin again" [John 8:11], thereby laying upon her the cross, that is, the mortifying of her flesh. This perverse error is greatly encouraged by the fact that we absolve sinners before the satisfaction has

204. Cf. Luke 17:20f.: "The kingdom of God is not coming with things that can be observed; nor will they say, 'Look, here it is!' or 'There it is!' For, in fact, the kingdom of God is among you." Luther's wordplay is on "observation" (*observantia*), which can also refer to the monastic observants; see n. 183, p. 171.

been completed, so that they are more concerned about completing the satisfaction, which is a lasting thing, than they are about contrition, which they suppose to be over and done with when they have made confession. Absolution ought rather to follow on the completion of satisfaction, as it did in the early church, with the result that, after completing the work, penitents gave themselves with much greater diligence to faith and the living of a new life.

But this must suffice in repetition of what I have said more fully in connection with indulgences, and *in general this must suffice for the present concerning the three sacraments*, which have been treated, and yet not treated, in so many harmful books on the *Sentences*[f] and on the laws. It remains to attempt some discussion of the other "sacraments" also, lest I seem to have rejected them without cause.

205. Confirmation was seen in connection with the gift of the Holy Spirit through apostolic laying on of hands (e.g., Acts 8:15f.) in the context of baptism. Alternatively, the sacrament has also been called chrism, especially in the Eastern church; in reference to the anointing of the Spirit it also was accompanied by the anointing of oil. Because of its origination with the apostles, confirmation was, like ordination, a sacramental act performed by the bishop. Cf., for example, Aquinas, *STh* III, q. 72, a. 11: "the conferring of this sacrament is reserved to bishops, who possess supreme power in the Church: just as in the primitive Church, the fullness of the Holy Ghost was given by the apostles, in whose place the bishops stand (Acts 8). Hence Pope Urban I (r. 222–230) says: "All the faithful should, after baptism, receive the Holy Ghost by the imposition of the bishop's hand, that they may become perfect Christians."

Confirmation

It is amazing that it should have entered the minds of these men to make a sacrament of confirmation out of the laying on of hands. We read that Christ touched the little children in that way,[g] and that by it the apostles imparted the Holy Spirit,[h] ordained presbyters,[i] and cured the sick;[j] as the Apostle writes to Timothy: "Do not be hasty in the laying on of hands" [1 Tim. 5:22]. Why have they not also made a "confirmation" out of the sacrament of the bread? For it is written in Acts 9[:19]: "And he took food and was strengthened," and in Ps. 104[:15]: "And bread to strengthen man's heart." Confirmation would thus include three sacraments—the bread, ordination, and confirmation itself. But if everything the apostles did is a sacrament, why have they not rather made preaching a sacrament?

f See n. 56, p. 120.

g Mark 10:16.

h Acts 8:17; 19:6.

i Acts 6:6.

j Mark 16:18.

I do not say this because I condemn the seven sacraments, but because I deny that they can be proved from the Scriptures. Would that there were in the church such a laying on of hands as there was in apostolic times, whether we chose to call it confirmation or healing! But there is nothing left of it now but what we ourselves have invented to adorn the office of bishops,[205] that they may not be entirely without work in the church. For after they relinquished to their inferiors those arduous sacraments together with the Word as being beneath their attention (since whatever the divine majesty has instituted they seem to need to despise!) it was no more than right that we should discover something easy and not too burdensome for such delicate and great heroes to do, and should by no means entrust it to the lower clergy as something common, for whatever human wisdom has decreed must be held in honor among all! Therefore, as the priests are, so let their ministry and duty be. For a bishop who does not preach the gospel or practice the cure of souls—what is he but an idol in the world [1 Cor. 8:4], who has nothing but the name and appearance of a bishop?

Ein Sermon von dem heiligen hoch wirdigen Sacrament der Tauffe doctoris Martini Luther Augustiner.

A woodcut of the seven sacraments of the Roman Catholic Church adorns the title page of this sermon on baptism (Leipzig, 1520) by Luther. The scene depicting the sacrament of confirmation is the center image on the left.

But *instead of this we seek sacraments that have been divinely instituted, and among these we see no reason for numbering confirmation.* For to constitute a sacrament there must be above all things else a word of divine promise, by which faith may be exercised. But we read nowhere that Christ ever gave a promise concerning confirmation, although he laid hands on many and included the laying on of hands among the signs in the last chapter of Mark [16:18]:

"They will lay their hands on the sick; and they will recover." Yet no one has applied this to a sacrament, for that is not possible.

For this reason it is sufficient to regard confirmation as a certain churchly rite or sacramental ceremony, similar to other ceremonies, such as the blessing of water and the like. For if every other creature is sanctified by the Word and by prayer,[k] why should not we much rather be sanctified by the same means? Still, these things cannot be called sacraments of faith, because they have no divine promise connected with them, neither do they save; but the sacraments do save those who believe the divine promise.

Marriage

[Marriage Is Not a Sacrament]

Not only is marriage regarded as a sacrament without the least warrant of Scripture,[206] but the very ordinances that extol it as a sacrament have turned it into a farce. Let us look into this a little.

We have said that in every sacrament there is a word of divine promise, to be believed by whoever receives the sign, and that the sign alone cannot be a sacrament. Nowhere do we read that the man who marries a wife receives any grace of God. There is not even a divinely instituted sign in marriage, nor do we read anywhere that marriage was instituted by God to be a sign of anything. To be sure, whatever takes place in a visible manner can be understood as a figure or allegory of something invisible. But figures or allegories are not sacraments, in the sense in which we use the term.

Furthermore, since marriage has existed from the beginning of the world and is still found among unbelievers, there is no reason why it should be called a sacrament of the New Law[207] and of the church alone. The marriages of the ancients were no less sacred than are ours, nor are those of unbelievers less true marriages than those of believers, and yet they are not regarded as sacraments. Besides, even among believers there are married folk who are wicked and worse than any heathen; why should marriage be called a sacrament in their case and not among

k 1 Tim. 4:4-5.

206. The Scripture most often cited in connected with marriage is Eph. 5:22-32, especially "the two will become one flesh. This is a great mystery . . . [Lat. *sacramentum*]." The sacramental character of marriage is articulated in the tradition in a variety of sources, though what constitutes a sacrament varied. For example, Augustine, in his work *On the Good of Marriage* (401), c. 32, notes the following: "Among all nations and all people the good that is secured by marriage consists in the offspring and in the chastity of married fidelity; but, in the case of God's people, it consists moreover in the holiness of the sacrament, by reason of which it is forbidden, even after a separation has taken place, to marry another as long as the first partner lives . . . just as priests are ordained to draw together a Christian community, and even though no such community be formed, the sacrament of orders still abides in those ordained, or just as the sacrament of the Lord, once it is conferred, abides even in one who is dismissed from his office on account of guilt, although in such a one it abides unto judgment." Peter Lombard lists marriage as one of the seven sacraments, noting that it offers only a remedy against sin rather than any helping grace, *Sentences* 4, d. 2, c. 1. In 1139, the Second Lateran Council assigned marriage along with the Eucharist and baptism as priestly acts, and at the Council of Verona, in 1184, marriage was designated as a sacrament.

207. "New Law" (*nova lex*) is a traditional designation for the gospel and the New Testament, set in contrast to the "Old Law" (*vetus lex*), i.e., the law of Moses.

A marriage ceremony presided over by a priest, depicted in a 1522 publication.

the heathen? Or are we going to talk the same sort of nonsense about baptism and the church and say that marriage is a sacrament only in the church, just as some make the mad claim that temporal power exists only in the church? That is childish and foolish talk, by which we expose our ignorance and foolhardiness to the ridicule of unbelievers.

But they will say, "The Apostle says in Eph. 5[:31-32], 'The two shall become one. This is a great sacrament.' Surely you are not going to contradict so plain a statement of the Apostle!" I reply: This argument like the others betrays great shallowness and a careless and thoughtless reading of Scripture. Nowhere in all of the Holy Scriptures is this word *sacramentum* employed in the sense in which we use the term; it has an entirely different meaning. For wherever it occurs it denotes not the sign of a sacred thing,[208] but the sacred, secret, hidden thing itself.[209]

208. Cf. Augustine, *The City of God* 10, 5: "a sacrament, that is, a sacred sign"; Lombard, *Sentences* 4, d. 1, c. 2: "A sacrament is a sign of a sacred thing"; Aquinas, *STh* III, q. 60, a. 3: "a sacrament properly speaking is that which is ordained to signify our sanctification. In which three things may be considered; viz. the very cause of our sanctification, which is Christ's passion; the form of our sanctification, which is grace and the virtues; and the ultimate end of our sanctification, which is eternal life. And all these are signified by the sacraments."

209. Cf. Aquinas, *STh* III, q. 60, a. 1: "a thing may be called a 'sacrament,' either from having a certain hidden sanctity, and in this sense a sacrament is a 'sacred secret'; or from having some relationship to this sanctity, which relationship may be that of a cause, or of a sign or of any other relation. But now we are speaking of sacraments in a special sense, as implying the habitude of sign: and in this way a sacrament is a kind of sign."

Thus Paul writes in 1 Cor. 4[:1]: "This is how one should regard us, as servants of Christ and stewards of the 'mysteries' of God," that is, the sacraments. For where we have the word *sacramentum* the Greek original has *mysterion*, which the translator sometimes translates and sometimes retains in its Greek form.[210] Thus our verse in the Greek reads: "They two shall become one. This is a great mystery." This explains how they came to understand a sacrament of the New Law here, a thing they would never have done if they had read *mysterium*, as it is in the Greek.

Thus Christ himself is called a "sacrament" in 1 Tim. 3[:16]: "Great indeed, is the sacrament (that is, the mystery): He was manifested in the flesh, vindicated in the Spirit, seen by angels, preached among the nations, believed on in the world, taken up in glory." Why have they not drawn out of this passage an eighth sacrament of the New Law, since they have the clear authority of Paul? But if they restrained themselves here, where they had a most excellent opportunity to invent new sacraments, why are they so unrestrained in the other passage? Plainly, it was their ignorance of both words and things that betrayed them. They clung to the mere sound of the words, indeed, to their own fancies. For, having once arbitrarily taken the word *sacramentum* to mean a sign, they immediately, without thought or scruple, made a "sign" of it every time they came upon it in the Holy Scriptures. Such new meanings of words, human customs, and other things they have dragged into the Holy Scriptures. They have transformed the Scriptures according to their own dreams, making anything out of any passage whatsoever. Thus they continually chatter nonsense about the terms: good work, evil work, sin, grace, righteousness, virtue, and almost all the fundamental words and things.[211] For they employ them all after their own arbitrary judgment, learned from the writings of men, to the detriment of both the truth of God and of our salvation.

Therefore, sacrament, or mystery, in Paul is that wisdom of the Spirit, hidden in a mystery, as he says in 1 Cor. 2, which is Christ, who for this very reason is not known to the rulers of this world, wherefore they also crucified him,[212] and for them he remains to this day folly, an offense, a stumbling stone,[213] and a sign that is spoken against.[214] The preachers he calls stewards of these mysteries[215] because they preach Christ, the power and the wisdom of God,[l] yet in such a way that, unless you believe, you cannot understand it. Therefore, a sacrament is a mystery, or

210. The common Latin translation of "mystery" (Gk.: *mysterion*) in the Vulgate Bible is *sacramentum*, though there are instances in which it retains a Latinized form of the original, i.e., *mysterium*.

211. In his Romans lectures (1515–16), Luther began to realize certain incompatibilities with the way the Scholastic tradition used and defined theological words and the manner in which Paul used them. Repeatedly he noted that there was a stark contrast between the way in which the apostle speaks (*modus loquendi apostoli*) and the way the Scholastics talked (*modus loquendi philosophiae . . . Aristoteli*). Exasperated, he famously wrote in his notes, "O pig-theologians . . . O ignorance of sin! O ignorance of God! O ignorance of the law!" In his 1522 translation of the New Testament, he included in his preface to Romans a list of biblical vocabulary that had been misinterpreted by the Scholastics, providing his own definitions for such key words as *law*, *sin*, *grace*, *faith*, *righteousness*, *flesh*, and *spirit*. See Leif Grane, *Modus Loquendi Theologicus: Luthers Kampf um die Erneuerung der Theologie 1515–1518*, Acta Theologica Danica, vol. 12 (Leiden: Brill, 1975).

212. 1 Cor. 2:7-8: "But we speak God's wisdom, secret and hidden, which God decreed before the ages for our glory. None of the rulers of this age understood this; for if they had, they would not have crucified the Lord of glory."

213. 1 Cor. 1:22-24: "For Jews demand signs and Greeks desire wisdom, but we proclaim Christ crucified, a stumbling block to Jews and foolishness to Gentiles, but to those who are the called, both Jews and Greeks, Christ the

secret thing, which is set forth in words, but received by the faith of the heart. Such a sacrament is spoken of in the passage before us: "The two shall become one. This is a great sacrament,"[m] which they understand as spoken of marriage,[216] whereas Paul himself wrote these words as applying to Christ and the church, and clearly explained them himself by saying: "I take it to mean Christ and the church" [Eph. 5:32]. See how well Paul and these men agree! Paul says he is proclaiming a great sacrament in Christ and the church, but they proclaim it in terms of man and a woman! If such liberty in the interpretation of the sacred Scriptures is permitted, it is small wonder that one finds here anything one pleases, even a hundred sacraments.

Christ and the church are, therefore, a mystery, that is, a great and secret thing which can and ought to be represented in terms of marriage as a kind of outward allegory. But marriage ought not for that reason to be called a sacrament. The heavens are a type of the apostles, as Ps. 19 declares; the sun is a type of Christ; the waters, of the peoples; but that does not make those things sacraments, for in every case there are lacking both the divine institution and the divine promise, which constitute a sacrament.[217] Hence Paul, in Ephesians 5, following his own mind, applies to Christ these words of Genesis 2 about marriage;[n] or else, following the general view, he teaches that the spiritual marriage of Christ is also contained therein, when he says: "As Christ cherishes the church, because we are members of his body, of his flesh and his bones. 'For this reason a man shall leave his father and mother and be joined to his wife, and the two shall become one.' This is a great sacrament, and I take it to mean Christ and the church." You see, he would have the whole passage apply to Christ, and is at pains to admonish the reader to understand that the sacrament is in Christ and the church, not in marriage.[o]

l 1 Cor. 1:24.

m Eph. 5:31-32.

n Gen. 2:24.

o At this point comes a paragraph that clearly breaks the flow of thought, though it is not clear how this might fit under Luther's treatment of penance earlier. It seems to have been an accidental

power of God and the wisdom of God." Cf. Rom. 9:32-33.

214. Luke 2:34: "Then Simeon blessed them and said to his mother Mary, 'This child is destined for the falling and the rising of many in Israel, and to be a sign that will be opposed.'"

215. 1 Cor. 4:1: "Think of us in this way, as servants of Christ and stewards of God's mysteries."

216. Lombard, *Sentences* 4, d. 26, c. 6: "since marriage is a sacrament, it is both a sacred sign and the sign of a sacred thing, namely of joining of Christ and the Church, as the Apostle says. . . . For just as there is between the partners to a marriage a joining according to the consent of souls and the intermingling of bodies, so the Church joins herself to Christ by will and nature." Aquinas, *STh* III Suppl., q. 42, a. 1.

217. Ps. 19:2-5: "The heavens are telling the glory of God; and the firmament proclaims his handiwork. . . . In the heavens he has set a tent for the sun, which comes out like a bridegroom from his wedding canopy." Luther's interpretation, which reflects the traditional allegorical interpretation of this Psalm in the history of exegesis, is first set forth in his lectures on the Psalms in 1513: "*the heavens tell*, [i.e.] the apostles and evangelists . . . *and the firmament proclaims*, [i.e.] the apostolic church . . . full of stars, i.e., the saints. . . . *for the sun*, in Christ . . . *he sets*, God . . . *his tabernacle*, his church" (WA 55/I:160; emphasis mine).

Granted that marriage is a figure of Christ and the church; yet it is not a divinely instituted sacrament, but invented by those in the church who are carried away by their ignorance of both the word and the thing. This ignorance, when it does not conflict with the faith, is to be borne in charity, just as many other human practices due to weakness and ignorance are borne in the church, so long as they do not conflict with the faith and the Holy Scriptures. But we are now arguing for the certainty and purity of faith and the Scriptures. We expose our faith to ridicule if we affirm that a certain thing is contained in the sacred Scriptures and in the articles of our faith, only to be refuted and shown that it is not contained in them; being found ignorant of our own affairs, we become a stumbling block to our opponents and to the weak. But most of all we should guard against impairing the authority of the Holy Scriptures. For those things which have been delivered to us by God in the sacred Scriptures must be sharply distinguished from those that have been invented by men in the church, no matter how eminent they may be for saintliness and scholarship.

So far concerning marriage itself.

insertion by the printer. The paragraph is reproduced here as a note for reference.

> I admit, of course, that the sacrament of penance existed in the Old Law, and even from the beginning of the world. But the new promise of penance and the gift of the keys are peculiar to the New Law. Just as we now have baptism instead of circumcision, so we have the keys instead of sacrifices and other signs of penance. We said above that the same God at various times gave different promises and diverse signs for the remission of sins and the salvation of men; nevertheless, all received the same. Thus it is said in 2 Cor. 4[:13], "Since we have the same spirit of faith, we too believe, and so we speak." And in 1 Cor. 10, "Our fathers all ate the same supernatural food and drank the same supernatural drink. For they drank from the supernatural Rock which followed them, and the Rock was Christ." Thus also in Heb. 11, "They all died, not having received what was promised, since God had foreseen something better for us, that apart from us they should not be made perfect." For Christ himself is, yesterday and today and forever the head of his church, from the beginning even to the end of the world. Therefore there are diverse signs, but the faith of all is the same. Indeed, without faith it is impossible to please God, yet by it Abel did please him.

p Cf. Gen. 10:8f. See n. 13, p. 105.

[Canonical Impediments to Marriage]

But what shall we say concerning the wicked laws of men by which this divinely ordained way of life has been ensnared and tossed to and fro? Good God! It is dreadful to contemplate the audacity of the Roman despots, who both dissolve and compel marriages as they please. I ask you, has humankind been handed over to the caprice of these men for them to mock them and in every way abuse them and make of them whatever they please, for the sake of filthy lucre?

There is circulating far and wide and enjoying a great reputation a book whose contents have been confusedly poured together out of all the dregs and filth of human ordinances. Its title is "The Angelic *Summa*,"[218] although it ought rather to be "The More than Devilish *Summa*." Among endless other monstrosities, which are supposed to instruct the confessors, whereas they most mischievously confuse them, there are enumerated in this book eighteen impediments to marriage. If you will examine these with the just and unprejudiced eye of faith, you will see that they belong to those things which the Apostle foretold: "There shall be those that give heed to the spirits of demons, speaking lies in hypocrisy, forbidding to marry" [1 Tim. 4:1-3]. What is "forbidding to marry" if it is not this—to invent all those hindrances and set those snares, in order to prevent people from marrying, or, if they are married to annul their marriage? Who gave this power to men? Granted that they were holy men and impelled by godly zeal, why should another's holiness disturb my liberty? Why should another's zeal take me captive? Let whoever will be a saint and a zealot, and to his heart's content, only let him not bring harm upon another, and let him not rob me of my liberty!

Yet I am glad that those shameful laws have at last reached their full measure of glory, which is this: that the Romanists of our day have through them become merchants. What is it that they sell? Vulvas and penises—merchandise indeed most worthy of such merchants, grown altogether filthy and obscene through greed and godlessness. For there is no impediment nowadays that may not be legalized through the intercession of mammon. These laws of men seem to have sprung into existence for the sole purpose of serving those greedy men and rapacious Nimrods[p] as snares for taking money and as nets for catching souls, and in

218. A fifteenth-century handbook on casuistry, the *Summa de casibus conscientiae* was popularly named after its author, Angelo Carletti di Chiviasso (1411–1495), and often used by priests as a guide to hearing confession. In the section on "Matrimony," the book listed eighteen impediments to marriage.

order that "abomination" might stand in "the holy place" [Matt. 24:15], the church of God, and openly sell to people the privy parts of both sexes, or (as the Scriptures say) "shame and nakedness,"[q] of which they had previously robbed them by means of their laws. O worthy trade for our pontiffs to ply, instead of the ministry of the gospel, which in their greed and pride they despise, being given up to a reprobate mind[r] with utter shame and infamy.

But what shall I say or do? If I enter into details, the treatise will grow beyond all bounds. Everything is in such dire confusion that one does not know where to begin, how far to go, and where to leave off. This I do know, that no state is governed successfully by means of laws. If rulers are wise, they[s] will govern better by a natural sense of justice than by laws. If they are not wise, they will foster nothing but evil through legislation, since they will not know what use to make of the laws nor how to adapt them to the case at hand. Therefore, in civil affairs more stress should be laid on putting good and wise leaders in office than on making laws; for such leaders will themselves be the very best of laws, and will judge every variety of ease with a lively sense of equity. And if there is knowledge of the divine law combined with natural wisdom, then written laws will be entirely superfluous and harmful. Above all, love needs no laws whatever.[219]

Nevertheless, I will say and do what I can. I ask and urge all priests and friars when they encounter any impediment to marriage from which the pope can grant dispensation but which is not stated in the Scriptures, by all means to confirm[220] all marriages that may have been contracted in any way[221] contrary to the ecclesiastical or pontifical laws. But let them arm themselves with the divine law which says: "What God has joined together, let no man put asunder" [Matt. 19:6]. For the joining together of a man and a woman is of divine law and is binding, however much it may conflict with the laws of men; the laws of men must give way before it without any hesitation. For if a man leaves father and mother and cleaves to his wife,[t] how much more will he tread underfoot the silly and wicked laws of men, in order to

q Cf. Lev. 18:6-18.

r Rom. 1:28.

s The male singular pronoun is replaced by the plural in this sentence.

t Matt. 19:5.

219. Luther's outspoken judgments about human institutions in this paragraph and elsewhere were evidently perceived as too radical and unreasonable. In the first editions of Luther's collected works, both the Wittenberg and Jena editions, this paragraph is entirely deleted.

220. Namely, by officiating the marriage ceremony.

221. Marriages were "contracted" by betrothal and most often arranged by parents. The secret engagement of young people without parental consent presented a problem at this time because marriage was often used to advance the family's fortunes. Many medieval theologians concluded that consent between two people constituted a valid marriage. Luther disagreed, but also encouraged both parents and children to deal with each other in a loving way. See *That Parents Should Neither Compel nor Hinder Marriage* . . . (1524), LW 45:385-93. Also, for apparently the same reasons as the previous paragraph, "in any way" (*quoquo modo*) is deleted from the Wittenberg and Jena editions of Luther's works.

cleave to his wife! And if pope, bishop, or official[222] should annul any marriage because it was contracted contrary to the laws of men, he is Antichrist, he does violence to nature, and is guilty of treason against the Divine Majesty, because this word stands: "What God has joined together, let no man put asunder" [Matt. 19:6].

Besides this, no human being had the right to frame such laws, and Christ has granted to Christians a liberty which is above all human laws, especially where a law of God conflicts with them. Thus it is said in Mark 2[:28]: "The Son of man is lord even of the Sabbath," and "Humankind was not made for the Sabbath, but the Sabbath for humankind" [Mark 2:27]. Moreover, such laws were condemned beforehand by Paul when he foretold that there would be those who forbid marriage.[223] Here, therefore, those inflexible impediments derived from affinity,[u] by spiritual or legal relationship, and from blood relationship must give way, so far as the Scriptures permit, in which the second degree of consanguinity alone is prohibited. Thus it is written in Lev. 18[:6-18], where there are twelve persons a man is prohibited from marrying: his mother, stepmother, full sister, half-sister by either parent, granddaughter, father's or mother's sister, daughter-in-law, brother's wife, wife's sister, stepdaughter, and his uncle's wife. Here only the first degree of affinity and the second degree of consanguinity are forbidden; yet not without exception, as will appear on closer examination, for the brother's or sister's daughter—the niece—is not included in the prohibition, although she is in the second degree.[224] Therefore, if a marriage has been contracted outside of these degrees, which are the only ones that have been prohibited by God's appointment, it should by no means be annulled on account of human laws. For marriage itself, being a divine institution, is incomparably superior to any laws, so that marriage should not be annulled for the sake of the law, rather the laws should be broken for the sake of marriage.

In the same way that nonsense about compaternities, commaternities, confraternities, consororities, and confilieties[225] must be completely abolished in the contracting of marriage.

u The Wittenberg and Jena editions delete this section from here to the end of the paragraph. See n. 219, p. 192.

222. The judge in the episcopal court.

223. 1 Tim. 4:1-3: "Now the Spirit expressly says that in later times some will renounce the faith by paying attention to deceitful spirits and teachings of demons, through the hypocrisy of liars whose consciences are seared with a hot iron. They forbid marriage and demand abstinence from foods, which God created to be received with thanksgiving by those who believe and know the truth."

224. The word *consanguinity* refers to kinship ties, while *affinity* refers to those who are related by marriage.

225. Relationships arising from sponsorship at baptism or through legal adoption.

What was it but superstition that invented this "spiritual affinity"? If one who baptized is not permitted to marry her whom he has baptized or stood sponsor for, what right has any Christian man to marry a Christian woman? Is the relationship that grows out of the external rite or sign of the sacrament more intimate than that which grows out of the blessing of the sacrament itself? Is not a Christian man the brother of a Christian woman, and is she not his sister? Is not a baptized man the spiritual brother of a baptized woman? How foolish we are! If a man instructs his wife in the gospel and in faith in Christ, does he not truly become her father in Christ? And is it not lawful for her to remain his wife? Would not Paul have had the right to marry a girl from among the Corinthians, of whom he boasts that he became their father in Christ?[v] See then, how Christian liberty has been suppressed through the blindness of human superstition.

There is even less in the "legal affinity," and yet they have set it above the divine right of marriage.[w] Nor would I agree to that impediment which they call "disparity of religion,"[x] which forbids one to marry an unbaptized person, either simply, or on condition that she be converted to the faith. Who made this prohibition? God or human beings? Who gave human beings the power to prohibit such a marriage? Indeed, the spirits that speak lies in hypocrisy, as Paul says.[y] Of them it must be said: "Godless men have told me fables which do not conform to your law" [Ps. 119:85].[226] The heathen Patricius married the Christian Monica, mother of St. Augustine;[z] why should that not be permitted today? The same stupid, or rather, wicked severity is seen in the "impediment of crime," as when a man has married a woman with whom he previously had committed adultery, or when he plotted to bring about the death of a woman's husband in order to be able to wed the widow.[a] I ask you, whence comes this cruelty of person toward person, which even God never demanded?

226. Luther is quoting the Latin Vulgate version of this psalm (118 in the Vulgate), which does not conform to modern English translations.

v 1 Cor. 4:15.

w The first sentence is also missing from the Wittenberg and Jena editions; see n. 219, p. 192.

x Cf. Aquinas, *STh* III Suppl., q. 59, "On the Disparity of Worship as an Impediment to Marriage."

y 1 Tim. 4:2.

z Cf. Augustine, *Confessions* 9, 9, 19.

a Cf. *Decr. Greg. IX*, lib. 4, tit. 7.

Do they pretend not to know that Bathsheba, the wife of Uriah, was wed by David, a most saintly man, after the double crime of adultery and murder?[b] If the divine law did this, what are these despotic men doing to their fellow servants?

They[c] also recognize what they call "the impediment of a tie," that is, when a man is bound to another woman by betrothal. Here they conclude that, if he has had sexual relations with a second woman, his engagement to the first becomes null and void. This I do not understand at all. I hold that he who has betrothed himself to one woman no longer belongs to himself. Because of this fact, by the prohibition of the divine law, he belongs to the first with whom he has not had intercourse, even though he has had intercourse with the second. For it was not in his power to give the latter what was no longer his own; he has deceived her and actually committed adultery. But they regard the matter differently because they pay more heed to the carnal union than to the divine command, according to which the man, having made a promise to the first woman, should keep it always. For whoever would give anything must give of that which is his own. And God forbids us to transgress and wrong a brother or sister in any matter.[d] This must be observed over and above all human ordinances.. Therefore I believe that such a man cannot with a good conscience live in marriage with a second woman, and this impediment should be completely reversed. For if a monastic vow makes a man no longer his own, why does not a pledge of mutual faithfulness do the same? After all, faithfulness is one of the precepts and fruits of the Spirit, in Gal. 5:[22], while a monastic vow is of human invention. And if a wife may claim her husband back, despite the fact that he has taken a monastic vow, why may not an engaged woman claim back her betrothed, even though he has intercourse with another? But we have said above that he who has promised to marry a girl may not take a monastic vow, but is in duty bound to marry her because he is in duty bound to keep faith with her; and this faith he may not break for any human ordinance, because it is commanded

b 2 Sam. 11:1-27.

c This entire paragraph is missing from the Wittenberg and Jena editions; see n. 219, p. 192.

d 1 Thess. 4:6.

by God. Much more should the man here keep faith with his first betrothed, since he could not promise marriage to a second except with a lying heart; and therefore did not really promise it, but deceived her, his neighbor, against God's command. Therefore, the "impediment of error"[227] enters in here, by which his marriage to the second woman is rendered null and void.

The "impediment of ordination" is also the mere invention of men, especially since they prate that it annuls even a marriage already contracted.[228] They constantly exalt their own ordinances above the commands of God. I do not indeed sit in judgment on the present state of the priestly order, but I observe that Paul charges a bishop to be the husband of one wife.[e] Hence, no marriage of deacon, priest, bishop, or any other order can be annulled, although it is true that Paul knew nothing of this species of priests and of the orders we have today. Perish then those cursed human ordinances which have crept into the church only to multiply perils, sins, and evils! There exists, therefore, between a priest and his wife a true and indissoluble marriage, approved by the divine commandment. But what if wicked men in sheer despotism prohibit or annul it? So be it! Let it be wrong among men; it is nevertheless right before God, whose command must take precedence if it conflicts with the commands of men.[f]

An[g] equally lying invention is that "impediment of public decency," by which contracted marriages are annulled. I am incensed at that foolhardy wickedness which is so ready to put asunder what God has joined together that one may well recognize Antichrist in it, for it opposes all that Christ has done and taught. What earthly reason is there for holding that no relative of a deceased fiancé, even to the fourth degree of consanguinity, may marry his fiancée? That is not a judgment of public decency, but ignorance of public decency. Why was not this judgment of public decency found among the people of Israel, who were endowed with the best laws, the laws of God? On the contrary, the next of kin was even compelled by the law of God to marry the widow of his relative.[229] Must the people of Christian lib-

e 1 Tim. 3:2.

f Acts 5:29.

g The following two paragraphs are not in the Wittenberg and Jena editions; see n. 219, p. 192.

227. Luther sarcastically pits one impediment against the other. Normally, the "impediment of error" has to do with mistaken identity. See Aquinas, *STh* III Suppl., q. 51, a. 2: "Wherefore error, in order to void marriage, must needs be about the essentials of marriage. Now marriage includes two things, namely the two persons who are joined together, and the mutual power over one another wherein marriage consists. The first of these is removed by error concerning the person, the second by error regarding the condition, since a slave cannot freely give power over his body to another, without his master's consent. For this reason these two errors, and no others, are an impediment to matrimony."

228. Cf. Aquinas, *STh* III Suppl., q. 53, a. 3: "Hence among the Greeks and other Eastern peoples a sacred order is an impediment to the contracting of matrimony but it does not forbid the use of marriage already contracted. . . . But in the Western Church it is an impediment both to marriage and to the use of marriage."

229. Cf. Deut. 25:5: "When brothers reside together, and one of them dies and has no son, the wife of the deceased shall not be married outside the family to a stranger. Her husband's brother shall go in to her, taking her in marriage, and performing the duty of a husband's brother to her."

erty be burdened with more severe laws than the people of legal bondage?[230]

But, to make an end of these—figments rather than impediments—I will say that so far there seem to me to be no impediments that may justly annul a contracted marriage except these: sexual impotence, ignorance of a previously contracted marriage, and a vow of chastity. Still, concerning this latter vow, I am to this day so far from certain that I do not know at what age such a vow is to be regarded as binding, as I also said above in discussing the sacrament of baptism. Thus you may learn, from this one question of marriage, how wretchedly and desperately all the activities of the church have been confused, hindered, ensnared, and subjected to danger through pestilent, ignorant, and wicked ordinances of men, so that there is no hope of betterment unless we abolish at one stroke all the laws of all men, and having restored the gospel of liberty we follow it in judging and regulating all things. Amen.

230. The "people of legal bondage" (*populum servitutis legalis*) is certainly a pejorative phrase regarding Israel in the Old Testament, but the language is shaped by Pauline usage, especially Galatians 4, rather than another kind of anti-Jewish sentiment.

[Impotence]

We must therefore speak of sexual impotence, in order that we may the more readily advise the souls that are laboring in peril. But first I wish to state that what I have said about impediments is intended to apply after a marriage has been contracted. I mean to say that no marriage should be annulled by any such impediment. But as to marriages which are yet to be contracted, I would briefly repeat what I have said above. If there is the stress of youthful passion or some other necessity for which the pope grants dispensation, then any brother may also grant a dispensation to another or even to himself, and following that counsel snatch his wife out of the power of tyrannical laws as best he can. For with what right am I deprived of my liberty by somebody else's superstition and ignorance? If the pope grants a dispensation for money, why should not I, for my soul's salvation, grant a dispensation to myself or to my brother? Does the pope set up laws? Let him set them up for himself, and keep hands off my liberty, or I will take it by stealth!

Now[h] let us discuss the matter of impotence.

h The next two paragraphs were left out of the Wittenberg and Jena editions; see n. 231, p. 199.

Consider the following case: A woman, wed to an impotent man, is unable to prove her husband's impotence in court, or perhaps she is unwilling to do so with the Mass of evidence and all the notoriety which the law demands; yet she is desirous of having children or is unable to remain continent. Now suppose I had counseled her to procure a divorce from her husband in order to marry another, satisfied that her own and her husband's conscience and their experience were ample testimony of his impotence; but the husband refused his consent to this. Then I would further counsel her, with the consent of the man (who is not really her husband, but only a dweller under the same roof with her), to have intercourse with another, say her husband's brother, but to keep this marriage secret and to ascribe the children to the so-called putative father. The question is: Is such a woman saved and in a saved state? I answer: Certainly, because in this case an error, ignorance of the man's impotence, impedes the marriage; and the tyranny of the laws permits no divorce. But the woman is free through the divine law, and cannot be compelled to remain continent. Therefore the man ought to concede her right, and give up to somebody else the wife who is his only in outward appearance.

Moreover, if the man will not give his consent, or agree to this separation—rather than allow the woman to burn with desire[i] or to commit adultery—I would counsel her to contract a marriage with another and flee to a distant unknown place. What other counsel can be given to one constantly struggling with the dangers of natural emotions? Now I know that some are troubled by the fact that the children of this secret marriage are not the rightful heirs of their putative father. But if it was done with the consent of the husband, then the children will be the rightful heirs. If, however, it was done without his knowledge or against his will, then let unbiased Christian reason, or better, charity, decide which one of the two has done the greater injury to the other. The wife alienates the inheritance, but the husband has deceived his wife and is defrauding her completely of her body and her life. Is not the sin of a man who wastes his wife's body and life a greater sin than that of the woman who merely alienates the temporal goods of her husband? Let him,

i 1 Cor. 7:9.

therefore, agree to a divorce, or else be satisfied with heirs not his own, for by his own fault he deceived an innocent girl and defrauded her both of life and of the full use of her body, besides giving her an almost irresistible cause for committing adultery. Let both be weighed in the same scales. Certainly, by every right, fraud should recoil on the fraudulent, and whoever has done an injury must make it good. What is the difference between such a husband and the man who holds another man's wife captive together with her husband? Is not such a tyrant compelled to support wife and children and husband, or else to set them free? Why should not the same hold true here? Therefore I maintain that the man should be compelled either to submit to a divorce or to support the other man's child as his heir. Doubtless this would be the judgment of charity. In that case, the impotent man, who is not really the husband, should support the heir of his wife in the same spirit in which he would at great expense wait on his wife if she fell sick or suffered some other ill; for it is by his fault and not by his wife's that she suffers this ill. This I have set forth to the best of my ability, for the strengthening of anxious consciences, because my desire is to bring my afflicted brothers and sisters in this captivity what little comfort I can.[231]

[Divorce]

As to divorce, it is still a question for debate whether it is allowable.[j] For my part I so greatly detest divorce that I should prefer bigamy to it;[232] but whether it is allowable, I do not venture to decide. Christ himself, the Chief Shepherd, says in Matt. 5[:32]: "Every one who divorces his wife, except on the ground of unchastity, makes her an adulteress; and whoever marries a divorced woman commits adultery." Christ, then, permits divorce, but only on the ground of unchastity. The pope must, therefore, be in error whenever he grants a divorce for any other cause; and no one should feel safe who has obtained a dispensation by this temerity (not authority) of the pope. Yet it is still a greater wonder to me, why they compel a man to remain unmarried after being separated from his wife by divorce, and why they will not permit him to remarry.[k] For if Christ permits divorce

j Cf. *Decr. Greg. IX*, lib. 5, tit. 19, *de divortiis*.

k Cf. *Decr. Greg. IX*, lib. 4, tit. 19, *de divortiis*, c. 2.

231. The advice given here was clearly found to be difficult by Luther's followers who removed it from the edition in his collected works. Still, several factors ought to be considered when judging the two preceding paragraphs: (1) Couched in the language of the scholars only, this Latin treatise was not intended for popular consumption but rather as a guide for bewildered and confused priests, who were called upon in the confessional to give practical advice and spiritual comfort to troubled souls. (2) The impediment of impotency was, even according to Roman church law, sufficient ground for declaring a marriage null and void. (3) But the legal process of securing an annulment demanded such an involved procedure for establishing proof that it was equally unpleasant for both parties. (4) Then, as now, divorce under any circumstances was absolutely forbidden by Roman church law. (5) As an alternate to an impossible legal solution, Luther's suggestion of a secret marriage was not without precedent; common law in parts of Westphalia and Lower Saxony, for example, prescribed that a man who could not perform his conjugal duty was required to seek satisfaction for his wife through a neighbor.

232. Luther famously gave this advice later to King Henry VIII of England and Landgrave Philip of Hesse, regarding it to be the lesser of two evils insofar as it was not without divinely sanctioned precedent in the Old Testament. This phrase, "that I should prefer bigamy to it," was deleted from the Wittenberg and Jena editions; see n. 231.

on the ground of unchastity and compels no one to remain unmarried, and if Paul would rather have us marry than burn with desire,[l] then he certainly seems to permit a man to marry another woman in the place of the one who has been put away. I wish that this subject were fully discussed and made clear and decided, so that counsel might be given in the infinite perils of those who, without any fault of their own, are nowadays compelled to remain unmarried; that is, those whose wives or husbands have run away and deserted them, to come back perhaps after ten years, perhaps never! This matter troubles and distresses me, for there are daily cases, whether by the special malice of Satan or because of our neglect of the Word of God.

I, indeed, who alone against all cannot establish any rule in this matter, would yet greatly desire at least the passage in 1 Cor. 7[:15] to be applied here: "But if the unbelieving partner desires to separate, let it be so; in such a case the brother or sister is not bound." Here the Apostle gives permission to put away the unbeliever who departs and to set the believing spouse free to marry again. Why should not the same hold true when a believer—that is, a believer in name, but in truth as much an unbeliever as the one Paul speaks of—deserts his wife, especially if he intends never to return. I certainly can see no difference between the two. But I believe that if in the Apostle's day an unbelieving deserter had returned and had become a believer or had promised to live again with his believing wife, it would not have been permitted, but he too would have been given the right to marry again. Nevertheless, in these matters I decide nothing (as I have said), although there is nothing that I would rather see decided, since nothing at present more grievously perplexes me, and many others with me. I would have nothing decided here on the mere authority of the pope and the bishops; but if two learned and good men agreed in the name of Christ[m] and published their opinion in the spirit of Christ, I should prefer their judgment even to such councils as are assembled nowadays, famous only for numbers and authority, not for scholarship and saintliness. Therefore I hang up my lyre[233] on this matter until a better man confers with me about it.

233. An allusion to Luther's remarks at the beginning of the treatise that he is writing a "prelude." Cf. Ps. 137:1-2: "By the rivers of Babylon—there we sat down and there we wept when we remembered Zion. On the willows there we hung up our lyres."

l 1 Cor. 7:9.

m Cf. Matt. 18:19-20.

Ordination

Of this sacrament the church of Christ knows nothing; it is an invention of the church of the pope. Not only is there nowhere any promise of grace attached to it, but there is not a single word said about it in the whole New Testament. Now it is ridiculous to put forth as a sacrament of God something that cannot be proved to have been instituted by God. I do not hold that this rite, which has been observed for so many centuries, should be condemned; but in sacred things I am opposed to the invention of human fictions. And it is not right to give out as divinely instituted what was not divinely instituted, lest we become a laughingstock to our opponents. We ought to see that every article of faith of which we boast is certain, pure, and based on clear passages of Scripture. But we are utterly unable to do that in the case of the sacrament under consideration.

This 1561 engraving illustrates one aspect of ordination to the priesthood: the laying on of hands. The bishop stands and lays his hands on the head of each person being ordained. The ordainee kneels and carries a chasuble, a priestly vestment, over one arm.

The church has no power to make new divine promises of grace, as some prate, who hold that what is decreed by the church is of no less authority than what is decreed by God, since the church is under the guidance of the Holy Spirit.[234] For the church was born by the word of promise through faith, and by this same word is nourished and preserved. That is to say, it is the promises of God that make the church, and not the church that makes the promise of God. For the Word of God is incomparably superior to the church, and in this Word the church, being a creature, has nothing to decree, ordain, or make, but only to be decreed, ordained, and made. For who begets his own parent? Who first brings forth his own maker?

This one thing indeed the church can do: It can distinguish the Word of God from the words of men; as Augustine confesses that he believed the gospel because he was moved by the authority of the church which proclaimed that this is the

234. Cf. John 14:16-17, 26: "And I will ask the Father, and he will give you another Advocate, to be with you forever. This is the Spirit of truth. But the Advocate, the Holy Spirit, whom the Father will send in my name, will teach you everything, and remind you of all that I have said to you"; John 16:13: "When the Spirit of truth comes, he will guide you into all the truth."

gospel.[235] Not that the church is therefore above the gospel; if that were true, the church would also be above God, in whom we believe, because it is the church that proclaims God is God. But, as Augustine says elsewhere,[236] the truth itself lays hold on the soul and thus renders it able to judge most certainly of all things; however, the soul is not able to judge the truth, but is compelled to say with unerring certainty that this is the truth. For example, our mind declares with unerring certainty that three and seven are ten; and yet it cannot give a reason why this is true, although it cannot deny that it is true. It is clearly taken captive by the truth; and, rather than judging the truth, it is itself judged by it. There is such a mind also in the church, when under the enlightenment of the Spirit she judges and approves doctrines; she is unable to prove it, and yet is most certain of having it. For as among philosophers no one judges the general concepts, but all are judged by them, so it is among us with the mind of the Spirit, who judges all things and is judged by no one, as the Apostle says.[237] But we will discuss this another time.

Let this then stand fast: The church can give no promises of grace; that is the work of God alone. Therefore she cannot institute a sacrament. But even if she could, it still would not necessarily follow that ordination is a sacrament. For who knows which is the church that has the Spirit? For when such decisions are made there are usually only a few bishops or scholars present; and it is possible that these may not be really of the church. All may err, as councils have repeatedly erred, particularly the Council of Constance,[n] which erred most wickedly of all. Only that which has the approval of the church universal, and not of the Roman church alone, rests on a trustworthy foundation. I therefore admit that ordination is a certain churchly rite, on a par with many others introduced by the church fathers, such as the consecration of vessels, houses, vestments, water, salt, candles, herbs, wine, and the like.[238] No one calls any of these a sacrament, nor is there in them any promise. In the same manner, to anoint a man's hands with oil, or to shave his head and the like is not to administer a sacrament, since no promise is attached to them; they are simply being prepared for a certain office, like a vessel or an instrument.

n See n. 52, p. 118.

235. Augustine, *Against the Epistle of Manichaeus Called "Fundamental"* 5, 6: "I should not believe the gospel except as moved by the authority of the church catholic."

236. Augustine, *On the Trinity* 9, 6, 10: "the judgment of truth from above is still strong and clear, and rests firmly upon the utterly indestructible rules of its own right; and if it is covered as it were by cloudiness of corporeal images, yet is not wrapped up and confounded in them."

237. Cf. 1 Cor. 2:11-13: "For what human being knows what is truly human except the human spirit that is within? So also no one comprehends what is truly God's except the Spirit of God. Now we have received not the spirit of the world, but the Spirit that is from God, so that we may understand the gifts bestowed on us by God. And we speak of these things in words not taught by human wisdom but taught by the Spirit, interpreting spiritual things to those who are spiritual."

238. Salt was used in connection with the rite of baptism, given to catechumens in the early church to signify purification, wisdom, and the promise of immortality; cf. Augustine, *Confessions* 1, 11. Candles were blessed especially for their use in Candelmas, the Feast of the Purification of Mary. Herbs, fruits, and flowers were often blessed at the beginning of the harvest season in connection with the Feast of the Assumption of Mary.

But you will say: "What do you do with Dionysius, who in his *Ecclesiastical Hierarchy* enumerates six sacraments, among which he also includes ordination?"[239] I answer: I am well aware that this is the one writer of antiquity who is cited in support of the seven sacraments, although he omits marriage and so has only six. But we read nothing at all about these "sacraments" in the rest of the fathers; nor do they ever regard them as sacraments when they speak of these things. For the invention of sacraments is of recent date.[240] Indeed, to speak more boldly, it greatly displeases me to assign such importance to this Dionysius, whoever he may have been, for he shows hardly any signs of solid learning. I would ask, by what authority and with what arguments does he prove his hodge-podge about the angels in his *Celestial Hierarchy*—a book over which many curious and superstitious spirits have cudgeled their brains? If one were to read and judge without prejudice, is not everything in it his own fancy and very much like a dream? But in his *Theology*, which is rightly called *Mystical*, of which certain very ignorant theologians make so much, he is downright dangerous, for he is more of a Platonist than a Christian. So if I had my way, no believing soul would give the least attention to these books. So far, indeed, from learning Christ in them, you will lose even what you already know of him. I speak from experience. Let us rather hear Paul, that we may learn Jesus Christ and him crucified.[o] He is the way, the life, and the truth;[p] he is the ladder[q] by which we come to the Father, as he says: "No one comes to the Father, but by me."[r]

Similarly, in the *Ecclesiastical Hierarchy*, what does this Dionysius do but describe certain churchly rites, and amuse himself with allegories without proving anything? Just as has been done in our time by the author of the book entitled *Rationale divinorum*.[241] Such allegorical studies are for idle people. Do you think I should find it difficult to amuse myself with allegories about anything in creation? Did not Bonaventura by allegory draw the liberal arts into theology?[242] And Gerson even converted the smaller Donatus into a mystical theologian.[243] It would not be

o 1 Cor. 2:2.

p John 14:6.

q Cf. Gen. 28:12; John 1:51.

r John 14:6.

239. Dionysius the Areopagite (a pseudonymous author from the sixth century) wrote several influential writings marked by a strong neo-Platonic structure. The *Ecclesiastical Hierarchy* lists as sacraments baptism, the Eucharist, unction, priestly ordination, monastic ordination, and burial.

240. A number of sacraments were listed in early Scholasticism with Peter Lombard's numbering of seven in his *Sentences* (4, d. 2, c. 1) winning general acceptance. These were not made official church doctrine until the bull *Exultate Deo* at the Council of Florence in 1439.

241. Guillaume Durandus (c. 1230–1296), bishop of Mende, wrote an explanation of the rites, ceremonies, and vestments used in the Mass: *Rationale divinorum officiorum* (i.e., "Explanation for the Divine Offices").

242. Like Aquinas, Bonaventure of Bagnoregio (1221–1274) sought to bring correlation and harmony between theological and philosophical knowledge. However, his *Opusculum de reductione artium ad theologiam* (*Little Work on the Restoration of the Arts to Theology*) takes a different approach than Aquinas, seeing the arts and sciences echoing in theology through types and figures.

243. Jean Gerson (1363–1429) was chancellor of the University of Paris. In addition to his influence in ecclesiastical affairs, Gerson also wrote several popular devotional and pastoral works. Luther is referring to his allegory of the *Ars minor*, a Latin grammar written by

difficult for me to compose a better hierarchy than that of Dionysius; for he knew nothing of pope, cardinals, and archbishops, and put the bishop at the top. Who has so weak a mind as not to be able to launch into allegories? I would not have a theologian devote himself to allegories until he has exhausted the legitimate and simple meaning of the Scripture; otherwise his theology will bring him into danger, as Origen discovered.[244]

Therefore a thing does not need to be a sacrament simply because Dionysius so describes it. Otherwise, why not also make a sacrament of the funeral processions, which he describes in his book, and which continue to this day? There will then be as many sacraments as there have been rites and ceremonies multiplied in the church. Standing on so unsteady a foundation, they have nevertheless invented "characters" which they attribute to this sacrament of theirs and which are indelibly impressed on those who are ordained.[245] Whence do such ideas come, I ask? By what authority, with what arguments, are they established? We do not object to their being free to invent, say, and assert whatever they please; but we also insist on our liberty, that they shall not arrogate to themselves the right to turn their opinions into articles of faith, as they have hitherto presumed to do. It is enough that we accommodate ourselves to their rites and ceremonies for the sake of peace; but we refuse to be bound by such things as if they were necessary to salvation, which they are not. Let them lay aside their despotic demand, and we shall yield free obedience to their wishes, in order that we may live in peace with one another. It is a shameful and wicked slavery for a Christian, who is free, to be subject to any but heavenly and divine ordinances.

We come now to their strongest argument. It is this: Christ said at the Last Supper: "Do this in remembrance of me."[s] "Look," they say, "here Christ ordained the apostles to the priesthood." From this passage they also concluded, among other things, that both kinds are to be administered to the priest alone. In fact, they have drawn out of this passage whatever they pleased, as men who would arrogate to themselves the liberty to prove anything whatever from any words of Christ. But is that interpreting the words of God? I ask you: Is it? Christ gives us no promise here, but only commands that this be done in remembrance of

s Luke 22:19; 1 Cor. 11:24-25.

the fourth-century Roman grammarian, Aelius Donatus (flourished mid-fourth century).

244. Nine statements of Origen were condemned as heretical after his death by an edict of Emperor Justinian I (c. 483-565) and published by the Council of Constantinople in 553; see n. 64, p. 122.

245. The "indelible character" (*character indelibilis*) as a special mark or seal left on the soul after receiving three of the seven sacraments: baptism, confirmation, and ordination. Because the soul has been impressed with this mark, the sacrament cannot be repeated. After ordination a priest, therefore, can never be a layman again. The notion was first officially set forth by the Council of Florence in 1439, "Among these sacraments there are three—baptism, confirmation, and orders—which indelibly impress upon the soul a character, i.e. a certain spiritual mark which distinguishes them from the rest."

him. Why do they not conclude that he also ordained priests when he laid upon them the office of the Word and baptism, and said: "Go into all the world and preach the gospel to the whole creation, baptizing them in the name, etc."[t] For it is the proper duty of priests to preach and to baptize. Or, since it is nowadays the chief, and (as they say) indispensable duty of priests to read the canonical hours,[246] why have they not discovered the sacrament of ordination in those passages in which Christ commanded them to pray, as he did in many places—particularly in the garden, that they might not enter into temptation?[u] But perhaps they will evade this argument by saying that it is not commanded to pray; it is enough to read the canonical hours. Then it follows that this priestly work can be proved nowhere in the Scriptures, and thus their praying priesthood is not of God; as, indeed, it is not.

But which of the ancient fathers claimed that in this passage priests were ordained? Where does this new interpretation come from? I will tell you. They have sought by this means to set up a seedbed of implacable discord, by which clergy and laypersons should be separated from each other farther than heaven from earth, to the incredible injury of the grace of baptism and to the confusion of our fellowship in the gospel. Here, indeed, are the roots of that detestable tyranny of the clergy over the laity.[247] Trusting in the external anointing by which their hands are consecrated, in the tonsure and in vestments, they not only exalt themselves above the rest of the lay Christians, who are only anointed with the Holy Spirit, but regard them almost as dogs and unworthy to be included with themselves in the church. Hence they are bold to demand, to exact, to threaten, to urge, to oppress, as much as they please. In short, the sacrament of ordination has been and still is an admirable device for establishing all the horrible things that have been done hitherto in the church, and are yet to be done. Here Christian brotherhood has perished, here shepherds have been turned into wolves, servants into tyrants, churchmen into worse than worldlings.

If they were forced to grant that all of us that have been baptized are equally priests, as indeed we are, and that only the

t Mark 16:15; Matt. 28:19.

u Matt. 26:41.

246. The canonical hours are the seven daily prayer offices part of the early monastic tradition. Inspired in part by the words of Ps. 119:164, "Seven times a day I praise you for your righteous laws," they are respectively: matins (including nocturns and lauds), prime, tierce, sext, nones, vespers, and compline.

247. Cf. Luther's earlier treatise *The Address to the Christian Nobility* (1520), in which he identifies this spiritual division between the laity and the priesthood as one of the "Roman walls" that the papacy has erected to protect itself from being reformed. It is in this place that Luther introduces the notion that the priesthood in the New Testament has been given to all people through baptism and that ordination only signifies an office that exercises publicly the spiritual authority that all Christians possess. Luther's most thorough articulation of this spiritual priesthood of the baptized was set forth in his subsequent treatise against Hieronymus Emser (see n. 11, p. 104.) *Answer to the Hyperchristian, Hyperspiritual and Hyperlearned Book by Goat Emser in Leipzig* (1521), LW 39:137–224.

ministry was committed to them, yet with our common consent, they would then know that they have no right to rule over us except insofar as we freely concede it. For thus it is written in 1 Pet. 2[:9]: "You are a chosen race, a royal priesthood, and a priestly royalty." Therefore we are all priests, as many of us as are Christians. But the priests, as we call them, are ministers chosen from among us. All that they do is done in our name; the priesthood is nothing but a ministry. This we learn from 1 Cor. 4[:1]: "This is how one should regard us, as servants of Christ and stewards of the mysteries of God."

From this it follows that whoever does not preach the Word, though he was called by the church to do this very thing, is no priest at all, and that the sacrament of ordination can be nothing else than a certain rite by which the church chooses its preachers. For this is the way a priest is defined in Mal. 2[:7]: "The lips of a priest should guard knowledge, and people should seek instruction from his mouth, for he is the messenger of the LORD of hosts." You may be certain, then, that whoever is not a messenger of the Lord of hosts, or whoever is called to do anything else than such messenger service—if I may so term it[248]—is in no sense a priest; as Hos. 4[:6] says: "Because you have rejected knowledge, I reject you from being a priest to me." They are also called shepherds[v] because they are to shepherd, that is, to teach. Therefore, those who are ordained only to read the canonical hours and to offer Masses are indeed papal priests, but not Christian priests, because they not only do not preach, but they are not even called to preach. Indeed, it comes to this, that a priesthood of that sort is a different estate altogether from the office of preaching. Thus they are hour-reading and Mass-saying priests—sort of living idols called priests—really such priests as Jeroboam ordained, in Beth-aven, taken from the lowest dregs of the people, and not of Levi's tribe.[w]

248. Luther is playing with the broader and narrower meanings of *angelus domini* in Malachi 2, i.e., messenger and angel.

See how far the glory of the church has departed! The whole earth is filled with priests, bishops, cardinals, and clergy; yet not one of them preaches so far as his official duty is concerned, unless he is called to do so by a different call over and above his sacramental ordination. Every one thinks he is doing full justice to his ordination by mumbling the vain repetitions of his

v Lat. *pastores*.

w 1 Kgs. 12:31.

prescribed prayers and by celebrating Masses. Moreover, he never really prays when he repeats those hours; or if he does pray, he prays them for himself. And he offers his Mass as if it were a sacrifice, which is the height of perversity because the Mass consists in the use made of the sacrament. It is clear, therefore, that the ordination, which, as a sacrament, makes clergymen of this sort of men, is in truth nothing but a mere fiction, devised by men who understand nothing about the church, the priesthood, the ministry of the Word, or the sacraments. Thus, as the "sacrament" is, so are the priests it makes. To such errors and such blindness has been added a still worse captivity: in order to separate themselves still farther from other Christians, whom they deem profane, they have emasculated themselves, like the Galli, who were the priests of Cybele,[249] and they have taken upon themselves the burden of a spurious celibacy.

To satisfy this hypocrisy and the working of this error it was not enough that bigamy should be prohibited, that is, the having of two wives at one time, as it was forbidden in the law (and as is the accepted meaning of the term); but they have called it bigamy if a man marries two virgins, one after the other, or if he marries one widow.[250] Indeed, so holy is the holiness of this most holy sacrament that no man can become a priest if he has married a virgin and his wife is still living.[x] And—here we reach the very summit of sanctity—a man is even prevented from entering the priesthood if he has married a woman who was not a virgin, though he did so in ignorance or by unfortunate mischance.[251] But if one has defiled six hundred harlots, or violated countless matrons and virgins, or even kept many Ganymedes,[252] that would be no impediment to his becoming bishop or cardinal or pope. Moreover, the Apostle's word "husband of one wife" [1 Tim. 3:2] must now be interpreted to mean "the prelate of one church," and this has given rise to the "incompatible benefices."[253] At the same time the pope, that munificent dispenser, may join to one man three, twenty, or a hundred wives, that is, churches, if he is bribed with money or power, that is, "moved by godly charity and constrained by the care of the churches."[y]

O pontiffs worthy of this venerable sacrament of ordination! O princes, not of the catholic churches, but of the synagogues of

x Cf. *Decr. Greg. IX*, lib. 1, tit. 21, *de bigamis non ordinandis*, c. 3.

y 2 Cor. 11:28.

249. Galli (sg. Gallus) was the name for the eunuch priests who served Cybele, the ancient Phrygian goddess of nature whose worship became part of the cultic practices in the Roman Empire.

250. Aquinas, *STh* III Suppl., q. 66, a. 1: "By the sacrament of order a man is appointed to the ministry of the sacraments; and he who has to administer the sacraments to others must suffer from no defect in the sacraments. . . . the perfect signification of the sacrament requires the husband to have only one wife, and the wife to have but one husband; and consequently bigamy, which does away with this, causes irregularity. And there are four kinds of bigamy: the first is when a man has several lawful wives successively; the second is when a man has several wives at once, one in law, the other in fact; the third, when he has several successively, one in law, the other in fact; the fourth, when a man marries a widow."

251. Aquinas, *STh* III Suppl., q. 66, a. 3: "Gregory says, 'We command thee never to make unlawful ordinations, nor to admit to holy orders a bigamist, or one who has married a woman that is not a virgin, or one who is unlettered, or one who is deformed in his limbs, or bound to do penance or to perform some civil duty, or who is in any state of subjection.'"

252. In Greek mythology, Ganymede was the youthful consort of Zeus.

253. Benefices, rents, and profits derived from lands endowed to the church (see the earlier note on the church and feudal system, p. 163) in exchange for spiritual services were part of the livelihood for bishops. Laws were originally enacted that prevented bishops from holding more than one benefice, but the distinction between "compatible" and "incompatible" benefices was used to justify plurality in a variety of cases, as sanctioned by the pope. This distinction was used toward widespread abuse and was part of the reforms taken up by the Council of Trent.

Satan[z] and of darkness itself! I would cry out with Isaiah, "You scoffers, who rule this people in Jerusalem";[a] and with Amos 6[:1], "Woe to those who are at ease in Zion, and to those who feel secure on the mountain of Samaria, the notable men of the first of the nations, that go in with state into the house of Israel, etc.!" O the disgrace that these monstrous priests bring upon the church of God! Where are there any bishops or priests who even know the gospel, not to speak of preaching it? Why then do they boast of being priests? Why do they desire to be regarded as holier and better and mightier than other Christians, who are merely laymen? To read the hours—what unlearned men, or (as the Apostle says) men speaking with tongues[b] cannot do that? But to pray the hours—that belongs to monks, hermits, and men in private life, even though they are laymen. The duty of a priest is to preach, and if he does not preach he is as much a priest as a picture of a man is a man. Does ordaining such babbling priests make one a bishop? Or blessing churches and bells? Or confirming children? Certainly not. Any deacon or layman could do as much. It is the ministry of the Word that makes the priest and the bishop.

Therefore my advice is: Begone, all of you that would live in safety; flee, young men, and do not enter upon this holy estate, unless you are determined to preach the gospel, and can believe that you are made not one whit better than the laity through this "sacrament" of ordination! For to read the hours is nothing, and to offer Mass is to receive the sacrament. What then is there left to you that every layperson does not have? Tonsure and vestments? A sorry priest, indeed, who consists of tonsure and vestments! Or the oil poured on your fingers? But every Christian is anointed and sanctified both in body and soul with the oil of the Holy Spirit. In ancient times every Christian handled the sacrament with his hands as often as the priests do now. But today our superstition counts it a great crime if the laity touch either the bare chalice or the corporal;[254] not even a nun who is a pure virgin would be permitted to wash the palls and the sacred linens of the altar. O God! See how far the sacrosanct sanctity of this "sacrament" of ordination has gone! I expect the time will

254. The "corporal" is the altar cloth upon which the consecrated bread and wine are placed.

z Rev. 2:9.

a Isa. 28:14

b Cf. 1 Cor. 14:23.

come when the laity will not be permitted to touch the altar—except when they offer their money. I almost burst with indignation when I contemplate the wicked tyrannies of these brazen men, who with their farcical and childish fancies mock and overthrow the liberty and glory of the Christian religion.

Let all, therefore, who know themselves to be Christian, be assured of this, that we are all equally priests, that is to say, we have the same power in respect to the Word and the sacraments. However, no one may make use of this power except by the consent of the community or by the call of a superior. (For what is the common property of all, no individual may arrogate to himself, unless he is called.) And therefore this "sacrament" of ordination, if it is anything at all, is nothing else than a certain rite whereby one is called to the ministry of the church. Furthermore, the priesthood is properly nothing but the ministry of the Word—the Word, I say; not the law, but the gospel. And the diaconate is the ministry, not of reading the Gospel or the Epistle, as is the present practice, but of distributing the church's aid to the poor, so that the priests may be relieved of the burden of temporal matters and may give themselves more freely to prayer and the Word. For this was the purpose of the institution of the diaconate, as we read in Acts 5.[255] Whoever, therefore, does not know or preach the gospel is not only no priest or bishop, but he is a kind of pest to the church, who under the false title of priest or bishop, or dressed in sheep's clothing, actually does violence to the gospel and plays the wolf[256] in the church.

Therefore, unless these priests and bishops, with whom the church abounds today, work out their salvation[c] in some other way; unless they realize that they are not priests or bishops, and bemoan the fact that they bear the name of an office whose duties they either do not know or cannot fulfill, and thus with prayers and tears lament their wretched hypocritical life—unless they do this, they are truly the people of eternal perdition, and the words of Isa. 5[:13f.] are fulfilled in them: "Therefore my people go into exile for want of knowledge; their nobles are dying of hunger, and their multitude is parched with thirst. Therefore, Hell has enlarged its appetite and opened its mouth beyond measure, and the nobility of Jerusalem and her multitude go down, her throng

255. Luther is referring to the setting apart of Stephen and six others to distribute food to the poor and widows in Acts 6:1-4.

256. Cf. Matt. 7:15: "Beware of false prophets, who come to you in sheep's clothing but inwardly are ravenous wolves."

c Cf. Phil. 2:12.

and he who exults in her." What a dreadful word for our age, in which Christians are swallowed up in so deep an abyss!

According to what the Scriptures teach us, what we call the priesthood is a ministry. So I cannot understand at all why one who has once been made a priest cannot again become a layperson;[257] for the sole difference between him and a layperson is his ministry. But to depose a man from the priesthood is by no means impossible, because even now it is the usual penalty imposed upon guilty priests. They are either suspended temporarily, or permanently deprived of their office. For that fiction of an "indelible character" has long since become a laughingstock. I admit that the pope imparts this "character," but Christ knows nothing of it; and a priest who is consecrated with it becomes the lifelong servant and captive, not of Christ, but of the pope, as is the case nowadays. Moreover, unless I am greatly mistaken, if this sacrament and this fiction ever fall to the ground, the papacy with its "characters" will scarcely survive. Then our joyous liberty will be restored to us; we shall realize that we are all equal by every right. Having cast off the yoke of tyranny, we shall know that the one who is a Christian has Christ; and that the one who has Christ has all things that are Christ's, and can do all things.[d] Of this I will write more,[258] and more vigorously, as soon as I perceive that the above has displeased my friends the papists.

257. Because of the notion of indelible character; see n. 245, p. 204.

258. Luther takes this up in his subsequent treatise, *The Freedom of the Christian* (1520), LW 31:327–77; TAL 1:466–538.

The Sacrament of Extreme Unction

To this rite of anointing the sick the theologians of our day have made two additions that are worthy of them: first, they call it a sacrament, and second, they make it the last sacrament. So it is now the sacrament of extreme unction, which is to be administered only to those who are at the point of death. Since they are such subtle dialectitians,[e] perhaps they have done this in order to relate it to the first unction of baptism and the two subsequent ones of confirmation and ordination.[259] But here they are able to cast in my teeth that, in the case of this sacrament, there are on the authority of the apostle James both promise

259. Cf. Lombard, *Sentences* 4, d. 23, c. 2: "And there are three kinds of anointing. For there is an anointing which is done with chrism [i.e., confirmation], which is called the principal anointing . . . there is also another anointing by which catechumens and neophytes are anointed on the breast and between the shoulders at the reception of baptism. But there is a third anointing which is called the oil of the sick."

d Cf. Phil. 4:13.

e See n. 25, p. 107.

and sign, which, as I have maintained all along, do constitute a sacrament. For the apostle says [Jas. 5:14-15]: "Are any among you sick? They should call for the elders of the church and have them pray over them, anointing them with oil in the name of the Lord. The prayer of faith will save the sick, and the Lord will raise them up; and anyone who has committed sins will be forgiven." There, they say, you have the promise of the forgiveness of sins and the sign of the oil.

This detail of the *Seven Sacraments* altarpiece by artist Roger van der Weyden (c. 1400–1464) shows the sacrament of extreme unction.

But I say: If ever folly has been uttered, it has been uttered especially on this subject: I will say nothing of the fact that many assert with much probability that this epistle is not by James the apostle, and that it is not worthy of an apostolic spirit;[260] although, whoever was its author, it has come to be regarded as authoritative. But even if the apostle James did write it, I still would say, that no apostle has the right on his own authority to institute a sacrament, that is, to give a divine promise with a sign attached. For this belongs to Christ alone. Thus Paul says that he received from the Lord the sacrament of the Eucharist,[f] and that he was not sent to baptize, but to preach the gospel.[g] And nowhere do we read in the gospel about the sacrament of extreme unction. But let us also pass over the point. Let us examine the words of the apostle, or whoever was the author of the epistle, and we shall see at once how little heed these multipliers of sacraments have given to them.

In the first place, if they believe the apostle's words to be true and binding, by what right do they change and contradict them? Why do they make an extreme and a special kind of unction out

f 1 Cor. 11:23.

g 1 Cor. 1:17.

260. The apostolicity and authorship of the epistle of James were long debated in the church. For example, Jerome regarded the text as pseudonymous, and Eusebius, in his *Church History*, numbers it among the New Testament texts whose authority had been contested, i.e., *antilegomena*. In Luther's day, Erasmus questioned its authorship, and Luther's Wittenberg colleague Andreas von Karlstadt published a treatise (*De canonicis scripturis* *libellus*) only a few months earlier that gave a detailed treatment of the question of James's authority and place in the canon.

261. Lombard takes up the question of a more general repetition of the sacrament of unction in *Sentences* 4, d. 23, c. 4.

262. For example, the Supplement to Aquinas's *Summa* discusses the fact that the *Ecclesiastical Hierarchy* does not mention extreme unction as one of the sacraments; *STh* III Suppl., q. 29, a. 1.

263. The concluding prayer of the rite of extreme unction, used since the eighth century, included the following: "In your mercy restore him inwardly and outwardly to full health, so that, having recovered through the help of your mercy, he may return to his former duties."

264. E.g., *Exultate Deo*, from the Council of Florence (1439), "this sacrament ought not to be given except to the sick of whom death is feared."

of that which the apostle wished to be general?[261] For the apostle did not desire it to be an extreme unction or administered only to the dying, but he says expressly: "Is any one sick?" He does not say: "Is any one dying?" I do not care what learned discussions Dionysius has on this point in his *Ecclesiastical Hierarchy*.[262] The apostle's words are clear enough, on which he as well as they rely; but they do not follow them. It is evident, therefore, that they have arbitrarily and without any authority made a sacrament and an extreme unction out of the words of the apostle which they have wrongly interpreted. And this works to the detriment of all other sick persons, whom they have deprived on their own authority of the benefit of the unction that the apostle enjoined.

But this is even a finer point: The apostle's promise expressly declares: "The prayer of faith will save the sick, and the Lord will raise them up, etc."[h] See, the apostle in this passage commands us to anoint and to pray, in order that the sick may be healed and raised up; that is, that they may not die, and that it may not be an extreme unction. This is proved also by the prayers that are used even to this day during the anointing, because the prayers are for the recovery of the sick.[263] But they say, on the contrary, that the unction must be administered to none but the dying;[264] that is, that they may not be healed and raised up. If it were not so serious a matter, who could help laughing at this beautiful, apt, and sensible exposition of the apostle's words? Is not the folly of the sophists here shown in its true colors? Because here, as in so many other places, it affirms what the Scriptures deny, and denies what the Scriptures affirm. Why should we not give thanks to these excellent masters of ours? Surely I spoke the truth when I said that they never uttered greater folly than on this subject.

Furthermore, if this unction is a sacrament, it must necessarily be (as they say)[i] an "effective sign" of that which it signifies and promises. Now it promises health and recovery to the sick, as the words plainly say: "The prayer of faith will save the sick, and the Lord will raise them up."[j] But who does not see that this promise is seldom, if ever, fulfilled? Scarcely one in a thousand is

h James 5:15.

i See nn. 163 and 164, p. 157.

j James 5:15.

restored to health, and when one is restored nobody believes that it came about through the sacrament, but through the working of nature or of medicine. Indeed to the sacrament they ascribe the opposite effect. What shall we say then? Either the apostle lies in making this promise or else this unction is no sacrament. For the sacramental promise is certain; but this promise fails in the majority of cases. Indeed—and here again we recognize the shrewdness and foresight of these theologians—for this very reason they would have it to be extreme unction, that the promise should not stand; in other words, that the sacrament should be no sacrament. For if it is extreme unction, it does not heal, but gives way to the disease; but if it heals, it cannot be extreme unction. Thus, by the interpretation of these masters, James is shown to have contradicted himself, and to have instituted a sacrament in order not to institute one; for they must have an extreme unction just to make untrue what the apostle intends, namely, the healing of the sick by it. If this is not madness, I ask you what is?

The word of the apostle in 1 Tim. 1[:7] describes these people: "Desiring to be teachers of the law, without understanding either what they are saying or the things about which they make assertions." Thus they read and follow everything uncritically. With the same carelessness they have also found auricular confession in the apostle's words: "Confess your sins to one another."[k] But they do not observe the command of the apostle, that the elders of the church be called, and prayer be made for the sick.[l] Scarcely one insignificant priest is sent nowadays, although the apostle would have many present, not because of the unction, but because of the prayer. That is why he says: "The prayer of faith will save the sick man, etc."[m] I have my doubts, however, whether he would have us understand "priests" when he says "presbyters," that is, "elders." For one who is an elder is not necessarily a priest or a minister. We may suspect that the apostle desired the older, graver men in the church to visit the sick, to perform a work of mercy, and pray in faith and thus heal him. Yet, it cannot be denied that the churches were once ruled by older persons,

k James 5:16.

l James 5:14.

m James 5:15.

chosen for this purpose without these ordinations and consecrations, solely on account of their age and long experience.

Therefore I take it that this unction is the same as that practiced by the apostles, of whom it is written in Mark 6[:13]: "They anointed with oil many that were sick and healed them." It was a rite of the early church, by which they worked miracles on the sick, and which has long since ceased. In the same way Christ, in the last chapter of Mark, gave to believers the power to pick up serpents, lay hands on the sick, etc.[n] It is a wonder that they have not made sacraments of those words also, for they have the same power and promise as these words of James. Therefore this extreme—which is to say fictitious—unction is not a sacrament, but a counsel of James, which anyone who will may follow; and it is derived from Mark 6[:13], as I have said. I do not believe that it was a counsel given to all sick persons, for the church's infirmity is her glory and death is gain;[o] but it was given only to such as might bear their sickness impatiently and with little faith, those whom the Lord allowed to remain in order that miracles and the power of faith might be manifest in them.

James made careful and diligent provision in this case by attaching the promise of healing and the forgiveness of sins not to the unction, but to the prayer of faith. For he says: "And the prayer of faith will save the sick, and the Lord will raise them up; and if anyone has committed sins, they will be forgiven."[p] A sacrament does not demand prayer and faith on the part of the minister, since even a wicked person may baptize and consecrate without prayer; a sacrament depends solely on the promise and institution of God, and requires faith on the part of the recipient. But where is the prayer of faith in our present use of extreme unction? Who prays over the sick one in such faith as not to doubt that he will recover? Such a prayer of faith James here describes, of which he said at the beginning of his epistle: "But ask in faith, with no doubting."[q] And Christ says of it: "Whatever you ask in prayer, believe that you receive it, and you will."[r]

There is no doubt at all that, even if today such a prayer were made over a sick person, that is, made in full faith by older,

n Mark 16:18.

o Cf. Phil. 1:21.

p James 5:15.

q James 1:6.

graver, and saintly men, as many as we wished would be healed. For what could not faith do? But we neglect this faith that the authority of the apostle demands above all else. Further, by "presbyters"—that is, men preeminent by reason of their age and faith—we understand the common herd of priests. Moreover, we turn the daily or temporally unrestricted unction into an extreme unction. And finally, we do not obtain the result promised by the apostle, namely, the healing of the sick, but we render the promise ineffective by doing the very opposite. And yet we boast that our sacrament, or rather figment, is established and proved by this saying of the apostle, which is diametrically opposed to it.[265] O what theologians!

Now I do not condemn this our "sacrament" of extreme unction, but I firmly deny that it is what the apostle James prescribes; for his unction agrees with ours neither in form, use, power, nor purpose. Nevertheless, we shall number it among those "sacraments" which we have instituted, such as the blessing and sprinkling of salt and water. For we cannot deny that any creature whatsoever may be consecrated by the Word and by prayer, as the apostle Paul teaches us.[s] We do not deny, therefore, that forgiveness and peace are granted through extreme unction; not because it is a sacrament divinely instituted, but because he who receives it believes that these blessings are granted to him. For the faith of the recipient does not err, however much the minister may err. For one who baptizes or absolves in jest,[266] that is, one who does not absolve so far as the minister is concerned, nevertheless does truly baptize and absolve if the person to be baptized or absolved believes. How much more will one who administers extreme unction confer peace, even though he does not really confer peace so far as his ministry is concerned, since there is no sacrament there! The faith of the one anointed receives even that which the minister either could not give or did not intend to give. It is sufficient for the one anointed to hear and believe the Word. For whatever we believe we shall receive, that we really do receive, no matter what the minister may or may not do, or whether he dissembles or jests. The saying of Christ holds good: "All things are possible to him who believes,"[t] and again: "Be it done for you

r Mark 11:24.

s 1 Tim. 4:4-5.

t Mark 9:32.

265. Luther uses a Greek proverbial expression here, *dis dia pason*, which signifies a great difference. In music, it was the greatest span in a given scale. Cf. Erasmus, *Adagia* 1, 2, 63.

266. On the Scholastic debate over this question, see, for example, Lombard, *Sentences* 4, d. 6, c. 5, "Concerning One Who Is Immersed in Jest." See also n. 161, p. 156.

as you have believed."[u] But in treating the sacraments our sophists say nothing at all of this faith, but only babble with all their might about the virtues of the sacraments themselves.[v] They will "listen to anybody and can never arrive at a knowledge of the truth."[w]

Still it was a good thing that this unction was made the extreme or "last" unction, for thanks to that, it has been abused and distorted least of all the sacraments by tyranny and greed. This one last mercy, to be sure, has been left to the dying—they may be anointed without charge, even without confession and communion.[267] If it had remained a practice of daily occurrence, especially if it had cured the sick, even without taking away sins, how many worlds, do you think, would not the pontiffs have under their control today? For through the one sacrament of penance and the power of the keys, as well as through the sacrament of ordination, they have become such mighty emperors and princes. But now it is a fortunate thing that they despise the prayer of faith, and therefore do not heal any sick, and that they have made for themselves, out of an ancient ceremony, a brand-new sacrament.

267. Luther is speaking of what was regarded as a widespread abuse of the sacrament, in which confession and communion were absent from the administration of extreme unction.

Let this now suffice for these four sacraments. I know how it will displease those who believe that the number and use of the sacraments are to be learned not from the sacred Scriptures, but from the Roman See. As if the Roman See had given these "sacraments" and had not rather received them from the lecture halls of the universities, to which it is unquestionably indebted for whatever it has. The papal despotism would not have attained its present position, had it not taken over so many things from the universities. For there was scarcely another of the celebrated bishoprics that had so few learned pontiffs as Rome. Only by violence, intrigue, and superstition has she till now prevailed over the rest. For the men who occupied the See a thousand years ago differed so vastly from those who have since come into power, that one is compelled to refuse the name of Roman pontiff to one group or the other.

u Matt. 8:13.

v Cf., for example, Aquinas, *STh* III, q. 69, a. 6.

w 2 Tim. 3:7.

[Other Sacraments]

There are still a few other things which it might seem possible to regard as sacraments; namely, all those things to which a divine promise has been given, such as prayer, the Word, and the cross. For Christ has promised, in many places, that those who pray should be heard; especially in Luke 11,[x] where by many parables he invites us to pray. Of the Word he says: "Blessed are those who hear the Word of God and keep it."[y] And who can count all the times God promises aid and glory to those who are afflicted, suffer, and are cast down? Indeed, who can recount all the promises of God? Why, the whole Scripture is concerned with provoking us to faith; now driving us with commands and threats, now drawing us with promises and consolations. In fact, everything in Scripture is either a command or a promise. The commands humble the proud with their demands; the promises exalt the humble with their forgiveness.

Nevertheless, it has seemed proper to restrict the name of sacrament to those promises which have signs attached to them. The remainder, not being bound to signs, are bare promises. Hence there are, strictly speaking, but two sacraments in the church of God—baptism and the bread.[z] For only in these two do we find both the divinely instituted sign and the promise of forgiveness of sins. The sacrament of penance, which I added to these two, lacks the divinely instituted visible sign, and is, as I have said, nothing but a way and a return to baptism. Nor can the scholastics say that their definition fits penance, for they too ascribe to the true sacrament a visible sign, which is to impress upon the senses the form of that which it effects invisibly.[a] But penance or absolution has no such sign. Therefore they are compelled by their own definition either to admit that penance is not a sacrament and thus to reduce their number, or else to bring forth another definition of a sacrament.

Baptism, however, which we have applied to the whole of life, will truly be a sufficient substitute for all the sacraments that we might need as long as we live. And the bread is truly the

x Luke 11:5-13.

y Luke 11:28.

z Cf. Luther's earlier remarks in which he initially proposes three sacraments; see p. 152, above.

a Cf. Lombard, *Sentences* 4, d. 1, c. 2.

sacrament of the dying and departing; for in it we commemorate the passing of Christ out of this world, that we may imitate him. Thus we may apportion these two sacraments as follows: baptism may be allotted to the beginning and the entire course of life, while the bread belongs to the end and to death. And the Christian should use them both as long as he is in this mortal frame, until, fully baptized and strengthened, he passes out of this world, and is born into the new eternal life, to eat with Christ in the kingdom of his Father, as he promised at the Last Supper, when he said: "Truly, I say to you, I shall not drink again of this fruit of the vine until it is fulfilled in the kingdom of God."[b] Thus he clearly seems to have instituted the sacrament of the bread with a view to our entrance into the life to come. For then, when the purpose of both sacraments is fulfilled, baptism and bread will cease.

[Conclusion]

Herewith I conclude this prelude, and freely and gladly offer it to all pious souls who desire to know the genuine sense of the Scriptures and the proper use of the sacraments. For it is a gift of no mean importance, to know the gifts that are given to us, as it is said in 1 Cor. 2[:12], and what use we ought to make of them. For if we are instructed with this judgment of the spirit, we shall not mistakenly rely on those things which are wrong. These two things our theologians never taught us; indeed, they seem to have taken pains to hide them from us. If I have not taught them, I certainly managed not to conceal them, and have given occasion to others to think out something better. It has at least been my endeavor to set them both forth. Nevertheless, "not all can do all things."[268] To the godless, on the other hand, and those who in obstinate tyranny force on us their own teachings instead of God's, I confidently and freely oppose these pages. I shall be completely indifferent to their senseless fury. Yet I wish even them a right understanding. And I do not despise their efforts; I only distinguish them from what is sound and truly Christian.

268. Luther is quoting Virgil, *Eclogues* 8, 63.

b Cf. Matt. 26:29; Mark 14:25; Luke 22:18.

I hear a rumor that new bulls[c] and papal maledictions are being prepared against me, in which I am urged to recant or be declared a heretic.[269] If that is true, I desire this little book to be part of the recantation that I shall make; so that the arrogant despots might not complain of having acted in vain. The remainder I will publish very soon;[270] please Christ, it will be such as the Roman See has never seen or heard before. I shall give ample proof of my obedience. In the name of our Lord Jesus Christ. Amen.

"Why doth that impious Herod fear
When told that Christ the King is near?
He takes not earthly realms away,
Who gives the realms that ne'er decay."[271]

269. The bull *Exsurge domine*, issued on 15 June 1520, gave Luther and his followers sixty days to recant before they would be declared of heresy. On 10 December, sixty days later, Luther and his colleagues invited the students of Wittenberg to a burning of papal and Scholastic books. There Luther publicly burned *Exsurge domine*. On 3 January 1521, the pope issued the bull *Decet Romanum pontificem*, formally excommunicating Luther.

270. On 29 November 1520, Luther published *Assertion of All the Articles Wrongly Condemned in the Roman Bull*. His treatise *On the Freedom of the Christian* was also published in the same month, with an accompanying letter to Pope Leo X (see LW 31:327–77; TAL 1:466–538).

271. The eighth stanza of Coelius Sedulius's *A solis ortus cardine* (fifth century). Luther would later translate stanzas 8, 9, 11, and 13 as an Epiphany hymn, *Was fürchtst du Feind, Herodes, sehr.*

c See n. 177, p. 169.

DE LIBER
TATE CHRISTIANA DIS-
SERTATIO MARTINI
LVTHERI, PER AV
TOREM RECO
GNITA.

EPISTOLA EIVSDEM AD
LEONEM DECIMVM
SVMMVM PON
TIFICEM.

Title page of *The Freedom of a Christian*
from a 1521 printing of the second edition.

The Freedom of a Christian

1520

TIMOTHY J. WENGERT

INTRODUCTION

The movement within Western Christianity that began in 1517 with the posting of Martin Luther's *95 Theses*, now known as the Reformation, was by no means a foregone conclusion in its earliest stages. Starting with the papal legate, Cardinal Cajetan's (1469–1534) interview of Luther in October 1518,[1] various attempts were made first to avoid or mitigate Luther's impending condemnation by the pope and, later, to find ways around the papal condemnation and the impending judgment of the imperial diet (parliament) that finally met in Worms in April 1521. One such embassy fell on the shoulders of Karl von Miltitz (c. 1490–1529), who throughout 1520 tried to find ways around the impasse between Luther and his supporters (along with his protector prince, the Elector Frederick of Saxony [1463–1525]) on the one side and the papal court and its defenders on the other.[2]

Luther left the final meeting with von Miltitz with instructions to write a reconciliation-minded letter to Pope Leo X (1475–1521), which he did in the weeks that followed and to which he appended a nonpolemical tract describing the heart of his beliefs. (Indeed, compared to other major tracts he produced in 1520, *The Freedom of a Christian* has

1. See *The Proceedings at Augsburg* in *The Annotated Luther*, Volume 1, pp 121–65.

2. For the details of the historical record, see Brecht 1:400–415, and Berndt Hamm, *The Early Luther: Stages in a Reformation Reorientation* (Grand Rapids: Eerdmans, 2014), 172–89.

a remarkably temperate tone.)[3] The dedicatory letter to Leo X represents what might be called a "case study" in the proposal found in *The Freedom of a Christian*, where Luther shows both his deep respect for the pope and his surprising freedom in proclaiming the gospel. While it is clear that these two documents should, therefore, be read in tandem, several accidents of history allowed for their own separate existence.[4]

In September 1520, probably working from a detailed Latin outline, Luther first completed the German version of *The Freedom of a Christian* and its epistle dedicatory to Leo X. Because the letter to Leo X arrived first at the printer, however, Johann Grünenberg (d. c. 1525)—knowing a bestseller when he saw one—printed it separately, forcing Luther to write a second, perfunctory preface for the German version to Hermann Mühlpfort (c. 1486–1534), mayor of Zwickau. Thus, some copies of the German version of *The Freedom of a Christian* circulated with both prefaces.[5] At nearly the same time and working off the same outline (so that many sections of the German and Latin correspond closely but were never quite word-for-word translations of each other), Luther then completed the Latin version, adding an introduction and a lengthy appendix not found in the German. The differences between the two tracts also arose in part out of the slightly different audiences for them: the one addressed to theologians, clerics, and church leaders (for whom Latin was the common language), and one addressed to the German-speaking public, which included the nobility, townsfolk, many from the lesser clergy, and others who could read (or have Luther's writings read to them).

3. These tracts include two others in this volume, *Sermon on Good Works* and *Address to the Christian Nobility*, and *The Babylonian Captivity of the Church*, in LW 36:3–126.

4. Hamm, *The Early Luther*, 172–89.

5. For a translation of the German preface, see LW 31:333. For a translation of the entire German tract, see Philip Krey and Peter Krey, eds., *Luther's Spirituality* (Mahwah, NJ: Paulist, 2007), 69–90.

Printing History

The Freedom of a Christian was a bestseller. Including the original Latin and German versions published in Wittenberg, there were between 1520 and 1526 thirty printings: nineteen in German, one in the dialect of the German lowlands, and eight in Latin, along with translations of the Latin into German (!) and English. It now appears that Luther sent a corrected copy to a cathedral canon in Augsburg, who forwarded it to Beatus Rhenanus, a famous humanist and early supporter in Basel (Switzerland), who added his own marginal headings and sent it on to the printer Adam Petri in Basel. The latter corrected typographical errors and probably in March 1521, published this corrected version in time for the Frankfurt book fair, titling it *A Discourse on Christian Freedom Revised by the Author.*[6] Later in the same year, Melchior Lotter reprinted this version, simply noting that it was "revised in Wittenberg."[a] With the few exceptions mentioned in the footnotes, all of the subheadings used in the following translation have been taken from Petri's edition.

The Letter to Leo X

The letter to Leo has all of the characteristics of polished Renaissance Latin prose expected for a writing that addresses the pope. Not only is the Latin itself among Luther's best writings, but the letter's argument also bears the marks of typical Latin style. Thus, Luther prosecutes two separate arguments, according to the painstaking analysis of the German linguist Birgit Stolt.[b] Her analysis is reflected in the headings of this translation. The Renaissance context of this letter, like that to Archbishop Albrecht von Brandenburg of Mainz (1490–1545), helps explain the tone of the

6. *De liberate Christiana dissertatio per autorem recognita* (Basel: A. Petri, 1521). Rhenanus (1485–1547) was an important humanist who worked from 1511 to 1526 in Basel at the famous Froben press and was favorable toward Luther's work. (In January 1520, Martin Bucer sent him a copy of Luther's commentary on Galatians.) Philipp Melanchthon was also a great supporter of the tract. His letter from April 1521 to an unknown recipient in Schaffhausen reflects many of the themes of *The Freedom of a Christian* and even refers his correspondent to it. See *Melanchthons Briefwechsel*, vol. T1: *Texte 1–254 (1514–1522)*, ed. Richard Wetzel (Stuttgart-Bad Cannstatt: Frommann-Holzboog, 1991), 276–78 (no. 137). Wetzel notes that in 1524 this letter was included with a Nuremberg printing of *The Freedom of a Christian*.

a See WA 7:40, "E": *Epistola Lutheriana ad Leonem Decimum summum pontificem. Liber de Christiana libertate, continens summam Christianae doctrinae, quo ad formandam mentem, & ad intelligendam Euangelii vim, nihil absolutius, nihil conducibilius neque a veteribus neque a recentioribus scriptoribus perditum est. Tu Christianae lector, relege iterum atque iterum, & Christum imbibe. Recognitus Wittembergae* (Wittenberg: Melchior Lotter, 1521). English: *A Lutheran Letter to Pope Leo X. A Book on Christian Freedom, Containing the Sum of Christian Teaching, Concerning Which Nothing More Absolute or More in Line with Either Ancient or More Recent Writers Has Been Produced for Forming the Mind and for Understanding the Power of the Gospel. You, Christian Reader, Reread This Again and Again and Drink in Christ. Reedited in Wittenberg.* For details, see James Hirstein's article in *Revue d'histoire et de philosophie religieuses* 95 (2015): 129–63.

b Birgit Stolt, *Studien zu Luthers Freiheitstraktat mit besonderer Rücksicht auf das Verhältnis der lateinischen und der deutschen Fassung zu einander und die Stilmittel der Rhetorik* (Stockholm: Almzvist & Wiksell, 1969).

piece—what to modern ears might appear stilted and even obsequious at times. *Not* to have addressed the pontiff with such respect would itself have been considered a shocking breech of etiquette and further proof of Luther's contempt for all authority in the church and government. To read this letter as if Luther were hiding his true feelings or even being deceitful imposes modern sensibilities on a very different age and with its very different expectations.

This letter also gives evidence of Luther's paradoxical view of the Christian's life as both free (in the gospel) and bound to the neighbor. To be sure, Luther was bound and determined to put to rest the (unfounded) rumor that he had attacked the pope's person. While he would insist that the papal court was to blame for the sorry state of the church in his day, he had no particular criticism of Leo X himself. Instead, he took direct aim at his bitterest opponent and one of the instigators of the papal bull of excommunication, Johann Eck (1486–1543). Thus, he expressed himself in the letter with remarkable freedom against his opponents—a freedom that arose for him from Christ himself. Luther could even call to mind the behavior of one of his favorite medieval theologians, Bernard of Clairvaux (1090–1153), who had written sternly to Pope Eugene III (1383–1447). This appeal to Leo, however, went unanswered.

The Freedom of a Christian

As the letter to Leo already indicates, Luther was a child of the Renaissance. This meant that his Latin prose especially was carefully shaped according to the rhetorical rules and conventions of his day. In the case of *The Freedom of a Christian*, this means that the reader today can still detect the basic outline of his argument as it followed these conventions.[c] Even the marginal notes added to the second edition often identify these various parts. Based upon classical writings on rhetoric by Cicero (106–43 BCE) and Quintilian (c. 35–c. 100), late medieval rhetorical handbooks divided a speech

c Ibid.

or tract into six parts: exordium, division of the tract, the exposition of the theme, confirmation or proof of the theme, an answer to objections to the theme, and a peroration.

Observing closely how Luther develops the argument in *The Freedom of a Christian* can help the reader in understanding the document. Luther begins by talking about the nature of faith, a key subject of debate in his case with Rome. Thereby, he intends to arouse his readers' interest in the subject and to present himself as a reliable witness or authority concerning faith. This constitutes a proper exordium, which Luther uses to encourage readers to see the importance of understanding faith, now defined not as a virtue but as an experience of struggle and mercy.

As the marginal gloss from the 1521 text notes, Luther then states the "themes" (*themata*) of his writing about Christian freedom and servitude. Yet, according to late medieval rules of rhetoric, these "themes" are not, as modern readers might think, outlining the subject of his essay (which was faith), but instead announce the proper division of the overall argument into two nearly equal sections, the first on the freedom of a Christian and the second on a Christian's servitude. It is first in the brief exposition of the themes, the so-called *narratio* following the themes' statement, that the reader discovers Luther's actual subject: *not* to divide freedom and servitude but to explain how, given their relation to faith and their use by the Apostle Paul, they cohere.

The body of the first part, or "theme," of the work consists in the *confirmatio* where Luther attempts to prove his claim that freedom and servitude cohere in the Christian life. Luther insists that the whole human being may be viewed as both inner and outer and that not works but only God's word received in faith constitutes true Christian freedom. From this premise, Luther then introduces three benefits or fruits of faith, concentrating most of his efforts on the third fruit: the marriage of the soul and Christ by faith alone. With this "joyous exchange" (as he calls it in the German version) between human sin and Christ's righteousness, the believing person receives, in addition, Christ's priesthood and kingship. Yet, by priesthood Luther does not mean having an office in the church but, rather, praying and proclaiming Christ's love; and by kingship Luther is not talking about power but the spiritual kingship of peace. Christian freedom then consists precisely in these gifts, fruits, and benefits of faith, so that Christians are lords over sin, death, the devil, and anything else that threatens them.

When Luther arrives at what he calls the second theme, that Christians are servants of all, he introduces it not as a separate theme at all but, rather, again following the rules of rhetoric, as an answer to the chief objections to the first section and its description of law and gospel, faith and its blessings. This standard component of good rhetoric since the time of Cicero, called the *confutatio*, anticipated opponents' arguments aimed at refuting the main point of a speech or writing. Here, the chief objection takes the form of derision. Opponents who were convinced that Luther's teaching on faith would lead to lawlessness and disorder, giving believers license to sin, had made exaggerated claims to that effect. Luther rebukes them ("Not so, you wicked people") and answers their objections using a series of examples from Scripture and experience that show how faith freely produces good works and, hence, serves the neighbor.[7] Throughout this section of the tract, however, Luther also restates his basic point that Christian faith does not depend upon works but only on God's mercy. Running throughout this section is a criticism of Aristotelian ethics, which dominated late medieval thinking, that a person becomes virtuous (or righteous) by doing virtuous acts. Luther argues the opposite, namely that only the one declared righteous by Christ through faith alone can bear fruit of righteousness.

The close of any proper speech or writing was the peroration, which consisted either of a summary conclusion to the argument or an appeal to the reader or listener. Indeed, Luther even signals this transition with the words, "We conclude."[8] In this case, Luther concludes that Christians live in Christ through faith and their neighbors through love. After his final "Amen," however, Luther adds a lengthy appendix that answers another misunderstanding of his argument by

7. See below, p. 264.

8. See below, p. 284.

ceremonialists, namely, that he really is supporting license and an abandonment of all good order among Christians.

His refusal to equate reform with abandoning past practices while still rebuking ceremonialists, coupled with his concern for the weak in faith, led Luther in 1522, upon returning from protective custody in the Wartburg Castle, to put the brakes on the reform movement that had arisen during his absence from Wittenberg—not on the basis of objections to the practices favored by these reform-minded colleagues (including not only Andreas Bodenstein from Karlstadt [1486-1541] but also Philip Melanchthon and Nicholas von Amsdorf [1483-1565], among others) but because such changes in practice would upset the faith of weak Christians who would not understand why they were taking place.[9] This reticence about changing forms of worship—foreign to his Roman opponents and to other leaders of reform (for example, Ulrich Zwingli [1484-1531] in Zurich and early Anabaptists)—stands as a unique mark of Wittenberg's brand of theology and may be traced to Luther's comments in *The Freedom of a Christian*.

9. See Martin Luther, *Invocavit Sermons* (March 1522), in LW 51:67-100.

LUTHER'S EPISTLE TO LEO X, SUPREME PONTIFF[10, d]

JESUS.[e]

MARTIN LUTHER sends greetings to Leo X, Roman Pontiff, in Christ Jesus our Lord. Amen.

[11, f]Surrounded by the monsters of this age, with which I have struggled and battled for three years, I am compelled at times to look to you and to think of you, Leo, most blessed father. Indeed, since you are widely held to be the sole cause of my battles, I cannot but think of you. And although the godless flatterers around you, who rage against me without cause, forced me to appeal from your see[12] to a future Council (given that I have no respect for the completely vain decrees of your predecessors, Pius and Julius, who with foolish tyranny prohibited such appeals),[13] nevertheless, throughout this time I have never turned my soul away from Your Holiness so as neither to desire with all my powers the very best for you and for your see nor, as far as was in me, to

10. The present translation is a revision of *Martin Luther, Freedom of a Christian: Luther Study Edition*, trans. Mark Tranvik (Minneapolis: Fortress Press, 2008), itself a revision of the version in LW 31:327–77, first translated by W. A. Lambert and revised by Harold J. Grimm. The present revision is based primarily upon WA 7:39–73, but also using the more recent version with extensive notes, ed. Hans-Ulrich Delius, in MLStA 2:260–309. The headings, except where noted, are translated from the Basel edition of 1521, printed by Adam Petri (1454–1527).

11. **EXORDIUM**

12. Referring to the pope's ecclesiastical jurisdiction in Rome.

13. Luther addresses here an important part of his case with Rome. In 1518, after Pope Leo X had reaffirmed his predecessors' statements about indulgences, Luther made a formal appeal to a general council. Especially to those theologians who championed papal authority over that of a church council, this was prima facie evidence of Luther's heresy, as decrees of Pius III (1439–1503) and Julius II (1443–1513) stated. By laying the blame on the pope's advisers and Leo's generally despised predecessors, Luther sought to defend his action. (This appeal remained an important part of the Evangelical struggle with Rome throughout Luther's lifetime and is reflected in the prefaces to the *Augsburg Confession* and Luther's own *Smalcald Articles*.)

d Using marginal notes found in WA 7:40, "D": *Epistola Lutheriana ad Leonem Decimum summum pontificem. Dissertatio de libertate Christiana per autorem recognita Wittembergae* (Basel: Adam Petri, 1521). See the Introduction above.

e Following a monastic tradition, Luther began many of his early writings and letters with this word.

f Throughout this letter, marginal notes on the letter's structure follow the structural analysis made by Stolt.

seek the same with earnest and heartfelt prayers to God.[14] I nearly started to despise and declare victory over those who up to now have tried to frighten me with the majesty of your authority and name, except I see that there remains one thing which I cannot despise and which has been the reason for my writing to Your Holiness for a second time.[g] That is, I realize that I am accused of impertinence, now twisted into my greatest vice,[15] because I am judged to have attacked your person.[16]

[Part One: Luther's Defense]

[17]However, so that I may confess this matter openly,[18] whenever your person has been mentioned, I am aware of having only said the greatest and best things. But if I had done otherwise, I could under no circumstances condone it; I would vote in favor of their judgment against me every time, and I would recant nothing more freely than this my impertinence and godlessness. I have called you a Daniel in Babylon, and every one of my readers knows fully well how, with extraordinary zeal, I have defended your remarkable innocence against your defiler, Sylvester [Prierias].[19] Your reputation and the fame of your blameless life, chanted in the writings of so many men the world over, are too well known and dignified to be possibly assailed in any way by anyone, no matter how great. Nor am I so foolish to attack someone whom absolutely everyone praises. As a matter of fact, I have even tried and will always try not to attack even those whom public opinion dishonors. For I take pleasure in no one's faults, since I myself am conscious enough of the log in my own eye.[h] Nor do I want to be the first who throws a stone at the adulteress.[i]

g The first time was the preface to the *Explanations of the Ninety-Five Theses* of 1518. See WA 1:527–29.

h Matt. 7:3.

i John 8:1-11.

14. The heightened rhetoric here and throughout this letter, addressed to a Renaissance pope, indicates the care with which Luther wrote it. None of the bracketed headings in this letter come from the original.

15. Luther's opponents often construed his highly charged language as impudence and exaggeration. Erasmus of Rotterdam (1466–1536) nicknamed him *doctor hyperbolicus*, "the exaggerating teacher."

16. Personal attacks of governmental or ecclesiastical rulers were viewed as especially inappropriate.

17. **Answering Three Questions in His Defense**
1. Whether He Committed the Offense

18. Luther answers the charges according to the three questions of the judicial genre of speech: whether he committed the offense; what he actually did; whether he acted rightly.

19. Luther stated this in his 1518 tract, *Response to the Dialogue of Sylvester Prierias concerning the Power of the Pope* (WA 1:679, 5–7). Sylvester (Mazzolini) Prierias (1456–1523) was named after the city of his birth (Prierio). A Dominican (as was Johann Tetzel [1460–1519]), he strongly defended papal authority and infallibility in matters of teaching and practice. Luther viewed this as an insult to the pope because it exalted him over Christ and the Scriptures.

20. *2. What Luther Actually Did and Whether This Was Proper*

[20] Now, generally I have sharply attacked ungodly teachings, and I have been quick to snap at my opponents not because of their bad morals but because of their godlessness. I do not repent of this in the least, as I have resolved in my soul, despite the contempt of others, to persist in this fervent zeal, following the example of Christ, who in his zeal called his adversaries "a brood of vipers," "blind," "hypocrites," and "children of the devil."[j] And Paul branded the Magician [Elymas] a "son of the devil . . . full of deceit and villainy."[k] Others he ridiculed as "dogs," "deceivers," and "adulterators."[l] If you consider any sensitive audience, no one will seem more biting and unrestrained than Paul. What is more biting than the prophets? The mad multitude of flatterers imitates the ever so sensitive ears of our rational age, so that, as soon as we sense disapproval of our ideas, we cry that we are bitten. As long as we can rebuff the truth by labeling it something else, we flee from it under the pretext of its being snappish, impatient, and unrestrained. What good is salt if it has lost its bite?[m] What use is the edge of a sword if it does not cut? "Accursed is the one who does the Lord's work deceitfully."[n]

21. *3. Summary Conclusion*

[21] For this reason, most excellent Leo, I beg you to admit that this letter vindicates me. And I beg you to convince yourself that I have never thought ill of your person and, moreover, that I am the kind of person who eternally wishes the very best things happen to you and that for me this strife is not with any person over morals but over the Word of truth alone. In everything else I will yield to anyone. I cannot and

j See Matt. 23:33, 13, 17; and John 8:44, respectively.

k Acts 13:10.

l Phil. 3:2; 2 Cor. 11:13; 2:17 (following the Latin; NRSV: "peddlers").

m Classical Latin authors often compared salt (especial "black salt") with sharpness (e.g., Pliny the Elder [23–79], *Historia naturalis*, 10, 72, 93, par. 198) and sarcasm (e.g., Catullus [c. 84-54 BCE] *Carmina*, 13, 5). See also Matt. 5:13.

n Jer. 48:10 (Vulgate).

will not yield or deny the Word. If a person has thought something else about me or otherwise interpreted my positions, then that one is not thinking straight nor interpreting my true positions.

[22] However, I have rightly cursed your see, called the Roman Curia,[23] which neither you nor any human being can deny is more corrupt than Babylon or Sodom[24] and, as far as I can tell, is composed of depraved, desperate, and notorious godlessness. And I have made known that, under your name and under the cover of the Roman Church, the people of Christ are being undeservedly deceived. Indeed, I have thus resisted and will continue to resist [the Curia], as long as the Spirit of faith lives in me—not that I would strive for the impossible or that I would hope that, given the furious opposition of so many flatterers, my works alone would improve anything in that chaotic Babylon, but I do acknowledge the debt owed to my fellow Christians,[o] whom I must warn so that fewer may perish or at least have milder symptoms from that Roman plague. Indeed, as you yourself know, for many years nothing else has been flooding the world from Rome than the devastation of possessions, bodies, and souls, and the worst examples of the worst possible things. All this is clearer than day to everyone. Moreover, out of the Roman Church, once the holiest of all, has been fashioned a completely licentious den of thieves, the most shameless of all brothels, the kingdom of sin, death, and hell, so that were the Antichrist to come, he could hardly think of anything that would add to its wickedness.[25]

22. Proof That Luther Acted Properly

1. The Corruption in the Roman Curia

23. The papal court (Latin: *curia*), consisting of cardinals, bishops, and other clerical functionaries.

24. Rev. 18:2-24 and 11:8, respectively names for the powers opposed to Christ and Christians during the end times.

25. Faced with what he perceived as the Roman Curia's intransigence, Luther moved from granting the papacy human authority over the churches to condemning it (but not individual bishops of Rome) as in league with or identified with the Antichrist. By the late Middle Ages, many Christian thinkers assumed that at the world's end an Antichrist would arise to do battle with God's elect.

o Literally, "brothers."

26. *2. Luther's Compassion for the Pope*

27. An attempt to poison Leo X had indeed been made in 1517.

28. Luther was quoting Baptista Mantuanus (1447–1516), *Varia ad Falconem Sinibaldum epigrammata*, a collection of epigrams against corruption in Rome. Luther also quoted this text in *On the Bondage of the Will* (LW 33:53) and used Mantuanus's work in his 1545 tract *Against the Roman Papacy: An Institution of the Devil* (LW 41:257–376). Gout was considered an incurable disease.

29. *3. What the Pope Should Do*

30. He was a member of the powerful de Medicis. From this point on, Luther uses the word *gloria* (glory or fame or boasting) to describe the situation in Rome and with his enemies.

[26] In the meantime, you, Leo, sit as a lamb in the midst of wolves, as Daniel in the midst of lions, and you dwell with Ezekiel among the scorpions.[p] How can you alone oppose these monsters? Add three or four of your best and most learned cardinals! "What are they among so many?"[q] Before you had even begun setting up the remedy, you would have all been poisoned to death.[27] It is all over for the Roman Curia. The wrath of God has fallen upon it completely. It hates councils; it fears being reformed; it cannot allay its raging godlessness; and it fulfills the eulogy written for its "mother," about whom is said, "We tried to heal Babylon, but she has not been healed. Let us forsake her."[r] To be sure, it was part of your office and that of your cardinals to heal these ills, but "this gout derided the physician's hands,"[28] and neither horse "nor chariot responds to the reins."[s] Touched by deep affection, I have always been grieved, most excellent Leo, that you, who were worthy of far better times, became pope in this day and age. For the Roman Curia is not worthy of you or people like you but only Satan himself, who now actually rules in that Babylon more than you do.

[29] O that, having cast aside the glory that your completely accursed enemies heap upon you, you would instead live on the small income of a parish priest or on your family's inheritance.[30] Only the Iscariots, sons of perdition,[t] are worthy of glorying in this kind of glory. For what are you accomplishing in the Curia, my Leo, except that the more wicked and accursed a person is, the more happily such a one uses your name and authority to destroy the wealth and souls of human beings, to increase wickedness, and to suppress faith and truth throughout the church of God? O truly most unhappy Leo, sitting on that most dangerous throne—I am telling you the truth, because I wish you well! For if Bernard

p Matt. 10:16; Dan. 6:16; and Ezek. 2:6, respectively.

q See John 6:9.

r Jer. 51:9 (Vulgate).

s Virgil (70–19 BCE), *Georgics*, 1, 514.

t The family of Judas Iscariot, as he was labeled in John 17:12.

had compassion on Pope Eugenius,[31] when the Holy See—although already then very corrupt—still governed with more hope [for improvement], why should we not complain about the three hundred years of corruption and ruin that has been added since then? Is it not true that under the great expanse of heaven nothing is more corrupt, pestilential, and despicable than the Roman Curia? For it even surpasses by any measure the godlessness of the Turks, so that, truth be told, what was once the gate of heaven is now the very gaping mouth of hell—such a mouth that because of the wrath of God cannot be blocked. This leaves only one option in these

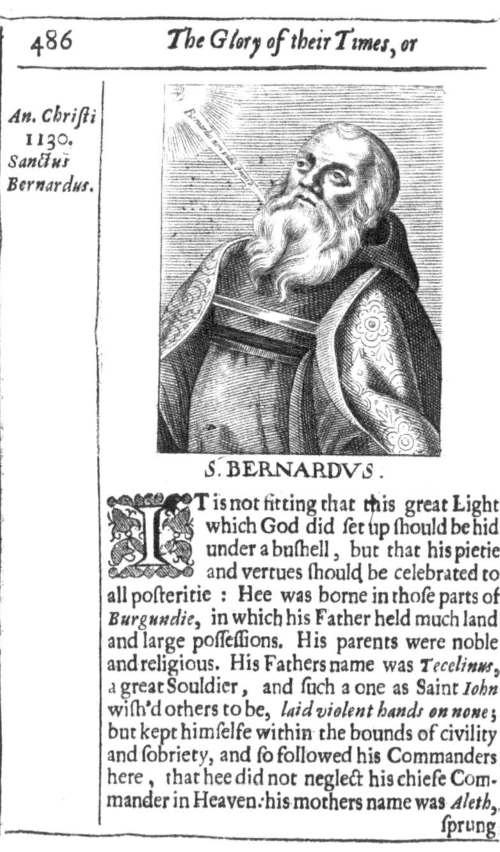

486 *The Glory of their Times, or*

An. Christi 1130. *Sanctus Bernardus.*

S. BERNARDVS.

IT is not fitting that this great Light which God did ſet up ſhould be hid under a buſhell, but that his pietie and vertues ſhould be celebrated to all poſteritie: Hee was borne in thoſe parts of *Burgundie*, in which his Father held much land and large poſſeſſions. His parents were noble and religious. His Fathers name was *Tecelinus*, a great Souldier, and ſuch a one as Saint *Iohn* wiſh'd others to be, *laid violent hands on none*; but kept himſelfe within the bounds of civility and ſobriety, and ſo followed his Commanders here, that hee did not neglect his chiefe Commander in Heaven: his mothers name was *Aleth*, ſprung

A seventeenth-century depiction of Bernard of Clairvaux (1090–1153), Cistercian monk and theologian.

31. Bernard of Clairvaux, a Cistercian monk, wrote *On Consideration* (MPL 182:727–808), addressing it to Pope Eugene III (d. 1153) and warning about the dangers connected to the papal office.

miseries: perhaps we can call back and rescue a few from this Roman abyss (as I said).[u]

32. *4. Recapitulation of Part One*

[32] Observe, my father Leo, my reason and design for raving against that pestilential see. For I completely avoided raging against your person because I even hoped that I would gain your favor and cause your rescue—if I could have quickly and decisively broken open that prison of yours or, rather, your hell. For it would have been useful for your sake and your rescue, along with that of many others, had an attack by all talented, able people been able to mitigate some of the confusion in that godless Curia. Those who harm the Curia serve your office; those who by any and all means curse it glorify Christ. In short, Christians are those who are not "Romans."

[Part Two: A Narrative of Luther's Case]

33. *1. The Real Cause of the Dispute*

34. Luther considered his unguarded remarks at the Leipzig Debate were the real cause of the problem and demanded explanation for a successful defense of his case before Leo. He returns to the debate in the next section when describing events chronologically.

[33] But, to enlarge upon this, attacking the Roman Curia or raising questions about it had never crossed my mind at all.[34] For seeing that all remedies for saving it had failed, I had only contempt for it, served it divorce papers,[v] and said to it, "Let the evildoer still do evil, and the filthy still be filthy."[w] I devoted my time to the peaceful and quiet studies of Holy Scripture, by which I wanted to assist my brothers around me. When I made some progress in this, Satan opened his

u See above, p. 229.

v See Jer. 3:8.

w Rev. 22:11.

eyes and goaded his servant Johann Eck,[35] a noted enemy of Christ, with an uncontrollable desire for glory. This resulted in Eck dragging me into an unexpected arena for combat and trapping me on one little word that in passing I let slip concerning the primacy of the Roman Church.[36] This glorious "Thraso,"[37] foaming at the mouth and gnashing his teeth, boasted that he would risk everything "for the glory of God" and "for the honor of the Holy Apostolic See." Puffed up with the prospect of abusing your power for himself, he expected nothing but certain victory, seeking not so much the primacy of Peter as his own preeminence among the theologians of this age. To achieve that goal, he imagined no small advantage in triumphing over Luther. When [the debate] ended unhappily for the Sophist,[38] an incredible madness seized the man, for he sensed that whatever of the Roman shame had come to light through me was his fault alone.[39]

35. Johann Eck, professor of theology at the University of Ingolstadt, opposed Luther already in 1518 and challenged Luther's colleague Andreas Bodenstein from Karlstadt to a debate in Leipzig, to which Luther then was added as an opponent. It took place in June 1519. See LW 31:307–25 for some of the 1519 documents from the proceedings.

36. Luther admitted in a publication leading up to the debate that the papacy of the last four hundred years was in error (proposition 13 in LW 31:318). At the debate, he admitted that councils could also err. Luther's intentions seemed more focused than he was admitting to Leo.

37. A vain character in the Roman author Terence's (d. 159 BCE) comedy *The Eunuch*, known for rhetorical bombast.

38. In the Renaissance, the label "sophist" implied someone who could nitpick about logic while missing the point of an argument. The universities established to judge the debate found in Eck's favor, but Luther won in the court of public opinion through the early publication of several accounts favorable to him.

39. After the Leipzig Debates, Eck made several trips to Rome to secure Luther's condemnation as a heretic. He also constantly wrote against Luther and his Wittenberg colleagues throughout his life.

[40] Therefore, most excellent Leo, allow me this once to make my case[41] here and to accuse your true enemies. I believe you are aware what your legate, Cardinal St. Sisto,[42] an unwise and unfortunate—indeed, untrustworthy—person, had wanted [to do] with me. When out of reverence for your name I placed myself and the entire affair into his hands, he did not attempt to establish peace—which he could easily have done with one simple word, since at the time I had promised to be silent and make an end to my case if he commanded my adversaries to do likewise. Instead, as a man seeking glory, he was not content with this agreement and instead began to defend my adversaries, to allow them freedom [of speech] and to command me to recant, even though this was not part of his mandate at all.[43] So, just when the case was in a very favorable place [for resolution], he came with his ill-natured tyranny and made it much worse. Thus, the blame for whatever followed this was not Luther's but totally Cajetan's, who did not permit me to remain silent and quiet as I at the time had requested with all my might. What more could I have possibly done?

Next followed Karl Miltitz, also a nuncio of Your Holiness.[44] He traveled back and forth in various negotiations, omitting nothing in regards to restoring the case's status quo, which Cajetan had rashly and arrogantly upset. Finally, with great difficulty but assisted by the Most Illustrious Prince, Elector Frederick,[45] he managed to speak with me several times privately, where once again I yielded to your authority and was prepared to keep silent, even accepting as a judge [in the case] either the Archbishop of Trier or the Bishop of Naumburg.[46] And thus it was settled and so ordered. While these good things were occurring and held the prospect [for success], behold, your other great enemy Eck[x] madly rushed in with the Leipzig disputation, which he set up with Dr. Karlstadt. And when a new question arose concerning the primacy of the pope, he turned

40. *2. The Progression of the Case*

41. Luther had to prove that he had done everything in his power to avoid this conflict.

42. Cardinal Cajetan (Tommaso de Vio), was also known by the name of St. Sisto's in Rome, where he was cardinal presbyter. As part of the Dominican order, he was a famous Renaissance interpreter of Thomas Aquinas (1225–1274). He was papal legate (ambassador) to the 1518 imperial Diet of Augsburg.

43. See Luther's *Proceedings at Augsburg*, above, pp 121–65. Although Luther describes Cajetan's behavior as overstepping his mandate as legate, Cajetan only may have violated the specific agreement with the Elector of Saxony, Luther's prince.

44. Karl von Miltitz was the papal ambassador north of the Alps in 1518 and 1519 with instructions to resolve the dispute with Luther.

45. Luther's own prince and the patron of the University of Wittenberg.

46. At the 1521 Diet of Worms, in addition to his public appearance before the diet, Luther met at several points with the archbishop of Trier, Richard von Greiffenklau zu Vollrads (1467–1531).

x Luther is making a play on words: "Ecce . . . Eck" (Behold . . . Eck).

his concealed weapons on me and thoroughly destroyed the plans for peace. In the meantime, Karl Miltitz waited. The disputation was held, judges were chosen, and yet no decision was reached. Small wonder, given Eck's lies, deceptions, and trickery, that everything everywhere was so completely stirred up, aggravated, and confused that, whatever the outcome of the decision, a greater conflagration would have flared up. For he sought glory not truth. Here, too, I left nothing undone that I should have carried out.

I concede that on this occasion much of Roman corruption came to light. But in this matter, whatever wrong was committed was Eck's fault. He took on a task beyond his abilities. While striving furiously for his own glory, he revealed the shame of Rome to the whole world. This one is your enemy, my Leo, or rather, the enemy of your Curia. We can learn from his example that no enemy is more pernicious than a flatterer.[y] For what did his flattery accomplish other than a kind of evil that not a single king would have been able to accomplish? For today the name "Roman Curia" reeks the world over, and papal authority languishes. Its notorious ignorance is now despised.[z] We would have heard nothing of this had Eck not upset the peace agreement between Karl and me. He himself senses this plainly and, too late and to no avail, is offended by the subsequent publication of my books. He should have thought of this earlier, when, just like a bleating goat, he madly raved about his own glory and sought nothing but his own advantage with you—at your great peril. That completely vain man hoped that I would stop and be silent out of fear for your name, since I do not believe that he supposed his own intelligence and learning would be enough. Now, because he realizes that I have confidence and continue to speak out, he understands albeit with overdue sorrow for his rash behavior—if he understands at

The coat of arms of Thomas Cardinal Cajetan, also called Tommaso de Vio.

y See Cicero, *De Amicitia*, 91 (25).

z See, e.g., the reference to "Roman ignorance" in Maurus Servius Honoratus (4th–5th century), *Commentary on the Aeneid of Virgil*, 8, 597.

all—that there is One in heaven who "resists the proud" and humbles the presumptuous.[a]

Therefore, after we had accomplished nothing by this disputation [in Leipzig] except greater confusion about the case in Rome, Karl von Miltitz came a third time, this time to the [Augustinian] fathers gathered for the chapter meeting of their order.[47] He asked their advice about how to resolve the case, which was now greatly disturbing and dangerous. Since there was no hope of proceeding against me by force (thanks to God's mercy!), some of their leaders were sent here to me. They requested that at least I show honor to the person of your Blessedness and in a humble letter plead that you and I are innocent. [They thought] that this matter was not yet completely hopeless as long as Leo X out of his innate goodness took a hand in it. Now, I have always offered and desired to keep the peace so that I might devote myself to quieter and more useful studies, since I have raged in this matter with such spirit in order that, by using great and forceful words and animus, I could restrain those whom I viewed as being no match for me at all. In this situation then, I not only freely yielded [to the delegation] but also accepted [the proposal] with joy and gratitude as a most welcomed kindness, provided that our hope could be realized.

47. This meeting of the heads of the German friaries of the Augustinian order met under the retiring vicar general, Johann von Staupitz (c. 1460–1524), in Eisleben on 28 August 1520, where von Miltitz also appeared. They sent a delegation to Wittenberg in early September. It consisted of von Staupitz, the new vicar general Wenceslaus Linck (1482–1547), and others.

48. *3. A Closing Plea for Mercy*

[48]So, most Holy Father, I come and, even now, prostrate myself before you, begging, if possible, that you lay your hands on those flatterers and enemies of peace (who only pretend to want peace) and rein them in. In turn, let no one presume, Most Holy Father, that I will recant, unless such a person wants to envelop this case in even greater turmoil. Furthermore, I will permit no binding laws for interpreting the Word of God, since "the Word of God must not be bound" because it teaches freedom in all other matters.[b] Save for these two things, there is nothing that I could not or would not freely do or endure. I hate contentions. I will

a See, e.g., 1 Pet. 5:5 and James 4:6.

b 2 Tim. 2:9, an indirect reference to the tract, *The Freedom of a Christian*, to which this letter became attached.

not provoke anyone at all. But, at the same time, I do not want to be provoked. But if I am provoked (with Christ as my teacher), I will not be at a loss for words. For, once this controversy has been brought before you and settled, Your Holiness could, with a short and simple word, command both parties to be silent and keep the peace, which is what I have always wanted to hear.

[Peroration: Advice for Pope Leo]

Consequently, My Father Leo, avoid listening to those sirens who turn you from being purely a human being into a demigod in order that you can command and decide whatever you wish. Do not let this happen; nor will you prevail in this way! You are a servant of servants and, more than all other human beings, in a most miserable and dangerous position. Do not let those deceive you who imagine that you are the lord of the world, who allow no one to be Christian outside of your authority and who babble on that you have power over heaven, hell, and purgatory.[49] They are your enemies and seek to destroy your soul, as Isaiah says, "O my people, those who call you blessed deceive you."[c] Those who place you above a council and the universal church err. Those who attribute to you alone the right to interpret Scripture err. For they seek to establish all manner of ungodliness in the Church under your name, and, alas, through them Satan has made great inroads among your predecessors.[d] In sum, believe none of those who exalt you but only those who humble you. For this is the judgment of God, who "has brought down the powerful from their thrones and lifted up the lowly."[e] Look at how different Christ is from his successors, although they still all want to be his vicars.[50] And I fear that most of them have been too literally his "vicars." For a person is a vicar only in the absence of a superior. But if the

49. Part of the original claims in the *95 Theses*. See *The Annotated Luther*, Volume 1, pp. 35–37.

50. This technical term designates the pope as a substitute (*vicarius*) ruler of the church in Christ's visible absence.

c Isa. 3:12 (Vulgate).

d See Luther's *Address to the Christian Nobility* (1520), above, pp. 19–21.

e Luke 1:52.

pope rules when Christ is absent and not present and dwelling in his heart, what is that but to be a Vicar of Christ? And then, what is the church other than a whole group of people without Christ? Truly, what is such a vicar except an Antichrist and idol? How much more correctly did the apostles call themselves servants of a present Christ than vicars of an absent Christ!

Perhaps I am presumptuous in attempting to teach such an exalted person, from whom all ought to be taught and (as your "plagues" boast)[51] from whom "the thrones of those who judge"[52] receive the [final] decree. But I emulate Saint Bernard in his book *On Consideration*, addressed to Pope Eugenius, which every pope should commit to memory.[f] I do this not from a desire to instruct you but from a sense of duty arising from pure and faithful solicitude that compels us to respect only the complete safety of our neighbors and that does not allow any consideration of their worthiness or unworthiness—being focused only on their dangers and particular situations. For since I know that Your Holiness is twisted and tossed about in Rome—that is, driven by unending dangers and surrounded by the highest seas—and that you are laboring on these things in miserable conditions such that you stand in need of even the smallest help from the least of the brothers, it did not seem foolish to me if for the moment I would forget your high majesty while fulfilling the duty of love. I do not want to flatter you in such a serious and dangerous situation. As far as that goes, if I am not understood to be your friend and most obedient servant, there is One who understands and judges.

51. Luther's description of the pope's flatterers. See above, p. 231.

52. That is, the bishops.

[Introduction to the Tract][53]

53. Renaissance dedications typically ended with a brief description of the book to which they were attached.

In conclusion, so that I might not approach you, Holy Father, empty-handed, I offer this little tract, published under your name, in the prospect of an established peace and good hope. In it you can get a taste of the kinds of studies with

f See above, p. 233.

which I could and would occupy myself far more fruitfully, if only your godless flatterers permitted it now and before. It is a small thing with respect to its size, but (unless I am mistaken) it contains a summary of the whole Christian life, if you understand its meaning. Poor man that I am, I have nothing else to present to you. But then you do not need to be enriched by any other gift save a spiritual one. Therefore, I commend myself to your fatherly goodness. May the Lord Jesus preserve you forever! Amen.

Wittenberg, September 6, 1520.

ON CHRISTIAN FREEDOM

[Introduction][g]

Many people view Christian faith as something easy, and quite a few people even count it as if it were related to the virtues.[54] They do this because they have not judged faith in light of any experience, nor have they ever tasted its great power.[h]

Faith Is Learned through Tribulations[i]

This is because a person who has not tasted its spirit in the midst of trials and misfortune cannot possibly write well about faith or understand what has been written about it. But one who has had even a small taste of faith can never write, speak, reflect, or hear enough about it. As Christ says in John 4[:14], it is a "spring of water welling up to eternal life."

g This subhead is not in sixteenth-century editions of the tract.

h The same Latin word is translated here "virtues" or "power."

i With few exceptions recorded in footnotes, all subtitles come from the second edition of the tract, printed in Basel by Adam Petri in 1521. See the introductory material, p. 222f, above.

54. In medieval moral theology, faith, hope, and love were the chief theological virtues (based on 1 Cor. 13:13). Over against this prevailing view, Luther understood faith relationally (experientially) as confidence or trust, arising in the midst of trials. He distinguished it from mere intellectual assent to doctrinal truths and thus opposed medieval theology, which derived its definition of faith from the basic Aristotelian distinction between "matter" and "form," interpreting the Latin version of Gal. 5:6 as "faith *formed* by love," meaning that faith by itself was insufficient (only the "material principle" of a saving disposition toward God), completed only by the "formal principle" of love for God.

Although I cannot boast of my own abundance of faith and I also know quite well how short my own supply is, nevertheless—given that I have been troubled by great and various trials[55]—I hope I can attain to at least a drop of faith. And I hope that I can talk about faith in a way that, if not more elegant, is certainly clearer than has been done in the past by the fancy writers and the subtle disputants alike, who have not even understood their own writings.[56]

The Main Themes[j]

In order to point out an easier way for common folk[k] (for I serve only them), I am proposing two themes[57] concerning the freedom and servitude of the spirit.

The Christian individual[l] is a completely free lord of all, subject to none.

The Christian individual is a completely dutiful servant[m] of all, subject to all.

Although these topics appear to contradict one another, nevertheless, if they can be found to be in agreement, they will serve our purposes beautifully. For both are from the Apostle Paul, when he says in 1 Cor. 9[:19], "For though I am free with respect to all, I have made myself a slave to all" and in Rom. 13[:8], "Owe nothing to anyone except to love one another." But "love" by its very nature is dutiful and serves the one who is loved. The same was true of Christ who,

55. For Luther, trials (*tentationes*; often denoted by the German word *Anfechtungen*, attacks or struggles) marked the Christian life of faith from beginning to end. Thus, Luther is not simply referring here to earlier struggles as an Augustinian friar concerned with God's righteousness and penitence but to his entire life as a believer. For an even earlier reflection on this notion, see his *Explanations of the Ninety-Five Theses*, thesis 15 (LW 31:125–30, esp. 129).

56. Luther probably had in mind both "fancy" humanist writers, such as Erasmus (in his *Handbook of the Christian Soldier*), and Scholastic theologians known for disputations, such as Gabriel Biel.

57. These two statements provide the basic themes of the entire tract, explicated below beginning on pp. 243 and 264, respectively.

j The word "themes" (*themata*) is a Greek loan word and a technical term in rhetoric and dialectics for the main topic or central proposition of a speech or an argument.

k Latin: *rudes*. This term can mean unlettered or uncultivated but here means the simple or common people, unfamiliar with the complexities of Scholastic theology. It is at this point that the German version begins. For further references to Luther's orientation toward the commoner, see his *Treatise on Good Works* in *The Annotated Luther*, Volume 1, pp. 265f.

l Latin here and in the next line: *Christianus homo*.

m *Servus* can be translated either servant or slave but here is rendered servant to correspond with Luther's German version (*Knecht*). In the Pauline letters, the NRSV translates the Greek *doulos* as "slave."

although Lord of all, was nevertheless "born of a woman, born under the law"[n] and who was at the same time free and slave, that is, at the same time "in the form of God" and "in the form of a slave."[58, o]

Let us approach these two themes from a rather distant and unsophisticated starting point.[p] Every human being consists of two natures: a spiritual and a bodily one. According to the spiritual nature, which people label the soul, the human being is called a spiritual, inner, and new creature. According to the bodily nature, which people label the flesh, a human being is called the fleshly, outer, and old creature.[59] Paul writes about this in 2 Cor. 4[:16], "Even though our outer nature is wasting away, our inner nature is being renewed day by day." This distinction results in the fact that in the Scripture these contrary things are said about the same person, because these two "human beings" fight against each other in the very same human being, as in Gal. 5[:17], "For what the flesh desires is opposed to the spirit, and what the spirit desires is opposed to the flesh."[q]

58. The basic themes of this tract first arose in Luther's *Two Kinds of Righteousness* from 1519 (LW 31:297–306, esp. 297), itself perhaps derived from a sermon on the appointed epistle lesson for Palm Sunday, Phil. 2:6-11.

59. By defining the whole human being according to these two aspects or natures, Luther is not simply taking over Platonic or other philosophical divisions between material and spiritual worlds. He often equated *soul* with the biblical term *heart*.

[The Spiritual, New, and Inner Person][60, r]

60. This begins the first main section of the tract on the first of the two themes introduced above. The second begins on p. 264.

In looking at the inner person first, we grasp how someone may become righteous,[s] free, and truly Christian, that is, "a spiritual, new, and inner person."[t]

n An allusion to Gal. 4:4.

o An allusion to Phil. 2:6-7.

p *Altior* could mean distant, deeper, or ancient. Coupled with *crassior*, it seems to indicate either an old, crude example or one that seems far removed from the two stated themes.

q In the Greek and Latin texts of Galatians, the word "spirit" can also refer to the Holy Spirit.

r This subtitle was not in any sixteenth-century text.

s Except where noted, the Latin words *iustus* and *iustitia* will be translated "righteous" and "righteousness," not "justice," which in current English usage denotes conformity to a legal principle.

t An allusion to the wording in the preceding paragraph.

What Christian Freedom Does Not Consist In

It is evident that no external thing at all, whatever its name, has any part in producing Christian righteousness or freedom. Nor does it produce unrighteousness or servitude. This can be proven by a simple argument. How can it benefit the soul if the body is in good health—free and active, eating and drinking and doing what it pleases—when even the most ungodly slaves to complete wickedness may overflow in such things? On the other hand, how could poor health or captivity or hunger or thirst or any other external misfortune harm the soul, when even the godliest, purest, and freest consciences[61] are afflicted with such things? Not one of these things touches upon the freedom or servitude of the soul. Thus, it does not help the soul if the body wears the sacred robes set apart for priests or enters sacred places or performs sacred duties or prays, fasts, abstains from certain foods, or does absolutely any work connected with the body.[62] Righteousness and freedom of the soul will require something completely different, since the things just mentioned could easily be done by some ungodly person and since such efforts result only in producing hypocrites. On the other side, the soul is not harmed if the body wears street clothes, goes around in secular places, eats and drinks like everyone else, does not pray aloud, and fails to do all the things mentioned above that hypocrites could do.

The Word of God Is Necessary for the Soul

Moreover, so that we may exclude everything—even contemplation, meditation, and whatever else can be done by the soul's efforts—all of this has no benefit. One thing and one thing alone is necessary for the Christian life, righteousness, and freedom, and that is the most holy word of God, the Gospel of Christ.[63] As John 11[:25] states: "I am the Resurrection and the Life, whoever believes in me will never die." And John 8[:36]: "If the Son makes you free, you will be free indeed." And Matt. 4[:4]: "One does not live by bread alone but by every word that comes from the mouth

61. Luther often used the term *conscience* not simply as an ethical category but to denote the entire human being standing before the righteous God, as here.

62. This argument implies criticism of late medieval popular piety, which assumed that pilgrimages to see relics, fasting, and sacred acts performed by priests did affect the soul's standing before God. Luther's readers might also have been familiar with even harsher criticism of the late medieval priesthood by humanists and other pamphleteers. See the "appendix" below, pp. 285–92.

63. For Luther, the phrase "word of God" rarely meant simply the Bible but more generally God's oral, direct proclamation. Thus, here he modifies the phrase with the words (capitalized in the original) "Gospel of Christ." The German version, also written by Luther, has: ". . . except the holy Gospel, the word of God preached by Christ." Luther understood God's word not simply as informative but as powerful and creative, present

of God." Therefore, we may consider it certain and firmly established, that the soul can lack everything except the word of God. Without it absolutely nothing else satisfies the soul. But when soul has the word, it is rich and needs nothing else, because the word of God is the word of life, truth, light, peace, righteousness, salvation, joy, freedom, wisdom, power, grace, glory, and every imaginable blessing.[64]

David in Psalm 119 [65]

This is why the prophet throughout Psalm 119 and in so many other places [in the Psalter] yearns and sighs with groans and cries for the word of God.

God's Cruelest Disaster

Again, there is no crueler disaster arising from God's wrath than when it sends "a famine of the hearing of his word," as stated in Amos 8[:11],[u] just as there is no greater grace than whenever God sends forth his word, as in Ps. 107[:20]. "He sent out his word and healed them and delivered them from their destruction." And Christ was not sent into the world for any other office than the word. Moreover, the apostles, bishops and the entire order of clerics[v] have been called and established only for the ministry of the word.

What the Word of God Is

You may ask, "What is this word and how should it be used, when there are so many words of God?" I respond as follows. Paul explains what this word is in Rom. 1[:1, 3]: "The gospel of God . . . concerning his Son," who was made flesh, suffered, rose, and was glorified through the Spirit, the Sanctifier.[w] Thus, to preach Christ means to feed, justify, free, and save the soul—provided a person believes the preaching. For faith

u Luther's citation of Amos is a paraphrase.

v Latin: *ordo clericorum*, that is, priests. Luther returns to this point later in the tract (p. 262f.).

w Paraphrasing Rom. 1:3-4. "Sanctificator" here means the One who makes holy.

in creation (Genesis 1) and in the church's proclamation of the good news of Christ (whom John 1 calls the Word of God). Luther's insistence on the Word "alone" (*solum*) is the basis for later comments about faith alone.

64. Luther uses one of his favorite rhetorical devices, congeries (a heaping up of words), to emphasize the wide-ranging work of God's word.

65. Luther and most of his contemporaries assumed that King David, whom they often called a prophet because of the association of many psalms with Christ, wrote many if not all of the psalms. Luther wrote similar things about Psalm 119 in his 1539 preface to his German works (LW 34:279–88).

alone is the saving and efficacious use of the word of God. Rom. 10[:9] states: "If you confess with your heart that Jesus is Lord and believe in your heart that God raised him from the dead, you will be saved," and again [in v. 4]: "For Christ is the end of the law, so that there may be righteousness for everyone who believes." And Rom. 1[:17] states: "The one who is righteous will live by faith."

Faith Alone Justifies

For the word of God cannot be received or honored by any works but by faith alone.[66] Therefore, it is clear that the soul needs the word alone for life and righteousness, because if the soul could be justified by anything else, it would not need the word and, consequently, would not need faith. Indeed, this faith absolutely cannot exist in connection with works, that is to say, in connection with any presumption of yours to be justified at the same time by any works whatsoever. For this would be "to limp in two different opinions" to worship Baal[x] and to "kiss [my] hand," which, as Job says, "is a great iniquity."[y]

What Must Be Believed

Therefore, when you begin to believe,[67] you discover at the same time that everything in you is completely blameworthy, damnable sins, as Rom. 3[:23] states: "All have sinned and fall short of the glory of God." And Rom. 3[:10-12] says, "There is no one who is righteous," no one does good, "all have turned aside, altogether they have done worthless things."[z] By this knowledge you will realize that you need Christ, who suffered and rose again for you, in order that, believing in him, you may become another human being by this faith, because all your sins are forgiven and you are justified by another's merits, namely, by Christ's alone.

66. First in the spring of 1518 (e.g., in his *Sermon on Penance* [*Sermo de poenitentia*; WA 1:324, 15]), Luther used the Latin phrase "faith alone justifies" (*sola fide iustificet*) in print. By stressing faith *alone*, he rejected the common medieval stance, based upon the Aristotelian notion that because everything consisted of matter and form, faith and love together justified. (See above, p. 241, n. 54.) For Luther, faith itself was not a human work. Thus, he was also attacking the notion, championed by Gabriel Biel and other Nominalist theologians, that "to those who do what is in them God will not deny grace." This whole paragraph is only in the Latin version.

67. In the German version, Luther uses the phrases "to believe firmly" and "to trust." In Latin, he uses "to believe" (*credere*) and "faith" (*fides*). Already here Luther is moving from law (commands that reveal and condemn sin) to gospel (promises that provide faith in Christ), a central part of his theology. See below, p. 248.

x An allusion to 1 Kgs. 18:21, Elijah's mocking of the priests of Baal.

y Job 31:27, which contrasts worship of God to worship of gold, nature, or the self.

z Reading with the Vulgate.

A Human Being Is Justified by No External Work

Because this faith can only rule the inner person, as Rom. 10[:10] says ("one believes with the heart and so is justified"), and because this faith alone justifies, it is clear that the inner person cannot be justified, freed, or saved by any external work or activity at all and that no works whatever have anything to do with the inner person. In the same way, on the other hand, the inner person becomes guilty and a condemned slave of sin only by ungodliness and unbelief of the heart and not by any external sin or work. It follows that the primary concern of each and every Christian ought to be that, by putting aside the supposition about works, they strengthen faith alone more and more and through that faith "grow . . . in knowledge" not of works but "of Christ Jesus," who suffered and rose again for them, as Peter in 2 Pet. 3[:18] teaches.[a] For no other work makes a Christian. Thus, when the Jews in John 6[:28] asked what they should do to perform the works of God, Christ dismissed their multitude of works, which he realized puffed them up, and prescribed one work for them, saying, "This is the work of God, that you believe in him whom he has sent," for "it is on him that God the Father has set his seal."[b]

Faith Is an Incomparable Treasure

Therefore, true faith in Christ is an incomparable treasure that includes with it complete salvation and protection from all evil, as it says in Mark 16[:16]: "The one who believes and is baptized will be saved; but the one who does not believe will be condemned." Isaiah contemplated this treasure and foretold it in chapter 10[:23, 22]: "The Lord will make an abbreviated and completed word upon earth," and "a

a Literally: "In the last chapter of 1 Peter," leading most editors and translators to refer to 1 Peter 5:10. However, the preceding language comes from the last chapter of 2 Peter (3:18): "But grow in the grace and knowledge of our Lord and Savior Jesus Christ."

b John 6:29, 27. See the *Treatise on Good Works* in *The Annotated Luther*, Volume 1, p. 267.

completed abbreviation will overflow with righteousness."[c] It is as if to say, "Faith, which is a compact and complete fulfillment of the law, will fill believers with such righteousness that they will need nothing else for righteousness." So, too, Paul says in Rom. 10[:10]: "For one believes with the heart and so is justified."

Scripture Contains Commands and Promises[d]

You may be asking, however, how it comes about that faith alone justifies and how it confers so many great treasures without works, given that so many works, ceremonies,[68] and laws are prescribed in the Scriptures. I answer this way. Before all else, remember what has been said above, namely, that faith alone without works justifies, frees, and saves. We shall make this clearer in a moment. In the meantime, it should be pointed out that the entire Scripture of God is divided into two parts: commands and promises. Commands, to be sure, teach what is good, but what is taught is not thereby done. For the commands show what we ought to do but do not give the power to do it. They were instead established for this: so that they may reveal individuals to themselves. Through the commands they know their inability to do good, and they despair of their own powers. This explains why commands are called and indeed are the *old* testament.[69]

68. Here and in the appendix, Luther uses the word *ceremonies* for all types of religious rules and regulations, not just for liturgical rites.

69. Emphasis added. It would appear that in this context Luther, rather than referring strictly to the books of the Old and New Testaments, equates "old testament" with any part of the Bible that commands something and "new testament" for language that contains God's promises. For Luther's later reflections on the relation between the Old and New Testaments, see *How Christians Should Regard Moses* (1525) in LW 35:155–74.

c Luther paraphrases v. 23 and then v. 22 of the Vulgate, adding the term "word." The Vulgate reads: "An abbreviated completion will overflow with righteousness. For the Lord God will make a completion and an abbreviation of troubles in the midst of all the earth." The NRSV states: "Destruction is decreed, overflowing with righteousness. For the Lord God of hosts will make a full end, as decreed, in all the earth." Here Luther treats this text, which refers to a remnant of believing Israel that will survive Assyria's destruction, allegorically.

d Luther introduced this theme earlier. See p. 246.

All Commands Are Equally Impossible for Us [70]

For example, "you shall not covet"[71,e] is a command that convicts us all of being sinners, because no one can avoid coveting, no matter how hard we might struggle against it. Thus, in order to keep this commandment and not covet, individuals are forced to despair of themselves and to seek help elsewhere from someone else. As it says in Hos. [13:9]: "Destruction is your own, O Israel. Your help is only in me."[f] However, what occurs with this single commandment occurs in the same way with them all. For all of them are equally impossible for us.

The Law Must Be Satisfied

Now, when through the commands individuals have been made aware of their powerlessness and now become anxious about how to satisfy the law (since the law must be satisfied so that "not one letter, not one stroke of a letter, will pass away"[g]—otherwise every person would be condemned without hope), they are then humbled and reduced to nothing in their own eyes. They find nothing in themselves by which to be justified and saved. At this point, the second part of Scripture (God's promises, which announce God's glory) arrives and says: "If you want to fulfill the law, 'You shall not covet,' as the law demands, then look here! Believe in Christ, in whom grace, righteousness, peace, freedom, and all things are promised to you. If you believe, you will have these things; if you do not believe, you will lack them."

We Fulfill Everything through Faith

For what is impossible for you to fulfill using all the works of the law, which though great in number are useless, you will fulfill easily and quickly through faith. Because God the Father has made all things depend on faith, whoever has

70. Luther is contradicting Jerome (c. 347–420), who in debates with Augustine (354–430) insisted that commands could be fulfilled, though not without God's grace.

71. See the discussion of this commandment in Rom. 7:7-13. See Luther's similar explanation of the Romans passage in his 1522 preface to the book for his German translation of the New Testament (LW 35:376–77).

e Exod. 20:17.

f Luther cites the Vulgate, which mirrors the Greek and Syriac. Following the Hebrew, the NRSV has: "I will destroy you, O Israel; who can help you?"

g Matt. 5:18.

faith has everything and whoever lacks faith has nothing. "For God has imprisoned all in unbelief, so that he may be merciful to all" (Rom. 11[:32]).[h] Thus, God's promises give what the law demands, so that everything may belong to God alone, both the commands and their fulfillment.

God Alone Commands and Fulfills[72]

72. This sentiment echoes Augustine's famous prayer in the *Confessions* X:29: "Give what you command, and command what you will."

God alone commands, and God alone fulfills. Therefore the promises of God pertain to and, indeed, are the *new* testament.[i]

The First Power of Faith

Now since these promises of God are holy, true, righteous, peaceful, and filled with total goodness, what happens is this: The soul that adheres to them with a firm faith is not simply united with them but fully swallowed up by them, so that it not only shares in them but also is saturated and intoxicated by their every power. For if Christ's touch healed, how much more will this tender touch in the spirit—or, better, this ingestion by the word—communicate to the soul all things that belong to the word. Therefore, by this means, through faith alone without works, the word of God justifies the soul and makes it holy, true, peaceful, and free, filled with every blessing and truly made a child of God, just as John 1[:12] says: "To all who . . . believe in his name, he gave power to become the children of God."

From these arguments it is easy to understand the source of faith's singular ability and why any good work—or all of them put together—cannot equal it at all. Why? Because no good work can cling to the word of God or even exist in the soul. Instead, faith alone and the word rule in it. For the word is of such a nature that the soul is formed by it. Just as heated iron glows like fire because of its union with fire, so it is clear that a Christian needs faith for everything and

h Luther cites the Vulgate. NRSV has "in disobedience."

i Emphasis added. See above, p. 248, n. 69.

will have no need of works to be justified. Now if works are unnecessary, then so is the law. If the law is unnecessary, then certainly such a person is free from the law. Moreover, it is true that "the law is not laid down for the righteous."[j] So, this is the Christian freedom referred to above, namely, our faith, which does not cause us to be lazy and lead evil lives but instead makes the law and works unnecessary for the righteousness and salvation of the Christian.[73]

73. Here Luther summarizes the first major theme of this tract and hints at the second (p. 264).

The Second Power of Faith

Let this suffice for the first power of faith. Let us now look at the second. Faith functions also in the following way. It honors the one in whom it trusts[k] with the most reverent and highest regard possible for this reason: Faith holds the one in whom it trusts to be truthful and deserving.

The Highest Honor

For no honor is equal to attributing truthfulness and righteousness to someone, which is how we honor the one in whom we trust. Could we ascribe to anyone anything greater than truthfulness, righteousness, and absolutely perfect goodness?

The Highest Contempt

Conversely, the greatest contempt is to suspect or to accuse someone publicly of being, in our opinion, a liar and wicked, which we do when we do not trust a person. So when the soul firmly believes the God who promises, it regards God as true and righteous. Nothing can show God greater respect!

j 1 Tim. 1:9, cited according to the Vulgate, which mirrors a literal translation of the Greek. NRSV has "for the innocent."

k The phrase *credere in* (literally, "to believe in") in this paragraph is best rendered "to trust." See Luther's comments on the equivalent German phrase (*glauben an*) in his *A Short Form of the Ten Commandments, Creed and Lord's Prayer* (1520), later printed in his *Personal Prayer Book* (1522) in LW 43:24: "The second kind of faith means believing in God—not just that I believe that what is said about God is true, but that I put my trust in him."

This is the highest worship of God: To bestow on God truthfulness and righteousness and whatever else ought to be ascribed to the One in whom a person trusts. Here the soul submits itself to what God wishes; here it hallows God's name and allows itself to be treated according to God's good pleasure. This is because, clinging to God's promises, the soul does not doubt that God is true, righteous, and wise—the One who will do, arrange, and care for everything in the best possible way.

Perfect Obedience

Is not such a soul completely obedient to God in all things by this very faith? What commandment remains that such obedience has not completely fulfilled? What fulfillment is fuller than obedience in every situation?[l] However, not works but faith alone offers this obedience.

Rebellion

Conversely, what greater rebellion against God, godlessness, and contempt of God is there than not to believe the One who promises? What is this but either to make God out a liar or to doubt that God is truthful? Or, to put it another way, is this not to ascribe truthfulness to oneself and falsehood and vanity to God? In so doing, is one not denying God and setting oneself up as an idol in one's very heart? Of what good are works done in this state of godlessness, even if they were angelic and apostolic works? Therefore, God rightly "imprisons everything under unbelief," not under anger or lust,[m] so that people do not imagine that by chaste and gentle works of the law[74] they fulfill the law (granted that such things are civic and human virtues). Such people assume they will be saved, even though they are caught in

74. The opposite of anger and lust. See Luther's commentary on Gal. 5:22 in his *Commentary on Galatians* (1519) in LW 27:377–78, where he condemns works of the law.

l Luther plays on the words for "fulfill," "fulfillment," and "fuller" (*impleverit, plenitudo, plenior*).

m Referring to Rom. 11:32, cited above.

the sin of unbelief and must thus either seek mercy or be justly condemned.

God Honors Those Who Believe in Him

But when God sees that we ascribe truthfulness to him and by our heart's faith honor him as is his due, then in return God honors us, ascribing to us truthfulness and righteousness on account of this faith. For faith results in truthfulness and righteousness, giving to God his own.[75] Thus, in return God gives glory to our righteousness. For it is true and righteous that God is true and righteous, and to ascribe this to God and to confess it means being true and righteous.[n] As 1 Sam. 2[:30] states: "For the ones who honor me I will honor, and those who despise me shall be treated with contempt." As Paul says in Rom. 4[:3] that Abraham's faith "was reckoned to him as righteousness," because through it he fully gave God the glory. For the same reason, if we believe it will be reckoned to us as righteousness.

The Third Benefit of Faith: Union with the Bridegroom[76, o]

The third incomparable benefit[77] of faith is this: that it unites the soul with Christ, like a bride with a bridegroom. By this "mystery" (as Paul teaches)[p] Christ and the soul are made one flesh. For if they are one flesh and if a true marriage—indeed by far the most perfect marriage of all—is culminated between them (since human marriages are but

n Given the standard definition of justice, *iustus* could be translated here "just" rather than "righteous."

o Combining consecutive marginal notes from the 2d ed.

p Luther uses here the term *sacramentum*, found in the Vulgate's translation of Eph. 5:32, applying what was said about the church to the soul. This translation of the Greek *mysterion* led eventually to the designation of certain rites in the church as sacraments (literally, in Latin, "oaths" or "vows" but also "mysteries"). First, in the 1522 German translation of the New Testament, Luther renders the phrase "secret" (*Geheimnis*), in line with the Greek, while adding a marginal comment noting the Latin and Greek words.

75. Throughout this discussion of faith's second power, Luther uses a standard definition of *iustitia* (righteousness or justice), proposed by Aristotle (384–322 BCE) and employed by Cicero and the Latin legal tradition, as "giving to each his [or her] own." Here, however, by attributing to God truth and righteousness (literally, "God's own"), the soul then receives them back from God as a divine gift. See also his preface to Romans in his translation of the New Testament (1522), in LW 35:371.

76. Luther borrows the marital image not only from Ephesians 5 and traditional Christian interpretations of the Song of Songs but more directly from Augustine's *Expositions on the Book of Psalms*, which Luther used in his lectures on the Psalms from 1513 to 1515. See, e.g., Augustine's comments on Ps. 38:3 (Vulgate: 37), par. 5 (English translation in NPNF ser. 1, 14 vols., 8:104), and Luther's glosses on the same psalm (WA 55/1:329). The union of the soul and Christ is also found in many medieval thinkers, including Bernard of Clairvaux and Johannes Tauler (c. 1300–1361).

77. In keeping with medieval usage, Luther can still use the word *grace* (*gratia*; here translated as "benefit") as a "bestowed power" and thus a synonym of the word *virtus*, the term for the first two "powers" of faith. By 1521 he would accept Erasmus's argument that in the Greek New Testament the word *charis* (traditionally translated *gratia*) means God's favor (*favor Dei*) or, as the Wittenberg reformers often rendered it, God's mercy (*misericordia Dei*). For

weak shadows of this one), then it follows that they come to hold all things, good and bad, in common. Accordingly, the faithful soul can both assume as its own whatever Christ has and glory in it, and whatever is the soul's Christ claims for himself as his own.[78]

Consider These Invaluable Things!

Let us examine these things in detail to see how invaluable they are. Christ is full of grace, life, and salvation; the soul is full of sins, death, and damnation. Now let faith intervene and it will turn out that sins, death, and hell are Christ's, but grace, life, and salvation are the soul's. For if he is the groom, then he should simultaneously both accept the things belonging to the bride and impart to the bride those things that are his. For the one who gives his body and his very self to her, how does he not give his all? And the one who receives the body of the bride, how does he not take all that is hers?[q]

Love's Duel in Christ

This is truly the most delightful drama,[79,r] involving not only communion but also a saving war, victory, salvation, and redemption. For Christ is God and a human being in one and the same person, who does not and cannot sin, die, or be damned; and his righteousness, life, and salvation are unconquerable, eternal, and all-powerful. When, I say, such a person shares in common and, indeed, takes as his own the sins, death, and hell of the bride on account of the wedding ring of faith, and when he regards them as if they were his own and as if he himself had sinned—suffering, dying, and descending into hell—then, as he conquers them all and as sin, death, and hell cannot devour him, they are devoured by

q Here, among other things, Luther echoes the language of 1 Cor. 7:4.

r Latin: *spectaculum*, literally, "a piece of theater."

Luther's early, still critical comments on Erasmus's proposal, see the commentary on Galatians (1519) in LW 27:252; and for his acceptance of it two years later, see the tract *Against Latomus* (1521) in LW 32:226–28.

78. Luther uses this traditional language about the marriage of Christ and the soul to illustrate his understanding of justification by faith. Roman marriage law distinguished between property (what one owned) and possession (what one had full use of) and held that in marriage the property of the one spouse became the possession of the other and vice versa. Similarly, Luther argues here and in the ensuing paragraphs that what is Christ's own (grace, life, and salvation) becomes the soul's and what is the soul's own (sin, death, and damnation) becomes Christ's, all by the marriage of faith. Luther first published his thoughts on this "joyous exchange" (the phrase used in the German version of *The Freedom of a Christian*) in *Two Kinds of Righteousness* (1519) in LW 31:297–99, a forerunner to this tract, although he employed it earlier in the lecture hall, pulpit, and correspondence. For one example, see the letter to Georg Spenlein (1486–1563) from 8 April 1516 (LW 48:12–13).

79. Luther's description of the extended metaphor of Christ's battle against sin for his bride is reminiscent of chivalry.

him in an astounding duel.[80] For his righteousness is superior to all sins, his life more powerful than death, and his salvation more invincible than hell.

80. This image of Christ as victor, popular among many Greek fathers and Augustine, was overshadowed in medieval theology by other explanations. Luther, however, uses this notion throughout his career. For just two examples of many, see his hymn "A Mighty Fortress" or his commentary on Gal. 3:13 (1535) in LW 26:276–91.

The Wedding Ring of Faith for the Bride of Christ

So it happens that the faithful soul, through the wedding ring of its faith in Christ her bridegroom, is free from all sins, secure against death, protected from hell, and given the eternal righteousness, life, and salvation of her bridegroom, Christ. Thus, "he takes to himself a glorious bride without spot or wrinkle . . . making her clean by washing . . . in the word of life,"[s] that is, through faith in the word, life, righteousness, and salvation [of Christ]. As Hos. 2[:19] says, [the Lord] becomes engaged to her "in faith, in mercy and compassion, in righteousness, and judgment."[t]

The Majesty of the Wedding Garments

Who can even begin to appreciate this royal marriage? What can comprehend the riches of this glorious grace? Here, this rich, upstanding bridegroom, Christ, marries this poor, disloyal little prostitute, redeems her from all her evil and adorns her with all his goodness. For now it is impossible for her sins to destroy her, because they have been laid upon Christ and devoured by him. In Christ, her bridegroom, she has her righteousness, which she can enjoy as her very own property. And with confidence she can set this righteousness over against all of her sins and in opposition to death and hell and can say, "Sure, I have sinned, but my Christ, in whom I trust, has not sinned. All that is his is mine and all that is mine is his." As it says in the Song of Sol. [2:16]: "My beloved is mine, and I am his." This is what Paul says in

s A fairly close rendering of Eph. 5:27a and 26b, leaving out the words "church" and "water."

t This citation matches the Vulgate: "And I will take you as my wife in righteousness and judgment and in mercy and in compassion, and I will take you as my wife in faith."

1 Cor. 15[:57]: "Thanks be to God, who gives us the victory through our Lord Jesus Christ." But this "victory" is over sin and death, as he notes in the previous verse [v. 56]: "The sting of death is sin, and the power of sin is the law."

Why Ascribe These Things Only to Faith?[u]

From the preceding, you may once again understand why the fulfillment of the law and justification without any works by faith alone may only be ascribed to faith. You observe that the first commandment, "You shall worship one God," is fulfilled by faith alone.[81]

81. This reflects Luther's interpretation of the first commandment, already expressed earlier in 1520 in his *Treatise on Good Works* (see *The Annotated Luther*, Volume 1, pp. 267–86) and later in his catechisms of 1529.

True Worship of God

For even if you were nothing but good works from the soles of your feet to the top of your head, you would still not be righteous, worship God, or fulfill the first commandment, since God cannot be worshiped unless the glory of truth and of complete goodness is ascribed to him, as truly must be due him.

Faith Does Works[v]

But works cannot do this—only faith of the heart can. For not by working but by believing do we glorify God and confess that God is truthful. On this basis, faith alone is the righteousness of a Christian and the fulfilling of all the commandments, because the one who fulfills the first commandment easily fulfills all the works of the others. Now works, being inanimate, cannot glorify God, although they can be done to God's glory if faith is present.[82] At this juncture, however, we are not asking about the kinds of works that are to be done but about the person who does them, who glorifies God and who produces works. This faith of the

82. Luther here distinguishes works, the fruits of faith, which he labels inanimate, from faith itself, which is alive in the heart of the believer. Works for him are an effect of faith; faith is the cause.

u This section summarizes Luther's argument regarding the three powers of faith.

v This refers to the second power of faith. See above, p. 251.

heart is the source and substance of all of our righteousness. Thus, it is a blind and dangerous instruction that teaches works must fulfill the commandments, because the commandments must be fulfilled before all works and thus works follow this fulfillment, as we will hear.[w]

The Prerogatives of the Firstborn[83]

In order to examine more closely this grace that our inner person possesses in Christ, it must be realized that God in the Old Testament consecrated to himself all firstborn males. And this birthright was highly prized, giving power over all others with a double honor: priesthood and kingship.[84] The firstborn brother was a priest and ruler over all others. This figure foreshadowed Christ who, as the true and only firstborn of God the Father and of the Virgin Mary, was true king and priest but not according to the flesh and this world.

What Christ's Kingdom and Priesthood Consist In[x]

For his "kingdom is not from this world."[y] He rules over and consecrates heavenly and spiritual things, such as righteousness, truth, wisdom, peace, and salvation. Not that everything on earth and in hell is not subjected to him (otherwise, how could he protect and save us from them?), but his kingdom does not consist in nor is it derived from such things. Similarly, his priesthood does not consist in the external pomp of robes and gestures, as did that human priesthood of Aaron then and as our ecclesiastical priesthood does today. But his consists in spiritual things, through which, in an invisible, heavenly office, he intercedes for us before God, offers himself there, and does all the things that a priest ought to do.

83. Here Luther introduces a new argument. For the law of the primogeniture of priests, see Exod. 13:2. For the primogeniture of kings, see, e.g., the struggle of succession at the time of David's death in 1 Kings 1–2 (esp. 2:22). Luther, following the longstanding practice of the church, views these historical facts in the Old Testament as types or figures, pointing to Christ.

84. Throughout, the word *sacerdos* is translated "priest," a term used in the Old Testament for the official priests and in the New only for Christ or for all believers in him. The word *priest* in English (as in many other European languages) is derived from the Greek word *presbyteros* ("elder").

w See the second major theme on p. 264 below.

x Combining two marginal glosses (2d ed.).

y John 18:36.

The Priestly Office

This is how Paul describes him in Hebrews [7], using the figure of Melchizedek.[z] Not only does he pray and intercede for us, but he also teaches us inwardly in the spirit by the living instruction of his Spirit. These two things are properly speaking the offices of a priest that are prefigured by the visible prayers and sermons of human priests.

How Faithful Christians Ought to Be Understood as Priests and Kings[a]

Now, just as Christ by his birthright possessed these two ranks, so he imparts them to and shares them with every believer legally in accord with the marriage described above, where whatever are the bridegroom's belong to the bride. Hence, all of us who trust in Christ are all priests and kings in Christ, as 1 Pet. 2[:9] states: "You are a chosen race, an acquired people, a royal priesthood and a priestly kingdom, so that you may recount the powers of the one who called you from darkness into his marvelous light."[b] The nature of these two ranks is as follows.

The Spiritual Kingdom[c]

First, what pertains to kingship is this: through faith every Christian is exalted over all things and, by virtue of spiritual power, is absolutely lord of all things. Consequently, nothing at all can ever harm such a one to whom, indeed, all things are subject and forced to serve for salvation. Paul states this in Rom. 8[:28]: "We know that all things work together for

z Based upon Genesis 14 and Ps. 110:4. The authorship of Hebrews was contested in the sixteenth century, so that on other occasions Luther admitted that Paul did not write this letter.

a Combining two marginal glosses (2d ed.).

b Here Luther follows the Vulgate, replacing "holy nation" with "priestly nation" and "announce" with "recount." Luther also uses this text in his *Address to the Christian Nobility* (p. 14).

c Mg. (2d ed.), moved slightly to correspond to the text.

good for the elect."[d] He says the same thing in 1 Cor. 3[:21b-23]: "All things are yours, whether . . . life or death or the present or the future . . . and you belong to Christ."

Note!

Now, this does not establish that Christians possess and exercise some sort of secular[e] power over everything—ecclesiastical leaders far and wide are possessed by such madness—for this is something that belongs to kings, princes, and human beings on earth.[f] We see from our daily experience in life that we are subjected to all kinds of things, suffer many things, and even die. Indeed, the more Christian a person is, the more he or she is subject to evils, suffering, or death, as we see in Christ, the firstborn prince himself, and in all his holy brothers [and sisters].

This power, which "rules in the midst of enemies"[g] and is powerful "in the midst of oppression,"[h] is spiritual. This is nothing other than "power made perfect in weakness" so that in "all things . . . I may gain" salvation.[i] In this way, the cross and death are forced to serve me and to work together for salvation. This is a lofty, splendid high rank and a true, omnipotent power and a spiritual sovereignty, in which there is nothing so good or nothing so evil that cannot "work together for good,"[j] if only I believe. Still, because faith alone suffices for salvation, I do not need anything else except for faith exercising its power and sovereignty of freedom in these things. Look here! This is the immeasurable power and freedom of Christians.

d NRSV: "for those who love God." Reference to the elect comes in the following verse.

e The word *corporali*, translated "secular," is literally, "bodily" or "physical."

f Luther expanded this distinction in 1523 in *On Secular Authority* (LW 45:75–129).

g Ps. 110:2.

h An allusion to 2 Cor. 4:8 as rendered in Erasmus's Latin translation of the Greek.

i Allusions to 2 Cor. 12:9 and Phil. 3:9.

j Rom. 8:28.

We Are Priests Forever[k]

Not only are we the freest kings of all, but we are also priests forever. This is more excellent by far than kingship, because through the priesthood we are worthy to appear before God, to pray for others, and to teach one another the things that are of God. For these are the priestly duties that absolutely cannot be bestowed on anyone who does not believe. Christ obtained this priesthood for us, if we trust in him, so that as we are confreres, coheirs, corulers, so we are co-priests with him, daring to come with confidence into God's presence in the spirit of faith and cry, "Abba, Father,"[l] to pray for another and to do all the things that we see are done and prefigured by the visible and corporeal office of priests.

Only Evil Comes to Nonbelievers

But nothing serves persons who do not believe, nor does anything "work together for good."[m] Instead, such individuals are slaves of all things and give themselves over to evil, because they use everything wickedly for their own advantage and not to the glory of God. Thus, they are not priests but profane people. Their prayers become sin, nor do they appear in God's presence, because God does not listen to sinners. Who, therefore, can comprehend the height of this Christian rank, which through its regal power is lord of all things—death, life, sin, and the like—but through its priestly glory can do all things before God, because God does what the priest asks and desires? As it is written: "He fulfills the desire of all who fear him; he also hears their cry, and saves them."[n] A person certainly arrives at this glory not by works but by faith alone.

k Referring back to Ps. 110:4.

l Rom. 8:15.

m Rom. 8:28. Luther uses the singular ("a" person) throughout this paragraph.

n Ps. 145:19.

The Freedom of Christians[85]

From the foregoing, anyone can clearly see how the Christian is free from all things and is over all things, so that such a person requires no works at all to be righteous or saved. Instead, faith alone bestows all these things in abundance. Now, if someone were so foolish as to presume to be made righteous, free, saved, and Christian through any good work, then such one would immediately lose faith along with all other good things. This foolishness is beautifully illustrated in that fable where a dog runs along a stream holding a piece of real meat in his mouth. When, deceived by the reflection of the meat in the water, the dog tries to get it by opening its mouth and loses both the meat and the reflection.[86]

[A Digression on the Meaning of Priesthood][87]

At this point, you may ask, "If all people in the church are priests, by what name do we distinguish those we now call priests from the laity?" I respond that an injustice has been done to these words—"priest," "cleric," "a spiritual one," and "a churchman"—when they are transferred from all other Christians to those few who now are called by this faulty usage "churchmen."[88] For Holy Scripture does not distinguish at all among them, except that it calls "ministers," "servants" and "stewards" those who now are proudly labeled popes, bishops, and lords but who should be serving others with the ministry of the word in order to teach the faith of Christ and the freedom of the faithful. For, although it is true that we are all equally priests, nevertheless we cannot all serve and teach nor, even if we can, ought we all to do so publicly. As Paul states in 1 Cor. 4[:1]: "Let a person regard us as servants of Christ and dispensers of God's mysteries."[o]

o Reading with the Vulgate.

85. This begins the conclusion to the first major theme, which Luther picks up again after the digression on priesthood and then applies it to preaching.

86. Luther filled his writings with allusions to classical sources, including *Aesop's Fables*, as here. His 1530 translation of these fables was published in 1557 (WA 50:432–60).

87. This subtitle was not in any sixteenth-century text. These two paragraphs form a digression from Luther's main argument, in order to discuss the proper meaning of "priest" (*sacerdos*). See also his discussion of what later became known as the "priesthood of all believers" in the *Address to the Christian Nobility* (pp. 14–16).

88. Although his main interest is in the use of the word *priest* (*sacerdos*), Luther employs other common terms for the ordained here: *cleros* ("cleric," a loan word into ecclesiastical Latin from the Greek, designating the clergy), *spiritualis* (a spiritual person [both priests and monks], as opposed to the laity, who live in the world) and *ecclesiasticus* ("ecclesiast," a church official [especially a teacher or preacher], but literally, "one who belongs to the church").

What the Ministry of Churchmen Has Become

Against this, such "dispensing" has now turned into such a display of power and a terrible tyranny that no national or worldly political power can be compared to it. It is as if the laity were something other than Christians. As a result of this perversity, the knowledge of Christian grace, faith, freedom, and Christ has perished entirely, only to be replaced by an intolerable captivity to human works and laws. As the Lamentations of Jeremiah puts it, we have become slaves of the vilest possible people on earth, who abuse our misery in all baseness and degradation of their desire.[p]

How Christ Must Be Preached

To return to my main topic, I believe that it has become clear that it is not sufficient or even Christian if, as those who are the very best preachers today do, we only preach Christ's works, life, and words just as a kind of story or as historical exploits (which would be enough to know for an example of how to conduct our lives). Much worse is when there is complete silence about Christ and human laws, and the decrees of the fathers[89] are taught instead of Christ. Moreover, some even preach Christ and recite stories about him for this purpose: to play on human emotions either to arouse sympathy for him or to incite anger against the Jews.[90] This kind of thing is simply childish and womanish nonsense.[91] Preaching, however, ought to serve this goal: that faith in Christ is promoted. Then he is not simply "Christ" but "Christ for you and me," and what we say about him and call him affect us.[92] This faith is born and preserved by preaching why Christ came, what he brought and gave, and what are the needs and the fruit that his reception entail. This kind of preaching occurs where Christian freedom, which we gain from him and which makes us Christians all kings and priests, is rightly taught. In him we are lords of all, and we trust that whatever we might do is pleasing and acceptable in God's sight, as we said above.

p Perhaps an allusion to Lamentations 1 or to the entire book.

89. Luther was probably thinking of canon law, the church rules from ancient and medieval teachers, popes, and councils that regulated the practice of penance, marriage, and all other aspects of church life.

90. For Luther's earlier criticism of this kind of preaching during Holy Week, see *A Meditation on Christ's Passion* in *The Annotated Luther*, Volume 1, p. 169.

91. Luther assumes, as did most men of his time (following Aristotle among others), that the emotions of children and women are especially easily manipulated by such preaching.

92. Luther reflects this conviction in comments about Christ in his catechisms, where he speaks of Christ as "my Lord, who redeemed me."

The Fruit of the Best Preaching[q]

What person's heart upon hearing these things would not rejoice from its very core and upon accepting such consolation would not melt[r] in love with Christ—something completely unattainable with laws and works? Who could possibly harm or frighten such a heart? If awareness of sin or dread of death overwhelms it, it is ready to hope in the Lord. It neither fears hearing about these evils nor is moved by them, until finally it despises its enemies.[s] For it believes that Christ's righteousness is its own and that its sin is now not its own but Christ's. More than that, the presence[t] of Christ's righteousness swallows up every sin. As noted above, this is a necessary consequence of faith in Christ. So the heart learns with the Apostle to scoff at death and sin and to say: "Where, O death, is your victory? Where, O death, is your sting? The sting of death is sin, and the power of sin is the law. But thanks be to God, who gives us the victory through our Lord Jesus Christ."[u] For death is swallowed up in victory—not only Christ's but ours—because through faith it becomes our victory and is in us and we are conquerors.

In a scene from the 1530 edition of the *Large Catechism* printed in Wittenberg, a preacher addresses a congregation from the pulpit, illustrating the petition in the Lord's Prayer, "Hallowed be your name."

q Luther moves from what preaching is to its effects.

r Literally, "become sweet."

s Perhaps an allusion to Ps. 110:1.

t Literally, "face."

u 1 Cor. 15:55-57.

Enough now has been said about the inner person, its freedom and its origin in the righteousness of faith. This inner person requires neither laws nor good works, which are harmful to it whenever someone presumes to be justified through them.

[The Outer Person][93, v]

93. This begins the second main section of the tract on the second of the two themes introduced above (p. 243). This theme serves as the confutation (see note *v* below).

Let us now turn to the second part, which concerns the outer person. Here we will respond to all those people who are offended by the word of faith and what has been said about it. They say, "If faith does all things and alone suffices for righteousness, why then are good works commanded? We will therefore be content with faith, take our ease and do no works." I respond, "Not so, you wicked people, not so!"[94] To be sure, this would be true if we were completely and perfectly inner, spiritual persons, which will not happen until the resurrection of the dead on the last day. As long as we live in the flesh, we are only beginning and advancing toward what will be perfected in the future life. The Apostle in Romans 8[:23] calls this the "first fruits of the Spirit," because in this life we will have received only a tenth but in the future life the fullness of the Spirit. So, this part of the essay pertains to what was said at the beginning: The Christian is a slave of all and subject to all.[w] Insofar as a Christian is free, he or she does nothing; insofar as the Christian is a slave, he or she does all things. Now we shall see how this can happen.

94. Luther is attacking moralistic opponents for pretending to make this argument as a way of destroying Christian freedom.

To be sure, as I have said, the inner person is in the spirit fully and completely justified through faith. Such a one has what he or she ought to have, except of course that this very faith and its riches ought to increase day by day toward the future life. For now, however, this person remains in this

v This subtitle was not in any sixteenth-century text. Instead, the marginal gloss in the second edition reads: "A question from those who do not understand Luther—or rather—what faith is."

w See above, p. 242.

mortal life on earth. In this life a person's own body must be ruled and be in relation with other human beings.

Where Works Begin [95]

Now here is where works begin. Here is not the time for leisure; here care must be taken to train the body by means of fasting, vigils, and other labors and to subdue it by the spirit.[96] In this way it may obey and be conformed to the inner person and faith, so that it may not rebel against or impede the inner person (as is its nature when not held in check).

The Single Concern of the Inner Person

For the inner person—conformed to God and created in the image of God through faith—is joyful and glad on account of Christ, in whom all good things have been conferred upon such a one. Because of this, that person has only one concern: to serve God joyfully, with boundless love and with no thought of earning anything. While acting this way, immediately the inner creature offends a contrary will in its own flesh, one that serves the world and tries seeking after what belongs to it. Because the spirit of faith cannot tolerate this at all, it attempts with joyful zeal to suppress and coerce the flesh. As Paul says in Rom. 7[:22-23]: "I delight in the law of God according to my inner person,[x] but I see in my members another law fighting against the law of my mind and making me captive to the law of sin." In another place,[y] he writes, "I punish my body and enslave it, so that after proclaiming to others I myself should not be disqualified." And in Gal. 5[:24] he states, "And those who belong to Christ Jesus have crucified the flesh with its passions and desires."[97]

x Reading with the Vulgate.

y 1 Cor. 9:27.

95. Here begins the first part of the second major theme on discipline of the flesh and works in general. For the second part (on love of neighbor), see below, p. 273.

96. Luther alludes to common practices of the day designed to restrain the flesh.

97. Throughout this section, Luther uses the technical term *concupiscentia*, translated here "desire." Concupiscence was said by medieval theologians to be the "matter" of sin that remained after baptism. Without the "form" of the willing conscience willing a sinful act, it was not viewed as sin. Luther and Reformation theologians rejected the imposition of medieval Aristotelian categories and insisted that such desires were themselves already sin. Thus, already in the lectures on Romans (1515–1516), in LW 25:336, and throughout his career (e.g., in the commentary on Galatians [1535] in LW 26:232), Luther declared that the justified person was *simul iustus et peccator* (at the same time justified and sinner).

Under What Supposition Are Works to Be Done?

These works, however, ought not to be done under the supposition that through them a person is justified before God. For faith, which alone is righteousness before God, does not endure this false opinion but supposes [that works be done] only so that "the body may be enslaved" and may be purified from its evil "passions and desires" so that the eye may not turn again to these expunged desires.[z] Because the soul has been cleansed through faith and made to love God, at the same time it wants all things (in particular the body) to be cleansed, so that all things may love and praise God with it. As a result, the human creature cannot be idle because of the demands of its body, and, because of the body, it attempts to do many good things to bring it under control. Nevertheless, these works are not what justify someone before God. Instead, the person does them in compliance to God out of spontaneous love, considering nothing else than the divine favor to which the person wishes to comply most dutifully in all things.

How to Discipline the Body

For this reason, all individuals[a] can easily figure out for themselves the "measure or discretion" (as people call it)[98,b] to which they ought to discipline their bodies. For they may only fast, perform vigils, and labor to the extent that they see it to be necessary for suppressing the body's wantonness and desire. Those who presume to be justified by works, however, have no regard for extinguishing[c] desires but only for the works themselves. They suppose that if they do so many great works, then they will fare well and be made righteous—sometimes even injuring their minds and destroying or at least rendering useless what makes them human. Wanting

98. Here Luther uses traditional language in relation to the freedom of faith, allowing the individual believer, not the confessor, to determine how much to discipline the body. See his *Treatise on Good Works* in *The Annotated Luther*, Volume 1, p. 324.

z Cf. 1 Cor. 9:27; Gal. 5:24; and 1 John 2:16.

a In the singular in the original.

b Latin: *mensura aut discretio*. This phrase is found in medieval books on virtues and vices and in medieval penitential manuals.

c Latin: *mortificatio*.

to be justified and saved through works without faith is simply monstrous foolishness and ignorance of the Christian life and faith!

An Excellent Analogy

So that we may make it easier to understand what we have said, let us illustrate these things with some analogies. The works of Christian individuals,[d] who are justified and saved through their faith by the pure and gracious mercy of God, ought not be considered from any other perspective than would be the works of Adam and Eve and their children had they not sinned. This is talked about in Gen. 2[:15]: God "placed the man," whom he had formed, "in paradise . . . so that he might work and take care of it."[e] Now, God created Adam to be righteous, upright, and without sin, so that through his work and care he had no need to be justified or made upright. Rather, so that he would not become idle, the Lord gave him a job, namely, that he care for and watch over paradise. These were truly the freest works, done neither "to make [a person] acceptable to anyone"[99] (except to divine favor) nor to obtain righteousness, which Adam already had fully and which would have been inborn in all of us.

In this engraving from a 1545 Leipzig publication of Luther's *Small Catechism*, God is shown marrying Adam and Eve.

Faith Puts a Person Back in Paradise

It is the same way with works of believing individuals,[f] who through their faith are once again put back in paradise and recreated from scratch. They would not do works to become or to be righteous but in order not to be idle and "to work and watch over" their bodies. For them these works arise

99. Medieval theologians defined justifying grace as *gratia gratum faciens*, the grace that makes acceptable, namely, by infusing a disposition (*habitus*) of love (*charitas*) into the soul and thus moving the soul from a state of mortal sin into a state of grace. Such a person then did good works acceptable to God.

d Singular in the original text.

e Cited according to the Vulgate.

f In the singular throughout this paragraph in the original.

from the same freedom [as Adam's], done only in consideration of divine favor—except that we are not yet fully recreated with perfect faith and love, which ought to increase not through works but through themselves.

Another Comparison

Here is another analogy. When a consecrated bishop dedicates a church building, confirms children, or performs some other duty pertaining to his office, he is not consecrated into office by performing these very works. Far from it! Unless he had already been consecrated a bishop beforehand, all of these works would be worthless; they would instead be foolish, childish, and silly. So also individual Christians,[g] who are consecrated by their faith, do good works, but through them they are not made holy[h] or Christian. For this arises from faith alone; indeed, unless they believed and were Christian beforehand, all of their works would be worthless and would be truly ungodly and damnable sins.

Two Statements Worth Remembering

Therefore, these two sayings are true: "Good works do not make a person good, but a good person does good works," and "Evil[i] works do not make a person evil, but an evil person does evil works." Thus, a person's essence or character must be good before all works, and good works follow and proceed from a good person.[100]

100. This is against the notion in Aristotelian ethics, followed by medieval theologians, that a person becomes good by doing good.

A Comparison

As Christ also says, "A good tree cannot bear bad fruit, nor can a bad tree bear good fruit."[j] It is obvious that fruit do not bear a tree nor does a tree grow on fruit, but just the reverse: trees bear fruit and fruit grow on trees. Therefore, just as it is necessary that trees exist prior to their fruit and

g In the singular throughout this paragraph in the original text.

h The same adjective translated "consecrated" above.

i In these paragraphs the Latin *malum* is translated either "evil" or "bad," depending on the context.

j Matt. 7:18.

that fruit make trees neither good nor bad, but that, on the contrary, specific kinds of trees make specific kinds of fruit, so it is necessary that first the very character of a person be good or evil before doing any good or evil work and that a person's works do not make one evil or good but rather that a person does evil or good works.

Another Comparison

Similar things can be seen in construction. A good or bad house does not make a good or bad builder, but a good or bad builder makes a good or bad house. As a general rule, no work makes its kind of artisan, but an artisan makes a particular kind of work. This same reality obtains for the works of human beings. Whatever kind of person one is—either in faith or unbelief—that determines one's work: good if done in faith, evil if done in unbelief. But this may not be reversed: as if whatever the kind of work determines the kind of human being—either in faith or unbelief. For just as works do not make someone a believer,[k] so also they do not make a person righteous. On the contrary, just as faith makes someone a believer and righteous, so also it produces good works.

Faith Alone Justifies

Since, therefore, works do not justify anyone and a person must be righteous before doing something good, these things are absolutely clear: that faith alone—because of the sheer mercy of God through Christ [given] in his word—properly and completely justifies and saves a person; and that no law is necessary for a Christian's salvation, since through faith one is free from every law and does everything that is done spontaneously, out of sheer freedom. Such a person seeks nothing for a payment or for salvation—already being satisfied and saved by God's grace from one's faith—but seeks only what pleases God.

k See above, p. 247.

Unbelievers Do Not Become Evil by Works

In the same way, no good work of an unbeliever contributes toward righteousness or salvation. On the other side, no evil work makes an unbeliever evil or damnable. Instead, unbelief, which makes an evil person and tree, does evil and damnable works. Thus, when someone is good or evil, this arises not from works but from faith or unbelief, as Sir. [10:14] says, "This is the beginning of sin, that a person falls away from God," that is, "does not believe." Paul states in Hebrews 11[:6]: "For whoever would approach God must believe." And Christ says the same thing: "Either make the tree good, and its fruit good; or make the tree bad and its fruit bad,"[l] as if he were saying, "Let whoever wants to have good fruit begin with the tree and plant a good one." Therefore, let whoever wants to do good things begin not with the doing but with the believing. For only faith makes a person good, and only unbelief makes someone evil.

Works Make a Human Being Good but Only in Human Eyes

To be sure, it is true that in the eyes of other human beings, works make a human being good or evil. But this happens the same way as when it is known or shown that someone is good or evil, as Christ says in Matt. 7[:20], "You will know them by their fruits." But all of this remains external and on the surface, which is just where many who presume to write and teach about "the good works by which we are justified"[101] are led astray.

101. Luther has in mind especially Gabriel Biel (c. 1420–1495) and Luther's own opponents who followed Biel's argument that a person merited justifying grace. See Heiko A. Oberman, *Harvest of Medieval Theology: Gabriel Biel and Late Medieval Nominalism*, 3d ed. (Durham, NC: Labyrinth, 1983), 141, esp. n.66.

The Source of Some Peoples' Error

Meanwhile, they do not even mention faith: going their false ways,[m] always leading astray, "progressing from bad to worse,"[n] "the blind leading the blind,"[o] wearying themselves

l Matt. 12:23.

m Echoing biblical condemnations, as in 2 Kgs. 8:18.

n Paraphrasing 2 Tim. 3:13.

o Matt. 15:14.

with many works and still never arriving at the true righteousness. Paul speaks about these people in 2 Tim. 3[:5, 7]: "Holding to the outward form of godliness but denying its power . . . who are always being instructed and can never arrive at knowledge of the truth."

Therefore, whoever does not want to fall into the same error with these blind people must look beyond works, laws, and teachings about works. More than that, one must focus on the person completely apart from works and on how such a one is justified. A person is justified and saved not by works or laws but by the Word of God (that is, by the promise of God's grace) and by faith. In this way, what remains firm is the glory of the divine majesty, which saves us who believe not by works of righteousness that we do but in accord with God's mercy through the word of his grace.

Rules for Understanding the Teachings of Many People Today

From all that has been said, it is easy to understand on what grounds good works must be rejected or accepted and by what rule everyone's current teachings about good works must be evaluated. For if works are coupled with righteousness and by that perverse Leviathan[102, p] and false persuasion take on such a character that you presume to be justified through them, then they become absolutely compulsory and extinguish freedom along with faith. By this kind of linkage, such works are no longer good but instead truly damnable. For they are not free, and they blaspheme against the grace of God, to whom alone belong justification and salvation through faith. What works are powerless to guarantee, they nevertheless pretend to do by this godless presumption and through this foolishness of ours, and thereby they intrude violently into the function of grace and its glory.

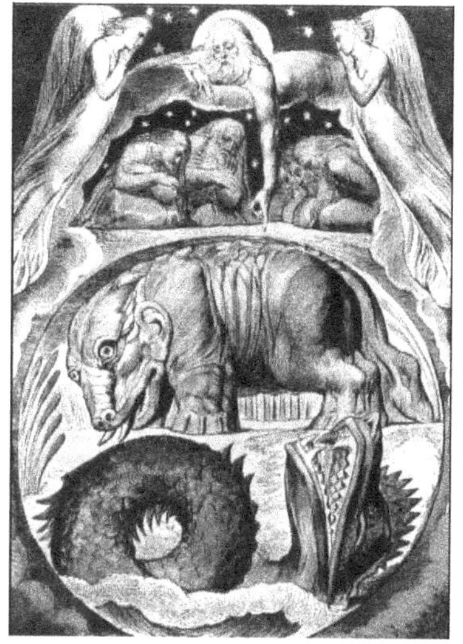

Leviathan and Behemoth.

102. As had medieval interpreters and even the Hebraist Johannes Reuchlin (1455–1522), Luther identifies Leviathan (a monster made up of a perverse mixture of parts) with the combination of sins or improper teachings prompted by the devil. See, e.g., the reference in his earliest lectures on the Psalms (1513–1515) in LW 10:273.

p See Job 41; Isa. 27:1; Pss. 74:14; 104:26; and Job 3:8.

The Basis of Luther's Teaching[q]

Therefore, we do not reject good works. On the contrary, we highly cherish and teach them. For we do not condemn them for their own sake but on account of this godless linkage and perverse opinion that try to seek righteousness [through them]. This makes them appear good on the surface when in reality they are not good. By such works people are deceived and, like ravenous wolves in sheep's clothing, they deceive [others].[r]

The Work of Leviathan

But this Leviathan and perverse opinion about works is impossible to overcome where genuine faith is lacking. These "work-saints" cannot get rid of this [monster] unless faith, its destroyer, comes and rules in the heart. Nature by itself cannot drive it out and, worse yet, cannot even recognize it but rather considers it the ground for the holiest of desires. In this situation, if (as godless teachers have done) custom invokes and strengthens this depravity of nature, it becomes an incurable evil that seduces and destroys countless people irreparably. Thus, while it is fine to preach and write about penitence, confession, and satisfaction,[103] nevertheless, they are without a doubt deceptive and diabolical teachings when placed here [with works] and not derived from faith as taught above.[104] For this is why Christ, like John [the Baptist], did not only say, "Repent,"[s] but added the word of faith, saying: "The kingdom of heaven has come near."[t]

Faith Ought to Be Awakened in Preaching

For we must preach not only one word of God but both, "bringing forth new and old from the treasure"[u]—both the

103. Here Luther is referring to the three parts of the sacrament of penance: contrition (sorrow for sin out of love of God), (private) confession, and (works of) satisfaction. For the first part he uses the more general term, *poenitentia*, which can refer either to the entire sacrament or to the sinner's penitence. For the role of penance in the origins of the Reformation, see *The 95 Theses* in *The Annotated Luther*, Volume 1, pp. 13–16.

104. This reframes Luther's basic argument in the first four of the *95 Theses*. See *The Annotated Luther*, Volume 1, p. 34f.

q The second of several marginal glosses from the second edition referring to Luther in the third person. See above, p. 264, note *v*.

r See Matt. 7:15.

s In the Latin Vulgate, the text (*poenitentiam agite*) may be translated either "Do penance" or "Repent."

t Matt. 4:17, also quoted in the *95 Theses*, thesis 1. See *The Annotated Luther*, Volume 1, p. 34.

u Matt. 13:52. In contrast, medieval commentators interpreted "old and new" as the Old and New Testaments. See above, p. 248, n. 94.

voice of the law and the word of grace. The voice of the law ought to be "brought forth" so that people may be terrified and led to a knowledge of their sins and thereby directed toward repentance[v] and a better basis for life. But the word must not stop here. For this would be only "to wound" and not "to bind up"; "to strike down" and not "to heal"; "to kill" and not "to make alive"; "to lead into hell" and not "to lead out"; "to humble" but not "to exalt."[w] Therefore, the word of grace and promised forgiveness ought also to be preached in order to instruct and awaken faith. Without this other word [of grace], law, contrition, penitence, and everything else are done and taught in vain.

The Origin of Repentance and Faith

To be sure, preachers of repentance and grace are still around, but they do not explain God's law and promise in light of their purpose and spirit, so that people can find out where repentance and grace come from. For repentance arises from God's law, but faith or grace come from the promise of God, as Rom. 10[:17] states: "So faith comes from what is heard, and what is heard comes through the word of Christ." It happens like this: A person, who has been humbled by the threats and fear of the divine law and led to self-knowledge, is consoled and raised up through faith in the divine promise. As Psalm 30[:6] says, "Weeping may linger for the night, but joy comes with the morning."

Concerning Works for the Neighbor[105]

Up to now we have spoken about works in general and, at the same time, about those specific things that a Christian must do to train his or her own body. Finally, we will discuss those things done for one's neighbor. For a human being does not live in this mortal body solely for himself or herself and work only on it but lives together with all other human

105. What follows constitutes a second major section of this part of the tract. For the first section (on discipline of the flesh), see above, p. 265.

v Latin: *poenitentia*, a word that may be translated as "repentance," "penitence," or the "sacrament of penance."

w A combination of Deut. 32:39; 1 Sam. 2:6-7; and Hos. 6:1.

beings on earth. Indeed, more to the point, each person lives only for others and not for himself or herself. The purpose of putting the body in subjection is so that it can serve others more genuinely and more freely. As Paul says in Rom. 14[:7-8], "We do not live to ourselves. If we live, we live to the Lord, and if we die, we die to the Lord." Thus, it can never happen that in this life a person is idle and without works toward one's neighbors. For it is necessary to speak, act, and live with other human beings, just as Christ was "made in human likeness and found in human form"[106, x] and "lived with humankind," as Bar. 3[:37] says.[107]

106. Luther's references to Phil. 2 throughout the tract suggest its origins as a sermon on the epistle for Palm Sunday. See p. 243, n. 58.

107. "Afterward she [Wisdom] appeared on earth and lived with humankind." Already the ancient church associated references to Wisdom (here and in Prov. 8) with Christ. Luther accorded some authority to the Apocrypha, and his complete translation of the Bible into German, first published in 1534, always included the Apocrypha, although his introduction to Baruch in LW 35:349–50 is rather harsh.

Serving All People

Nevertheless, no one needs even one of these works to attain righteousness and salvation. For this reason, in all of one's works a person should in this context be shaped by and contemplate this thought alone: to serve and benefit others in everything that may be done, having nothing else in view except the need and advantage of the neighbor. So the Apostle commands that "we work with our hands so that we may give to those in need."[y] Although he could have said, "so that we may support ourselves," he said instead, "give to those in need."

Why the Body Must Be Taken Care Of

For, under these circumstances, it is also Christian to care for the body. At times when the body is healthy and fit, we can work and save money and thereby can protect and support those who are in need. In this way, the stronger members may serve the weaker[z] and we may be sons [and daughters] of God: one person caring and working for another, "bearing

x Phil. 2:7, according to the Latin Vulgate.

y Luther here paraphrases the Latin Vulgate of Eph. 4:28. The Vulgate reads: "Let [the former thief] labor by working with his hands, which is a good thing, so that he may have a source from which he might contribute to the one who suffers need."

z Luther was combining images from Rom. 14 and 1 Cor. 8–9, 12.

one another's burdens and so fulfilling the law of Christ."[a] Look here! This is truly the Christian life; here truly "faith is effective through love."[108] That is, with joy and love [faith] reveals itself in work of freest servitude, as one person, abundantly filled with the completeness and richness of his or her own faith, serves another freely and willingly.

108. Luther's own rendering of Gal. 5:6. The Vulgate's "faith which works through love" (*fides per charitatem operatur*) led to the medieval insistence that love (*caritas*) provided the (Aristotelian) "form" for the material of faith. Luther not only uses the word *efficax* ("efficacious") but also, following Erasmus, *dilectio* ("ardent love") for *caritas*. See his discussion of this verse in the commentary on Galatians (1519) in LW 27:335-36.

The Christian Life

Thus, after Paul had taught the Philippians how they were made rich through faith in Christ (in which faith they had obtained all things), he then teaches them by saying, "If then there is any encouragement in Christ, any consolation from love, any sharing in the Spirit, any compassion and sympathy, make my joy complete: be of the same mind, having the same love, being in full accord and of one mind. Do nothing from selfish ambition or conceit but in humility regard others as better than yourselves. Let each of you look not to your own interests but to the interests of others."[b] Here we see clearly that the Apostle places the life of Christians into this framework,[c] so that all of our works may be ordered toward the advantage of others. Since each and every person thus thrives through their own faith—so that all other works and the sum total of life flows out from that very faith—by these works each may serve and benefit the neighbor with willing benevolence. To this end, Paul introduces Christ as an example, stating: "Let the same mind be in you that was also in Christ Jesus, who, though he was in the form of God, did not regard himself to be equal to God, but emptied himself, taking the form of a servant, made in human likeness, and being found in human vesture . . . became obedient to the point of death."[d]

a Gal. 6:2.

b Phil. 2:1-4. This precedes the biblical text on which the original sermon may have been based. See p. 243, n. 58.

c Latin: *regula* (rule).

d Phil. 2:5-8, according to the Vulgate.

Perverters of Apostolic Teaching

To be sure, those who have completely misunderstood the apostolic vocabulary ("form of God," "form of a servant," "vesture," "human likeness") and have transferred it to the divine and human natures [of Christ] have obscured for us this most salutary word of the Apostle—even though Paul wanted to say the following.[109] Although Christ was filled with "the form of God" and abounded in all good things—so that he required no work or suffering in order to be righteous and saved (for he possessed all these things right from the very beginning)—nevertheless he was not puffed up by these things nor did he raise himself above us and arrogate to himself some kind of power over us, even though he could by rights have done so. But he acted contrary to this: living, working, suffering, and dying just like other humans, and in "vesture" and action he was nothing other than a human being, as if he lacked all of these things and possessed nothing of God's "forms." Yet he did all of this for our sake, in order to serve us and in order that all things that he had accomplished in the "form of a servant" might become ours.

109. The christological interpretation of Phil. 2 was standard from the time of the ancient church. Luther here is complaining that applying this verse only to the doctrine of Christ's two natures loses sight of its relation to the life of faith.

Let the Christian Be Conformed to Christ

As Christ, their head, was rich and full through his faith, so each and every Christian ought to be content with this "form of God" obtained through faith, except that (as I have said) this very faith ought to increase until it is made perfect. For this faith is one's life, righteousness, and salvation: preserving and making each person acceptable and giving the Christian all things that Christ possesses, as stated above.[e] Paul also confirms this in Gal. 2[:20] when he says, "And the life I now live in the flesh I live by faith in the Son of God." Although individual Christians[f] are thereby free from all works, they should nevertheless once again "humble themselves" in this freedom, take on "the form of a servant," "be made in human form and found in human vesture," and serve, help, and do everything for their neighbor, just as they

e See p. 253.

f Singular in the original throughout this paragraph.

Passional Christi vnd Antichristi.

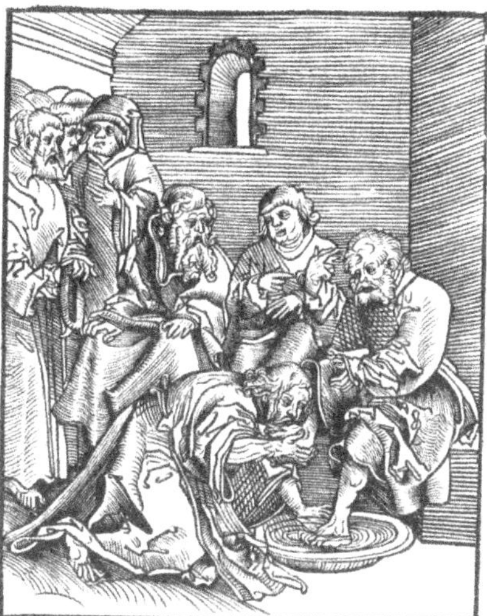

Christus.
Szo ich ewre fuesze habe gewaschen d ich ewir herr vñ meyster bin/vill mehr solt yr einander vnter euch die fusze waschen. Hie-mit habe ich euch ein antzeygung vñ beyspiel geben/ wie ich ym than habe/ alszo solt yr hinfur auch thuen. Warlich warlich sage ich euch/d knecht ist nicht mehr dan seyn herre/ szo ist auch nicht d geschickte botte mehr dā d yn gesandt hat/ Wist yr das? Selig seyt yr szo yr das thuen werdent. Johan. 13.

Antichristus.
Der Babst mast sich an itzlichen Tyrannen vnd heydnischen fursten/ szo yre fuesz den leuten zu kuszen dar gereicht/ nach zu-volgen/ damit es waer werde das geschrieben ist. Wilcher dieser bestien bilde nicht anbettet/ sall getōd werden. Apocalip. 13. Ditz kussens darff sich der Bapst yn seynē decretalen vnuor-schembt rūmen. c. cū oli de pri. cle. Si summus pon. de sen. ex cō.

Jesus washing his disciples' feet contrasted with the pope's feet being kissed from the Passion of Christ and Antichrist (1521). See also pp. 49–50.

see God has done and does with them through Christ. And they should do this freely, having regard for nothing except divine approval.

Christian Trust

Moreover, a Christian should think as follows: "Although I am unworthy and condemned, in Christ my God devotes to my insignificant person, without any merit and by sheer gracious mercy, all the riches of righteousness and salvation, so that I need absolutely nothing else further except faith, which believes that it is so. Thus, to such a Father as this, who overwhelms me with these his inestimable riches, why should I not freely, joyfully, with a whole heart and willing eagerness do everything that I know is pleasing and acceptable to him? Therefore, I will give myself as a kind of Christ to my neighbor, just as Christ offered himself to me. I will do nothing in this life except what I see will be necessary, advantageous, and salutary for my neighbor, because through faith I am overflowing with all good things in Christ."

The Fruits of Faith (See, My Reader, How Worthily Luther Is Condemned!)[110]

Look at what love and joy in the Lord[g] flow from faith! Moreover, from love proceeds a joyful, gladsome, and free soul,[111] prepared for willing service to the neighbor, which takes no account of gratitude or ingratitude, praise or blame, profit or loss. For such a soul does not do this so that people may be obligated to it, nor does it distinguish between friends and enemies, nor does it anticipate thankfulness or ingratitude. Instead, it expends itself and what it has in a completely free and happy manner, whether squandering these things on the ungrateful or on the deserving. For as its Father also does—distributing everything to all people abundantly and freely and making "his sun to rise on the evil and on the good,"[h] so the son [or daughter] only does or suffers everything with spontaneous joy, as each person has through Christ been filled with delight in God, the lavish dispenser of all things.

Recognizing How Great the Things Given to Us Are

Therefore, you see that if we recognize those great and precious things that have been given to us, then, as Paul says, "love . . . is poured out in our hearts through the . . . Spirit."[i] By this love we are free, joyful, all-powerful workers and victors over all tribulations, servants of our neighbors and, nev-

110. The papal bull threatening excommunication, *Exsurge Domine*, condemned Luther for saying that the righteous sin in all their good works. See *Defense and Explanation of All the Articles* (1521) in LW 32:83–87.

111. Luther does not usually use this word to designate some more spiritual, less material part of the human being, but as a way of talking about the entire human creature standing before God. See p. 243, n. 59 above.

g See Phil. 4:4.

h Matt. 5:45.

i Rom. 5:5.

ertheless, still lords of all.[j] But for all who do not recognize what has been given to them through Christ, Christ was born in vain, and such people carry on using works, never attaining a taste or sense of the things just described. Therefore, just as our neighbor has need and lacks what we have in abundance, so also we had need before God and lacked God's mercy. For this reason, as our heavenly Father supported us freely in Christ, so also we ought freely to support our neighbor with our body and its actions, and each person ought to become to the other a kind of Christ, so that we may be Christs to one another and be the same Christ in all, that is, truly Christians!

The Glory of the Christian Life

Therefore, who can comprehend the riches and glory of the Christian life? It can do all things and has all things and lacks nothing. It is lord of sin, death, and hell but, at the same time, is servant and obedient and beneficial to all.[112] And yet how terrible it is that in our day this life is unknown! It is neither preached about nor sought after.

112. For this contrast, see p. 242.

Why We Are Called Christians

What is more, we are also completely ignorant of our very name, why we are Christians and bear that name. Without a doubt we are named after Christ—not absent from us but dwelling in us; in other words: provided that we believe in him and that, in turn and mutually, we are a second Christ to one another, doing for our neighbors as Christ does for us.[k] But nowadays, using human doctrines,[l] we are taught to seek nothing but merits, rewards, and the things that are ours, and we have made out of Christ nothing but a slave driver[m] far harsher than Moses.[113]

113. Luther, following John 1:17, often contrasted "Moses" to Christ as harsh lawgiver to gracious savior. He did not, however, think that there was no grace in the "books of Moses" (Genesis through Deuteronomy). See, e.g., *How Christians Should Regard Moses* (1525) in LW 35:161–74.

j See above, p. 242.

k See Matt. 7:12 and John 13:34.

l See Mark 7:7.

m Latin: *exactor.*

The Holy Mother of God as an Example of Faith[114]

The blessed Virgin provides a preeminent example[115] of this very faith, when (as is written in Luke 2[:22]) she was purified "according to the Law of Moses," as was the custom of all women. Although she was not bound by such a law and had no need of purification,[116] nevertheless, she subjected herself to the law out of free and voluntary love, doing just as other women did, so that she did not offend or disdain them. She was therefore not justified by this work, but as one already righteous, she did it freely and spontaneously. So also our works ought not be done for the purpose of being justified, since—already justified by faith—we ought to do all things freely and joyfully for the sake of others.

Paul Teaches Works

St. Paul also circumcised his disciple Timothy,[n] not because circumcision was necessary for righteousness but rather so that he would not offend or disdain the Jews who were weak in faith and who could not yet grasp faith's freedom. However, on the contrary, when in contempt of this freedom of faith they insisted upon circumcision as necessary for righteousness, he resisted and did not permit Titus to be circumcised (Gal. 2[:3]). For just as he did not want to offend or disdain any person's weakness in faith, yielding to their wishes as appropriate, so also he did not want the freedom of faith to be offended against or disdained by hardened "justices."[117] He took a middle course, sparing the weak as appropriate and always resisting the hardened, so that he might convert everyone to the freedom of faith. Our actions also ought to be done with the same devotion, so that we support the weak in faith (as Rom. 14[:1] teaches) but resist boldly the hardened "masters" of works, about which we will say more below.[118]

n Acts 16:3.

114. Although rejecting the notion that Mary should be worshiped, Luther often pointed to Mary as an example of faith. See his *Commentary on the Magnificat* (written at Wartburg and published in 1522) in LW 21:297–358 and his exposition of the Ave Maria (Hail, Mary) in the *Personal Prayer Book* (1522) in LW 43:39–41. The marginal gloss uses the equivalent of *theotokos*, "Divine God-bearer" (*diva Dei genitrix*).

115. In this section of his argument, Luther provides a series of biblical examples to prove his point.

116. Luther held that Mary had herself conceived Jesus of the Holy Spirit without sin. Thus, she had no need of any purifying sacrifice.

117. Luther uses here a medieval term for court judges, *iustitiarii*, which contains within it the Latin word for righteousness (*iustitia*).

118. Luther uses the term *Magister*, which means teachers in general but in medieval Latin more specifically designated those Scholastic "masters" of theology. Luther takes up Romans 14 on p. 288.

The Example of Christ the Lord

Moreover, in Matt. 17[:24-27], when a tax payment was demanded from the disciples, Christ discussed with Peter whether or not a king's sons were exempt from paying taxes. But when Peter affirmed that they were exempt, Jesus nevertheless commanded him to go to the sea, saying [v. 27]: "However, so that we do not give offense to them, go to the sea and cast a hook; take the first fish that comes up; and when you open its mouth you will find a coin; take that and give it to them for you and me." This example beautifully supports our argument,[119] in that Christ refers to himself and his own as free sons of the king, who need nothing, and yet he willingly submits and pays the tax. As little as this deed was necessary or useful for righteousness or salvation, so all of his other works and those of his followers contribute nothing to righteousness, since all of these things are a result of righteousness and free, done only as an example and a service to others.

Let All the Religious Understand and Let Luther Be Your Teacher[o]

The same thing goes for what Paul commands in Rom. 13[:1] and Titus 3[:1], saying, "Let" them "be subject to the governing authorities" and "be ready for every good work"—not that they may be justified through this (since they are already justified by faith) but so that through these things and in the freedom of the Spirit they may serve the authorities, among others, and may obey them out of willing, spontaneous love. The works of all clerical institutions,[120] monasteries, and priests should be of this kind, too. Thus, each would only do works of his own profession and walk of life,[121] in order to work not toward righteousness but, in the first place, toward the subjection of his own body as an example for the sake of others, who have need to discipline their own bodies, too. In the second place, they would

119. A *propositio* meant either the theme of a speech or the major premise of a logic syllogism.

120. Literally, "colleges," a designation for legally constituted groups of clergy supported by a foundation or cathedral for the purpose of performing certain religious observances.

121. Luther uses the Latin *status* here as a synonym for the German *stand*, "station in life" or "walk of life."

o Latin: *religiosi*, a technical term encompassing the ordained (priests and bishops) and those under a vow (monks, nuns, and friars).

also obey others and do their bidding out of spontaneous love. Nevertheless, here the utmost care must be taken, so that a false trust does not presume that such works justify, earn reward, or save—which is all from faith alone, as I have repeatedly said.

A True Christian's Knowledge

Therefore, whoever has this knowledge can easily and without danger manage those countless rules and commands of the pope, bishops, monasteries, churches, princes, and magistrates. Some foolish shepherds[p] insist that these things are all necessary for righteousness and salvation, calling them "commands of the church,"[122] although they are nothing of the kind. For a free Christian will say instead, "I will fast, pray, and do this or that because it is commanded by human beings—not because this is necessary for righteousness or salvation but because in this behavior I may conduct myself toward the pope, bishop, community, this or that magistrate, or my neighbor as an example. I will do or suffer all things, as Christ often did and suffered many things for me—none of which he needed for himself at all, having been 'placed under the law' on my account, although he was not under the law.[q] And although tyrants may harm or use force [to effect compliance], it will still not do harm, as long as [what they commanded] was not against God."[123]

Distinguishing Good Shepherds from Evil Ones

From all these examples,[124,r] any person can derive firm judgment and reliable distinction among all works and laws and can recognize who are the blind, foolish shepherds and who are the true and good ones. For any work not directed toward the purpose of either disciplining the body

122. For example, this phrase occurs in Thomas Aquinas, *Summa Theologica* II/II q. 39 a. 1, ad 2 (a discussion of schism in the church), but it was more commonly used in moral theology, which listed five or six precepts of the church that must be followed. Lists might include receiving the Lord's Supper during the Easter season, following appointed fasts, supporting the church monetarily, obeying the church's marriage laws, hearing the Mass on Sundays and holy days, and going to private confession yearly.

123. This double attitude toward authority is reflected in Luther's letter to Pope Leo X, toward whom he tries to demonstrate both obedience and freedom (see above, p. 222). Later he applies this respect toward and limits of authority to secular authority as well. See *On Secular Authority* (1523) in LW 45:81–129.

124. There are four examples beginning with Mary.

p Latin: *pastores.*

q Some modern versions end the quotation here. Quotation marks were not employed in sixteenth-century printings. The reference is to Gal. 4:4-5.

r Literally, "things."

or serving the neighbor (as long as the neighbor demands nothing against God) is neither good nor Christian. As a result, I greatly fear that nowadays few if any clerical institutions, monasteries, high altars,[125] or ecclesiastical offices are Christian, along with special fasts and prayers for certain saints. To repeat, I fear that in all of these things nothing is sought after except what has to do with us, because we think that through them our sins are cleansed and salvation is attained. In this way, Christian freedom is completely obliterated, because [this attitude] arises from ignorance of Christian faith and freedom.

Many completely blind shepherds zealously support such ignorance and suppression of freedom, while at the same time inciting and encouraging the people in their devotion by praising these things and inflating them with indulgences,[126] and yet never teaching faith at all.

Advice

Instead, I desire each of you to consider that if you really want to pray, fast, or establish a foundation in churches (as they say),[127] pay attention to whether you are doing it for the purpose of obtaining some temporal or eternal reward!

Be Concerned for Faith Alone

You may harm your faith, which alone offers you all things. For this reason, let faith be your sole concern, so that faith may be increased by exercising it either through works or suffering. Meanwhile, whatever you give, give freely and without reward, so that others may experience increase and reap benefits from you and what is yours. For in this way, you will be truly good and Christian. For what are your good works (which function most fully for bodily discipline) to you, when for yourself you are filled through your faith, in which God gives you all things?[s]

125. Latin: *altaria*. Luther is probably referring to altars reserved for saying Masses for the dead.

126. In late medieval piety and connected with the sacrament of penance, many works, such as special fasts, prayers, or pilgrimages, were made even more meritorious with the addition of specially crafted indulgences. These limited indulgences, designed to encourage a variety of works, differed in scope from the plenary "Peter's Indulgence," which Luther attacks in the *95 Theses*. See *The Annotated Luther*, Volume 1, p. 15f.

127. Luther is referring to the practice of establishing monetary foundations so priests could recite perpetual Masses for one's deceased family members.

s Luther uses the word *you* (singular: *tu*) five times in this sentence, including *pro te* ("for you").

128. Luther is alluding to the baptismal language of "taking off" and "putting on" found in Col. 3:1-17.

129. Luther reworks the "joyous exchange" (see above, p. 253f.) to describe relations between the believer and the neighbor.

130. This verb begins the concluding section of Luther's tract, similar to the peroration in good Latin rhetoric of the time. It summarizes the chief argument, introduced on p. 242.

131. The *Postilla moralis* of Nicholas of Lyra (1270–1349), provides a similar allegory, in that preachers ascend to the deity of Christ and descend "when they seek the need of the neighbor raised up for their love." For a different interpretation of this text by Luther, in sermons from 1538, see LW 22:200–211.

The Rule for "Brotherly Love"

Look here! This should be the rule: that the good things we have from God may flow from one person to the other and become common property. In this way each person may "put on" his [or her] neighbor[128] and conduct oneself toward him [or her] as if in the neighbor's place. These good things flowed and flow into us from Christ, who put us on and acted for us, as if he himself were what we are. They now flow from us into those who have need of them. Just as my faith and righteousness ought to be placed before God to cover and intercede for the neighbor's sins, which I take upon myself, so also I labor under and am subject to them as if they were my very own.[129] For this is what Christ did for us. For this is true love and the genuine rule of the Christian life. Now where there is true and genuine faith, there is true and genuine love. Hence, the Apostle in 1 Cor. 13[:5] attributes to love that "it does not seek its own."[t]

The Christian Lives in Christ and the Neighbor

Therefore, we conclude[130] that Christian individuals[u] do not live in themselves but in Christ and their neighbor, or else they are not Christian. They live in Christ through faith and in the neighbor through love. Through faith they are caught up beyond themselves into God; likewise through love they fall down beneath themselves into the neighbor—remaining nevertheless always in God and God's love, as Christ says in John 1[:51]: "Very truly I say to you, you will see the heavens opened and the angels of God ascending and descending upon the Son of Man."[131]

Let this suffice concerning that freedom, which, as you see, is spiritual and true, making our hearts free from all sin, laws, and commands, as Paul says in 1 Tim. 1[:9], "The law is not laid down for the righteous person."[v] This freedom is

t Following here the more literal Latin Vulgate.

u This is singular in the original throughout this paragraph.

v A literal rendering of the Latin Vulgate and the Greek text.

far above all other external freedoms, as high as heaven is above the earth. May Christ cause us to know and preserve this freedom! Amen.

[Appendix][132] Against the Freedom of the Flesh[w]

Finally, this must be added because of those for whom nothing can be stated well enough that they cannot distort it by warped understanding—if they could even understand what is said here at all. There are so many people who, when they hear about this freedom of faith, immediately turn it into "an occasion for the flesh."[x] They imagine that straightaway all things are permitted for them, and they want to be free and seem Christian in no other way than by showing contempt and disdain for ceremonies,[y] traditions, and human laws. As if they were Christians precisely because they do not fast on the stated days or because they themselves eat meat while others fast[133] or they refrain from saying the customary prayers! They stick up their noses, make fun of human commands, and hold the other things that in fact pertain to the Christian religion in low esteem.

Against Trust in Works

These people are stubbornly resisted by those who strive for salvation solely by reverent observance of ceremonies—as if they might be saved because they fast on the appointed days or abstain from meat or pray certain prayers. They boast about the precepts of the church and the Fathers while not caring one wit about those things that concern our genuine faith. Both sides are plainly in error, because they are so confused and troubled about unnecessary and silly things while neglecting the more serious things that are necessary for salvation.

132. This marginal word is not in sixteenth-century editions, which simply put a larger space between the preceding and what follows. This appendix, found only in the Latin edition, deals with a persistent charge against Luther and his followers: that their understanding of Christian freedom resulted only in license to sin and, hence, fostered civil disobedience. Dealing with this issue also gives Luther opportunity to attack what he views as his opponents' legalism. Thus, each section, as the marginal notations from the second edition help make clear, deals with both sides of the problem. The Latin here is somewhat more complicated than the preceding, perhaps because of the absence of a German text.

133. In late medieval practice, people were to abstain from meat on certain days (especially Fridays) and seasons (especially Lent)—religious regulations enforced by local authorities. In 1523 in Zurich, eating of meat during Lent by a prominent printer led to the wholesale rejection of episcopal authority and the establishment of an important center for what became Reformed Christianity.

w "Against the Freedom of the Flesh" is from the 2nd ed.

x Gal. 5:13 according to the Vulgate and Greek text. NRSV: "an opportunity for self-indulgence."

y For Luther's use of this word throughout this section, see above, p. 248, n. 68.

How much more correct is the Apostle Paul, who teaches taking the middle way and condemns both sides completely when he says, "Those who eat must not despise those who abstain, and those who abstain must not pass judgment on those who eat."[z] You see here that those who neglect or despise ceremonies—not out of a sense of piety but rather out of sheer contempt—are upbraided, since Paul teaches not to condemn, for "knowledge puffs them up."[a] On the other hand, he teaches those other, obstinate people not to judge the former group. For neither side cares about the "love that builds up" the neighbor.[b] Therefore, Scripture must be listened to, which teaches that we "will turn aside neither to the right nor to the left"[c] but will follow "the acceptable righteousness of the Lord that gladdens the heart."[d] For just as no one is righteous by preserving or being a slave to the works and rites of ceremonies, so also no one is deemed righteous by simply omitting and condemning them.

For we are not free from works through faith in Christ but from conjectures about works, that is, from the foolish presumption of justification acquired through works. For faith redeems, makes right, and guards our consciences, so that we realize that righteousness is not in works—although works can and should not be lacking. For example, we cannot exist without food and drink and all the other works of this mortal body, and yet our righteousness is not built upon them but upon faith. Still these things must not be condemned or omitted. Thus, in this world we are bound by the necessities of this bodily life, but we are not righteous because of them. Christ said, "My kingdom is not from this world . . . not from here," but he did not say, "My kingdom is not here in this world."[e] Paul also says, "For though we walk

z Rom. 14:3.
a Paraphrasing 1 Cor. 8:1.
b Paraphrasing 1 Cor. 8:1.
c Paraphrasing Deut. 2:27 and 28:14.
d Paraphrasing Ps. 19:8.
e John 18:36.

in the flesh, we do not war according to the flesh."[f] And in Gal. 2[:20] he says, "The life I now live in the flesh I live by faith in the Son of God." Thus, the necessities of life and the need to control the body cause us to act and live and exist with works and ceremonies. Nevertheless, we are righteous not through these things but through faith in the Son of God. For this reason, the same middle way is set out for each Christian, who must also keep in mind these two types of people.

How to Deal with the Stubborn

On the one hand, the Christian encounters the stubborn and obstinate ceremonialists. Like deaf adders,[g] they do not want to hear freedom's truth, but instead they boast about their ceremonies as the means of justification, imperiously commanding and insisting on them quite apart from faith. The Jews of old, who did not want to understand anything about how to behave properly, were like this.[134] Against these people one ought to resist, do the opposite, and boldly offend them, so that they do not mislead many others as well by this ungodly opinion. In their presence it is appropriate to eat meat, to break fasts, and for the freedom of faith to do other things that they take for the greatest of sins. It must be said of them, "Let them alone; they are blind guides of the blind."[h] In line with this, Paul did not want Titus to be circumcised when some demanded it,[i] and Christ defended the apostles because they wanted [to pluck] grain on the Sabbath and in many other instances.[j]

134. As what follows makes clear, Luther had in mind conflicts between Jesus and the Pharisees over keeping the law. See, e.g., Mark 2:1–3:6.

f 2 Cor. 10:3, using the more literal rendering of the Greek, which matches the Latin Vulgate.

g Ps. 58:4 (see also Mic. 7:16-17).

h Matt. 15:14.

i Gal. 2:3.

j Matt. 12:1-8.

Regarding the Common Folk

On the other hand, the Christian encounters the simple, uneducated, ignorant, and (as Paul calls them) weak in faith, who cannot yet understand this freedom of faith, even if they want to. Care must be taken not to offend these people but to defer to their weakness until they are more fully instructed. For fasts and other things that they think are necessary must be kept to avoid causing them to fall—not because their actions or thoughts are motivated by deep-seated wickedness but only because they are weak in faith. For love, which seeks to harm no one but only to serve all, demands it. After all, they are weak not by their own fault but by that of their shepherds,[135] who have taken them captive and wickedly beaten them using the snares and rods of their traditions, from which they should have been freed and healed with the teaching of faith and freedom! As the Apostle teaches in [1 Cor. 8:13],[k] "I will never eat meat, so that I may not cause one of them to fall." And he says elsewhere, "I know and am persuaded by the Lord Jesus that nothing is unclean . . . but to anyone who thinks it is unclean it is unclean . . . [and] it is evil for that person who eats to give offense."[l]

135. A reference to Luther's Roman opponents, especially the priests and bishops.

Concerning Laws and the Lawgivers

Therefore, although those master teachers of traditions must be boldly resisted and the papal laws, by which they plunder God's people, must be sharply criticized, nevertheless one must refrain from injuring the frightened masses—which those ungodly tyrants hold captive with these very laws—until they may be set free from them. Thus, fight vigorously against the wolves but *for* the sheep and not, in the same breath, against the sheep. Each of you may do this by inveighing against the laws and the lawgivers while at the same time guarding the weak from being offended, until

k The original text refers to Romans 14, the passage Luther cites next.

l Rom. 14:14, 20, where Luther cites the Vulgate, which provides a more literal rendering of the Greek.

they themselves recognize this tyranny and understand their own freedom. If you desire to exercise your freedom, do it in secret, as Paul says in Rom. 14[:22], "The faith that you have, have for yourself before God."[m] But be careful not to exercise [faith's freedom] before the weak. Contrariwise, before tyrants and stubborn people you may exercise that freedom with contempt and without ever letting up at all. Then they, too, will understand that they are ungodly, that their laws contribute nothing to righteousness, and that, frankly, they did not even have the right to enact them.

For the Young and Untrained

Thus, it is clear that in this life one cannot live without ceremonies and works. Indeed, hotheaded and untrained adolescents need to be held back and guarded by such restraints. Moreover, individual Christians must discipline their bodies with such efforts. The servant of Christ[n] must be wise and faithful, so that he may so rule and teach Christ's people about all these things, so that their conscience and faith are not offended. Otherwise, an opinion or "root of bitterness" may arise in them "and through it many become defiled," as Paul warns in Heb. [12:15].[136] That is to say, "so that, in the absence of faith, they begin to be defiled by the opinion about works, as if they were justified through them." This happens quite easily and defiles many people. Unless faith is constantly inculcated at the same time, it is impossible to avoid the situation where (faith having been silenced) human regulations alone are taught. This has happened today through the pestilent, ungodly, soul-destroying, traditions of our popes and the opinions of our theologians.[137] With an infinite number of souls being dragged to hell by these snares, you can recognize Antichrist.[138]

m Following Luther's citation of the Vulgate, which renders the Greek more literally.

n Latin: *minister Christi*, Luther's favorite designation for the public minister.

136. In the sixteenth century, biblical interpreters debated whether Paul wrote Hebrews. Luther was of a divided mind on the subject but here supports the traditional viewpoint.

137. See above, *Address to the Christian Nobility*, p. 62.

138. Luther uses the widespread depiction of the devil, who at the end of time binds the souls of the damned around the neck and leads them into hell. By this stage of the Reformation, Luther was convinced that the Antichrist ruled in Rome and was associated with the institution of the Roman papacy. See, e.g., *On the Papacy in Rome against the Most Celebrated Romanist in Leipzig* (1520), in LW 39:49–104.

Danger in Ceremonies

In conclusion, just as riches endanger poverty; business dealings, honesty; honors, humility; banquets, abstinence; or pleasures, chastity; so also ceremonies endanger the righteousness of faith. Solomon asks, "Can fire be carried in the bosom without burning one's clothes?"[o] And yet, as with riches, business dealings, honors, pleasures, and feasts, so also one must take part in ceremonies—that is, in dangers. To say this as strongly as possible:[p] Just as infant boys need to be attentively caressed at a young woman's bosom, in order that they may not perish (even though as adults it endangers salvation for them to be consorting with young women), so also hotheaded, untrained youth need to be restrained and disciplined by the iron bars of ceremonies, so that their unrestrained heart may not go blindly into corruption. And yet it would be the death of them if they insisted on imagining that justification came from them. Instead, they should be taught that they have been imprisoned in this way not to be righteous or to merit something but so that they would be kept from evil and might more easily be instructed in the righteousness of faith. For, unless their impulsiveness be put in check, they would not put up with such instruction.

The Place for Ceremonies

Thus, ceremonies are to have the same place in the Christian life as a builder's construction plans or an artisan's instructions. They are not prepared to be the substance and lasting part of a building but because without them nothing can be built or made. For they are set aside once the structure is finished. Here you can see that they are not being despised but rather are especially required. What is being despised is a [false] opinion about them: because no one imagines that plans are the real and permanent structure. Who would be so silly that they would care for nothing in life other than

o Prov. 6:27.

p Latin: *immo*, an adversative much beloved by Luther, who used it to introduce radical or even contrary ideas from what had just been stated. It is similar to the archaic "forsooth" or "nay, verily."

plans that they had most lavishly, carefully, and stubbornly[q] prepared while never thinking about the structure itself and only being pleased with and boasting about their work in making plans and such vain first steps? Would not everybody have pity on such insanity and judge that something great could have been built by this wasted expense? In the same way, we do not despise ceremonies or works but rather especially require them. However, we despise the [false] opinion about works, so that a person may not imagine that they are true righteousness, as hypocrites do. They waste their whole life by tying their life to works, and yet they never arrive at the goal for which works are done. As the Apostle says, they "are always being instructed and can never arrive at knowledge of the truth."[r] For it seems that they want to build and to prepare themselves and yet never actually build anything. So they remain with "the outward form of godliness and do not" attain "its power."[s]

On Hyper-Religious[t] People

All the while these people are pleased with their efforts and dare to judge everyone else whom they do not see glowing with a similar display of works. Instead, had they been filled with faith, by properly using God's gifts (rather than vainly wasting and abusing them) they could have brought about great things for their salvation and the salvation of others. But human nature and natural reason (as they call it)[139] are naturally hyper-religious and, whenever some laws and works are proposed, promptly jump to the conclusion that justification may be attained through them. Added to this, reason is trained and strengthened in this very point of view by the practice of all earthly lawgivers. Therefore, it

139. This term went back to Cicero and was a central concept in Roman law.

q Latin: *pertinacissime*. In this context, Luther means "meticulously," but he is using the same word that he had already used to describe "*stubborn* ceremonialists."

r 2 Tim. 3:7.

s 2 Tim. 3:5.

t Here and below *superstitiosus* (here translated "hyper-religious") means fixed on one's own unreasonable ideas about religion.

is impossible that by its own powers [reason] may free itself from servitude to this view of works and come into the necessary knowledge of faith's freedom. For this reason, prayer is needed, so that the Lord may "draw us" and make us "*theodidaktos*," that is, "taught by God."[u] Moreover, as he promised, he will "write the law in our hearts."[v] Otherwise, it is all over for us. For unless God teaches this wisdom hidden in mystery[w] inwardly, [human] nature, because it is offended and regards it as foolish, can only condemn it and judge it to be heretical.[x] What we observe happened to the prophets and Apostles, those godless and blind pontiffs and their flatterers are now doing to me and people like me. In the end, "may God be merciful to us . . . and cause his face to shine upon us, so that we may know his way on earth, among all nations the saving power of the one"[y] who is blessed forever. Amen.

u Luther is quoting John 6:44-45, mixing the Latin and Greek text.

v Jer. 31:33.

w See Col. 1:26.

x See 1 Cor. 1:23.

y A close paraphrase of Ps. 67:1-2.

Image Credits

xiv, 6, 9, 50, 54, 56, 75, 220, 233, 237, 263, 267, 271: Courtesy of the Digital Image Archive, Pitts Theology Library, Candler School of Theology, Emory University.

11: Photo © photos.com

23: Photo © Chris Dascher / iStock

24: Photo © somor / iStock

31: Photo © photos.com, Thinkstock

66: (Foto Marburg) Art Resource, NY.

81: Gianni Dagli Orti / The Art Archive at Art Resource, NY.

98: The Lutheran School of Theology at Chicago (Gruber Rare Books Collection). Used by permission.

102, 104, 106, 124, 129, 145, 175, 183, 211: Wikimedia Commons.

150, 185, 187, 201: Courtesy of the Richard C. Kessler Reformation Collection, Pitts Theological Library, Candler School of Theology, Emory University.